Numerical and Analytical Methods with MATLAB® for Electrical Engineers

CRC Series in
COMPUTATIONAL MECHANICS and APPLIED ANALYSIS

Series Editor: J.N. Reddy
Texas A&M University

Published Titles

ADVANCED THERMODYNAMICS ENGINEERING, Second Edition
Kalyan Annamalai, Ishwar K. Puri, and Milind Jog

APPLIED FUNCTIONAL ANALYSIS
J. Tinsley Oden and Leszek F. Demkowicz

COMBUSTION SCIENCE AND ENGINEERING
Kalyan Annamalai and Ishwar K. Puri

CONTINUUM MECHANICS FOR ENGINEERS, Third Edition
Thomas Mase, Ronald Smelser, and George E. Mase

DYNAMICS IN ENGINEERING PRACTICE, Tenth Edition
Dara W. Childs

EXACT SOLUTIONS FOR BUCKLING OF STRUCTURAL MEMBERS
C.M. Wang, C.Y. Wang, and J.N. Reddy

THE FINITE ELEMENT METHOD IN HEAT TRANSFER AND FLUID DYNAMICS, Third Edition
J.N. Reddy and D.K. Gartling

MECHANICS OF LAMINATED COMPOSITE PLATES AND SHELLS: THEORY AND ANALYSIS, Second Edition
J.N. Reddy

MICROMECHANICAL ANALYSIS AND MULTI-SCALE MODELING USING THE VORONOI CELL FINITE ELEMENT METHOD
Somnath Ghosh

NUMERICAL AND ANALYTICAL METHODS WITH MATLAB®
William Bober, Chi-Tay Tsai, and Oren Masory

NUMERICAL AND ANALYTICAL METHODS WITH MATLAB® FOR ELECTRICAL ENGINEERS
William Bober and Andrew Stevens

PRACTICAL ANALYSIS OF COMPOSITE LAMINATES
J.N. Reddy and Antonio Miravete

SOLVING ORDINARY AND PARTIAL BOUNDARY VALUE PROBLEMS IN SCIENCE and ENGINEERING
Karel Rektorys

STRESSES IN BEAMS, PLATES, AND SHELLS, Third Edition
Ansel C. Ugural

Numerical and Analytical Methods with MATLAB® for Electrical Engineers

William Bober • Andrew Stevens

CRC Press
Taylor & Francis Group
Boca Raton London New York

CRC Press is an imprint of the
Taylor & Francis Group, an **informa** business

Reprint 2019

CRC Press
Taylor & Francis Group
6000 Broken Sound Parkway NW, Suite 300
Boca Raton, FL 33487-2742

CRC Press is an imprint of Taylor & Francis Group, an Informa business

ISBN: 978-1-138-04650-4

Library of Congress Cataloging-in-Publication Data

Bober, William, 1930-
Numerical and analytical methods with MATLAB for electrical engineers / William Bober and Andrew Stevens.
p. cm. -- (Computational mechanics and applied analysis)
ISBN 978-1-4398-5429-7 (hardback)
1. Engineering mathematics--Data processing. 2. Numerical analysis--Data processing. 3. MATLAB. I. Stevens, Andrew, 1964- II. Title.

TA345.B63 2012
515.0285'53--dc23 2012005856

Visit the Taylor & Francis Web site at
http://www.taylorandfrancis.com

and the CRC Press Web site at
http://www.crcpress.com

Printed and bound in India

For sale in India, Pakistan, Nepal, Bhutan, Bangladesh and Sri Lanka only.

Contents

Preface

I have been teaching two courses in computer applications for engineers at Florida Atlantic University (FAU) for many years. The first course is usually taken in the student's sophomore year; the second course is usually taken in the student's junior or senior year. Both computer classes are run as lecture-laboratory courses, and the MATLAB® software program is used in both courses. To familiarize students with engineering-type problems, approximately six or seven projects are assigned during the semester. Students have, depending on the difficulty of the project, either one week or two weeks to complete each project. I believe that the best source for students to complete the assigned projects in either course is this textbook.

This book has its origin in a previous textbook, *Numerical and Analytical Methods with MATLAB®* by William Bober, Chi-Tay Tsai, and Oren Masory, also published by CRC Press. The previous book was primarily oriented toward mechanical engineering students. I and Jonathan Plant of CRC Press envisioned that a similar text would fill a need in electrical engineering curricula; as a result, I enlisted Dr. Andrew Stevens to replace the projects in the existing textbook with those oriented toward electrical engineering students. This new textbook retains the philosophy of teaching that exists in the original textbook.

The advantage of using the MATLAB software program over other packages is that it contains built-in functions that numerically solve systems of linear equations, systems of ordinary differential equations, roots of transcendental equations, integrals, statistical problems, optimization problems, signal-processing problems, and many other types of problems encountered in engineering. A student version of the MATLAB program is available at a reasonable cost. However, to students, these built-in functions are essentially black boxes. By combining a textbook on MATLAB with basic numerical and analytical analysis (although I am sure that MATLAB uses more sophisticated numerical techniques than are described in these textbooks), the mystery of what these black boxes might contain is somewhat alleviated. The text contains many sample MATLAB programs that should provide guidance to the student on completing the assigned projects. Many of the projects in this book are non-trivial and, I believe, will be good training for a graduating engineer entering industry or in an advanced degree program.

Furthermore, I believe that there is enough material in this textbook for two courses, especially if the courses are run as lecture-laboratory courses. The advantage of running these courses (especially the first course) as a lecture-laboratory course is that the instructor is in the computer laboratory to help the students debug their programs. This includes the sample programs as well as the projects.

The common core of the book is the introduction to the MATLAB programming environment in Chapter 2. Then, depending on the individual curriculum (but typically sophomore year), a course might proceed with mathematical techniques for matrix algebra, root finding, integration, and differential equations (Chapters 3 through 6). A more advanced course (perhaps in junior or senior year) might include transform techniques (Chapters 7 and 8) and advanced topics in curve fitting and optimization (Chapters 9 and 10). MATLAB's graphical design environment, Simulink®, is introduced in Chapter 11 and could be relocated elsewhere in the syllabus.

We have tried to make each chapter stand alone so that each may be rearranged based on the preference of the instructor. In many cases, we have used the resistor-inductor-capacitor (RLC) circuit as an example, and we have put the basic derivation of this circuit in Appendix A to minimize the chapter dependencies and facilitate reordering. In all cases, we have attempted to provide illustrative examples using modern topics in electrical engineering.

All chapters (except for Chapter 1) contain projects, and some also contain several exercises that are less difficult than the projects and might be assigned prior to a project assignment. All projects require the student to write a computer program, most requiring the use of MATLAB built-in functions and solvers.

Additional materials, including down loadable copies of all examples in the textbook, are available from the CRC press website:

http://www.crcpress.com/product/isbn/9781439854297

William Bober
Florida Atlantic University
Department of Civil Engineering

Acknowledgments

We wish to thank Jonathan Plant of CRC Press for his confidence and encouragement in writing this textbook. In addition, we would like to express thanks to Chris LeGoff for help in preparing the artwork and to Patrick Farrell and Michael Rohan for their technical expertise.

We also wish to express our deep gratitude to Selma Bober, Theresa Stevens, and Emma Stevens for tolerating the many hours we spent on the preparation of the manuscript, the time that otherwise would have been devoted to our families.

About the Authors

William Bober, Ph.D., received his B.S. degree in civil engineering from the City College of New York (CCNY), his M.S. degree in engineering science from Pratt Institute, and his Ph.D. degree in engineering science and aerospace engineering from Purdue University. At Purdue University, he was on a Ford Foundation Fellowship; he was assigned to teach one engineering course each semester. After receiving his Ph.D., he went to work as an associate engineering physicist in the Applied Mechanics Department at Cornell Aeronautical Laboratory in Buffalo, New York. After leaving Cornell Labs, he was employed as an associate professor in the Department of Mechanical Engineering at the Rochester Institute of Technology (RIT) for the following twelve years. After leaving RIT, he obtained employment at Florida Atlantic University (FAU) in the Department of Mechanical Engineering. More recently, he transferred to the Department of Civil Engineering at FAU. While at RIT, he was the principal author of a textbook, *Fluid Mechanics*, published by John Wiley & Sons. He has written several papers for *The International Journal of Mechanical Engineering Education* (IJMEE) and more recently coauthored a textbook, *Numerical and Analytical Methods with MATLAB®*.

Andrew Stevens, Ph.D., P.E., received his bachelor's degree from Massachusetts Institute of Technology, his master's degree from the University of Pennsylvania, and his doctorate from Columbia University, all in electrical engineering. He did his Ph.D. thesis work at IBM Research in the area of integrated circuit design for high-speed optical networks. While at Columbia, he lectured a course in the core undergraduate curriculum and won the IEEE Solid-State Circuits Fellowship. He has held R&D positions at AT&T Bell Laboratories in the development of T-carrier multiplexer systems and at Argonne National Laboratory in the design of radiation-hardened integrated circuits for colliding beam detectors. Since 2001, he has been president of Electrical Science, an engineering consulting firm specializing in electrical hardware and software. He has published articles in several scientific journals and holds three patents in the areas of analog circuit design and computer user interfaces.

Chapter 1

Numerical Methods for Electrical Engineers

1.1 Introduction

All disciplines of science and engineering use numerical methods for the analysis of complex problems. However, electrical engineering particularly lends itself to computational solutions due to the highly mathematical nature of the field and its close relationship with computer science. It makes sense that engineers who design high-speed computers would also use the computers themselves to aid in the design (a process known as bootstrapping). In fact, the entire field of computer-aided design (CAD) is dedicated to the creation and improvement of software tools to enable the implementation of highly complex designs.

This book describes various methods and techniques for numerically solving a variety of common electrical engineering applications, including circuit design, electromagnetic field theory, and signal processing. Classical engineering curricula teach a variety of methods for solving these problems using techniques such as linear algebra, differential equations, transforms, vector calculus, and the like. However, in many cases, the search for a closed-form solution leads to extreme complexity, which can cause us to lose physical insight into the problem. In solving these same problems numerically, we will often revert to fundamental physical relations, such as the differential relationship between capacitor current and voltage or the electric field of a point charge. Often, a problem that seems intractable when solved symbolically can become trivial when solved numerically. And sometimes, the simpler numerical solution can be elusive because we are so used to thinking in terms of advanced calculus (a classic case of not being able to see the forest but for the trees).

1.2 Engineering Goals

Some fundamental goals in engineering include

- Design new products or improve existing ones
- Improve manufacturing efficiency
- Minimize cost, power consumption, and nonreturnable engineering (NRE) cost
- Maximize yield and return on investment (ROI)
- Minimize time to market

The engineer will frequently use the laws of physics and mathematics to achieve these goals.

Many electrical engineering processes involve expensive manufacturing steps that are both delicate and time consuming. For example, the fabrication of integrated circuits can involve thousands of manufacturing steps, including wafer preparation, mask creation, photolithography, diffusion and implantation, dicing, testing, packaging, and more. These steps can take weeks or months to perform at substantial expense and in clean rooms. Any design mistakes require repeating the process; thus, it is our job as designers to model and simulate designs as much as possible in advance of manufacture to eliminate flaws and minimize the iterations necessary to produce the final product.

Using integrated circuit design as an example, we might use computers for the

a. Design stage: Solve mathematical models of physical phenomena (e.g., predicting the behavior of PN junctions)
b. Testing stage: Store and analyze experimental data (e.g., comparing the laboratory-measured actual behavior of PN junctions to the prediction)
c. Manufacturing stage: Controlling machine operations to fabricate and test silicon wafers and dice

1.3 Programming Numerical Solutions

Physical phenomena are always described by a set of governing equations, and numerical methods can be used to solve the set of governing equations even in the absence of a closed-form solution. Numerical methods invariably involve the computer, and the computer performs arithmetic operations on discrete numbers in a defined sequence of steps. The sequence of steps is defined in the program. A useful solution is obtained if

a. The mathematical model accurately represents the physical phenomena; that is, the model has the correct governing equations.
b. The numerical method is accurate.
c. The numerical method is programmed correctly.

This text is mainly concerned with items (b) and (c).

The advantage of using the computer is that it can carry out many calculations in a fraction of a second; at the time of this writing, computer speeds are measured in teraflops (trillions of floating point operations per second). However, to leverage this power, we need to write a set of instructions, that is, a program. For the problems of interest in this book, the digital computer is only capable of performing arithmetic, logical, and graphical operations. Therefore, arithmetic procedures must be developed for solving differential equations, evaluating integrals, determining roots of an equation, solving a system of linear equations, and so on. The arithmetic procedure usually involves a set of algebraic equations. A computer solution for such problems involves developing a computer program that defines a step-by-step procedure for obtaining an answer to the problem of interest. The method of solution is called an *algorithm*. Depending on the particular problem, we might write our own algorithm, or as we shall see, we can also use the algorithms built into a package like MATLAB® to perform well-known algorithms such as the Runge-Kutta method for solving a set of ordinary differential equations or use Simpson's rule for evaluating an integral.

1.4 Why MATLAB?

MATLAB was originally written by Dr. Cleve Moler at University of New Mexico in the 1970s and was commercialized by MathWorks in the 1980s. It is a general-purpose numerical package that allows complex equations to be solved efficiently and subsequently generate tabular or graphical output. While there are many numerical packages available to electrical engineers, many are highly focused toward a particular application (e.g., SPICE for modeling electronic circuits). Also, MATLAB is not to be confused with CAD software for schematic capture, layout, or physical design, although this software often integrates with an accompanying numerical package.

Originally, MATLAB was a command-line program that ran on MS-DOS and UNIX hosts. As computers have evolved, so has MATLAB, and modern editions of the program run in windowed environments. As of the time of this writing, MATLAB R2011b runs natively on Microsoft Windows, Apple MacOS, and Linux. In this text, we assume that you are running MATLAB on your local machine in a Microsoft Windows environment. It should be straightforward for non-Windows users to translate the usage descriptions to their preferred environment. In any case, these differences are largely limited to the cosmetics and presentation of the program and not the MATLAB commands themselves. All versions of MATLAB (on any platform) use the same command set, and the Command Window on all platforms should behave identically.

MATLAB is offered with accompanying "toolboxes" at additional cost to the user. A wide variety of toolboxes are available in fields such as control systems, image processing, radio frequency (RF) design, signal processing, and more. However, in this text, we largely focus on fundamental numerical concepts and limit ourselves to basic MATLAB functionality without requiring the purchase of any additional toolboxes.

1.5 The MATLAB Programming Language

There are many methodologies for computer programming, but the tasks at hand boil down to the following:

a. Study the problem to be programmed.
b. List the algebraic equations to be used in the program based on the known physical phenomena and geometries of the problem.
c. Create a general design for the program flow and algorithms, perhaps by creating a flowchart or by writing high-level pseudocode to outline the main program modules.
d. Carry out a sample calculation by hand to prove the algorithm.
e. Write the program using the list of algebraic equations and the outline.
f. Debug the program by running it and fixing any syntax errors.
g. Test the program by running it using parameters with a known (or intuitive) solution.
h. Iterate over these steps to refine and further debug the algorithm and program flow.
i. If necessary, revise the program to obtain faster performance.

Experienced programmers might omit some of these steps (or do them in their head), but the overall process resembles any engineering project: design, create a prototype, test, and iterate the process until a satisfactory product is achieved.

MATLAB may be considered a programming or scripting language unto itself, but like every programming language, it has the following core components:

a. Data types, i.e., formats for storing numbers and text in the program (e.g., integers, double-precision floating point, strings, vectors, matrices)
b. Operators (e.g., commands for addition, multiplication, cosine, log)
c. Control flow directives for making decisions and performing iterative operations (e.g., `if`, `while`, `switch`)
d. Input/output ("I/O") commands for receiving input from a user or file and for generating output to a file or the screen (e.g., `fprintf`, `fscanf`, `plot`, `stem`, `surf`)

MATLAB borrows many constructs from other languages. For example, the `while`, `switch`, and `fprintf` commands are from the C programming language (or its descendents C++, Java, and Perl). However, there are some fundamental differences as well. For example, MATLAB stores *functions* (known in other languages as "subroutines") in separate files. The first entry in a *vector* (known in most other languages as an *array*) is indexed by the number 1 and not 0. However, the biggest difference is that all MATLAB variables are vectors, thus providing the ability to manipulate large amounts of data with a terse syntax and allowing for the solution of complicated problems in just a few lines of code. In addition, because MATLAB is normally run interactively, it is also rich in presentation functions to display sophisticated plots and graphs.

1.6 Conventions in This Book

We use the following typographical conventions in this text:

- All input/output to and from MATLAB are in `typewriter` font.
- In cases where you are typing directly into the computer, the typed text is displayed in **`bold`**.

We illustrate this in the following example, for which we use MATLAB to find the value $x = \sin\frac{\pi}{4}$:

```
>> x = sin(pi/4)
x =
   0.7071
```

In this case, >> represents MATLAB's prompt, **`x=sin(pi/4)`** represents text typed into the MATLAB command window, and `x = 0.7071` represents MATLAB's response.

1.7 Example Programs

The example programs in this book may be downloaded from the publisher's Web site at http://www.crcpress.com/product/isbn/9781439854297. Students may then run the example programs on their own computer and see the results. It also may be beneficial for students to type in a few of the sample programs (along with some inevitable syntax and typographical errors), thereby giving them the opportunity to see how MATLAB responds to program errors and subsequently learn what they need to do to fix the problem.

Chapter 2

MATLAB Fundamentals

2.1 Introduction

MATLAB® is a software program for numeric computation, data analysis, and graphics. One advantage that MATLAB has for engineers over programming languages such as C or C++ is that the MATLAB program includes functions that numerically solve large systems of linear equations, systems of ordinary differential equations, roots of transcendental equations, integrals, statistical problems, optimization problems, control systems problems, and many other types of problems encountered in engineering. MATLAB also offers toolboxes (which must be purchased separately) that are designed to solve problems in specialized areas.

In this chapter, the following items are covered:

- The MATLAB desktop environment
- Constructing a script (also called a program) in MATLAB
- MATLAB fundamentals and basic commands, including `clear`, `clc`, colon operator, arithmetic operators, trigonometric functions, logarithmic and exponential functions, and other useful functions such as `max`, `min`, and `length`
- Input/output in MATLAB, including the `input` and `fprintf` statements
- MATLAB program flow, including `for` loops, `while` loops, `if` and `elseif` statements, and the `switch` group statement
- MATLAB function files and anonymous functions
- MATLAB graphics, including the `plot` and `subplot` commands

- Working with matrices
- Working with functions of a vector
- Working with characters and strings
- Interpolation and MATLAB's `interp1` function
- MATLAB's `textscan` function
- Exporting MATLAB data to other software, such as Microsoft Excel
- Debugging a program

Many example scripts are included throughout the chapter to illustrate these various topics.

2.2 The MATLAB Windows

Under Microsoft Windows, MATLAB may be started via the Start menu or clicking on the MATLAB icon on the desktop. On startup, a new window will open containing the MATLAB "desktop" (not to be confused with the Windows desktop), and one or more MATLAB windows will open within the desktop (see Figure 2.1 for the

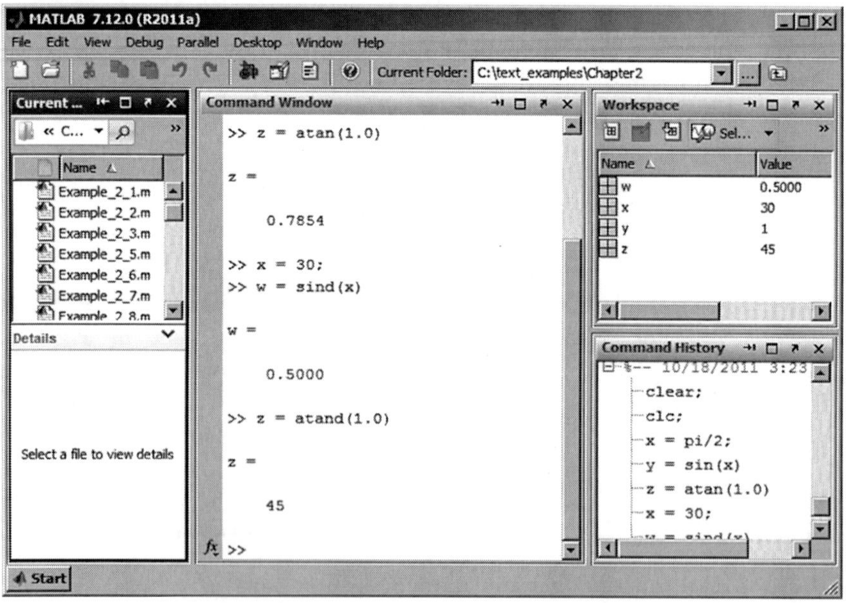

Figure 2.1 MATLAB desktop windows. (From MATLAB, with permission.)

default configuration). The main windows are the Command window, Command History, Current Folder, and Workspace. You can customize the MATLAB windows that appear on startup by opening the *Desktop* menu and checking (or unchecking) the windows that you wish to appear on the MATLAB desktop. Figure 2.1 shows the Command window (in the center), the Current Folder (on the left), the Workspace (on the top right), the Command History (on the bottom right), and the Current Folder box (in the icon toolbar, second from the top, just above the Command window). These windows and the current folder box are summarized as follows:

- *Command Window:* In the Command window you can enter commands and data, make calculations, and print results. You can write a program in the Command window and execute the program. However, writing a program directly into the Command window is discouraged because it will not be saved, and if an error is made, the entire program must be retyped. By using the up arrow (↑) key on your keyboard, the previous command can be retrieved (and edited) for reexecution.
- *Command History Window:* This window lists a history of the commands that you have executed in the Command window.
- *Current Folder Box:* This box lists the active Current Folder (also called the Current Directory in older versions of MATLAB). **To run a MATLAB script (program), the script of interest needs to be in the folder listed in this box.** By clicking on the down arrow within the box, a drop-down menu will appear that contains names of folders that you have previously used. This will allow you to select the folder in which the script of interest resides (see Figure 2.2). If the folder containing the script of interest is not listed in the drop-down menu, you can click on the adjacent little box containing three dots, which allows you to browse for the folder containing the program of interest (see Figure 2.3).
- *Current Folder Window* (on the left): This window lists all the files in the Current Folder. By double clicking on a file in this window, the file will open within MATLAB.
- *Script Window* (also called the Editor window in older MATLAB versions): To open this window, use the *File* menu at the top of the MATLAB desktop and choose *New* and then *Script* (or in older versions of MATLAB, click on *New M-File*) (see Figure 2.4). The Script Window may be used to create, edit, and execute MATLAB scripts. Scripts are then saved as *M-Files.* These files have the extension *.m*, such as *circuit.m*. To execute the program, you can click the *Save and Run* icon (the green arrow) in the Script window or return to the Command window and type in the name of the program (without the *.m* extension).

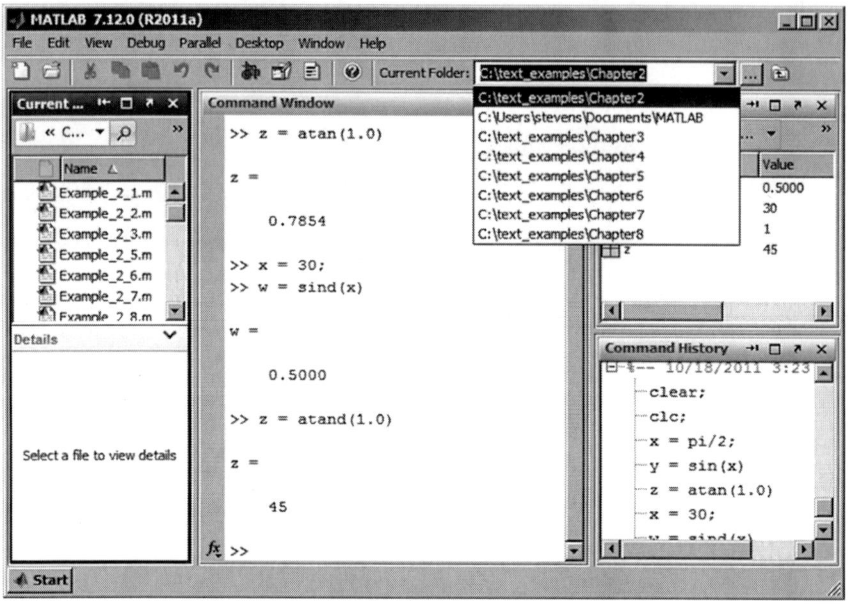

Figure 2.2 Drop-down menu in the Current Folder window. (From MATLAB, with permission.)

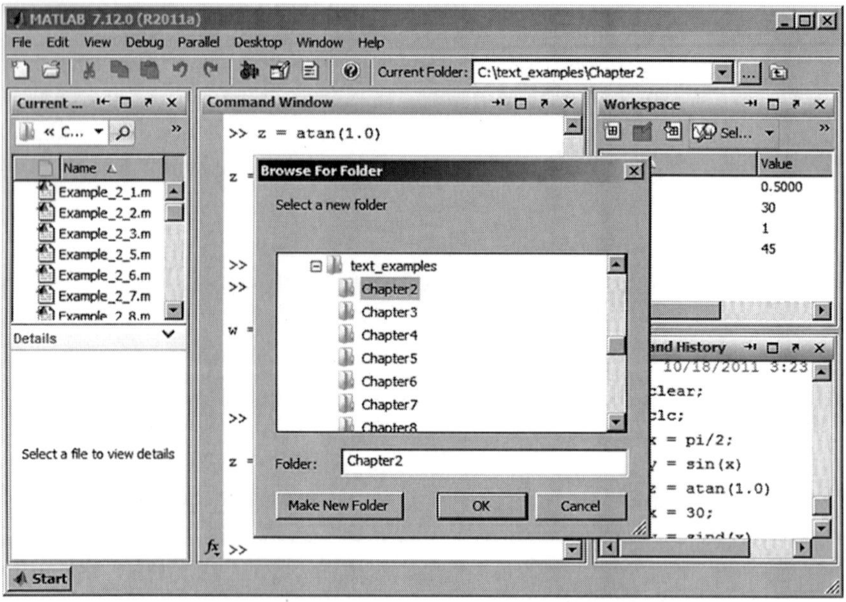

Figure 2.3 Drop-down menu for selecting folder containing program of interest. (From MATLAB, with permission.)

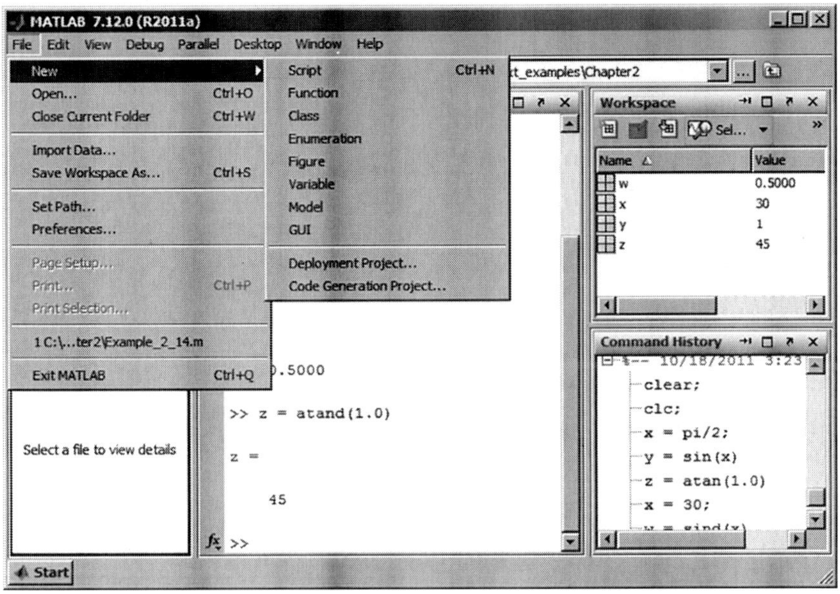

Figure 2.4 Opening up the Script window. (From MATLAB, with permission.)

2.3 Constructing a Program in MATLAB

This list summarizes the steps for writing your first MATLAB program:

1. Start the MATLAB desktop via the Windows Start menu or by double clicking on the MATLAB icon on the desktop.
2. Click on *File-New-Script*. This brings up a new Script window.
3. Type your script into the Script window.
4. Save the script by clicking on the *Save* icon in the icon toolbar or clicking on *File* in the menu bar and selecting *Save* in the drop down menu. In the dialog box that appears, select the folder where the script is to reside and type in a file name of your own choosing. It is best to use a folder that contains only your own MATLAB scripts.
5. Before you can run your script, you need to go to the Current Folder box at the top of the MATLAB desktop, clicking on the down arrow and in the drop down menu, selecting (or browsing to) the folder that contains your new script.
6. You may run your script from the Script window by clicking on the *Save and Run* green arrow in the icon toolbar (see Figure 2.5) or alternatively, from the

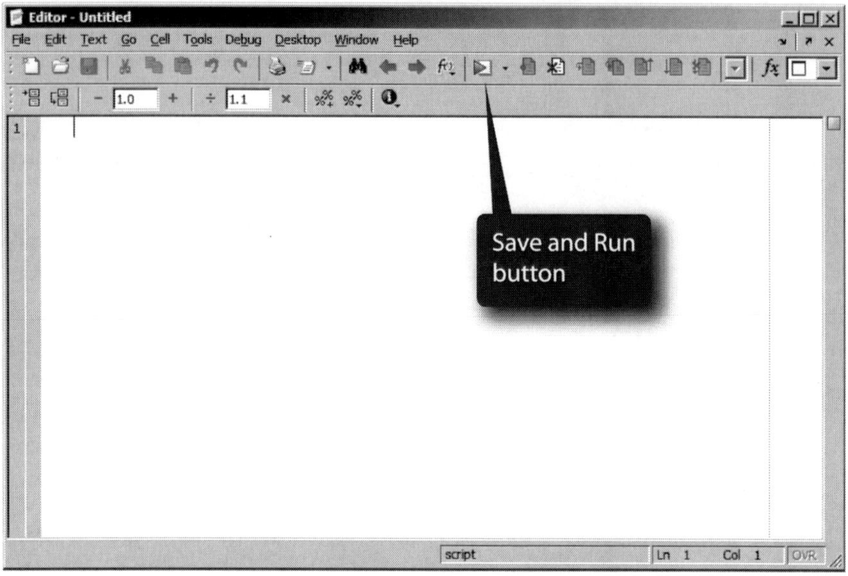

Figure 2.5 Save and run button in the script window. (From MATLAB, with permission.)

command window by typing the script name (without the *.m* extension) after the MATLAB prompt (>>). For example, if the program has been saved as *circuit.m,* then type `circuit` after the MATLAB prompt (>>), as shown below:

```
>> circuit
```

If you need additional help getting started, you can click on *Help* in the menu bar in the MATLAB window and then select *Product Help* from the drop-down menu. This will bring up the help window as shown in Figure 2.6. By clicking on the little '+' box next to the MATLAB listing in the left column, you will get additional help topics as shown in Figure 2.7. Once you select one of the help topics, the help information will be in the right-hand window. You can also type in a topic in the search window to obtain information on that topic.

2.4 MATLAB Fundamentals

- Variable names
  - must start with a letter.

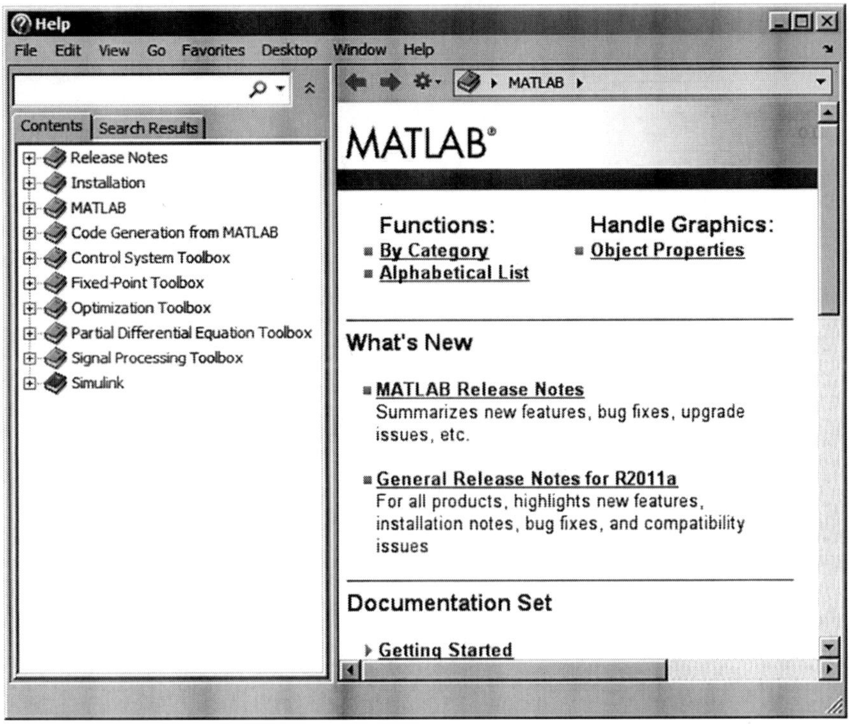

Figure 2.6 Product help window. (From MATLAB, with permission.)

  - can contain letters, digits and the under score character.
  - can be of any length, but must be unique within the first 19 characters.

  Note: Do not use a variable name that is the same name as the name of a file, a MATLAB function, or a self written function.

- MATLAB command names and variable names are case sensitive. Use lower case letters for commands.
- Semicolons are usually placed after variable definitions and program statements when you do not want the command echoed to the screen. In the absence of a semicolon, the defined variable appears on the screen. For example, if you entered the following assignment in the command window:

```
>> A = [3 4 7 6]
```

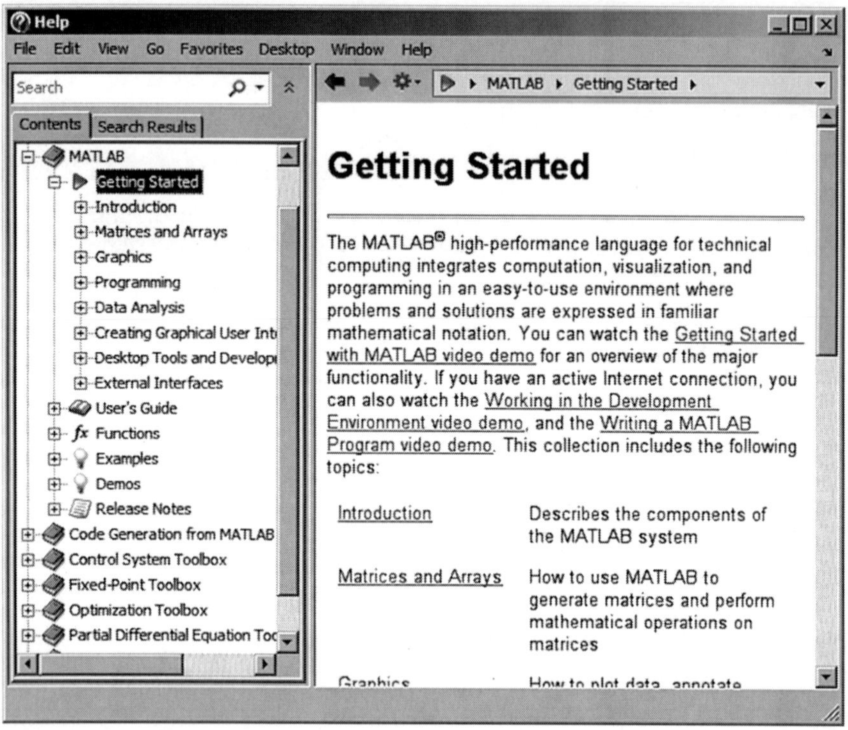

Figure 2.7 Getting started in product help window. (From MATLAB, with permission.)

In the command window, you would see

```
A =
    3  4  7  6
>>
```

Alternatively, if you add the semicolon, then your command is executed but there is nothing printed to the screen, and the prompt immediately appears for you to enter your next command:

```
>> A = [3 4 7 6];
>>
```

- Percent sign (%) is used for a comment line.
- A separate Graphics window opens to display plots and graphs.
- There are several commands for clearing windows, clearing the work space and stopping a running program.

`clc`	clears the Command window
`clf`	clears the Graphics window
`clear`	removes all variables and data from the workspace
Ctl-C	aborts a program that may be running in an infinite loop

- the `quit` or `exit` commands terminate MATLAB.
- the `save` command saves variables or data in the workspace of the current directory. The file name containing the data will have *.mat* extension.
- User-defined functions (also called *self-written* functions) are also saved as M-files.
- Scripts and functions are saved as ASCII text files. Thus, they may be written either in the built-in Script window, Notepad, or any word processor (saved as a text file).
- The basic data structure in MATLAB is a matrix.
- A matrix is surrounded by brackets and may have an arbitrary number of rows and columns; for example, the matrix $A = \begin{bmatrix} 1 & 3 \\ 6 & 5 \end{bmatrix}$ may be entered into MATLAB as

```
>> A = [1 3 <enter>
        6 5]; <enter>
```

or

```
>> A = [1 3 ; 6 5]; <enter>
```

where the semicolon within the brackets indicates the start of a new row within the matrix.

- A matrix of one row and one column is a scalar; for example:

```
>> A = [3.5];
```

Alternatively, MATLAB also accepts **A = 3.5** (without brackets) as a scalar.

- A matrix consisting of one row and several columns or one column and several rows is considered a vector; for example:

```
>> A = [2 3 6 5] (row vector)

>> A = [2
        3
        6
        5] (column vector)
```

A matrix can be defined by including a second matrix as one of the elements; example:

```
>> B = [1.5 3.1];
>> C = [4.0 B];    (thus C = [4.0 1.5 3.1])
```

- A specific element of matrix C can be selected by writing

  `>> a = C(2);` (thus $a = 1.5$)

  If you wish to select the last element in a vector, you can write

  `>> a = c(end);` (thus $a = 3.1$)

- The colon operator (:) may be used to create a new matrix from an existing matrix; for example:

$$\text{if} \quad A = \begin{bmatrix} 5 & 7 & 10 \\ 2 & 5 & 2 \\ 1 & 3 & 1 \end{bmatrix}$$

then `x = A(:,1)` gives $x = \begin{bmatrix} 5 \\ 2 \\ 1 \end{bmatrix}$

The colon in the expression `A(:,1)` implies all the rows in matrix A, and the 1 implies column 1.

`x = A(:,2:3)` gives $x = \begin{bmatrix} 7 & 10 \\ 5 & 2 \\ 3 & 1 \end{bmatrix}$

The first colon in the expression `A(:,2:3)` implies all the rows in A, and the 2:3 implies columns 2 and 3.

We can also write

`y = A(1,:)`, which gives $y = [5 \;\; 7 \;\; 10]$

The 1 implies the first row, and the colon implies all the columns.

- A colon can also be used to generate a series of numbers. The format is:

  n = starting value : step size : final value. If omitted, the default step size is 1. For example:

  `n = 1:8` gives $n = [1 \quad 2 \quad 3 \quad 4 \quad 5 \quad 6 \quad 7 \quad 8]$.

  To increment in steps of 2, use

  `n=1:2:7` gives $n = [1 \quad 3 \quad 5 \quad 7]$

  These types of expressions are often used in a `for` loop, which is discussed later in this chapter.

- Arithmetic operators:

+	addition
-	subtraction
*	multiplication
/	division
^	exponentiation

- To display a variable value, just type the variable name without the semicolon, and the variable will appear on the screen.

  Examples (try typing these statements into the Command window):

```
clc;
x = 5;
y = 10;
z = x + y
w = x - y
z = y/x
z = x*y
z = x^2
```

  Note that in the arithmetic statement `z = x + y`, the values for `x` and `y` were assigned in the two prior lines. In general, all variables on the right-hand side of an arithmetic statement must be assigned a value before they are used.

- Special values:

`pi`	π
`i` or `j`	$\sqrt{-1}$
`inf`	∞
`ans`	the last computed unassigned result to an expression typed in the Command window

Examples (try typing these statements in the command window):

```
x = pi;
z = x/0 (gives inf)
```

- Trigonometric functions:

`sin`	sine
`sinh`	hyperbolic sine
`asin`	inverse sine
`asinh`	inverse hyperbolic sine
`cos`	cosine
`cosh`	hyperbolic cosine
`acos`	inverse cosine
`acosh`	inverse hyperbolic cosine
`tan`	tangent
`tanh`	hyperbolic tangent
`atan`	inverse tangent
`atan2`	four-quadrant inverse tangent
`atanh`	inverse hyperbolic tangent
`sec`	secant
`sech`	hyperbolic secant
`asec`	inverse secant
`asech`	inverse hyperbolic secant
`csc`	cosecant
`csch`	hyperbolic cosecant
`acsc`	inverse cosecant
`acsch`	inverse hyperbolic cosecant
`cot`	cotangent
`coth`	hyperbolic cotangent
`acot`	inverse cotangent
`acoth`	inverse hyperbolic cotangent

The arguments of these trigonometric functions are in radians. However, the arguments can be made in degrees if a "`d`" is placed after the function name, such as `sind(x)`.

Examples (try typing these statements into the Command window):

```
clc;
x = pi/2;
y = sin(x)
```

```
z = atan(1.0)
x = 30;
w = sind(x)
z = atand(1.0)
```

- Exponential, square root, and error functions:

`exp`	exponential
`log`	natural logarithm
`log10`	common (base 10) logarithm
`sqrt`	square root
`erf`	error function

Examples (try typing these statements into the Command window):

```
clc;
x = 2.5;
y = exp(x)
z = log(y)
w = sqrt(x)
```

- Complex numbers:

Complex numbers may be written in two forms: Cartesian, such as `z = x + yj`; or polar, such as `z = r * exp(j*theta)`. Note that we use `j` for $\sqrt{-1}$ throughout this text. However, MATLAB allows the use of `i` for $\sqrt{-1}$ as well. Note: `i` and `j` are also legal MATLAB variable names which are often used within loops. To avoid confusion, programs which involve complex numbers should not use `i` or `j` as variable names.

`abs`	absolute value (magnitude)
`angle`	phase angle (in radians)
`conj`	complex conjugate
`imag`	complex imaginary part
`real`	complex real part

Examples (try typing these statements into the Command window):

```
clc;
z1 = 1 + j;
z2 = 2 * exp(j * pi/6)
y = abs(z1)
```

```
w = real(z2)
v = imag(z1)
phi = angle(z1)
```

■ Other useful functions:

`length(X)`	Gives the number of elements in the vector *X*.
`size(X)`	Gives the size (number of rows and the number of columns) of matrix *X*.
`sum(X)`	For vectors, `sum(X)` gives the sum of the elements in *X*. For matrices, gives a row vector containing the sum of the elements in each column of the matrix.
`max(X)`	For vectors, `max(X)` gives the maximum element in *X*. For matrices, `max(X)` gives a row vector containing the maximum in each column of the matrix. If *X* is a column vector, it gives the maximum value of *X*.
`min(X)`	Same as `max(X)` except it gives the minimum element in *X*.
`sort(X)`	For vectors, `sort(X)` sorts the elements of *X* in ascending order. For matrices, `sort(X)` sorts each column in the matrix in ascending order.
`factorial(n)`	$n! = 1 \times 2 \times 3 \times \cdots \times n$
`mod(x,y)`	modulo operator, gives the remainder resulting from the division of *x* by *y*. For example, `mod(13,5) = 3`, that is, 13 ÷ 5 gives 2 plus remainder of 3 (the 2 is discarded). As another example, `mod(n,2)` gives zero if *n* is an even integer and one if *n* is an odd integer.

Examples (try typing these statements into the Command window):

```
clc;
A = [2 15 6 18];
length(A)
y = max(A)
z = sum(A)
A = [2 15 6 18; 15 10 8 4; 10 6 12 3];
x = max(A)
y = sum(A)
size(A)
mod(21,2)
mod(20,2)
```

■ A list of the complete set of elementary math functions can be obtained by typing **help elfun** in the Command window.

- Sometimes, it is necessary to preallocate a matrix of a given size. This can be done by defining a matrix of all zeros or ones; for example:

$$\texttt{A = zeros(3)} = \begin{bmatrix} 0 & 0 & 0 \\ 0 & 0 & 0 \\ 0 & 0 & 0 \end{bmatrix}$$

$$\texttt{B = zeros(3,2)} = \begin{bmatrix} 0 & 0 \\ 0 & 0 \\ 0 & 0 \end{bmatrix}$$

$$\texttt{C = ones(3)} = \begin{bmatrix} 1 & 1 & 1 \\ 1 & 1 & 1 \\ 1 & 1 & 1 \end{bmatrix}$$

$$\texttt{D = ones(2,3)} = \begin{bmatrix} 1 & 1 & 1 \\ 1 & 1 & 1 \end{bmatrix}$$

The function to generate the identity matrix (main diagonal of ones; all other elements are zero) is `eye`; example:

$$\texttt{I = eye(3)} = \begin{bmatrix} 1 & 0 & 0 \\ 0 & 1 & 0 \\ 0 & 0 & 1 \end{bmatrix}$$

2.5 MATLAB Input/Output

- If you wish to have your program pause to accept input from the keyboard, use the `input` function; for example, to enter a 2 by 3 matrix, use

```
Z = input('Enter values for Z in brackets \n');
```

then type in:

```
[5.1  6.3  2.5;  3.1  4.2  1.3]
```

Thus,

$$Z = \begin{bmatrix} 5.1 & 6.3 & 2.5 \\ 3.1 & 4.2 & 1.3 \end{bmatrix}$$

Note that the argument to `input()` is a character string enclosed by single quotation marks, which will be printed to the screen. The `\n` (newline) tells MATLAB to move the cursor to the next line. Alternatively, `\t` (tab) tells MATLAB to move the cursor several spaces along the same line.

If you wish to enter text data to `input`, you need to enclose the text with single quotation marks. However, you can avoid this requirement by entering a second argument of `'s'` to `input` as shown in the following statement:

```
response = input('Plot function? (y/n):\n', 's');
```

In this case, the user can respond with either a `y` or `n` (without single quotation marks).

Examples (try typing these statements into the Command window):

```
z = input ('Enter a 2x3 matrix of your choosing\n')
name=input('Enter name enclosed by single quote marks:')
response = input('Plot function? (y/n):\n', 's');
```

- The `disp` command prints *just* the contents of a matrix or alphanumeric information; for example (assuming that matrix X has already been entered in the Command window):

```
>>     x = [3.6 7.1]; disp(X); disp('volt');
```

The following will be displayed on the screen:

```
        3.6000 7.1000
        volt
>>
```

- The `fprintf` command prints formatted text to the screen or to a file; for example:

```
>> I = 2.2;
>> fprintf ('The current is %f amps \n', I);
```

The following will appear on the screen:

```
The current is 2.200000 amps
```

The `%f` refers to a formatted floating point number, and the default is six decimal places (although in earlier versions of MATLAB, the default for `%f` format was four decimal places).

`fprintf` uses format strings based on the C programming language [1]. Thus, you can specify the minimum number of spaces for the printed variable as well as the number of decimal places using

```
%8.2f
```

This will allow eight spaces for the variable, to two decimal places. You can also specify just the number of decimal places, for example, say three decimal places, and then let MATLAB automatically decide the number of spaces for the variable using

```
%.3f
```

However, to create neat looking tables, it is best to specify the number of spaces in the format statement that allows for several spaces between variables in adjacent columns.

Other formats are as follows:

`%i` or `%d`	used for integers
`%e`	scientific notation (e.g., `6.02e23`), with default six decimal places
`%g`	automatically use the briefest of `%f` or `%e` format
`%s`	used for a string of characters
`%c`	used for a single character

Unlike C, the format string in MATLAB's `fprintf` must be enclosed by single quotation marks (and *not* double quotes).

Sometimes, the format part of the `fprintf` command may be too long to fit on a single line in your script. When this happens, you can use three dots (...) to tell MATLAB to continue the statement on a second line, as shown by the following example:

```
fprintf('resistance = %f volts = %f current = %f \n',...
      R,V,I);
```

Three dots may be used to continue any MATLAB statement onto additional lines to improve the readability of your script, as shown by the following statement:

```
a = (-4*pi^2*omega^2*r^2*(cos(arg1))^2/sqrt(arg2) +...
    4*pi^2*omega^2*r^2*(sin(arg1))^2/sqrt(arg2)) *...
    exp(j*pi*omega);
```

An alternative to using the three dots to extend a lengthy arithmetic statement onto more than one line is to break up the statement into several smaller statements and then combine them. As an example, we could break up the previous statement into three shorter statements to calculate a:

```
a1 = -4*pi^2*omega^2*r^2*(cos(arg1))^2/sqrt(arg2);
a2 = 4*pi^2*omega^2*r^2*(sin(arg1))^2/sqrt(arg2);
a = (a1+a2) * exp(j*pi*omega);
```

- Printing to a file: It is often useful to print the results of a MATLAB program to a file, possibly for inclusion in a report. In addition, program output that is printed to a file can subsequently be edited within the file, such as aligning or editing column headings in a table. Before you can print to a file, you need to open a file for printing with the command fopen. The syntax for fopen is

```
fo = fopen('filename','w')
```

Thus, fo is a pointer to the file named filename, and the w indicates writing.

To print to filename use

```
fprintf(fo,'format',var1,var2,...);
```

where the format string contains the text format for var1, var2, and so on. When you are finished with all of your print statements, you should close the file with the fclose command, as shown in the following example.

Example (write this simple program in the Script window and save it as *io_example.m*):

```
% io_example.m
% This program is a test for printing to a file.
clear; clc;
V = 120;
I = 2.2;
fo = fopen('output.txt','w');
fprintf (fo, 'V = %4i volt, I = %5.2f amp \n',V,I);
fclose(fo);
```

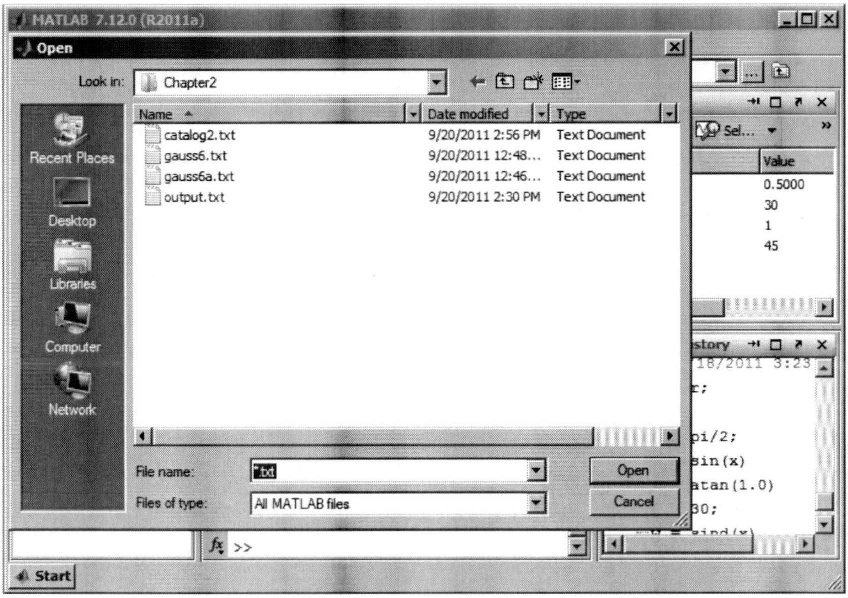

Figure 2.8 Files with extension *.txt*. (From MATLAB, with permission.)

The extension on the output file should be *.txt* (otherwise, MATLAB will start the import wizard). The resulting output file can be opened from either the Script window or the Command window. To access the output file, click on *File-Open*, which brings up the screen shown in Figure 2.8. In the box labeled *File name*, type in **.txt*. This will bring up all the files with the extension *.txt*. To open the file of interest, double click on the name of the output file (in this example, the file name is *output.txt*). In earlier versions of MATLAB, you would not be able to open the output file without including the `fclose(fo)` statement in the program. None the less it is still good practice to include the `fclose` statement after all the output statements in the program or at the end of the program itself.

- The `fscanf` command may be used to read from an existing file as follows:

```
A = zeros(n,m);
fi = fopen('filename.txt', 'r');
[A] = fscanf(fi, '%f', [n,m]);
```

where $n \times m$ is the number of elements in the data file. The 'r' in the fopen statement indicates that the file is for reading data into the program.

The $n \times m$ matrix is filled in column order. Thus, rows become columns, and columns become rows. To use the data in its original order, transpose the read-in matrix. To transpose a matrix `A` in MATLAB, simply type in `A'`. This changes columns to rows and rows to columns.

- An existing data file can also be entered into a program by the `load` command. The `load` command, unlike the `fscanf` command, leaves rows as rows and columns as columns.

For example:

```
load filename.txt
x = filename(:,1);
y = filename(:,2);
```

The input file must have the same number of rows in each column.

2.6 MATLAB Program Flow

- The `for` loop provides the means to carry out a series of statements with just a few lines of code.

Syntax:

```
for m = 1:20
    statement;
       :
    statement;
end
```

MATLAB sets the index `m` to 1, carries out the statements between the `for` and `end` statements, then returns to the top of the loop, changes `m` to 2, and repeats the process. After the 20th iteration, the program exits the loop. Any statement that is not to be repeated should not be within the `for` loop. For example, table headings that are not to be repeated should be outside the `for` loop.

Example (write this simple program in the Script window, save it as *for_loop_example.m,* and run the script):

```
% for_loop_example.m
clear; clc;
% Table headings:
fprintf(' n          y1                y2 \n');
fprintf(' ------------------------------\n');
% Using the index in the for loop in an arithmetic statement
for j = 1:10
    y1 = j^2/10;
    y2 = j^3/100;
    fprintf('%5i    %10.3f %10.3f \n',j,y1,y2);
end
```

Note: If the index in a `for` loop is used to select an element of a matrix, then the index *must* be an integer. However, if you are not using the `for` index as a matrix index, then the `for` index need not be an integer as shown in the following example (write this simple program in the Script window, save it as *for_loop_example2.m,* and run the script):

```
% for_loop_example2.m
% Using a range of non-integer x values in a for loop.
% The range of x is from -0.9 to +0.9 in steps of 0.1.
clear; clc;
% print the table header outside of the 'for' loop:
fprintf(' x          y1                 y2     \n');
fprintf(' ------------------------------\n');
for x = -0.9:0.1:0.9
    y1 = x/(1-x);
    y2 = y1^2;
    fprintf('%5.2f  %10.3f %10.3f \n',x,y1,y2);
end
```

■ The `while` loop

Syntax:

```
n = 0;
while n < 10
   n = n+1;
   statement;
      ⋮
   statement;
end
```

In the `while` loop, MATLAB will carry out the statements between the `while` and `end` statements as long as the condition in the `while` statement is satisfied. If an index in the program is required, the use of the `while` loop statement (unlike the `for` loop) requires that the program create its own index, as shown above. Note that the statement "`n=n+1`" may not make sense algebraically but does makes sense in the MATLAB language. The "=" operator in MATLAB (as in many computer languages) is the *assignment* operator, which tells MATLAB to fetch the contents of the memory cell containing the variable `n`, put its value into the arithmetic unit of the CPU (central processing unit), increment by 1, and put the new value back into the memory cell designated for the variable `n`. Thus, the old value of `n` has been replaced by the new value for `n`.

■ `if` statement

Syntax:

`if` logical expression

```
        statement;
            ⋮
        statement;
    else
        statement;
            ⋮
        statement;
    end
```

If the logical expression is true, then only the upper set of statements is executed. If the logical expression is false, then only the bottom set of statements is executed.

- Logical expressions are of the form

```
a == b;        a <= b;
a < b;         a >= b;
a > b;         a ~= b;
```
(*a* not equal to *b*)

- Compound logical expressions

```
a > b  &&   a ~= c
a > b  ||   a < c
```
($a > b$ AND $a \neq c$)

($a > b$ OR $a < c$)

- The `if-elseif` ladder

Syntax:

```
    if logical expression 1
            statement(s);
    elseif logical expression 2
            statements(s);
    elseif logical expression 3
            statement(s);
    else
            statement(s);
    end
```

The `if-elseif` ladder works from top down. If the top logical expression is true, the statements related to that logical expression are executed, and the program will leave the ladder. If the top logical expression is not true, the program moves to the next logical expression. If that logical expression is true, the program will execute the group of statements associated with that logical expression and leave the ladder. If that logical expression is not true, the program moves to the next logical expression and continues the process. If none of the logical expressions are true, the program will execute the statements associated with the `else` statement. The `else` statement is not required. In that case, if none of the logical expressions are true, no statements within the ladder will be executed.

- The `break` command may be used within a for or while loop to end the loop; for example:

```
for m = 1:20
    statement;
       ⋮
    statement;
    if m > 10
        break;
    end
end
```

In this example, when *m* becomes greater than 10, the program leaves the `for` loop and moves on to the next statement in the program.

- The switch group

Syntax:

```
switch(var)
    case var1
        statement(s);
    case var2
        statement(s);
    case var3
        statement(s);
    otherwise
        statement(s);
end
```

where `var` takes on the possible values `var1`, `var2`, `var3`, and so on.

If `var` equals `var1`, those statements associated with `var1` are executed, and the program leaves the switch group. If `var` does not equal `var1`, the program tests if `var` equals `var2`, and if yes, the program executes those statements associated with `var2` and leaves the switch group. If `var` does not equal any of `var1`, `var2`, and so on, the program executes the statements associated with the `otherwise` statement. If `var1`, `var2`, and so on are strings, they need to be enclosed by single quotation marks. It should be noted that `var` cannot be a logical expression, such as `var1 >= 80`. For example (write this simple program in the Script window, save it as *switch_example.m,* and run the program):

```
% switch_example.m
% This program is a test of the switch statement.
clear; clc;
```

```
var = 'a';
x = 5;
switch(var)
    case 'b'
          z = x^2;
    case 'a'
          z = x^3;
end
fprintf('z = %6.1f \n',z);
```

Additional example programs follow that demonstrate the use of the `for` loop, nested `for` loops, the `while` loop, the `if` statement, the `if-elseif` statements, the `break` statement, the `input` statement, and the `fprintf` statement. Since a number of these sample programs involve determining e^x by a Taylor series expansion, we start with a discussion of the series expansion of e^x.

Example 2.1: Calculation of e^x

The Taylor series expansion of e^x to n terms is

Term index:	1	2	3	4	⋯	n

$$e^x = 1 + x + \frac{x^2}{2!} + \frac{x^3}{3!} + \frac{x^4}{4!} + \cdots + \frac{x^n}{n!}$$

There are several possible programming algorithms to calculate this series. The simplest method is to start with `sum = 1` and then evaluate each term using exponentiation and MATLAB's `factorial` function and add the obtained term to `sum`. An alternative approach would be to evaluate each term individually, save them in an array, and then use MATLAB's `sum` function to add them all. However, for some series expressions it is best to compute each term in the series based on the value of the preceding term. For example, in the above series, we can see that the third term in the series can be obtained from second term by multiplying the second term by x and dividing by 3; that is, term3 = term2 · x/3. In general, term (n) = term$(n–1)$ · x/n.

```
% Example_2_1.m
% This program calculates e^x by series and by MATLAB's
% exp() function. The 'for' loop ends when the term only
% affects the seventh significant figure.
% Note: e^x = 1 + x + x^2/2! + x^3/3! + x^4/4! + ...
clear; clc;
x=5.0;
s=1.0;
for n=1:100
    term=x^n/factorial(n);
    s=s+term;
```

```
    if(abs(term) <= s*1.0e-7)
        break;
    end
end
ex1=s;
ex2=exp(x);
fprintf('x=%3.1f   ex1=%8.5f  ex2=%8.5f \n',x,ex1,ex2);
-------------------------------------------------------------
```

Example 2.2: Nested Loops

```
% Example_2_2.m
% This program illustrates the use of nested loops, i.e.
% an inner 'for' loop inside an outer 'for' loop.
% The program calculates e^x by both MATLAB's 'exp'
% command (variable 'ex2'), and by a Taylor series
% expansion (variable 'ex1'), where -0.5 < x < 0.5.
% The outer 'for' loop is used to determine the x
% values. The inner loop is used to determine the Taylor
% series method for evaluating e^x. In this example,
% term(n+1) is obtained by multiplying term(n) by x/n.
% The variable 'term' is established as a vector so that
% MATLAB's built-in 'sum' function can be used to sum
% all the terms calculated in the Taylor series method.
% A maximum of fifty terms is used in the series.
% Program output is sent both to the screen and to a
% file. By printing the output to a file, you can easily
% edit the output file to line up column headings,
% etc. (which you can't do when printing to the screen).
% Note: e^x = 1 + x + x^2/2! + x^3/3! + x^4/4! + ...
clear; clc;
xmin=-0.5; dx=0.1;
fo=fopen('output.txt','w');
% Table headings
fprintf(' x          ex1          ex2 \n');
fprintf('------------------------------------\n');
fprintf(fo,' x          ex1          ex2 \n');
fprintf(fo,'------------------------------------\n');
for i=1:11
    x=xmin+(i-1)*dx;
    ex2=exp(x);
    term(1)=1.0;
    for n=1:49
        term(n+1)=term(n)*x/n;
        if abs(term(n+1)) <= 1.0e-7
            break;
        end
    end
    ex1 = sum(term);
    fprintf('%5.2f    %10.5f    %10.5f \n',x,ex1,ex2);
    fprintf(fo,'%5.2f    %10.5f    %10.5f \n',x,ex1,ex2);
end
fclose(fo);
-------------------------------------------------------------
```

Note: In this example, the two statements

```
for i = 1:11
      x = xmin+(i-1)*dx;
```

could be replaced with the following single statement:

```
for x = -0.5:0.1:0.5
```

This approach is acceptable when the `for` loop index is not used to select an element of a matrix. In MATLAB, the variable selecting an element of a matrix must be an integer.

Example 2.3: While Loop

```
% Example_2_3.m
% Calculation of e^x by both MATLAB's exp function and
% the Taylor series expansion of e^x. The input()
% function is used to establish the exponent x.
% A 'while' loop is used in determining the series
% solution. A 'break' statement is used to end the loop
% if the number of terms becomes greater than 50. The
% display statement is used to display the values of x,
% ex and ex2 in the command window.
% Note: e^x = 1 + x + x^2/2! + x^3/3! + x^4/4! + ...
clear; clc;
x=input('Enter a value for the exponent x \n');
n=1; ex=1.0; term=1.0;
while abs(term) > ex*1.0e-6
    term=x^n/factorial(n);
    ex=ex+term;
    n=n+1;
    if n > 50
        break;
    end
end
ex2=exp(x);
disp(x);
disp(ex);
------------------------------------------------------------
```

2.7 MATLAB Function Files

MATLAB functions are useful if you have a complicated program and wish to break it down into smaller parts. Also, if a series of statements is to be used many times, it is convenient to place them in a function. Functions are equivalent to subroutines in most programming languages, but in MATLAB they are usually stored in separate files instead of in the main program (although small functions can be defined in the same file as your main script. This is described in the next section).

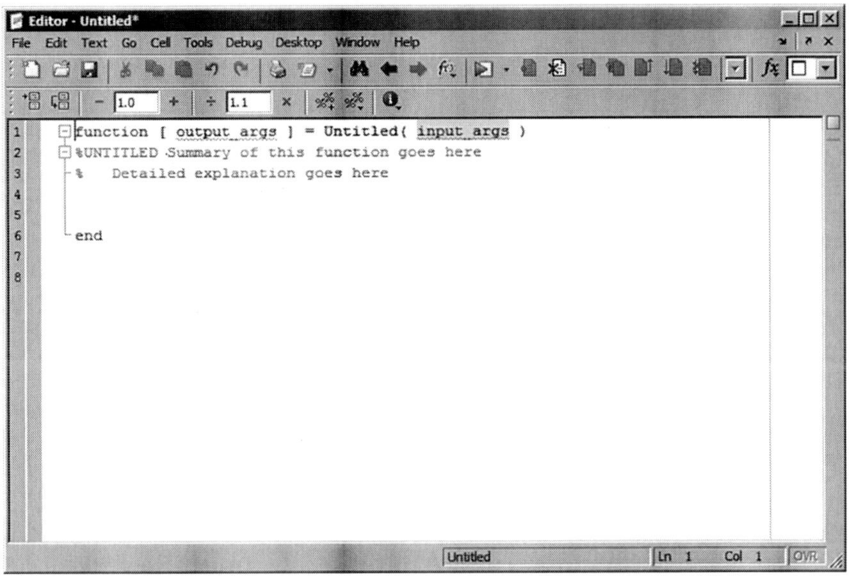

Figure 2.9 Function template. (From MATLAB, with permission.)

- The function file name must be saved as *function_name.m.*
- MATLAB has a template for writing a function (see Figure 2.9). The first executable statement in the function file must be `function`. As can be seen from Figure 2.9, the function template is of the form:

  `function` [output arguments] = `Untitled`(input arguments)

  see above figure

  Some example function definitions are shown in Table 2.1.

  If the function has more than one output value, then the output variables must be in brackets. If there is only one output value, then no brackets are necessary. If there are no output values, use empty brackets.
- A function differs from a script in that the return arguments may be passed to another function or to the Command window. Variables defined and manipulated inside the function are local to the function.

Table 2.1 Example of Function Usage

Function Definition Line	*Function File Name*
`function [P,V] = power(i,v)`	*power.m*
`function ex = exf(x)`	*exf.m*
`function[] = output(x,y)`	*output.m*

- Many of MATLAB's "built-in" functions are actually implemented as *.m* files. For example, `factorial` is implemented in the file *factorial.m*. You can find *factorial.m* by typing **`which factorial`** in the Command window.

Example 2.4: MATLAB Function Definition

```
% exf1.m (Example 2.4)
% Define a function, 'exf1', that evaluates e^x.
% This function takes 'x' as an input argument and is
% called either from the Command Window or from another
% program. The resulting output, 'ex', is available to
% be used in another program or in the Command Window.
% In this example, term(n+1) is obtained from term(n)
% by multiplying term(n) by x/n.
% Note: e^x = 1 + x + x^2/2! + x^3/3! + x^4/4! + ...
function ex = exf1(x)
term(1)=1.0;
for n=1:99
   term(n+1)=term(n)*x/n;
   if abs(term(n+1)) <= 1.0e-7
      break;
   end
end
ex=sum(term);
----------------------------------------------------------------
```

To test out this function, run it from the Command window. Some examples follow:

```
>> exf1(1.0)
ans =
     2.7183
>> y = exf1(5.0)
y =
    148.4132
```

Example 2.5: Using a MATLAB Function

```
% Example_2_5.m
% This program uses the function exf1 (defined in
% Example 2.4) in several arithmetic statements, i.e to
% calculate w, y and z. In this program, the output is
% sent to a file.
clear; clc;
fo=fopen('output.txt','w');
fprintf(fo,'  x         y          w          z     \n');
fprintf(fo,'---------------------------------- \n');
for x=0.1:0.1:2.0
    y=exf1(x);
    w=5*x*exf1(x);
    z=10*x/y;
    fprintf(fo,'%4.2f  %8.3f  %8.3f  %8.3f \n',x,y,w,z);
end
fclose(fo);
------------------------------------------------------------
```

The following example demonstrates that the names of the arguments in the calling program need not be the same as those in the function. It is only the argument list in the calling program that needs to be in the same order as the argument list defined in the function. This feature is useful when a function is to be used with several different scripts, each script having different variable names but with each of the variable names corresponding to variables in the function.

Example 2.6: Defining and Using a MATLAB Function

```
% Example_2_6.m
% This program uses the function exf2 to calculate
% q=e^w/z .  w and z are input variables to function
% exf2.  The function exf2 calculates q and returns it
% to this program.  The input variables to function exf2
% need not be the same names as those used in the
% calling program. For one-to-one correspondence, the
% argument positions in the calling program have to be
% the same as the argument positions in the function.
% Note: function exf2 (defined below) must be created
% before this program is executed because the function
% exf2 calculates exy and returns it to the calling program.
% q is set equal to exy.
clear; clc;
z=5;
for w=0.1:0.1:2.0
    q=exf2(w,z);
    fprintf('Values of w,z and q from main program: ');
    fprintf('w=%.2f  z=%.0f    q=%.5f \n', w, z, q);
end
-----------------------------------------------------------------
% exf2.m
% This script is used with script Example_2_6.m and creates a
% function 'exf2' that evaluates e^x/y.  In this
% function, x and y are input variables that need to be
% defined in another program. The output variable in the
% function exf2 is sent back to the calling program.
% This example demonstrates that the names of the
% arguments in the calling program need not be the same
% as those in the function. It is the order list in the
% calling program that needs to be the same as the order
% list in the function.
% In this example, term(n+1) is obtained from term(n) by
% multiplying term(n) by x and dividing by index n. The
% program does its own summing of terms.
% Note: e^x = 1 + x + x^2/2! + x^3/3! + x^4/4! + ...
function exy = exf2(x,y)
% Note: x and y are set equal to w and z respectively.
s=1.0; term=1.0;
for n=1:100
    term=term*x/n;
    s=s+term;
    if abs(term) <= s*1.0e-5
        break;
    end
```

```
end
exy=s/y;
% These fprintf statements demonstrate the equivalence
% between function input variables (x,y) and calling
% program variables (w,z) in the program Example_2_6.m.
% Compare the printout of x,y and exy with w,z and q.
fprintf('Values of x,y and exy from exf2():     ');
fprintf('x=%.2f  y=%.0f  exy=%.5f \n', x, y, exy);
------------------------------------------------------------
```

2.8 Anonymous Functions

Sometimes, it is more convenient to define a function inside your script rather than in a separate file. For example, if a function is brief (perhaps a single line) and unlikely to be used in other scripts, then the *anonymous* form of a function can be used. This will save you from having to create another *.m* file. An example is

```
fh = @(x,y)(y*sin(x)+x*cos(y));
```

MATLAB defines the @ sign as a *function handle*. A function handle is equivalent to accessing a function by calling its function name, which in this case is `fh`. The `(x,y)` defines the input arguments to the function, and the `(y*sin(x)+x*(cos(y))` is the actual function. Anonymous functions may be used in a script or in the command window.

For example, in the Command window, type in the following two lines:

```
>> fh = @(x,y)(y*sin(x)+x*cos(y));
>> w = fh(pi,2*pi)
w =
   3.1416
```

Additional information on anonymous functions can be obtained by typing **`help function _ handle`** in the Command window.

2.9 MATLAB Graphics

- Plot commands:

`plot(x,y)`	linear plot of *y* versus *x*
`semilogx(x,y)`	semilog plot (log scale for *x* axis, linear scale for *y* axis)
`semilogy(x,y)`	semilog plot (linear scale for *x* axis, log scale for *y* axis)
`loglog(x,y)`	log-log plot (log scale for both *x* and *y* axes)

■ Multiple plots:

`plot(x,y,w,z)` gives multiple plots on the same axes: in this case y versus x and z versus w.

For example, suppose

$$A = \begin{bmatrix} t_1 & y_1 & z_1 & w_1 \\ t_2 & y_2 & z_2 & w_2 \\ \vdots & \vdots & \vdots & \vdots \\ t_n & y_n & z_n & w_n \end{bmatrix}$$

Let $T = A(:,1)$, $Y = A(:,2)$, $Z = A(:,3)$, and $W = A(:,4)$, giving

$$T = \begin{bmatrix} t_1 \\ t_2 \\ \vdots \\ t_n \end{bmatrix} \quad Y = \begin{bmatrix} y_1 \\ y_2 \\ \vdots \\ y_n \end{bmatrix} \quad Z = \begin{bmatrix} z_1 \\ z_2 \\ \vdots \\ z_n \end{bmatrix} \quad W = \begin{bmatrix} w_1 \\ w_2 \\ \vdots \\ w_n \end{bmatrix}$$

Then, to plot Y versus T, Z versus T, and W versus T all on the same figure, write

```
plot(T,Y,T,Z,T,W);
```

Of course, we could have avoided the additional step by writing

```
plot(A(:,1),A(:,2),A(:,1),A(:,3),A(:,1),A(:,4))
```

■ Customizing plots:

You can add a grid to the plot with the command,

```
grid
```

To label the x and y axes and to add a title to the plot, add the following commands to your program:

```
xlabel('T');
ylabel('Y, Z, W');
title('Y, Z, W vs T');
```

You can also add text to the plot with the command

`text(`*x* position, *y* position, `'text statement'`);

Greek letters and mathematical symbols can be used in `xlabel`, `ylabel`, `title`, and `text` by spelling out the Greek letter and preceding it with a '\' (backslash character). Thus, to display ω, use `\omega`, and to display γ, use `\gamma`. For example:

```
ylabel('\omega'), title('\omega vs. \gamma'), text(10,5,'\Phi');
```

For a complete list of Greek symbols and additional special characters, see Appendix B. You may also occasionally need to print a "`'`" character in your label or title. In this case, use a double `'` to "escape" the single-quote character in your string. Thus, to generate the plot title "`Signal 'A' vs. Signal 'B'` ", you would type

```
title('Signal ''A'' vs. Signal ''B''')
```

In most cases, you can let MATLAB select the scaling for the *x* and *y* axes of a two-dimensional plot. However, if you are unsatisfied with MATLAB's automatic selection, then you can use the `axis` command to set the plot limits explicitly:

```
axis([xmin xmax ymin ymax])
```

where `xmin` and `xmax` set the scaling for the *x* axis, and `ymin` and `ymax` set the scaling for the *y* axis.

- Interactively annotating plots:
  As an alternative to adding the `xlabel`, `ylabel,` and `title` commands to your program, you can create the plot, then click on the *Insert* menu in the plot window and choose *X Label* from the drop-down menu. This will highlight a box in which you can type in the abscissa variable name. You can repeat this process for the *Y Label* and the *Title* of the plot. Other options available in the *Insert* menu are *TextBox, Text Arrow, Arrow,* and others. When you click any one of these options, a cross hair will appear, and you can then move the item to the location where you want it to appear, then left click the mouse to fix the location. You can then type in the desired text. To remove the outlines of a *TextBox*, place the cursor in the *TextBox* and right click the mouse. This will bring up a drop-down menu; select *Line Style* and then left click on *none.*

- Saving plots:
  To save a plot, click on *File* in the plot window and select the *Save* option from the drop-down menu. This produces a window where you can enter a file name. The disadvantage of this method is that if you decide to rerun the

script, the items that you manually inserted will not be saved. If you wish to copy the figure into a report, you can click on *Edit* in the plot window, then select *Copy Figure* from the drop-down menu. You can then paste the figure into your report. If you need a monochrome version of your plot (for best reproduction on a photocopier), you can make all of your curves black by choosing the File menu and then selecting *Export Setup* from the drop-down menu. This will open a window in which you need to click on *Rendering* and change the *Colorspace* to *black and white.*

There are many more options available in the plot window; however, we leave it up to the student to explore further.

Example 2.7: Creating Plots

```
% Example_2_7.m
% This program creates a simple table and a simple plot.
% First, the vectors y1, y2 and t are calculated.
% Next a table of y1 = n^2/10 and y2 = n^3/100 is created.
% Then y1 and y2 are plotted.
clear; clc;
for n=1:10
    t(n)=n;
    y1(n)=n^2/10;
    y2(n)=n^3/100;
end
% By making t, y1 and y2 as vectors, their values can be
% printed out outside the 'for' loop that created them.
% Print column headings
fprintf('     t           y1            y2    \n');
fprintf('-------------------------------------\n');
for n=1:10
    fprintf('%8.1f    %10.2f    %10.2f \n', ...
        t(n),y1(n),y2(n));
end
% Create the plot. y1 is red, y2 is in green.
plot(t,y1,'r',t,y2,'g');
xlabel('t'), ylabel('y1,y2'), grid;
title('y1 and y2 vs. t');
% Plot identification is also established by adding text
% to the plot.
text(6.5,2.5,'y1');
% In the above statement, 6.5 is the abscissa position
% and 2.5 is the ordinate position where the 'y1' label
% will be positioned.
text(4.2,2.4,'y2');
% Other MATLAB plot options:
% Available color types:
%   blue         'b'
%   green        'g'
%   red          'r'
%   cyan         'c'
%   yellow       'y'
% Curves y1 and y2 can also be distinguished by using
```

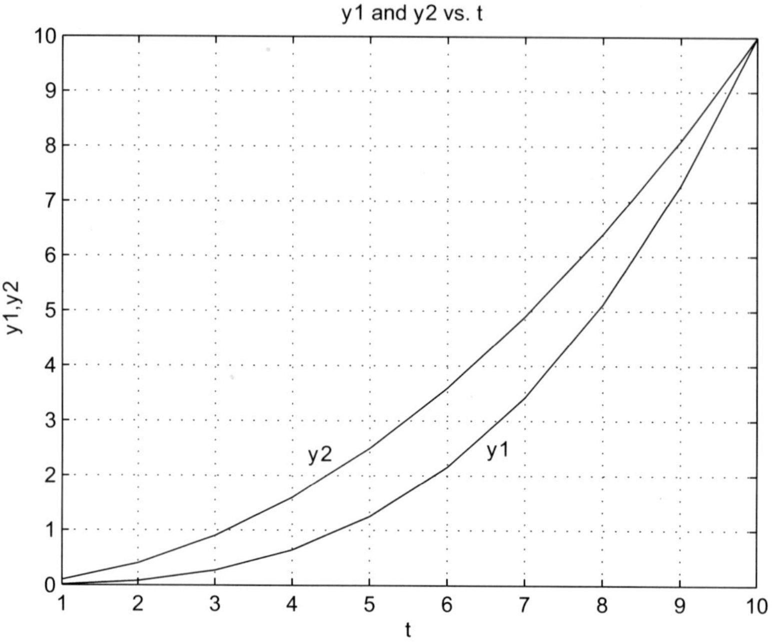

Figure 2.10 Example plot generated with the `plot` command.

```
% different types of lines as listed below.
% Available line types:
%    solid          (default)
%    dashed         '--'
%    dashed-dot     '-.'
%    dotted         ':'
% Alternatively, you can create a marker plot of
% discrete points (without a line) by using one of these
% marker styles:
%    point          '.'
%    plus           '+'
%    star           '*'
%    circle         'o'
%    x-mark         'x'
% The 'legend' command may also be used in place of the
% text command to identify the curves. The legend box
% may be moved by clicking on the box and dragging it to
% the desired position.
-----------------------------------------------------------------------------
```

The resulting plot is shown in Figure 2.10.

Example 2.8: The Subplot Command

Suppose you want to plot each of the curves in the previous example as a separate plot, but all on the same page. The `subplot` command provides the means to do so. The command `subplot(m,n,p)` breaks the page into an `m` by `n` matrix of small plots, and `p` selects the matrix position of the plot. The following example demonstrates the use of the `subplot` command:

```
% Example_2_8.m
% This program is an example of the use of the subplot
% command and the elseif ladder. Values of y1, y2, y3
% and y4 are constructed as vectors.  Separate plots of
% y1 vs. t, y2 vs. t and y3 vs. t are plotted on the
% same page.
clc; clear;
for n=1:11
    t(n)=n-1;
    y1(n)=t(n)^2/10;
    y2(n)=sin(pi*t(n)/10);
    y3(n)=exp(t(n)/2);
    y4(n)=sqrt(t(n));
end
for n=1:4
    subplot(2,2,n)
    if n==1
        plot(t,y1), grid, title('y1 vs. t');
        xlabel('t'), ylabel('y1');
    elseif n==2
        plot(t,y2), grid, title('y2 vs. t');
        xlabel('t'), ylabel('y2');
    elseif n==3
        plot(t,y3), grid, title('y3 vs. t');
        xlabel('t'), ylabel('y3');
    elseif n==4
        plot(t,y4), grid, title('y4 vs. t');
        xlabel('t'), ylabel('y4');
    end
end
------------------------------------------------------------------------
```

Example 2.9: The `sprintf` Function

Sometimes, we might wish to enter formatted data into the `xlabel`, `ylabel`, or `title` of a graph. We can do this with the `sprintf` command, which allows data to be formatted using a similar mechanism as `fprintf` but sends the result to a function or variable instead of to the screen or a file. This is shown in the following example:

```
% Example_2_9.m
% This program demonstrates the use of sprintf command
% to pass formatted data to ylabel and title in a graph.
% The subplot command is also demonstrated.
clear; clc;
% Define the data to plot
x = -10:2:10;
m = 2:5;
b = [1 10 100 1000];
% Create table and plot
for i=1:4
```

```
        fprintf('m = %i \n',m(i));
        % print table headings
        fprintf('x          yc \n');
        fprintf('----------------------\n');
        % (x to power m(i)) divided by b(i)
        for j=1:length(x)
            yc(j) = x(j)^ m(i) / b(i);
            fprintf('%5.0f  %8.2f \n',x(j),yc(j));
        end
        fprintf('\n\n');
        % plot
        subplot(2,2,i);
        plot(x,yc);
        xlabel('x');
        ylabel(sprintf('(x to power %d) / %.0f',m(i),b(i)));
        grid, title(sprintf('m = %d, b = %d',m(i),b(i)));
end
-----------------------------------------------------------------------
```

See Figure 2.11 for the resulting plot.

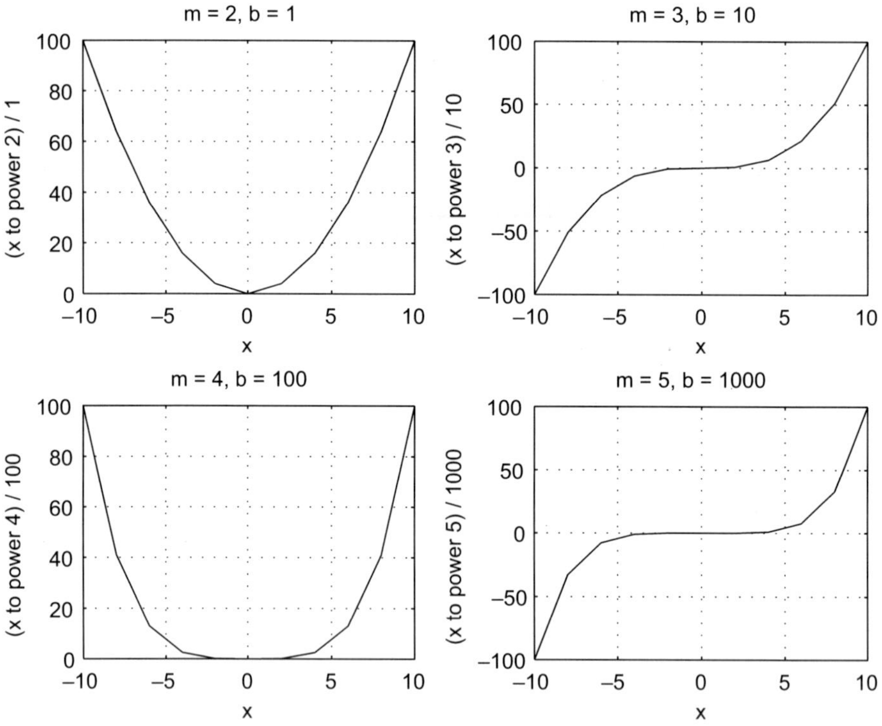

Figure 2.11 Example subplots and example use of the `sprintf` command in the plot titles and labels.

Example 2.10: The Stem Plot

In discrete-time signal processing, a *stem* plot is often used to display signal sequences. Given a signal $x[n]$ that is defined for integer values of n, the command `stem(n,x)` will plot `x` as vertical "lollipops" stemming from the horizontal axis. The following script generates a stem plot for the following data:

$$x[0] = 2.4,\ x[1] = 3.8,\ x[2] = -1.8,\ x[3] = 2.1,\ x[4] = 1.9$$

$$x[5] = 0.8,\ x[6] = 0.0,\ x[7] = -0.8,\ x[8] = 1.5$$

```
% Example_2_10.m
% This script uses the 'stem' command to plot discrete
% data.
clc; clear;
x = [2.4  3.8  -1.8  2.1  1.9  0.8  0.0 -0.8 1.5];
n = [ 0    1     2    3    4    5    6    7   8];
stem(n,x);
xlabel('n'), ylabel('x[n]');
axis([ -1 9 -3 5]);
---------------------------------------------------------------
```

The resulting plot is shown in Figure 2.12.

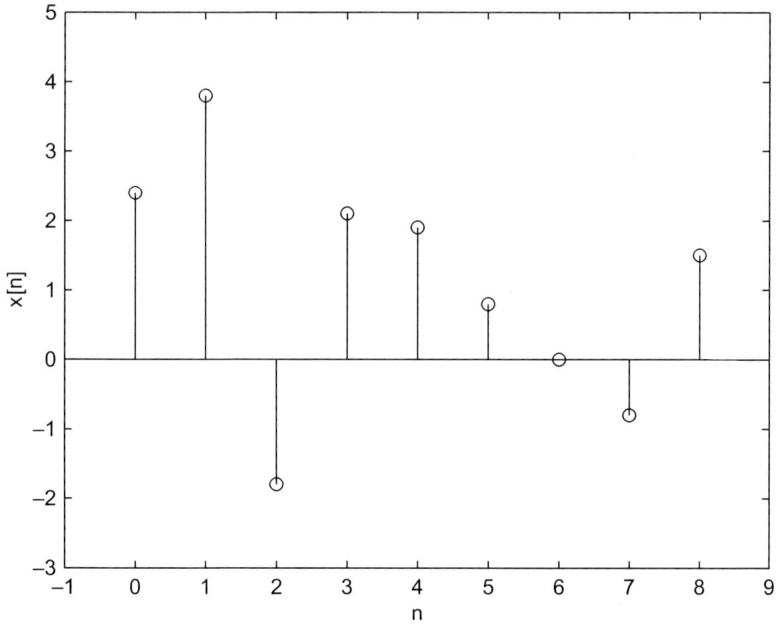

Figure 2.12 A stem plot.

Example 2.11: Creating a Data File to be Used in an External Program

```
% Example_2_11.m
% This program is used to create a data file that can be
% loaded in another program for use in a variety of ways.
clear; clc;
for n=1:20
    t(n)=n;
    y1(n)=n^2/10;
    y2(n)=n^3/100;
    y3(n)=n^4/1000;
end
fo=fopen('ydata.txt','w');
for i=1:20
    fprintf(fo,'%6.1f  %10.5f   %10.5f  %10.5f \n',...
        t(i),y1(i),y2(i),y3(i));
end
% Running the program creates the data file 'ydata.txt':
fprintf('Data is saved to file ''ydata.txt''\n');
% Adding the clear statement removes all data from the
% work space:
clear;
------------------------------------------------------------
```

Example 2.12: Loading Data Created in an External Program

```
% Example_2_12.m
% This program demonstrates the use of the load command.
% A data file named ydata.txt (created in Example_2_11.m)
% is loaded into this program. Then, variables t,y1,y2,y3
% are extracted from the loaded data and plotted all on
% one graph.
clear; clc;
fprintf('Reading data from ''ydata.txt''\n');
load ydata.txt
t = ydata(:,1);
y1 = ydata(:,2);
y2 = ydata(:,3);
y3 = ydata(:,4);
plot(t,y1,t,y2,'--',t,y3,'-.');
xlabel('t'), ylabel('y1,y2,y3'),
title('y1, y2 and y3 vs. t'), grid;
legend('y1','y2','y3');
------------------------------------------------------------
```

An alternative to the `load` command is the `dlmread` command. This command will read an ASCII delimited file. All data in the file must be numeric. In Example 2.12, we could replace the lines starting with `load ydata.txt` and ending with `y3 = ydata(:,4)` with

```
Y = dlmread('ydata.txt');
t = Y(:,1);
y1 = Y(:,2);
y2 = Y(:,3);
y3 = Y(:,4);
```

Example 2.13: Semilog Plots

```
% Example_2_13.m
% This program is a demonstration of a semilog plot
% command
clc; clear;
x=1:0.5:5;
for i=1:length(x)
    y(i)=3.0*exp(x(i));
end
semilogy(x,y), title('Semilog plot of y vs. x');
xlabel('x'), ylabel('y'),grid;
----------------------------------------------------------
```

Example 2.14: Plotting Trigonometric Functions

```
% Example_2_14.m
% This script calculates functions sin(2x/3) and cos(3x+pi)
% for -pi <= x <= pi. The x domain is subdivided into 50
% subdivisions. The functions at each data point is
% calculated and stored in the vectors 'fsin' and 'fcos'.
% Then the two vectors are printed as a table to a file
% named 'output.txt'. Plots of both functions on the same
% axis are created. Finally, the maximum values of
% 'fsin' and 'fcos' are determined and printed.
clear; clc;
xmin=-pi; dx= 2*pi/50;
for i=1:51
    x(i)=xmin+(i-1)*dx;
    arg1=2*x(i)/3;
    arg2=3*x(i)+pi;
    fsin(i)=sin(arg1);
    fcos(i)=cos(arg2);
end
fo=fopen('output.txt','w');
% Table headings
fprintf(fo,'      x           fsin         fcos \n');
fprintf(fo,'--------------------------------------\n');
for i=1:51
    fprintf(fo,'%10.5f    %10.5f  %10.5f \n', ...
        x(i),fsin(i),fcos(i));
end
fprintf(fo,'--------------------------------------\n\n');
% Print maximum values:
fsin_max=max(abs(fsin));
fcos_max=max(abs(fcos));
fprintf(fo,'fsin_max=%10.5f\n',fsin_max);
fprintf(fo,'fcos_max=%10.5f\n',fcos_max);
% Plot data:
plot(x,fsin,x,fcos,'--');
xlabel('x'), ylabel('fsin,fcos'), grid,
title('fsin and fcos vs. x');
legend('fsin','fcos');
-------------------------------------------------------------
```

2.10 Working with Matrices

Additional examples follow demonstrating the use of

1. nested `for` loops for entering a 3 × 3 matrix from the keyboard.
2. the `input` command.
3. the `load` command.
4. an example of a self-written function.
5. the `fscanf` command.

Example 2.15: Interactive Keyboard Input of a Matrix

```
% Example_2_15.m
% Input a 3 by 3 matrix from the keyboard.
% Nested loops are used to create a 3 by 3 matrix.
% An element in the matrix is established by the indices
% of both the inner and outer loops.
clear; clc;
for n=1:3
    for m=1:3
        fprintf('n=%i  m=%i    ',n,m);
        a(n,m)=input('Enter a(n,m): ');
        fprintf('\n');
    end
end
% Print the resulting matrix:
a
-------------------------------------------------------------
```

Example 2.16: Loading a Matrix from a File

```
% Example_2_16.m
% Matrices A and B are loaded from a file named
% data216.txt, then printed to the screen. Matrices A and
% B are combined into matrix C, which is sent to function
% signal_out. This function subdivides matrix C back into
% matrices A and B and prints them out to the screen.
% Note: Before running this program, the data file
% data216.txt and function file signal_out.m need to be
% created (see below).
clear; clc;
n = 5;
load data216.txt
A = data216(:,1:n);
B = data216(:,n+1);
fprintf('Matrix A elements: \n');
A
fprintf('\n');
fprintf('Matrix B elements: \n');
B
C=[A B];
signal_out(C);
-------------------------------------------------------------
```

```
% Data file 'data216.txt' (do not include this header line)
8.77  2.40  5.66  1.55  1.0 -32.04
4.93  1.21  4.48  1.10  1.0 -20.07
3.53  1.46  2.92  1.21  1.0 -8.53
5.05  4.04  2.51  2.01  1.0 -6.30
3.54  1.04  3.47  1.02  1.0 -12.04
-------------------------------------------------------------
% signal_out.m
% This function accepts matrix A & matrix B and prints
% them to the screen and is used with Example 2.16.
function [] = signal_out(C)
n=5;
A=C(:,1:n);
fprintf('This output is from signal_out: \n\n');
fprintf('Matrix A elements: \n')
for i=1:n
    for j=1:n
        fprintf('  %8.3f ',A(i,j));
    end
    fprintf('\n');
end
fprintf('\n\n Matrix B elements: \n');
B=C(:,n+1);
for i=1:n
    fprintf('  %8.3f \n',B(i));
end
------------------------------------------------------------
```

Example 2.17: Loading a Matrix with **fscanf**

```
% Example_2_17.m
% This program uses the fscanf command to enter an M by N
% matrix into MATLAB. The M by N matrix is entered in
% column order. Thus, rows become columns and columns
% become rows. The script creates matrices A and B and
% then prints them out to the screen.
% Note: Before running this program, the data file
% data217.txt needs to be created (see data below).
clear; clc;
n=5;
A=zeros(n); B=zeros(5,1);
fin=fopen('data217.txt','r');
[A]=fscanf(fin,'%f ',[n,n]);
fprintf('  Matrix A elements: \n');
A
[B]=fscanf(fin,'%f',[n]);
fclose(fin);
fprintf('\n');
fprintf('  Matrix B elements: \n');
B
fprintf('\n');
fprintf('  Matrix C elements: \n');
C=[A' B]
% Comparing the data217 data file with matrices A and B,
```

```
% we see that the data217 data file has been transposed
% (rows become columns and columns become rows).
------------------------------------------------------------
% Data file 'data217' (do not include this header line)
  8.77    2.40   5.66   1.55    1.0
  4.93    1.21   4.48   1.10    1.0
  3.53    1.46   2.92   1.21    1.0
  5.05    4.04   2.51   2.01    1.0
  3.54    1.04   3.47   1.02    1.0
-32.04 -20.07  -8.53  -6.30  -12.04
------------------------------------------------------------
```

2.11 Working with Functions of a Vector

MATLAB allows functions to have vectors as arguments. The return value can also be a vector. For example (write this simple script in the script window, save it as *vector_function.m,* and run the script):

```
% vector_function.m
clear; clc;
% Define vector x;
x = 0:30:360;
% Let y1 be the sine of a vector x where x is in degrees.
% Running sind on a vector will return a vector:
y1 = sind(x);
% Let y2(n) be the sine of the nth element of x. We will
% use a for loop to calculate each value y2(n) and then
% compare y1 and y2.
for n = 1:length(x)
    y2(n) = sind(x(n));
end
% Table headings
fprintf(' x       y1      y2      \n');
fprintf(' ------------------------------------------ \n');
for n = 1:length(x)
    fprintf('%5.1f  %8.5f  %8.5f \n', x(n),y1(n),y2(n))
end
```

In the generated output, does `y1 = y2`?

We see that in some scripts, we could replace the use of a `for` loop by taking a function of a vector, which produces a vector, thus reducing the number of lines in the script. This concept is demonstrated above in the script *vector_function.m*. However, if the script requires a mathematical operation of two functions (such as a product of two vector functions), then the operation will require an element-by-element operation. Element-by-element operations are discussed in Chapter 3.

2.12 Additional Examples Using Characters and Strings

Additional examples follow that demonstrate

- printing a string of characters
- the use of the `switch` statement
- the use of the `if-elseif` ladder
- the use of a `for` loop to select the proper interval in a matrix for establishing a grade or for interpolation.

Example 2.18: Printing a Character String Matrix from a Loop

```
% Example_2_18.m
% Sometimes you might wish to print out a string of
% characters in a loop. This can be done by declaring a
% 2-D character string matrix as shown in this example.
% Note that all row character strings must have the same
% number of columns and that character strings must be
% enclosed by single quotation marks.
clear; clc;
parts=['Internal modem   '
       'Graphics adapter'
       'CD drive         '
       'DVD drive        '
       'Floppy drive     '
       'Hard disk drive '];
for i=1:5
    fprintf('%16s \n', parts(i,1:16));
end
------------------------------------------------------------
```

Example 2.19: Printing Strings to the Screen or to a File Based on User Input

```
% Example_2_19.m
% This example is a modification of Example 2.18. The
% program asks the user if they want to have the output
% go to the screen or to a file. This example illustrates
% the use of the switch statement.
clear; clc;
char=['Internal modem         '
      'External modem         '
      'Graphics circuit board'
      'CD drive               '
      'Hard disk drive        '];
fprintf('Choose whether to send the output to the\n');
fprintf('screen or to a file named ''output.txt''.\n');
fprintf('\n');
fprintf('Enter ''s'' for screen or ''f'' for file\n');
var = input('(without quotes): ','s');
switch(var)
```

```
    case 's'
        for i=1:5
            fprintf('%22s \n',char(i,1:22));
        end
    case 'f'
        fo=fopen('output.txt','w');
        for i=1:5
            fprintf(fo,'%22s \n',char(i,1:22));
        end
        fclose(fo);
    otherwise
        fprintf('You did not enter an ''s'' or an ');
        fprintf('''f'', try again.\n');
end
-------------------------------------------------------------
```

Example 2.20: The `if-elseif` Ladder

```
% Example_2_20.m
% This example uses the if-elseif ladder.
% The program determines a letter grade depending on the
% score the user enters from the keyboard.
clear; clc;
gradearray=['A'; 'B'; 'C';'D';'F'];
score=input('Enter your test score: ');
fprintf('Score is: %i \n',score);
if score > 100
    fprintf('Error: score is out of range.\n');
    fprintf('Rerun program.\n');
    break;
elseif (score >= 90 && score <= 100)
    grade=gradearray(1);
elseif (score >= 80 && score < 90)
    grade=gradearray(2);
elseif (score >= 70 && score < 80)
    grade=gradearray(3);
elseif (score >= 60 && score < 70)
    grade=gradearray(4);
elseif (score < 60)
    grade=gradearray(5);
end
fprintf('Grade is: %c \n', grade);
-------------------------------------------------------------
```

Example 2.21: Interactive User Input Establishing a Grade

```
% Example_2_21.m
% This program determines a letter grade depending on the
% score the user enters from the keyboard. This version
% uses a loop to determine the correct interval of
% interest. For a large number of intervals, this method
% is more efficient (fewer statements) than the method in
% Example 2.20
clear; clc;
gradearray=['A'; 'B'; 'C';'D';'F'];
```

```
sarray=[100 90 80 70 60 0];
score=input('Enter your test score: ');
fprintf('Score is: %i \n', score);
% The following 2 statements are needed for the case
% when score = 100.
if score == 100
    grade=gradearray(1);
else
    for i=1:5
        if (score >= sarray(i+1) && score < sarray(i))
            grade=gradearray(i);
        end
    end
end
fprintf('Grade is: %c \n', grade);
-------------------------------------------------------------
```

Example 2.22: Printing String Arrays

```
% Example_2_22.m
% This program determines the letter grades of several
% students. Student's names and their test scores are
% entered in the program. This example uses nested 'for'
% loops and an 'if' statement to determine the correct
% letter grade for each student.
clear; clc;
gradearray=['A'; 'B'; 'C';'D';'F'];
sarray=[100 90 80 70 60 0];
Lname=['Smith       '
       'Lambert     '
       'Kurtz       '
       'Jones       '
       'Hutchinson  '
       'Diaz        '];
Fname=['Joe       '
       'Jane      '
       'Howard    '
       'Martin    '
       'Peter     '
       'Carlos    '];
score=[84; 72; 93; 64; 81; 75];
% The score = 100 is treated separately.
for j=1:6
    if score(j) == 100
        grade(j)=gradearray(1);
    else
        for i=1:5
           if score(j)>=sarray(i+1) && score(j)<sarray(i)
               grade(j)=gradearray(i);
           end
        end
    end
end
fprintf('Last name    First name     Grade \n');
fprintf('----------------------------------\n');
for j=1:6
```

```
    fprintf('%12s   %10s      %c \n', ...
        Lname(j,1:12), Fname(j,1:10), grade(j));
end
------------------------------------------------------------
```

Example 2.23: A Self-Written Function and String Arrays

An important building block in program development is the self-written function. In the following, we construct the function `func_grade` to determine the grade in the previous example. The input to `func_grade` is the score, and the output is the corresponding grade. Remember that a user-defined function is saved in a separate *.m* file.

```
% Example_2_23.m
% This program uses func_grade.m (defined below) to
% determine the grade of a student. The input to the
% function is score and the function returns the grade
% to the calling program.
clear; clc;
Lname=['Smith       '
       'Lambert     '
       'Kurtz       '
       'Jones       '
       'Hutchinson  '
       'Diaz        '];
Fname=['Joe       '
       'Jane      '
       'Howard    '
       'Martin    '
       'Peter     '
       'Carlos    '];
% The scores of the students named above are given in the
% vector score in the order listed in Lname.
score = [84; 72; 93; 64; 81; 75];
fprintf('Last name     First name   Grade \n');
fprintf('--------------------------------\n');
for j=1:6
    grade(j)=func_grade(score(j));
    fprintf('%12s   %10s    %c   \n', ...
        Lname(j,1:12), Fname(j,1:10), grade(j));
end
------------------------------------------------------------
% func_grade.m
% This function works with Example_2_23.m
function grade=func_grade(score)
gradearray=['A'; 'B'; 'C';'D';'F'];
sarray=[100 90 80 70 60 0];
if score == 100
    grade=gradearray(1);
else
    for i=1:5
        if (score >= sarray(i+1) && score < sarray(i))
            grade=gradearray(i);
        end
    end
end
------------------------------------------------------------
```

2.13 Interpolation and MATLAB's `interp1` Function

For many physical phenomena, we frequently find that a property of a given material will be computed as a function of some other variable. For example, the mobility of electrons in silicon is dependent on temperature and is often presented as a table of laboratory measurements for a few distinct temperatures. If we wish to determine the electron mobility at a temperature that is not in the table, we need to interpolate. The general linear interpolation formula is

$$\mu = \mu_1 + \frac{(T - T_1) \times (\mu_2 - \mu_1)}{T_2 - T_1}$$

where T_2 and T_1 are the closest surrounding measured temperatures to T, and μ_2 and μ_1 are the electron mobilities at temperatures T_2 and T_1, respectively. The next example illustrates the computation of the mobility for an arbitrary temperature based on a table of known values at known temperatures.

Example 2.24: Interpolation Using an Anonymous Function

```
% Example_2_24.m
% This program uses an anonymous function to linearly
% interpolate the electron mobility of silicon.  Measured
% values of the mobility (cm^2/V-s) vs temperature (K)
% are given [2].
clear; clc;
% Anonymous function (avoids creating an extra .m file):
Muf = @(T,T1,T2,Mu1,Mu2) (Mu1+(T-T1)*(Mu2-Mu1)/(T2-T1));
% Table values
Tt = [100 150 200 250 300 350 400 450];
Mut = [19650 7427 3723 2180 1407 972.0 705.5 531.8 ];
fprintf('This program interpolates for the electron\n');
fprintf('mobility (Mu) at a specified temperature T.\n');
fprintf('The valid temperature range is 100-450K.\n\n');
T=input('Enter T at which Mu is to be determined: ');
% Determining the closest surrounding temperatures to
% temperature T.
for n=1:length(Tt)-1
    if T >= Tt(n) && T <= Tt(n+1)
        T1=Tt(n); T2=Tt(n+1); Mu1=Mut(n); Mu2=Mut(n+1);
    end
end
Mu=Muf(T,T1,T2,Mu1,Mu2);
fprintf(' T=%.1f (K)   Mu=%.3f (cm^2/V-s) \n',T,Mu);
-------------------------------------------------------------
```

MATLAB has a function named `interp1` that performs interpolation. The next example demonstrates the use of this function for interpolating for electron mobility. In addition, MATLAB's `interp1` function can do multiple interpolations by just calling the function once.

The syntax for `interp1` is:

```
Yi = interp1(X,Y,Xi)
```

where X and Y are a set of known *x,y* data points, and Xi is the set of *x* values at which the set of *y* values Yi are to be determined by linear interpolation. Arrays X and Y must be of the same length. The function `interp1` can also be used for interpolation methods other than linear interpolation, and this is covered in Chapter 9 on curve fitting.

Example 2.25: Interpolation Using interp1 and Saving to a .mat File

```
% Example_2_25.m
% This program uses MATLAB's function interp1 to
% interpolate for the electron mobility of silicon.
% Measured values of the mobility (cm^2/V-s) vs
% temperature (K) are given [2]. Table values for
% temperature are specified in matrix T_data. Table
% values for mobility are specified in Mu_data. The
% temperature at which the electron mobility is to be
% determined is entered from the keyboard.
clear; clc;
T_data = [ 100 150 200 250 300 350 400 450 ];
Mu_data = [ 19650 7427 3723 2180 1407 972.0 705.5 531.8];
fprintf('This program interpolates for the electron\n');
fprintf('mobility (Mu) at a specified temperature T.\n');
fprintf('The valid temperature range is 100-450K.\n\n');
T=input('Enter T at which Mu is to be determined: ');
Mu = interp1(T_data,Mu_data,T);
fprintf(' T=%.1f (K)   Mu=%.3f (cm^2/V-s)\n\n', T, Mu);
% The data T_data and Mu_data can be saved in a data file
% and loaded later in another program. By the use of the
% 'clear' command the data file is removed from the
% workspace. Another script can brings the data back into
% the workspace by the load command. The script can then
% use the data for some other purpose. We want T_data and
% Mu_data to be column vectors, so save the transpose.
T_Mu_data = [T_data' Mu_data'];
save T_Mu_data;
% T_Mu_data is saved in a .mat file and will be used
% in Example 2.25.
fprintf('Mobility vs. temperature data saved to file ');
fprintf('T_Mu_data.mat\n');
clear;
% T_Mu_data has been removed from the work space
% T_Mu_data will be used in Example_2_26.
------------------------------------------------------------
```

If we wish to interpolate for electron mobility at several different temperatures, we can modify Example 2.25 by replacing all lines after (and including) the lines

```
fprintf('This program interpolates for the electron \n');
fprintf('mobility (mu) at a specified temprature T. \n');
```

with the following lines:

```
T2 = [432 182 343 210 385];
fprintf('This program interpolates for the electron \n')
fprintf('mobility (Mu) at a specified temprature T. \n');
fprintf('specified temperatures, T2. \n');
fprintf('The allowable temperature range is 100-450K. \n\n');
Mu = interp1(T_data,Mu_data,T2);
fprintf(' T2(K) Mu(cm^2/V-s) \n');
fprintf(' ---------------------------\n');
for i = 1:5
  fprintf('%6.1f  %9.3f \n',T2(i),Mu(i));
end
-----------------------------------------------------------
```

Example 2.26: Interpolating Data Stored in a `.mat` File

```
% Example_2_26.m
% This script is a sample of a plot program loading data
% obtained in another program. Make sure you run Example
% 2.25 before running this example.
clear; clc;
fprintf('Loading data from file "T_Mu_data.mat"\n');
load T_Mu_data
T= T_Mu_data(:,1);
Mu= T_Mu_data(:,2);
plot(T,Mu);
xlabel('T'), ylabel('Mu'), title('Mu vs. T'), grid;
-----------------------------------------------------------
```

2.14 MATLAB's `textscan` Function

There may be occasions when you wish to read a data file into a program that contains both numerical data and a string of characters. MATLAB's `textscan` function is best suited for this operation.

Syntax:

```
C = textscan(fid, format)
```

The function will read data from an open text file identified by `fid` into a cell array `C`.

The format is of the form `%f, %d, %c, %s,` and so on. The number of format specifiers determines the number of cells in the cell array `C`. Each cell will contain the number of lines contained in the data file and be of the type specified by the format statement. String specifiers also include `%q,` which is a string enclosed by double quotation marks. For a single character, use `%c`.

Note: To reference the contents of a cell, enclose the cell number with {}. See the following examples.

If you wish to read in `N` lines from the open data file, use

```
C = textscan(fid, format, N)
```

Example 2.27: Loading Mixed Text and Numerical Data from a File

```
% Example_2_27.m
% Load the product data from inv4.txt into the arrays
% 'sku', 'desc', and 'cost', and print.
% sku, desc and cost stands for item #,
% item description and item cost respectively.
clear; clc;
% Note: inventory227.txt is defined below.
fid=fopen('inventory227.txt');
C = textscan(fid, '%d %14c %f', 5);
% Contents of cell block C contains 1 row and 3 columns
sku = C{1};
desc = C{2};
cost = C{3};
fclose(fid);
count = length (sku)
for i=1:count
    fprintf('%5i   %14s   %6.2f\n\n', ...
        sku(i), desc(i,1:14), cost(i));
end
------------------------------------------------------------
% inventory227.txt file (do not include this header line)
1  'hammer         '  2.58
2  'plier          '  1.20
3  'screwdriver    '  1.56
4  'soldering iron'  3.70
5  'wrench         '  2.60
------------------------------------------------------------
```

Example 2.28: Another Example of Loading Mixed Text and Numerical Data from a File

```
% Example_2_28.m
% Read product inventory into a matrix using textscan.
% The file 'inventory228.txt' is listed below.
clc; clear;
fid=fopen('inventory228.txt');
C = textscan(fid,'%d  %q  %f' );
% Need to designate contents in cell C{2} as characters.
sku = C{1};
desc = char(C{2});
cost = C{3};
count = length(sku);
fprintf(' sku#  description          cost    \n');
fprintf('----------------------------------\n');
for i=1:count
    fprintf('%4i    %14s    %6.2f     \n\n', ...
        sku(i), desc(i,1:14), cost(i));
end
fclose(fid);
------------------------------------------------------------
% inventory228.txt file (Do not includ this header line)
1 "hammer           "  2.58
2 "plier            "  1.20
```

```
3 "screwdriver      "   1.56
4 "soldering iron  "   3.70
5 "wrench           "   2.60
------------------------------------------------------------
```

2.15 Exporting MATLAB Data to Excel

MATLAB can write its data directly to spreadsheet software such as Microsoft Excel. To do this, follow these steps:

1. In your MATLAB program, create a matrix of the output data, say `M`.
2. Write the data to an Excel file with the following statement:

   ```
   xlswrite('filename.xls',M);
   ```

   This will create an Excel file named *filename.xls* of your data, `M`, which you can then edit within Excel (see Figure 2.13).
3. You can now use all of the formatting and data manipulation commands available in Excel. For example, to add table headings, open the Excel file, place the cursor in the top left cell (cell A1), and type in table headings in each

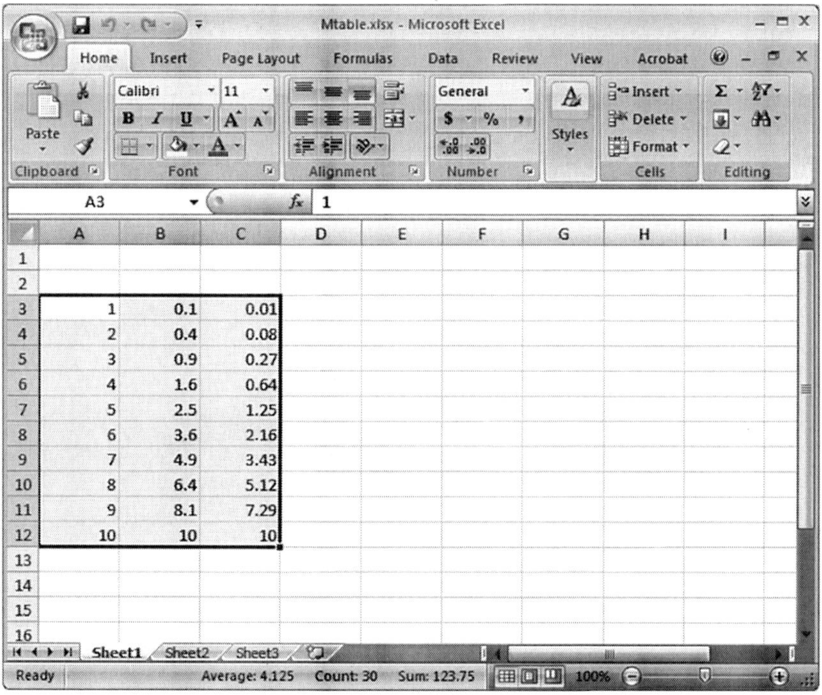

Figure 2.13 Example of sending output to Excel.

of the cell columns. To add up the second column, place the cursor in cell B13 and type = `SUM(B3:B12)`. You can also apply bold, italics, and cell borders.

2.16 Debugging a Program

It is common when writing a program to make typographical errors, such as omitting a parenthesis, forgetting a comma in a two-dimensional array, and so on. This type of bug is called a *syntax error.* When this occurs, MATLAB will provide an error message pointing out the line in which the error has occurred. However, there are cases when there are no syntax errors, but the program still fails to run or gives an obvious incorrect answer. When this occurs, you can utilize the debug feature in MATLAB. The debug feature allows you to set break points in your program. The program will run up to the line containing the break point. To set a break point, left click the mouse in the narrow column next to the line number that you wish to be a break point. A small red circle will appear next to the break point line as shown in Figure 2.14. The script will now run up to, but not including, the line containing the break point, as shown in Figure 2.15 (at the command to print matrix A). The `K>>` prompt indicates that you are in the debug mode. You can then click on the debug listing in the MATLAB toolbar and select from several options in the drop-down menu (see Figure 2.16). If the program contains self-written functions, you can continue execution one line at a time in the function. To do this, you first need to clear all the break points in the main program, then select the *Step In* option in the debug drop-down menu (see Figure 2.16). The *Step Out* option returns the control

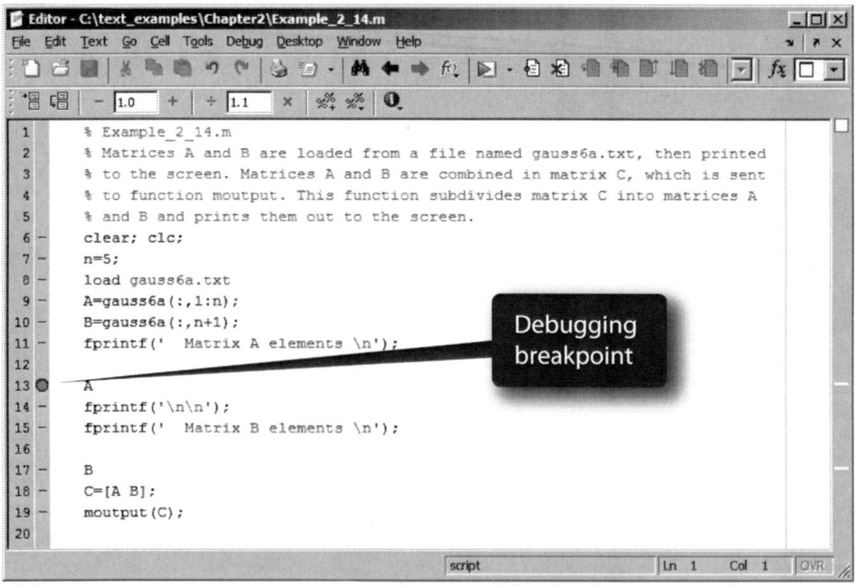

Figure 2.14 Setting a break point. (From MATLAB, with permission.)

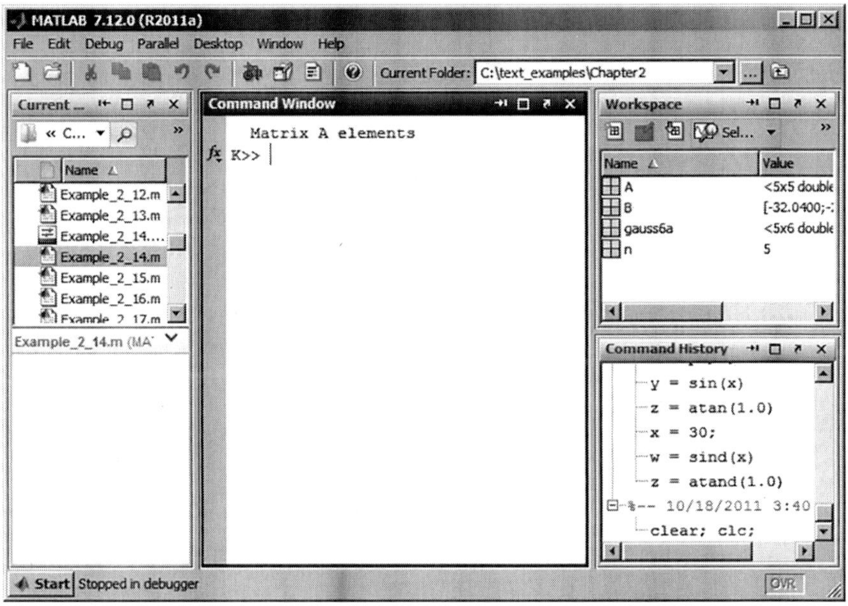

Figure 2.15 Program execution is halted when the break point is reached in the program. (From MATLAB, with permission.)

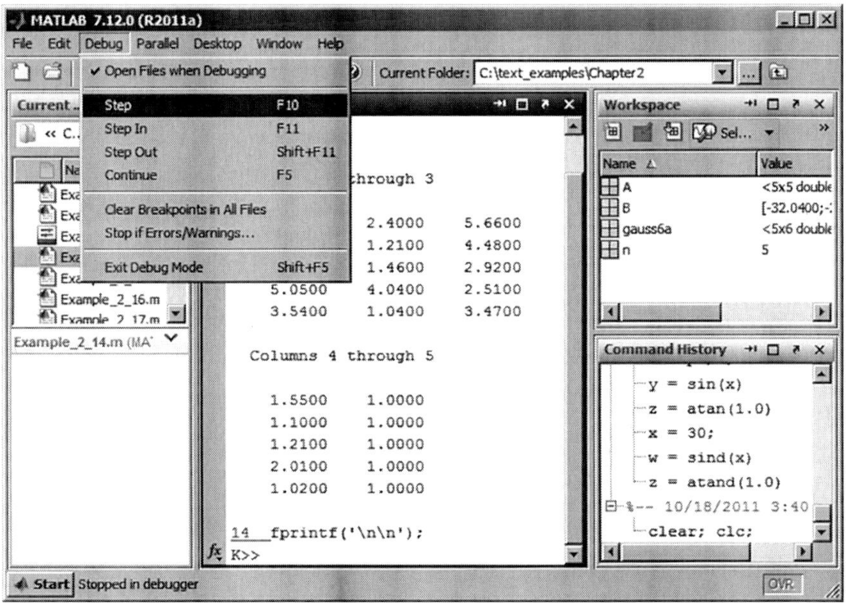

Figure 2.16 The Debug drop-down menu. (From MATLAB, with permission.)

to the main program. Selecting *Clear Breakpoints in All Files* will remove all break points from the program.

2.17 The Parallel RLC Circuit

The resistance, inductor, capacitor (RLC) circuit is a fundamental problem in electrical engineering that we revisit several times in this text (see Figure 2.17 and Appendix A). This section derives the governing equations describing the voltages and currents for the circuit components. The circuit is driven by a current source $I_o(t)$ via a switch that is opened at time $t = 0$. We do not (for the moment) concern ourselves with the definition of $I_o(t)$ other than that it is used to determine the initial conditions of the circuit elements. We start the analysis with the constituent voltage-current relations for resistors, inductors, and capacitors:

$$\text{Resistor (Ohm's law): } v_R = R\, i_R \tag{2.1}$$

$$\text{Inductor: } \quad v_L = L\frac{d\, i_L}{dt} \tag{2.2}$$

$$\text{Capacitor: } i_C = C\frac{dv_C}{dt} \tag{2.3}$$

where R, L, and C are the component values for the resistor (in ohms), inductor (in henries), and capacitor (in farads), respectively, and the voltages v and currents i are as defined in the Figure 2.17. In addition, we assume that the stateful circuit elements L and C have known initial conditions $i_L(0)$ and $v_C(0)$ at the moment that the switch is opened.

Kirchhoff's current law (KCL) states that the sum of currents at any circuit node is zero. Applying KCL at the top right node in the circuit gives

$$i_R + i_L + i_C = 0 \tag{2.4}$$

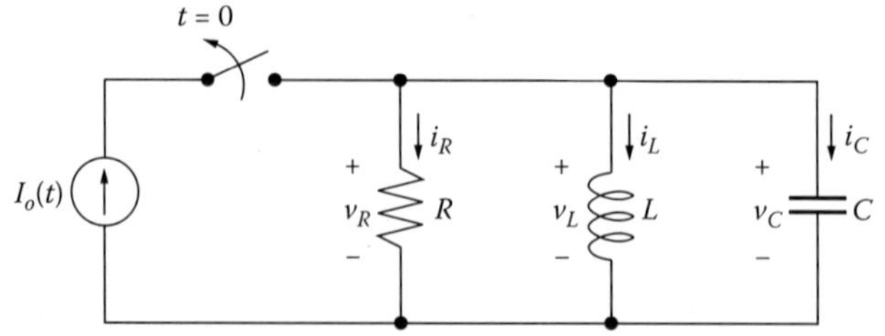

Figure 2.17 Parallel RLC circuit.

Also, the parallel topology of the circuit gives

$$v_R = v_L = v_C \equiv v \tag{2.5}$$

Substituting Equation (2.5) into Equation (2.2) gives

$$\frac{di_L}{dt} = \frac{1}{L}v \tag{2.6}$$

and substituting Equations (2.1) and (2.3) into Equation (2.4) gives

$$\frac{dv}{dt} = -\frac{1}{RC}v - \frac{1}{C}i_L \tag{2.7}$$

Equations (2.6) and (2.7) are a system of two first-order differential equations with two unknowns. We can combine these into one second-order differential equation by differentiating both sides of Equation (2.7):

$$\frac{d^2v}{dt^2} = -\frac{1}{RC}\frac{dv}{dt} - \frac{1}{C}\frac{di_L}{dt} \tag{2.8}$$

Substituting Equation (2.6) into Equation (2.8) gives the second-order differential equation

$$\frac{d^2v}{dt^2} + \frac{1}{RC}\frac{dv}{dt} + \frac{1}{LC}v = 0 \tag{2.9}$$

To solve this second order homogeneous differential equation, we seek a function $v(t)$ such that the derivatives $v'(t)$ and $v''(t)$ reproduce the form of $v(t)$. A function that satisfies this condition is $Ae^{\alpha t}$, where A and α are arbitrary constants. If we assume that $v = Ae^{\alpha t}$, then

$$v'(t) = \alpha A e^{\alpha t} \quad \text{and} \quad v''(t) = \alpha^2 A e^{\alpha t}$$

Substituting these terms into the differential Equation (2.9) gives

$$\left(\alpha^2 + \frac{1}{RC}\alpha + \frac{1}{LC}\right)A\,e^{\alpha t} = 0 \tag{2.10}$$

Since $e^{\alpha t} \neq 0$, solving this equation involves solving the quadratic part

$$\left(\alpha^2 + \frac{1}{RC}\alpha + \frac{1}{LC}\right) = 0 \tag{2.11}$$

The solutions are

$$\alpha = -\frac{1}{2RC} \pm \sqrt{\left(\frac{1}{2RC}\right)^2 - \frac{1}{LC}} \tag{2.12}$$

Thus, there are two solutions that satisfy the differential equation for the two values of α in Equation (2.12). The general solution to Equation (2.9) is the sum of all known solutions:

$$v = A\exp\left(-\frac{1}{2RC}t + \sqrt{\left(\frac{1}{2RC}\right)^2 - \frac{1}{LC}}\,t\right) + B\exp\left(-\frac{1}{2RC}t - \sqrt{\left(\frac{1}{2RC}\right)^2 - \frac{1}{LC}}\,t\right)$$

or equivalently

$$v = \exp\left(-\frac{1}{2RC}t\right)\left\{A\exp\left(\sqrt{\left(\frac{1}{2RC}\right)^2 - \frac{1}{LC}}\,t\right) + B\exp\left(-\sqrt{\left(\frac{1}{2RC}\right)^2 - \frac{1}{LC}}\,t\right)\right\} \tag{2.13}$$

where $\exp(x) = e^x$, and A and B are constants that are dependent on the initial conditions of the circuit.

Note that this solution has two regions of interest:

a) *Overdamped:* If $\left(\frac{1}{2RC}\right)^2 > \frac{1}{LC}$, then the solutions are decaying exponentials over time.

b) *Underdamped:* If $\left(\frac{1}{2RC}\right)^2 < \frac{1}{LC}$, then the solutions are decaying sinusoids over time.

For the underdamped case, we can show the sinusoidal behavior by applying the identities $e^{jx} = \cos x + j\sin x$ and $e^{-jx} = \cos x - j\sin x$ to Equation (2.13), giving

$$v = \exp\left(-\frac{1}{2RC}t\right)\left\{A'\cos\left(\sqrt{\frac{1}{LC} - \left(\frac{1}{2RC}\right)^2}\,t\right) + B'\sin\left(\sqrt{\frac{1}{LC} - \left(\frac{1}{2RC}\right)^2}\,t\right)\right\} \tag{2.14}$$

where the coefficients A' and B' are to be determined by initial conditions.

If $\left(\frac{1}{2RC}\right)^2 = \frac{1}{LC}$, then the square root term is zero, and the system is said to be *critically damped*. For this case [3], the solution is

$$v = (A' + B't)\exp\left(-\frac{1}{2RC}t\right) \tag{2.15}$$

The equations developed in this section are used in projects starting with Project 2.7.

Exercises

Exercise 2.1 Show that the Taylor series expansion of *cos x* about $x = 0$ is

$$\cos(x) = 1 - \frac{x^2}{2!} + \frac{x^4}{4!} - \frac{x^6}{6!} + \cdots$$

Exercise 2.2 Show that the Taylor series expansion of *sin x* about $x = 0$ is

$$\sin(x) = x - \frac{x^3}{3!} + \frac{x^5}{5!} - \frac{x^7}{7!} + \cdots$$

Exercise 2.3 Using the Taylor series expansion of e^x about $x = 0$ (see Example 2.1), show that $e^{jx} = \cos x + j \sin x$ and that $e^{-jx} = \cos x - j \sin x$, where $j = \sqrt{-1}$.

Projects

Project 2.1

Using the Taylor series expansion of cos x about $x = 0$ (see Exercise 2.1) develop a computer program in MATLAB that will evaluate cos x from $-\pi \le x \le \pi$ in steps of 0.1 π. Compute the series by determining each term according to the equation

$$\text{term}(k+1) = \text{term}(k) \times \text{a multiplication factor}$$

where the multiplication factor needs to be determined. Use as many as 50 terms; however, stop adding terms when the last term only affects the sixth decimal place in the answer. Also, compute the value of cos x using MATLAB's built-in `cos()` function over the same interval and step size. Print a table of your results to a file using the table format in Table P2.1. Use six decimal places for cos x.

Also, create a plot of cos x for $-\pi \le x \le \pi$.

Table P2.1 Table Format for Project 2.1

x	cos x by cos ( )	cos x by series	Terms in the series
–1.0 π			
–0.9 π			
–0.8 π			
⋮			
0.9 π			
1.0 π			

Project 2.2

Using the Taylor series expansion of sin x about $x = 0$ (see Exercise 2.2), develop a computer program in MATLAB that will evaluate sin x from $-\pi \le x \le \pi$ in steps of 0.1 π. Compute the series by using MATLAB's `factorial` function and use as many as 50 terms. However, stop adding terms when the last term only affects the sixth decimal place in the answer.

Also, compute the value of sin x using MATLAB's built-in `sin()` function over the same interval and step size. Create a table similar to the table shown in Project 2.1, except replace cos x with sin x. Create a plot of sin x for $-\pi \le x \le \pi$.

Project 2.3

Develop a computer program in MATLAB that will evaluate the following function for $-0.9 \le x \le 0.9$ in steps of 0.1 by:

1. an arithmetic statement.
2. a series allowing for as many as 50 terms. However, stop adding terms when the last term only affects the sixth decimal place in the answer.

The function and its series expansion, valid for $x^2 < 1$, is

$$f(x) = (1+x^2)^{-1/2} = 1 - \frac{1}{2}x^2 + \frac{1\cdot 3}{2\cdot 4}x^4 - \frac{1\cdot 3\cdot 5}{2\cdot 4\cdot 6}x^6 + \frac{1\cdot 3\cdot 5\cdot 7}{2\cdot 4\cdot 6\cdot 8}x^8 - \cdots + \cdots$$

Print out a table (to a file) in the format shown in Table P2.3; use six decimal places for $f(x)$.

Table P2.3 Table Format for Project 2.3

x	f(x) (arithmetic statement)	f(x) (by series)	No. of Terms Used in the Series
–0.9			
–0.8			
–0.7			
⋮			
0.7			
0.8			
0.9			

Project 2.4

Develop a computer program in MATLAB that will evaluate the function

$$f(x) = (1+x)^{1/3}$$

for $-0.9 \le x \le 0.9$ in steps of 0.1 by

1. an arithmetic statement.
2. series allowing for as many as 50 terms. However, stop adding terms when the last term only affects the sixth decimal place in the answer.

By using a Taylor series expansion, it can be seen that the relationship between successive terms is

$$\text{term}(k+1) = \text{term}(k) \times \left(\frac{1}{3} - (k-1)\right) \times \frac{x}{k}$$

for $k = 1, 2, 3, \ldots$.

Print out a table (to a file) in the format shown in Project 2.3; use six significant figures for $f(x)$.

Project 2.5

The binomial expansion for $(1+x)^n$, where n is an integer, is as follows:

$$(1+x)^n = 1 + nx + \frac{n(n-1)x^2}{2!} + \frac{n(n-1)(n-2)x^3}{3!} + \cdots + \frac{n(n-1)(n-2)\ldots(n-r+2)x^{r-1}}{(r-1)!} + \cdots + x^n$$

Construct a MATLAB program that will evaluate $(1+x)^n$ by both the preceding series and an arithmetic statement for $n = 10$ and $1.0 \le x \le 10.0$ in steps of 0.5. Print out the results in a table as shown in Table P2.5.

Table P2.5 Table Format for Project 2.5

x	$(1+x)^n$ *(arithmetic statement)*	$(1+x)^n$ *(by series)*
1.0		
1.5		
2.0		
2.5		
⋮		
9.5		
10.0		

Project 2.6

This project examines a 340 $V_{\text{peak-to-peak}}$ sinusoidal waveform at 60 Hz that has no DC component (i.e., it is centered around 0 V).

1. Plot this waveform in MATLAB by using the `sin()` function. Plot over the interval $0 \le t \le 50$ msec in steps of 0.2 msec.
2. Compute and print to the screen the root-mean-square (RMS) voltage for this waveform by performing the following operations in MATLAB:
   a. Squaring it.
   b. Computing the mean value of the squared waveform by averaging it over the 100-msec time interval.
   c. Taking the square root of the average.
3. In North America, residential electrical service is usually delivered as two 340 $V_{\text{peak-to-peak}}$ sinusoids, each 180° out of phase with each other (Figure P2.6a), referred to as *one-phase* service. For high-power appliances (e.g., air conditioners and stoves), the current is drawn from both "legs" of the service.

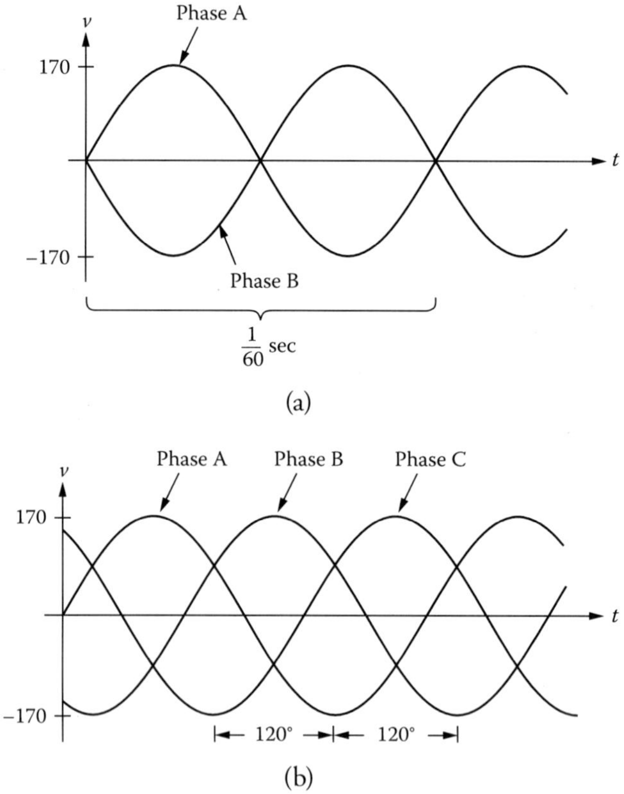

Figure P2.6 (a) One-phase power is delivered as two sinusoids that are out of phase by 180°. (b) Three-phase power is delivered as three sinusoids that are out of phase by 120°.

a. Plot the *difference* waveform between the two legs of one-phase service.
b. Compute and print to the screen the RMS value of the difference waveform (as in part 2).

4. In many commercial and industrial buildings, *three-phase* electrical service is delivered as three 340 $V_{\text{peak-to-peak}}$ sinusoids, with each leg 120° out of phase with the others (see Figure P2.6b).
   a. Plot the waveform of the voltage difference between any two of the three legs
   b. Compute and print to the screen the RMS value of this waveform. Most high-voltage appliances are rated to work at either of the RMS voltages computed in part 3 or part 4.

Project 2.7

Given the following component values in the parallel RLC circuit described in Section 2.17

$$R = 100\ \Omega,\ L = 1\ \text{mH},\ C = 1\ \mu\text{F}$$

and the following initial conditions, determine the coefficients A and B for the following three cases:

1. $i_L(0) = 0.25\ \text{A}, \quad v_C(0) = 6\ \text{V}$

   [Hint: convert $i_L(0)$ to $v'(0)$ with Equation (2.7).]

2. $i_L(0) = -0.25\ \text{A}, \quad v_C(0) = 6\ \text{V}$
3. $i_L(0) = 0, \quad v_C(0) = 6\ \text{V}$

For each case, determine an expression for A and B in terms of R, L, C, $v_C(0)$ and $i_L(0)$ and write a MATLAB program that will

a. Determine $v(t)$ for $0 \le t \le 500$ μsec in steps of 1 μsec.
b. Print out a table of v versus t every 10 μsec.
c. Plot v versus t for all three cases on the same graph. Label each curve with the value of $i_L(0)$.

Project 2.8

The envelope of the voltage waveform for the parallel RLC circuit described in Section 2.17 is given by

$$v(t) = \pm Ae^{\left(-t/2RC\right)} \tag{P2.8}$$

Given the following component values

$$R = 5000\ \Omega,\ L = 1\ \mu\text{H},\ C = 10\ \text{pF}$$

$$i_L(0) = 0\ \text{A}, \quad v_C(0) = 3.3\ \text{V}$$

determine $v(t)$ for $0 \le t \le 50$ nsec in steps of 1 nsec. Plot v versus t for both the oscillating function and its envelope on the same graph.

Project 2.9

Instead of using v as the state variable in the analysis of the parallel RLC circuit, we can use i_L by differentiating both sides of Equation (2.6) and combining with Equation (2.7) to obtain the differential equation

$$\frac{d^2 i_L}{dt^2} + \frac{1}{RC}\frac{di_L}{dt} + \frac{1}{LC} i_L = 0 \tag{P2.9a}$$

Note that Equation (P2.9a) has the identical form as Equation (2.12) and thus has solutions of the identical form. For the underdamped case,

$$i_L = \exp\left(-\frac{1}{2RC}t\right)\left\{\alpha \cos\left(\sqrt{\frac{1}{LC} - \left(\frac{1}{2RC}\right)^2}\; t\right) + \beta \sin\left(\sqrt{\frac{1}{LC} - \left(\frac{1}{2RC}\right)^2}\; t\right)\right\} \tag{P2.9b}$$

where α and β are constants to be determined by initial conditions and have amperes as units.

For the component values $R = 100\ \Omega$, $L = 1$ mH, $C = 1\ \mu$F, and initial conditions $i_L(0) = 0$ and $v_C(0) = 6\text{ V}$,

1. Solve for the coefficients α and β.
2. Plot $i_L(t)$ for $0 \le t \le 500\ \mu$sec in steps of 0.5 μsec
3. Plot $i_L(t)$ and $v_C(t)$ (solved in Project 2.7) on the same axes. Note that when v_C is at a maximum, i_L is zero and vice versa. This illustrates how the energy in the circuit oscillates back and forth between the capacitor and inductor.

Project 2.10

The classical form for a second-order differential equation is

$$\frac{d^2 y}{dt^2} + 2\zeta\omega_n \frac{dy}{dt} + \omega_n^2 y = 0 \tag{P2.10a}$$

where ζ is the *damping factor,* and ω_n is the *natural frequency*. We can match the terms of Equation (P2.9a) with Equation (P2.10a) to find the damping factor and natural frequency for the parallel RLC circuit. Thus,

$$\omega_n = \frac{1}{\sqrt{LC}} \quad \text{and} \quad \zeta = \frac{1}{2RC\omega_n} = \frac{\sqrt{LC}}{2RC} \tag{P2.10b}$$

Note that for $\zeta < 1$ the circuit is underdamped, for $\zeta > 1$ the circuit is overdamped, and for $\zeta = 1$, it is critically damped.

For the component values $L = 1$ mH, $C = 1\ \mu$F, and initial conditions $i_L(0) = 0.25$ A and $v_C(0) = 6$ V:

1. Determine the resistor value R_{crit} that makes the circuit critically damped.
2. Plot the inductor current i_L versus time for the three values of R: $R = R_{crit}$, $R = 5\ R_{crit}$, and $R = \frac{1}{2} R_{crit}$. Assume the interval $0 \le t \le 500\ \mu$sec in steps of 0.5 μsec. Plot all of the waveforms on one graph.

Project 2.11

We wish now to consider the RLC circuit described in Section 2.17 to be subjected to a driving current such that instead of opening the switch at $t = 0$, we close the switch. In this case, the sum of the currents at the top left node is

$$i_R + i_L + i_C - I_o = 0 \qquad \text{(P2.11a)}$$

Note that the I_o term is negative because I_o is arbitrarily defined in Figure 2.17 as flowing *into* the node instead of *away* from the node (as is true for the other three currents).

The governing equation then becomes

$$\frac{d^2 i_L}{dt^2} + \frac{1}{RC}\frac{di_L}{dt} + \frac{1}{LC} i_L = I_o \qquad \text{(P2.11b)}$$

The complete solution of this differential equation is equal to the homogeneous solution (found in Project 2.9) plus a *particular solution.*

Let us assume that the driving current is a sinusoid of the form $I_o(t) = A_o \sin \omega_o t$. To obtain the particular solution i_p, we seek a solution whose first and second derivatives can be summed to equal the form of the driving current. Thus, assume

$$i_p = A_p \sin \omega_o t + B_p \cos \omega_o t \qquad \text{(P2.11c)}$$

where A_p and B_p are constants. Then,

$$i_p' = \omega_o \left(A_p \cos \omega_o t - B_p \sin \omega_o t \right)$$

and

$$i_p'' = \omega_o^2 \left(- A_p \sin \omega_o t - B_p \cos \omega_o t \right)$$

Substituting these expressions into Equation (P2.11b) gives

$$\left(-A_p \omega_o^2 - \frac{1}{RC} \omega_o B_p + \frac{1}{LC} A_p \right) \sin \omega_o t + \left(-B_p \omega_o^2 + \frac{1}{RC} \omega_o A_p + \frac{1}{LC} B_p \right) \cos \omega_o t = A_o \sin \omega_o t$$

(P2.11d)

Collecting coefficients of the sine and cosine terms on the left side of Equation (P2.11d) and equating them to the sine and cosine coefficients on the right side of that equation gives

$$\left(\frac{1}{LC} - \omega_o^2 \right) A_p - \frac{\omega_o}{RC} B_p = A_o$$

$$\frac{\omega_o}{RC} A_p + \left(\frac{1}{LC} - \omega_o^2 \right) B_p = 0$$

Solving these two equations for A_p and B_p gives

$$A_p = A_o \times \frac{\frac{1}{LC} - \omega_o^2}{\left(\frac{\omega_o}{RC}\right)^2 + \left(\frac{1}{LC} - \omega_o^2\right)^2} \tag{P2.11e}$$

$$B_p = - A_o \times \frac{\frac{\omega_o}{RC}}{\left(\frac{\omega_o}{RC}\right)^2 + \left(\frac{1}{LC} - \omega_o^2\right)} \tag{P2.11f}$$

Substituting Equations (P2.11e) and (P2.11f) into Equation (P2.11c) gives

$$i_p = A_o \times \frac{1}{\left(\frac{\omega_o}{RC}\right)^2 + \left(\frac{1}{LC} - \omega_o^2\right)^2} \left\{ \left(\frac{1}{LC} - \omega_o^2\right) \sin \omega_o t - \frac{\omega_o}{RC} \cos \omega_o t \right\} \tag{P2.11g}$$

We can rewrite Equation (P2.11g) using the trigonometric identity

$$\alpha \sin \omega t + \beta \cos \omega t = \gamma \sin(\omega t - \phi)$$

where

$$\gamma = \sqrt{\alpha^2 + \beta^2}$$

and

$$\phi = \tan^{-1} \frac{\beta}{\alpha}$$

Applying these relations to Equation (P2.11g) gives

$$i_p = A_o \times \frac{1}{\sqrt{\left(\frac{1}{LC} - \omega_o^2\right)^2 + \left(\frac{\omega_o}{RC}\right)^2}} \sin(\omega_o t - \phi) \tag{P2.11h}$$

Using the definitions from Project 2.10 for natural frequency $\omega_n = \sqrt{\frac{1}{LC}}$ and damping factor $\zeta = \frac{1}{2RC\omega_n}$, we can algebraically manipulate Equation (P2.11h) into

$$i_p = \frac{A_o}{\omega_n} \frac{1}{\sqrt{\left(1 - \frac{\omega_o}{\omega_n}\right)^2 + \left(2\zeta \frac{\omega_o}{\omega_n}\right)^2}} \sin(\omega_o t - \phi) \tag{P2.11i}$$

The term

$$\frac{A_o}{\omega_n}\frac{1}{\sqrt{\left(1-\frac{\omega_o}{\omega_n}\right)^2+\left(2\zeta\frac{\omega_o}{\omega_n}\right)^2}}$$

is the amplitude of the oscillation. For a given $\frac{A_o}{\omega_n}$,

the larger the term $\frac{1}{\sqrt{\left(1-\frac{\omega_o}{\omega_n}\right)^2+\left(2\zeta\frac{\omega_o}{\omega_n}\right)^2}}$, the larger is the amplitude.

$$\text{Let ampl} = \frac{1}{\sqrt{\left(1-\frac{\omega_o}{\omega_n}\right)^2+\left(2\zeta\frac{\omega_o}{\omega_n}\right)^2}}$$

1. Construct a MATLAB program to create a plot of ampl versus $\frac{\omega_o}{\omega_n}$ for values of $\zeta = 1.0, 0.5, 0.25, 0.10, 0.05$, and $0 < \frac{\omega_o}{\omega_n} < 2$ in steps of 0.01.
2. What happens as $\omega_o \rightarrow \omega_n$?

Project 2.12

Modify Example 2.25 as follows:

1. Use a self-written function saved as an *.m* file to do the interpolation. The linear interpolation formula for $y(x) = f(x)$ expression is

$$y = y_1 + \frac{x - x_1}{x_2 - x_1} \times (y_2 - y_1)$$

   where points (x_1, x_2) are the nearest surrounding points to x and (y_1, y_2) are the y values at (x_1, x_2), respectively. Use a global statement to bring T_1, T_2, μ_1, and μ_2 into the self-written function, where T_1, T_2 are the closest temperature table values to the temperature at which μ is to be determined and μ_1, μ_2 are the μ values at T_1, T_2 respectively.
2. Print out the table data to the screen, then ask the user if he or she wishes to interpolate for μ at a temperature other than those temperatures given in the table. If the answer is yes, ask the user to enter the temperature, do the interpolation, and print out the result. Use the `switch` group to determine whether to do the interpolation. If the answer to your query is no, exit the program.
3. If the answer to the query in part 2 is yes, then ask the user if he or she wishes to enter another temperature; if yes, ask the user to enter the temperature, do the interpolation, and print out the result. The process is to continue until the answer to the query is no. The user is to enter the following five temperatures (k), one at a time: 125, 180, 218, 334, 427.

Project 2.13

This project is a modification of Example 2.24 in which the "anonymous function" that does the interpolation is to consist of arguments of x, x_1, x_2, y_1, y_2 .and uses the interpolation formula

$$y = y_1 + \frac{x - x_1}{x_2 - x_1} \times (y_2 - y_1)$$

where points (x_1, x_2) are the nearest surrounding points to x and (y_1, y_2) are the y values at (x_1, x_2), respectively. In Example 2.6, it was shown that the input variables to a function need not have the same names as those used in the calling program. For one-to-one correspondence, the argument *positions* in the calling program must be the same as the argument *positions* in the function. Table values for electron mobility μ as a function of temperature T are as follows:

$$T = [100\ 150\ 200\ 250\ 300\ 350\ 400\ 450]$$

$$\mu = [19650\ 7427\ 3723\ 2180\ 1407\ 972.0\ 705.5\ 531.8]$$

The units for T are (K) and the units for μ are (cm^2/V-s).

1. Create a MATLAB program that contains the anonymous function as described and that interpolates for the electron mobility μ at the following temperatures TT:

$$TT = [110\ 165\ 215\ 365\ 440]$$

2. Print out a table of values of μ at temperatures TT.

Project 2.14

In discrete-time signal processing, signals are represented as a sequence of discrete numerical values, as opposed to the "smooth" waveforms in continuous-time signal processing.

Figure P2.14a shows a continuous-time waveform (a 1-kHz sine wave) and its discrete-time counterpart, which is generated by sampling the continuous-time signal at a rate of 8000 samples/sec (every 125 μsec). This sampling rate is commonly used for voice-grade telephony equipment, and the resulting discrete-time sequence might subsequently be transmitted by methods such as PAM (pulse amplitude modulation) or PCM (pulse code modulation).

Now, suppose we want to use this sampled waveform in a movie soundtrack to be recorded on DVD. The digital audio on DVDs typically uses a sampling rate of 48,000 samples/sec (every 20.8333 μsec); thus, we will need to *upsample* our 8000-sample/sec waveform to use it on DVD.

In upsampling, we augment a given discrete waveform by adding samples to the sequence to achieve the desired higher sampling rate. In this case, upsampling from 8000 to 48,000 samples/sec will require adding five new samples for every one in the original waveform. There are many methods for doing this, and one simple approach is to compute values for the added samples by interpolating between adjacent values of the original waveform (Figure P2.14b).

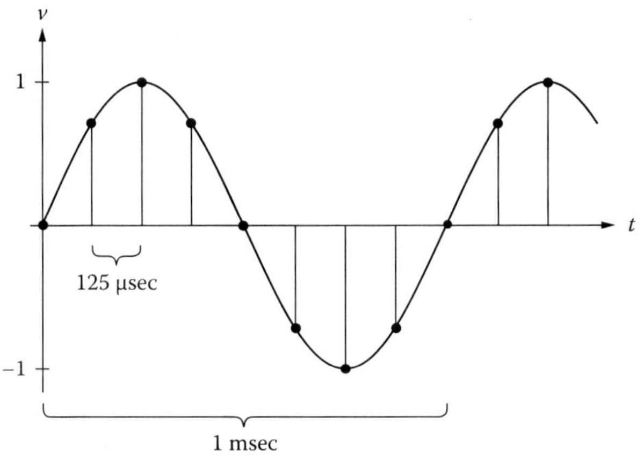

(a)

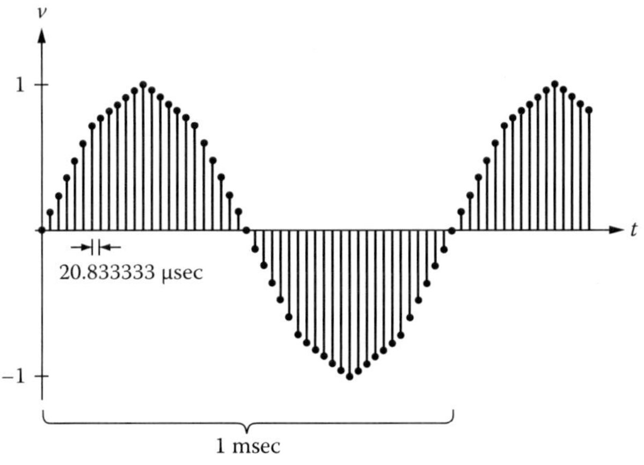

(b)

Figure P2.14 (a) A 1-kHz sine wave is sampled at 8000 samples/sec. (b) If we want to upsample the sine wave to 48,000 samples/sec, we need to interpolate five additional samples between points of the original waveform.

Develop a MATLAB program that will

1. Compute the signal values of the original 8000-samples/sec waveform over the period of $0 < t \leq 2$ msec, for a total of 17 samples. Assume signal peak values of ±1 for the sine wave.
2. Create a table consisting of sample number, sample time, and sample signal value.
3. Use MATLAB's `interp1` function to calculate the upsampled waveform (i.e., at a sample rate of 48,000 samples/sec). To avoid round-off error, use $\Delta t = 20.833333$ μsec. You should end up with a sample size of 97 values.

4. Plot the original and the upsampled waveforms on the same graph. For the original sample waveform, use circles to display the data points. For the upsampled waveform, use × s to display the data points.

Project 2.15

This project involves determining the quality of the upsampled waveform of Project 2.14. This is accomplished by comparing the upsampled waveform with an ideal 1-kHz sine wave. A common performance metric for audio systems is the *total harmonic distortion* (THD), which is a measure of the noise at harmonic frequencies other than the frequency of interest (1 kHz in our case). Because our signal is periodic and of known frequency, we can assume that *all* the imperfections will contribute to the THD. Develop a MATLAB program that will

1. Compute the values of an ideal 48,000-samples/sec waveform V_{ideal} over the period of $0 < t \leq 2$ msec, for a total of 97 samples. Assume waveform peak values of ±1 for the sine wave.
2. Subtract this ideal waveform from our upsampled 48,000-samples/sec waveform to calculate the waveform error V_{error} for the interpolation method that was used in Project 2.14.
3. Calculate the THD of the upsampled waveform as follows:

$$\text{THD} = \sqrt{\frac{\left(V_{error,RMS}\right)^2}{\left(V_{ideal,RMS}\right)^2}} \tag{P2.15}$$

Use the method described in Project 2.6 to calculate $\left(V_{error,RMS}\right)$ and $\left(V_{ideal,RMS}\right)$.

4. Print out $V_{error,RMS}$, $V_{ideal,RMS}$, and THD.

Project 2.16

Mathematician Joseph Fourier is credited with the theorem that any periodic waveform may be expressed as a summation of pure sines and cosines. For example, the square wave of Figure P2.16a can be written as a sum of sines:

$$\begin{aligned} v(t) &= \frac{4}{\pi}\sin\frac{2\pi t}{T} + \frac{4}{3\pi}\sin\frac{6\pi t}{T} + \frac{4}{5\pi}\sin\frac{10\pi t}{T} + \cdots \\ &= \sum_{\substack{k=1 \\ k \text{ odd}}}^{\infty} \frac{4}{\pi k}\sin\frac{2\pi k t}{T} \end{aligned}$$

Figure P2.16b shows the first three terms of the series and their summation.

1. Write a MATLAB script that implements a self-written function `sqwave(n,T,i)`, which takes the following arguments:

`n`	the number of terms of the Fourier series
`T`	the period of the square wave in seconds
`i`	the number samples per period

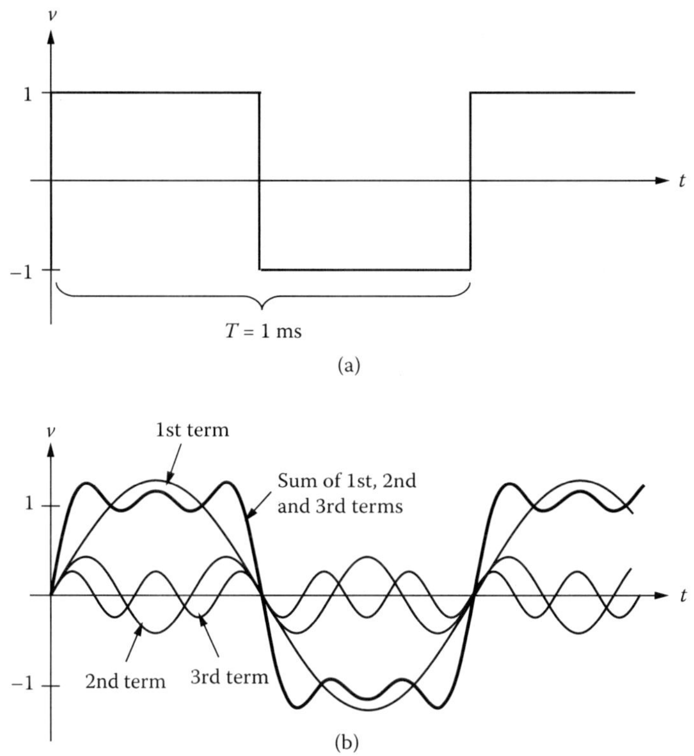

Figure P2.16 (a) Square wave. (b) Three terms in a Fourier series of a square wave.

The function should return two arrays, `t` and `V`, each containing `i` elements, where

`t` = an array of `i` time points.
`V` = an array of `i` computed values of the `n`th-degree approximated square wave

2. Run your `sqwave(n,T,i)` function and plot the results for the following arguments:

   `T` = 1 msec, `i` = 1001, `n` = 1, 3, 10, 100

3. For n = 100, print out a table of `(t,V)` at every 20 timepoints.

Project 2.17

Bob's Hardware Store wishes to create an online program to sell inventory items in its store. You are to create an interactive MATLAB program for this purpose. The program is to contain the following items: a data file, a main script and a billing function.

Data file:
The data file is to contain a description of the inventory items for sale, their cost, and the quantity available for sale. The list should contain at least 10 items. This data file will be read into the main script. Whenever an item is purchased, the inventory available for sale should be updated in the data file.

Main script:
1. The script is to print to the screen the items for sale, their cost, and the quantity available for purchase.
2. The script is to ask the user if he or she wishes to make a purchase. If yes, the script is to ask the user the line number of the item he or she wishes to purchase and the quantity.
3. If the user does not wish to make a purchase, exit the program. If the user does not respond correctly to the query, print an error message to the screen and inform the user to restart the program. Then, exit the program.
4. If the user does make a purchase, the program is to continue asking the user if he or she wishes to make another purchase. If yes, print to the screen the list of items, their cost, and the updated items available for purchase. Then, the script is to ask the user the line number of the item he or she wishes to purchase and the quantity. If the answer is no, exit the program.

Billing function:
When the user is finished making all of his or her purchases, the main script is to call the billing function that prints out a bill for the items purchased. The bill should contain the name and address of the store, the user's first and last names, the user's address, bill headings, a list of all the items purchased, the items' unit prices, the total price for each item purchased, and finally the total price of all the items purchased.

References

1. Kernighan, B.W., and Ritchie, D.M., *The C Programming Language*, 2nd ed., Prentice-Hall, Englewood Cliffs, NJ, 1988.
2. Sze, S.M., *Physics of Semiconductor Devices*, 2nd ed., Wiley, New York, 1981.
3. Kreyszig, E. *Advanced Engineering Mathematics*, 8th ed., Wiley, New York, 1999.

Chapter 3

Matrices

3.1 Introduction

In engineering, we are frequently confronted with matrices or a problem involving a set of linear equations. In addition, the basic element in MATLAB® is a matrix, and it is therefore appropriate to have a chapter on matrices. First, we discuss some basic matrix concepts and operations and the treatment of matrices in MATLAB, including several sample MATLAB programs involving matrices. This is followed by a discussion of several methods for solving a system of linear equations, including the use of MATLAB's `inv` function, Gauss elimination, and the Gauss-Jordan methods. An example of the use of matrices to solve a problem in resistive circuits is included. Finally, the matrix eigenvalue problem is discussed, including an application to a resonant circuit problem.

3.2 Matrix Operations

- A rectangular array of numbers of the following form is called a *matrix*.

$$\mathbf{A} = \begin{bmatrix} a_{11} & a_{12} & \cdots & a_{1n} \\ a_{21} & a_{22} & \cdots & a_{2n} \\ \vdots & \vdots & \ddots & \vdots \\ a_{m1} & a_{m2} & \cdots & a_{mn} \end{bmatrix}$$

The numbers a_{ij} in the array are called the elements of the $m \times n$ matrix **A**.

- A matrix of m rows and one column is called a column vector.
- A matrix of one row and n columns is called a row vector.
- Matrices obey certain rules of addition, subtraction, and multiplication.
- Addition and subtraction: If matrices **A** and **B** have the same number of rows and columns, then

$$\mathbf{C} = \mathbf{A} + \mathbf{B} = \begin{bmatrix} (a_{11}+b_{11}) & (a_{12}+b_{12}) & \cdots & (a_{1n}+b_{1n}) \\ (a_{21}+b_{21}) & (a_{22}+b_{22}) & \cdots & (a_{2n}+b_{2n}) \\ \vdots & \vdots & \ddots & \vdots \\ (a_{m1}+b_{m1}) & (a_{m2}+b_{m2}) & \cdots & (a_{mn}+b_{mn}) \end{bmatrix}$$

$$\mathbf{C} = \mathbf{A} - \mathbf{B} = \begin{bmatrix} (a_{11}-b_{11}) & (a_{12}-b_{12}) & \cdots & (a_{1n}-b_{1n}) \\ (a_{21}-b_{21}) & (a_{22}-b_{22}) & \cdots & (a_{2n}-b_{2n}) \\ \vdots & \vdots & \ddots & \vdots \\ (a_{m1}-b_{m1}) & (a_{m2}-b_{m2}) & \cdots & (a_{mn}-b_{mn}) \end{bmatrix}$$

- Addition and subtraction of the matrices **A** and **B** are only defined if **A** and **B** have the same number of rows and columns.
- Multiplication: The product **AB** is only defined if the number of columns in **A** equals the number of rows in **B**. If **C** = **AB**, where

$$\mathbf{A} = \begin{bmatrix} a_{11} & a_{12} & a_{13} \\ a_{21} & a_{22} & a_{23} \end{bmatrix} \quad \text{and} \quad \mathbf{B} = \begin{bmatrix} b_{11} & b_{12} \\ b_{21} & b_{22} \\ b_{31} & b_{32} \end{bmatrix}$$

then

$$\mathbf{C} = \begin{bmatrix} (a_{11}b_{11} + a_{12}b_{21} + a_{13}b_{31}) & (a_{11}b_{12} + a_{12}b_{22} + a_{13}b_{32}) \\ (a_{21}b_{11} + a_{22}b_{21} + a_{23}b_{31}) & (a_{21}b_{12} + a_{22}b_{22} + a_{23}b_{32}) \end{bmatrix}$$

- If **A** has m rows and **B** has K columns, then **C** = **AB** will have m rows and K columns. A general expression for the element c_{ij} is

$$c_{ij} = \sum_{k=1}^{K} a_{ik} b_{kj}$$

In MATLAB, the multiplication of matrices **A** and **B** is entered as `A * B`.

- Transpose: The transpose of a matrix is the operation of exchanging the rows and columns. If

$$\mathbf{A} = \begin{bmatrix} 2 & 5 & 1 \\ 7 & 3 & 8 \\ 4 & 5 & 21 \\ 16 & 3 & 10 \end{bmatrix}$$

then

$$\mathbf{A}^T = \begin{bmatrix} 2 & 7 & 4 & 16 \\ 5 & 3 & 5 & 3 \\ 1 & 8 & 21 & 10 \end{bmatrix}$$

In MATLAB, the transpose of matrix **A** is entered as `A'`.

- Summing the elements of a vector or the columns of a matrix:

$$\text{If} \quad \mathbf{A} = [\, a_1 \;\; a_2 \;\; a_3 \,], \text{ then } \operatorname{sum}(\mathbf{A}) = a_1 + a_2 + a_3 .$$

If

$$\mathbf{B} = \begin{bmatrix} b_{11} & b_{12} & b_{13} \\ b_{21} & b_{22} & b_{23} \\ b_{31} & b_{32} & b_{33} \end{bmatrix}$$

then

$$\operatorname{sum}(\mathbf{B}) = [\,(b_{11} + b_{21} + b_{31}) \quad (b_{12} + b_{22} + b_{32}) \quad (b_{13} + b_{23} + b_{33})\,]$$

In MATLAB, the sum of matrix **A** is entered as `sum(A)`.

- Dot product: The dot product of two vectors is defined as

$$\mathbf{A} \cdot \mathbf{B} = \sum a_i b_i$$

For example, if $\mathbf{A} = [4 \;\; -1 \;\; 3]$ and $\mathbf{B} = [-2 \;\; 5 \;\; 2]$, then

$$\mathbf{A} \cdot \mathbf{B} = (4)(-2) + (-1)(5) + (3)(2) = -7$$

The result of a dot product is always a scalar (i.e., a single number). In MATLAB, the dot product $\mathbf{A} \cdot \mathbf{B}$ is entered as `dot(A,B)`.

- Identity: The identity matrix **I** is a matrix where the main diagonal elements are all one and all other elements are zero.

$$\mathbf{IA} = \mathbf{AI} = \mathbf{A}$$

For example, for the case of a three-by-three matrix **A**,

$$\mathbf{AI} = \begin{bmatrix} a_{11} & a_{12} & a_{13} \\ a_{21} & a_{22} & a_{23} \\ a_{31} & a_{32} & a_{33} \end{bmatrix} \begin{bmatrix} 1 & 0 & 0 \\ 0 & 1 & 0 \\ 0 & 0 & 1 \end{bmatrix}$$

$$= \begin{bmatrix} (a_{11}+0+0) & (0+a_{12}+0) & (0+0+a_{13}) \\ (a_{21}+0+0) & (0+a_{22}+0) & (0+0+a_{23}) \\ (a_{31}+0+0) & (0+a_{32}+0) & (0+0+a_{33}) \end{bmatrix}$$

In MATLAB, you can generate an $n \times n$ identity matrix with `eye(`n`)`.

- Inverse: The inverse of a matrix, denoted $\mathbf{A}^{-1}$, is a matrix such that

$$\mathbf{A}^{-1}\mathbf{A} = \mathbf{A}\mathbf{A}^{-1} = \mathbf{I} = \begin{bmatrix} 1 & 0 & 0 \\ 0 & 1 & 0 \\ 0 & 0 & 1 \end{bmatrix} \quad \text{(for a } 3\times 3 \text{ matrix)}$$

In MATLAB, the matrix inverse $\mathbf{A}^{-1}$ is entered as `inv(A)`.

- Determinant:

Before the use of computers, determinants were developed as a method for obtaining a solution to a system of linear equations. Computationally, it is only practical for a system involving just a few equations [1]. However, determinants do have an application in the eigenvalue problem that is discussed at the end of this chapter.

The determinant of a 2×2 matrix is

$$D = \begin{vmatrix} a_{11} & a_{12} \\ a_{21} & a_{22} \end{vmatrix} = a_{11}a_{22} - a_{12}a_{21}$$

Note that the determinant of a matrix is written with two straight lines that enclose the matrix elements.

The determinant of a 3×3 matrix is

$$D = \begin{vmatrix} a_{11} & a_{12} & a_{13} \\ a_{21} & a_{22} & a_{23} \\ a_{31} & a_{32} & a_{33} \end{vmatrix} = a_{11}\begin{vmatrix} a_{22} & a_{23} \\ a_{32} & a_{33} \end{vmatrix} - a_{12}\begin{vmatrix} a_{21} & a_{23} \\ a_{31} & a_{33} \end{vmatrix} + a_{13}\begin{vmatrix} a_{21} & a_{22} \\ a_{31} & a_{32} \end{vmatrix}$$

In MATLAB, the determinant of the matrix **A** is entered as **`det(A)`**.

- Dimensions: You can obtain the size of matrix **A** by running `size(A)`. This command is useful when you run a script and you get an error message like "Index exceeds matrix dimensions." Adding the `size()` command in the script will help you determine the problem.
- Element-by-element operations: Given two matrices of the same dimensions, we can perform element-by-element multiplication and division in MATLAB with the .* and ./ operators.

Given $\mathbf{A} = \begin{bmatrix} a_1 & a_2 & a_3 \end{bmatrix}$ and $\mathbf{B} = \begin{bmatrix} b_1 & b_2 & b_3 \end{bmatrix}$, then

$$\mathbf{C} = \mathbf{A}\ .*\ \mathbf{B} = \begin{bmatrix} a_1b_1 & a_2b_2 & a_3b_3 \end{bmatrix}$$

$$\mathbf{D} = \mathbf{A}\ ./\ \mathbf{B} = \begin{bmatrix} \frac{a_1}{b_1} & \frac{a_2}{b_2} & \frac{a_3}{b_3} \end{bmatrix}$$

Also, note the dot product can be expressed as a combination of an element-by-element multiplication and a sum:

$$\mathbf{A} \cdot \mathbf{B} = \text{sum}(\mathbf{A}\ .*\ \mathbf{B}) = \text{sum}\left(\begin{bmatrix} a_1b_1 & a_2b_2 & a_3b_3 \end{bmatrix}\right) = a_1b_1 + a_2b_2 + a_3b_3$$

- Product of functions of two vectors:

As described in Chapter 2, MATLAB allows taking a function of a vector and that the result is also a vector. However, if a script requires a mathematical operation of two functions (such as a product of two vector functions), then the operation will require an element-by-element operation.

In the following example, we compute the product of two vector functions, both directly and indirectly, by using a `for` loop and multiplying the elements of each function. Write this simple script into a new script window, save it as *matrix_example.m*, and run the script:

```
% matrix_example.m
clear; clc;
x = 0:30:360;
% y1 is the product of two vector functions
y1 = sind(x).* cosd(x);
fprintf(' x     y1      y2\n');
fprintf(' ------------------------------------- \n');
for n = 1:length(x);
    % y2(n) is the product of the elements of the two
    % functions.
    y2(n) = sind(x(n)) * cosd(x(n));
    fprintf('%5.1f %8.5f %8.5f \n',x(n),y1(n),y2(n));
end
-------------------------------------------------------
```

Do the two different methods for computing `y1` and `y2` give the same answer?

Example 3.1: Matrix Operations

The following example illustrates several matrix operations, including addition, dot product, element-by-element multiplication and division, sum, and transpose.

```
% Example_3_1.m
% This program demonstrates matrix algebra in MATLAB
clear; clc;
a=[1 5 9]
b=[2 6 12]
c=a+b
d=dot(a,b)
e=a.*b
f=a./b
g=sum(a.*b)
h=a*b'
------------------------------------------------------------------------
```

3.3 System of Linear Equations

In engineering, we are frequently confronted with the problem of solving a set of linear equations.

Given the set of equations

$$
\begin{aligned}
a_{11}x_1 + a_{12}x_2 + a_{13}x_3 + \cdots + a_{1n}x_n &= c_1 \\
a_{21}x_1 + a_{22}x_2 + a_{23}x_3 + \cdots + a_{2n}x_n &= c_2 \\
\vdots \qquad\qquad\qquad &\quad \vdots \\
a_{n1}x_1 + a_{n2}x_2 + a_{n3}x_3 + \cdots + a_{nn}x_n &= c_n
\end{aligned}
\tag{3.1}
$$

The set contains n equations in n unknowns. It is convenient to express the set as a matrix equation of the form

$$\mathbf{AX} = \mathbf{C} \tag{3.2}$$

where

$$\mathbf{A} = \begin{bmatrix} a_{11} & a_{12} & \cdots & a_{1n} \\ a_{21} & a_{22} & \cdots & a_{2n} \\ \vdots & \vdots & \ddots & \vdots \\ a_{n1} & a_{n2} & \cdots & a_{nn} \end{bmatrix}, \quad \mathbf{X} = \begin{bmatrix} x_1 \\ x_2 \\ \vdots \\ x_n \end{bmatrix}, \quad \mathbf{C} = \begin{bmatrix} c_1 \\ c_2 \\ \vdots \\ c_n \end{bmatrix}$$

Matrix **A** has n rows and n columns.
Matrix **X** has n rows and 1 column.
Note: The number of columns in **A** must equal the number of rows in **X**; otherwise, matrix multiplication is not defined.
Matrix **C** has n rows and 1 column
In matrix algebra, **X** can be obtained by multiplying both sides by $\mathbf{A}^{-1}$, that is,

$$\underbrace{\mathbf{A}^{-1}\mathbf{A}}_{\mathbf{I}}\mathbf{X} = \mathbf{A}^{-1}\mathbf{C} \quad \Rightarrow \quad \mathbf{IX} = \mathbf{X} = \mathbf{A}^{-1}\mathbf{C}$$

MATLAB offers the following functions for solving a set of linear equations:

- The `inv` function:

  To solve a system of linear equations in MATLAB, you can use

  ```
  X = inv(A) * C
  ```

  The method of solving a system of linear equations by using the `inv` function is more computationally complicated than a method called Gauss elimination, which is discussed next.
- The Gauss elimination function:

  MATLAB allows for the solution of the linear system, **AX** = **C**, by Gauss elimination by writing

  ```
  X = A \ C
  ```

  Note the use of MATLAB's backslash operator to solve for `X` by Gauss elimination.

Example 3.2

The following example solves the three equation linear system shown and writes the results to a file:

$$
\begin{aligned}
3x_1 + 2x_2 - x_3 &= 10 \\
-x_1 + 3x_2 + 2x_3 &= 5 \\
x_1 - x_2 - x_3 &= -1
\end{aligned}
$$

```
% Example_3_2.m
% This program solves a simple linear system of equations
% by both the use of MATLAB's inverse matrix function and
% by the Gauss elimination method.
clc; clear;
A=[3 2 -1; -1 3 2; 1 -1 -1]
C=[10 5 -1]'
% X1 is the solution using matrix inverse function:
X1=inv(A)*C
% X2 is the solution using Gauss elimination method:
X2=A\C
% check solution:
A*X1
% Use the size() command to determine the number of rows
% and the number of columns in matrix A.
[A_rows  A_cols] = size(A)
% Print matrix A, matrix C and the solution of the linear
% system of equations to the file output.txt:
fid=fopen('output.txt','w');
fprintf(fid,'A matrix:\n');
for i=1:A_rows
    for j=1:A_cols
        fprintf(fid,' %6.1f',A(i,j));
    end
    fprintf(fid,'\n');
end
fprintf(fid,'C vector:\n');
for i=1:length(C)
    fprintf(fid,' %6.1f', C(i));
end
fprintf(fid,'\n');
fprintf(fid,'Solution X1 (using inverse matrix):\n');
for i=1:length(X1)
    fprintf(fid,' %6.1f', X1(i));
end
fprintf(fid,'\n');
fprintf(fid,'Solution X2 (using Gauss elimination):\n');
for i=1:length(X2)
    fprintf(fid,' %6.1f',X2(i));
end
fprintf(fid,'\n');
fclose(fid);
```

Example 3.3: An Example in Resistive Circuits

A typical example involving a system of linear equations can be found in the resistive circuit of Figure 3.1. The goal is to solve for the node voltages v_1, v_2, and v_3 as functions of the input voltages V_1 and V_2 and the input current I_1.

Using Ohm's law ($v = iR$) and Kirchhoff's current law (KCL), we can write expressions for the sum of currents at each node of interest. KCL states that the total current entering any circuit node must sum to zero. In Figure 3.1, the resistor currents are written as i_n and are arbitrarily defined in the directions as drawn. Writing three KCL equations for the currents *entering* each node (and noting that currents drawn as *leaving* the node are written mathematically as negative numbers) gives

$$\text{At node ①: } i_1 + i_2 + i_3 = 0 \tag{3.3}$$

$$\text{At node ②: } I_1 - i_2 + i_4 = 0 \tag{3.4}$$

$$\text{At node ③: } -i_3 - i_4 + i_5 = 0 \tag{3.5}$$

We now rewrite these three equations in terms of voltages using Ohm's law. Note that in these types of problems, it is often easier to write the equa-

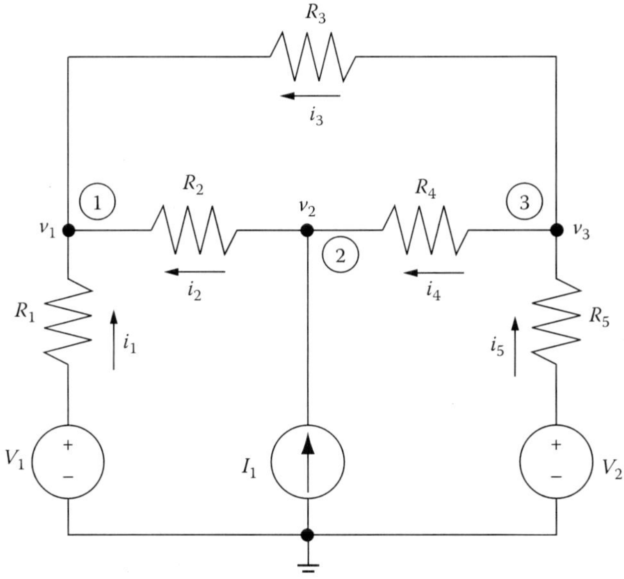

Figure 3.1 Resistive circuit.

tions in terms of conductances G_n instead of resistances (where $G_n = 1/R_n$), and Ohm's law may be rewritten as $i = vG$. Thus,

$$i_1 = \frac{V_1 - v_1}{R_1} \rightarrow i_1 = (V_1 - v_1)G_1 \tag{3.6}$$

$$i_2 = \frac{v_2 - v_1}{R_2} \rightarrow i_2 = (v_2 - v_1)G_2 \tag{3.7}$$

$$i_3 = \frac{v_3 - v_1}{R_3} \rightarrow i_3 = (v_3 - v_1)G_3 \tag{3.8}$$

$$i_4 = \frac{v_3 - v_2}{R_4} \rightarrow i_4 = (v_3 - v_2)G_4 \tag{3.9}$$

$$i_5 = \frac{V_2 - v_3}{R_5} \rightarrow i_5 = (V_2 - v_3)G_5 \tag{3.10}$$

Substituting these expressions for i_1 through i_5 into Equations (3.3) to (3.5) gives

$$(V_1 - v_1)G_1 + (v_2 - v_1)G_2 + (v_3 - v_1)G_3 = 0 \tag{3.11}$$

$$I_1 - (v_2 - v_1)G_2 + (v_3 - v_2)G_4 = 0 \tag{3.12}$$

$$-(v_3 - v_1)G_3 - (v_3 - v_2)G_4 + (V_2 - v_3)G_5 = 0 \tag{3.13}$$

These expressions can be rearranged into a system of three equations with three unknowns:

$$\begin{bmatrix} (G_1 + G_2 + G_3) & -G_2 & -G_3 \\ -G_2 & (G_2 + G_4) & -G_4 \\ -G_3 & -G_4 & (G_3 + G_4 + G_5) \end{bmatrix} \begin{bmatrix} v_1 \\ v_2 \\ v_3 \end{bmatrix} = \begin{bmatrix} V_1 G_1 \\ I_1 \\ V_2 G_5 \end{bmatrix} \tag{3.14}$$

This equation has the form **AX** = **C** and may be solved by Guass elimination as shown previously in Example 3.2.

The following script solves for the node voltages for the following circuit values:

$$R_1 = 2200\,\Omega,\ R_2 = 10\,\text{k}\Omega,\ R_3 = 6900\,\Omega,\ R_4 = 9100\,\Omega,\ R_5 = 3300\,\Omega$$

$$V_1 = 12\,\text{V},\ V_2 = 3.3\,\text{V},\ I_1 = 2\,\text{mA}$$

```
% Example_3_3.m Resistive Circuit
% This program solves for the internal node voltages for
% the circuit shown in Figure 3.1.
% The conductances G are in units of siemens
% The node voltage V are in units of volts
% The currents I are in units of amps
clear; clc;
g1 = 1/2200;
g2 = 1/10000;
g3 = 1/6900;
g4 = 1/9100;
g5 = 1/3300;
V1 = 12;
V2 = 3.3;
I1 = .002;
% Put the problem into standard form AX=C:
A = [ g1+g2+g3 -g2 -g3; -g2 g2+g4 -g4; -g3 -g4 g3+g4+g5];
C = [ V1*g1; I1; V2*g5 ];
X = A \ C ;
% print the results
fprintf('V1=%9.1f V\nV2=%9.1f V\nI1=%9.1e A\n',V1,V2,I1);
fprintf('g1=%9.5f S\ng2=%9.5f S\ng3=%9.5f S\n',g1,g2,g3);
fprintf('g4=%9.5f S\ng5=%9.5f S\n',g4,g5);
fprintf('\n');
fprintf('  Node #     v (volts)  \n');
fprintf('------------------------\n');
for n=1:length(C)
    fprintf('  %3i     %9.1f\n', n,X(n));
end
----------------------------------------------------
```

3.4 Gauss Elimination

As previously discussed, the Gauss elimination method is computationally more efficient than the inverse matrix method or the method of determinants with Cramer's rule. We wish to use the Gauss elimination method to solve the system of linear equations described by Equation (3.1) and represented in matrix form by Equation (3.2). In the Gauss elimination method, the original system is reduced to an equivalent triangular set that can readily be solved by back substitution. The reduced equivalent set would appear like the following set of equations:

$$\begin{aligned}
\tilde{a}_{11}x_1 + \tilde{a}_{12}x_2 + \tilde{a}_{13}x_3 + \quad \cdots \quad + \tilde{a}_{1n}x_n &= \tilde{c}_1 \\
\tilde{a}_{22}x_2 + \tilde{a}_{23}x_3 + \quad \cdots \quad + \tilde{a}_{2n}x_n &= \tilde{c}_2 \\
\tilde{a}_{33}x_3 + \quad \cdots \quad + \tilde{a}_{3n}x_n &= \tilde{c}_3 \\
\ddots \qquad \vdots &= \vdots \\
\tilde{a}_{n-1,n-1}x_{n-1} + \tilde{a}_{n-1,n}x_n &= \tilde{c}_{n-1} \\
\tilde{a}_{n,n}x_n &= \tilde{c}_n
\end{aligned} \tag{3.15}$$

where the tilde (~) variables are a new set of coefficients (to be determined) and where the new coefficient matrix $\tilde{\mathbf{A}}$ is *diagonal* (i.e., all of the coefficients left of the main diagonal are zero. Then,

$$x_n = \tilde{c}_n / \tilde{a}_{n,n}$$

$$x_{n-1} = \frac{1}{\tilde{a}_{n-1,n-1}}(\tilde{c}_{n-1} - \tilde{a}_{n-1,n}x_n)$$

$$\vdots$$

etc.

To determine the reduced equivalent set $\tilde{\mathbf{A}}$ and $\tilde{\mathbf{C}}$, it is convenient to augment the original coefficient matrix **A** with the **C** matrix as shown below:

$$\mathrm{A}_{aug} = \left[\begin{array}{cccc|c} a_{11} & a_{12} & \cdots & a_{1n} & c_1 \\ a_{21} & a_{22} & \cdots & a_{2n} & c_2 \\ \vdots & \vdots & \ddots & \vdots & \vdots \\ a_{n1} & a_{n2} & \cdots & a_{nn} & c_n \end{array}\right] \tag{3.16}$$

The following procedure is used to obtain the reduced equivalent set:

1. Multiply the first row of Equations (3.1) by a_{21}/a_{11} and subtract from the second row, giving

$$a'_{21} = a_{21} - \frac{a_{21}}{a_{11}} \times a_{11}, \quad a'_{22} = a_{22} - \frac{a_{21}}{a_{11}} \times a_{12}, \quad a'_{23} = a_{23} - \frac{a_{21}}{a_{11}} \times a_{13}, \ldots \quad \text{etc.}$$

and

$$c'_2 = c_2 - \frac{a_{21}}{a_{11}} \times c_1$$

This gives $a'_{21} = 0$

2. For the third row: multiply the first row of Equations (3.1) by a_{31} / a_{11} and subtract from row 3, giving

$$a'_{31} = a_{31} - \frac{a_{31}}{a_{11}} \times a_{11}, \quad a'_{32} = a_{32} - \frac{a_{31}}{a_{11}} \times a_{12}, \quad a'_{33} = a_{33} - \frac{a_{31}}{a_{11}} \times a_{13}, \ldots \text{ etc.}$$

and

$$c_3' = c_3 - \frac{a_{31}}{a_{11}} \times c_1$$

This gives $a_{31}' = 0$.

3. This process is repeated for the remaining rows 4, 5, 6, … , n. The original row 1 is kept in its original form. All other rows have been modified and the new coefficients are designated by a ($'$). Except for the first row, the resulting set will not contain x_1.
4. For the preceding steps, the first row of Equations (3.1) was used as the *pivot row,* and a_{11} was the *pivot element*. We now use the new row 2 as the pivot row and repeat steps 1–3 for the remaining rows below row 2. Thus, multiply the new row 2 by $\frac{a_{32}'}{a_{22}'}$ and subtract from row 3, giving

$$a_{32}'' = a_{32}' - \frac{a_{32}'}{a_{22}'} \times a_{22}', \quad a_{33}'' = a_{33}' - \frac{a_{32}'}{a_{22}'} \times a_{23}', \; a_{34}'' = a_{34}' - \frac{a_{32}'}{a_{22}'} \times a_{24}', \ldots \text{ etc.}$$

and

$$c_3'' = c_3' - \frac{a_{32}'}{a_{22}'} \times c_2'$$

This gives $a_{32}'' = 0$.

Similarly, multiply the new row 2 by $\frac{a_{42}'}{a_{22}'}$ and subtract from row 4, giving

$$a_{42}'' = a_{42}' - \frac{a_{42}'}{a_{22}'} \times a_{22}', \quad a_{43}'' = a_{43}' - \frac{a_{42}'}{a_{22}'} \times a_{23}', \; a_{44}'' = a_{43}' - \frac{a_{42}'}{a_{22}'} \times a_{24}', \ldots \text{ etc.}$$

and

$$c_4'' = c_4' - \frac{a_{42}'}{a_{22}'} \times c_2'$$

This gives $a_{42}'' = 0$.

This process is continued for the remaining rows 5, 6, … , n. Except for the new row 2, the set does not contain x_2.

5. The next row is now used as a pivot row, and the process is continued until the $(n-1)$th row is used as the pivot row. When this is complete, the new system is triangular and can be solved by back substitution.

The general expression for the new coefficients is

$$a'_{ij} = a_{ij} - \frac{a_{ik}}{a_{kk}} \times a_{kj} \qquad \text{for } i = k+1, k+2, \ldots, n \quad \text{and} \quad j = k+1, k+2, \ldots, n$$

where k is the pivot row.

These operations only affect the a_{ij} and c_j. Thus, we need only operate on the **A** and **C** matrices.

Example 3.4: Given

$$\begin{aligned} x_1 - 3x_2 + x_3 &= -4 \\ -3x_1 + 4x_2 + 3x_3 &= -10 \\ 2x_1 + 3x_2 - 2x_3 &= 18 \end{aligned}$$

The augmented coefficient matrix is

$$\mathbf{A}_{aug} = \left[\begin{array}{ccc|c} 1 & -3 & 1 & -4 \\ -3 & 4 & 3 & -10 \\ 2 & 3 & -2 & 18 \end{array}\right]$$

multiply row 1 by $\frac{a_{21}}{a_{11}} = \frac{-3}{1}$ and subtract from row 2

Row 2 becomes (−3 + 3), (4−9), (3 + 3), (−10−12) = (0, −5, 6, −22)
The new matrix is

$$\mathbf{A}_{aug,Equiv} = \left[\begin{array}{ccc|c} 1 & -3 & 1 & -4 \\ 0 & -5 & 6 & -22 \\ 2 & 3 & -2 & 18 \end{array}\right]$$

multiply row 1 by $\frac{a_{31}}{a_{11}} = \frac{2}{1}$ and subtract from row 3

Row 3 becomes (2−2), (3 + 6), (−2−2), (18 + 8) = (0, 9, −4, 26)
The new matrix is

$$\mathbf{A}_{aug,Equiv} = \left[\begin{array}{ccc|c} 1 & -3 & 1 & -4 \\ 0 & -5 & 6 & -22 \\ 0 & 9 & -4 & 26 \end{array}\right]$$

We now use row 2 as the pivot row.

$$\mathbf{A}_{aug,Equiv} = \left[\begin{array}{ccc|c} 1 & -3 & 1 & -4 \\ 0 & -5 & 6 & -22 \\ 0 & 9 & -4 & 26 \end{array}\right]$$

multiply row 2 by $\dfrac{a_{32}}{a_{22}} = -\dfrac{9}{5}$ and subtract from row 3

Row 3 becomes

$$(0-0), \left(9 - \frac{9}{5} \times 5\right), \left(-4 + \frac{9}{5} \times 6\right), \left(26 - \frac{9}{5} \times 22\right) = \left(0,\ 0,\ \frac{34}{5},\ -\frac{68}{5}\right)$$

The new matrix is

$$\mathbf{A}_{aug,Equiv} = \left[\begin{array}{ccc|c} 1 & -3 & 1 & -4 \\ 0 & -5 & 6 & -22 \\ 0 & 0 & \frac{34}{5} & -\frac{68}{5} \end{array}\right]$$

The system is now triangular, and the system can be rewritten as

$$\mathbf{A}_{Equiv}\mathbf{X} = \mathbf{C}_{Equiv}$$

which gives

$$\begin{aligned} x_1 - 3x_2 + x_3 &= -4 \\ -5x_2 + 6x_3 &= -22 \\ \frac{34}{5}x_3 &= -\frac{68}{5} \end{aligned}$$

Solving:

$$\frac{34}{5}x_3 = -\frac{68}{5} \quad \Rightarrow \quad x_3 = -2$$

$$-5x_2 + 6(-2) = -22 \quad \Rightarrow \quad x_2 = 2$$

$$x_1 - 3(2) + (-2) = -4 \quad \Rightarrow \quad x_1 = 4$$

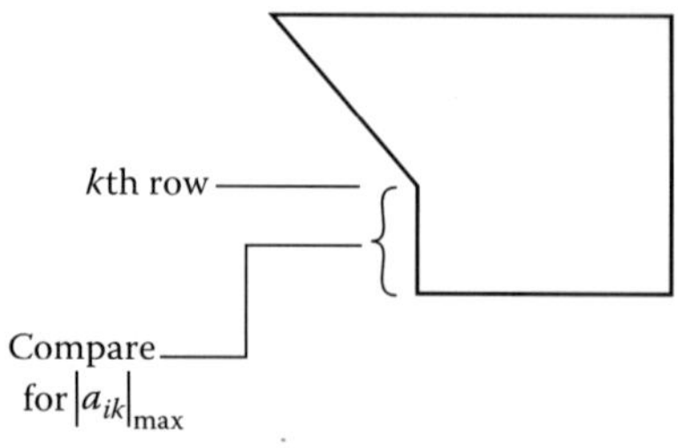

Figure 3.2 Row interchange.

There are two important considerations:

1. If a_{kk} is zero, where k is the pivot row, then the process cannot be carried out.
2. Greater accuracy in the solution is obtained if the pivot element is the absolute maximum available from the set. That is; if the pivot row is k, one compares the a_{ik}'s for $i = k + 1, k + 2, \ldots, n$ (see Figure 3.2). If $|a_{ik}|_{max} \neq |a_{kk}|$, then the row containing the $|a_{ik}|_{max}$ is interchanged with the kth row. This only affects the ordering of the equations and does not affect the solution.

If after row interchange is carried out and one of the a_{kk}'s remains zero, then the system is singular, and no solution can be obtained.

One last consideration: it can be shown that if the magnitude of the pivot element is much smaller than other elements in the matrix, the use of the small pivot element will cause a decrease in the accuracy of the solution. To check if this is the case, you can first scale the equations, that is, divide each equation by the absolute maximum coefficient in that equation. This makes the absolute maximum coefficient in that equation equal to 1.0. If $|a_{kk}| \ll 1$, then the solution is likely to be inaccurate.

3.5 The Gauss-Jordan Method

The Gauss-Jordan method is a modification of the Gauss elimination method and can be used to solve a system of linear equations of the form **AX** = **C**. In this method, the objective is to obtain an equivalent coefficient matrix such that, except for the main diagonal, all elements are zero. The method starts out, as in the Gauss elimination method, by finding an equivalent matrix that is triangular. It then continues, assuming that **A** is an $n \times n$ matrix, using the nth row as the pivot row, multiplying the nth row by $a_{n-1,n}/a_{n,n}$ and subtracting the result from row $n - 1$, thus making the new $a_{n-1,n} = 0$. The process is repeated for rows $n - 2, n - 3, \ldots, 1$.

Example 3.5

As an example, the Gauss-Jordan method is applied as follows: Starting with the triangular equivalent matrix of Example 3.4,

$$\mathbf{A}_{aug,Equiv} = \left[\begin{array}{ccc|c} 1 & -3 & 1 & -4 \\ 0 & -5 & 6 & -22 \\ 0 & 0 & \frac{34}{5} & -\frac{68}{5} \end{array}\right]$$

Multiply row 3 by $\frac{a_{23}}{a_{33}} = 6 \times \frac{5}{34}$ and subtract from row 2. Row 2 becomes

$$\left(0 - \frac{30}{34} \times 0\right), \left(-5 - \frac{30}{34} \times 0\right), \left(6 - \frac{30}{34} \times \frac{34}{5}\right), \left(-22 + \frac{30}{34} \times \frac{68}{5}\right) = (0, -5, 0, -10)$$

Next, multiply row 3 by $\frac{a_{13}}{a_{33}} = \frac{5}{34}$ and subtract from row 1. Row 1 becomes

$$\left(1 - \frac{5}{34} \times 0\right), \left(-3 - \frac{5}{34} \times 0\right), \left(1 - \frac{5}{34} \times \frac{34}{5}\right), \left(-4 + \frac{5}{34} \times \frac{68}{5}\right) = (1, -3, 0, -2)$$

The new $\mathbf{A}_{aug,Equiv}$ becomes

$$\mathbf{A}_{aug,Equiv} = \left[\begin{array}{ccc|c} 1 & -3 & 0 & -2 \\ 0 & -5 & 0 & -10 \\ 0 & 0 & \frac{34}{5} & -\frac{68}{5} \end{array}\right]$$

Now, row 2 is used as the pivot row. Multiply row 2 by $\frac{a_{12}}{a_{22}} = \frac{3}{5}$ and subtract from row 1. Row 1 then becomes

$$\left(1 - \frac{3}{5} \times 0\right), \left(-3 + \frac{3}{5} \times 5\right), \left(0 - \frac{3}{5} \times 0\right), \left(-2 + \frac{3}{5} \times 10\right) = (1, 0, 0, 4)$$

The new $\mathbf{A}_{aug,Equiv}$ becomes

$$\mathbf{A}_{aug,Equiv} = \left[\begin{array}{ccc|c} 1 & 0 & 0 & 4 \\ 0 & -5 & 0 & -10 \\ 0 & 0 & \frac{34}{5} & -\frac{68}{5} \end{array}\right]$$

Thus, the equivalent set of equations becomes

$$x_1 = 4$$

$$-5x_2 = -10$$

$$\frac{34}{5}x_3 = -\frac{68}{5}$$

And thus $x_1 = 4$, $x_2 = 2$, and $x_3 = -2$, which is the same answer that was obtained previously by the Gauss elimination method.

3.6 Number of Solutions

Suppose a Gauss elimination program is carried out and the following results are obtained:

$$\begin{aligned} a_{11}x_1 + a_{12}x_2 + a_{13}x_3 + \quad \cdots \quad + a_{1n}x_n &= c_1 \\ a_{22}x_2 + a_{23}x_3 + \quad \cdots \quad + a_{2n}x_n &= c_2 \\ a_{33}x_3 + \quad \cdots \quad + a_{3n}x_n &= c_3 \\ \ddots \qquad \vdots \;&= \vdots \\ a_{rr}x_r + \cdots + a_{rn}x_n &= c_r \\ 0 &= c_{r+1} \\ 0 &= c_{r+2} \\ &\vdots \\ 0 &= c_n \end{aligned}$$

where $r < n$ and $a_{11}, a_{12}, \ldots, a_{rr}$ are not zero. There are two possible cases:

1. No solution exists if any one of the c_{r+1} through c_n is not zero.
2. Infinitely many solutions exist if c_{r+1} through c_n are all zero.

If $r = n$ and $a_{11}, a_{12}, \ldots, a_{nn}$ are not zero, then the system would appear as follows:

$$\begin{aligned}
a_{11}x_1 + a_{12}x_2 + a_{13}x_3 + \quad \cdots \quad + a_{1n}x_n &= c_1 \\
a_{22}x_2 + a_{23}x_3 + \quad \cdots \quad + a_{2n}x_n &= c_2 \\
a_{33}x_3 + \quad \cdots \quad + a_{3n}x_n &= c_3 \\
\ddots \qquad \vdots &= \vdots \\
a_{nn}x_n &= c_n
\end{aligned}$$

For this case, there is only one solution.

3.7 Inverse Matrix

Given a matrix system of equations of the general form

$$\mathbf{AX} = \mathbf{C}$$

We can solve by front-multiplying both sides of the equation by the matrix inverse $\mathbf{A}^{-1}$:

$$\mathbf{A}^{-1}\mathbf{AX} = \mathbf{IX} = \mathbf{X} = \mathbf{A}^{-1}\mathbf{C}$$

MATLAB's method of solution is

`X = inv(A) * C` (solves by $\mathbf{A}^{-1}$)

or

`X = A/C` (solves by Gauss elimination)

Let us see what is involved by determining $\mathbf{A}^{-1}$.

Let $\mathbf{B} = \mathbf{A}^{-1}$. Then, $\mathbf{BA} = \mathbf{I}$. We will demonstrate for a 3 × 3 matrix:

$$\begin{bmatrix} b_{11} & b_{12} & b_{13} \\ b_{21} & b_{22} & b_{23} \\ b_{31} & b_{32} & b_{33} \end{bmatrix} \begin{bmatrix} a_{11} & a_{12} & a_{13} \\ a_{21} & a_{22} & a_{23} \\ a_{31} & a_{32} & a_{33} \end{bmatrix} = \begin{bmatrix} 1 & 0 & 0 \\ 0 & 1 & 0 \\ 0 & 0 & 1 \end{bmatrix}$$

First row of **BA**:

$$\text{Element (1,1): } b_{11}a_{11} + b_{12}a_{21} + b_{13}a_{31} = 1$$

$$\text{Element (1,2): } b_{11}a_{12} + b_{12}a_{22} + b_{13}a_{32} = 0$$

$$\text{Element (1,3): } b_{11}a_{13} + b_{12}a_{23} + b_{13}a_{33} = 0$$

Here, b_{11}, b_{12}, b_{13} are the unknowns. Also, note that the transpose matrix

$$\mathbf{A}^T = \begin{bmatrix} a_{11} & a_{21} & a_{31} \\ a_{12} & a_{22} & a_{32} \\ a_{13} & a_{23} & a_{33} \end{bmatrix}$$

Let

$$\mathbf{B}_1 = \begin{bmatrix} b_{11} \\ b_{12} \\ b_{13} \end{bmatrix}$$

Then,

$$\mathbf{A}^T\mathbf{B}_1 = \begin{bmatrix} 1 \\ 0 \\ 0 \end{bmatrix}$$

Solve for b_{11}, b_{12}, b_{13} by Gauss elimination.

Second row of **BA**:

$$\text{Element (2,1): } b_{21}a_{11} + b_{22}a_{21} + b_{23}a_{31} = 0$$

$$\text{Element (2,2): } b_{21}a_{12} + b_{22}a_{22} + b_{23}a_{32} = 1$$

$$\text{Element (2,3): } b_{21}a_{13} + b_{22}a_{23} + b_{23}a_{33} = 0$$

Here, b_{21}, b_{22}, b_{23} are the unknowns.

Let

$$\mathbf{B}_2 = \begin{bmatrix} b_{21} \\ b_{22} \\ b_{23} \end{bmatrix}$$

Then,

$$\mathbf{A}^T\mathbf{B}_2 = \begin{bmatrix} 0 \\ 1 \\ 0 \end{bmatrix}$$

Solve for b_{21}, b_{22}, b_{23} by Gauss Elimination.

Third row of **BA**:

$$\text{Element (3,1):} \quad b_{31}a_{11} + b_{32}a_{21} + b_{33}a_{31} = 0$$

$$\text{Element (3,2):} \quad b_{31}a_{12} + b_{32}a_{22} + b_{33}a_{32} = 0$$

$$\text{Element (3,3):} \quad b_{31}a_{13} + b_{32}a_{23} + b_{33}a_{33} = 1$$

Here, b_{31}, b_{32}, b_{33} are the unknowns.

Let

$$\mathbf{B}_3 = \begin{bmatrix} b_{31} \\ b_{32} \\ b_{33} \end{bmatrix}$$

Then,

$$\mathbf{A}^T\mathbf{B}_3 = \begin{bmatrix} 0 \\ 0 \\ 1 \end{bmatrix}$$

Solve for b_{31}, b_{32}, b_{33} by Gauss elimination.

An alternative [1] to the method described is to augment the coefficient matrix with the identity matrix, then apply the Gauss-Jordan method, making the coefficient matrix the identity matrix. The original identity matrix then becomes $\mathbf{A}^{-1}$. The starting augmented matrix for a 3 × 3 coefficient matrix is as follows:

$$\left[\begin{array}{ccc|ccc} a_{11} & a_{12} & a_{13} & 1 & 0 & 0 \\ a_{21} & a_{22} & a_{23} & 0 & 1 & 0 \\ a_{31} & a_{32} & a_{33} & 0 & 0 & 1 \end{array}\right]$$

Example 3.6

This method is illustrated by the following example:

$$\begin{aligned} x_1 - 3x_2 + \ x_3 &= -4 \\ -3x_1 + 4x_2 + 3x_3 &= -10 \\ 2x_1 + 3x_2 - 2x_3 &= 18 \end{aligned}$$

Writing the augmented matrix:

$$\mathbf{A}_{aug} = \left[\begin{array}{ccc|ccc} 1 & -3 & 1 & 1 & 0 & 0 \\ -3 & 4 & 3 & 0 & 1 & 0 \\ 2 & 3 & -2 & 0 & 0 & 1 \end{array}\right]$$

Multiply row 1 by $\frac{-3}{1}$ and subtract from row 2, giving

(−3+3×1), (4−3×3), (3+3×1), (0+3×1), (1+3×0), (0+3×0) = (0,−5, 6, 3, 1, 0)

Multiply row 1 by $\frac{2}{1} = 2$ and subtract from row 3, giving

(2−2×1), (3−2×(−3)), (−2−2×1), (0−2×1), (0−2×0), (1−2×0) = (0, 9, −4, −2, 0, 1)

$$\mathbf{A}_{aug,Equiv} = \left[\begin{array}{ccc|ccc} 1 & -3 & 1 & 1 & 0 & 0 \\ 0 & -5 & 6 & 3 & 1 & 0 \\ 0 & 9 & -4 & -2 & 0 & 1 \end{array}\right]$$

Multiply row 2 by $\frac{-9}{5}$ and subtract from row 3, giving

$$\left(0+\frac{9}{5}\times 0\right), \left(9+\frac{9}{5}\times(-5)\right), \left(-4+\frac{9}{5}\times 6\right), \left(-2+\frac{9}{5}\times 3\right), \left(0+\frac{9}{5}\times 1\right), \left(1+\frac{9}{5}\times 0\right)$$

$$=\left(0, 0, \frac{34}{5}, \frac{17}{5}, \frac{9}{5}, 1\right)$$

$$\mathbf{A}_{aug,Equiv} = \left[\begin{array}{ccc|ccc} 1 & -3 & 1 & 1 & 0 & 0 \\ 0 & -5 & 6 & 3 & 1 & 0 \\ 0 & 0 & \frac{34}{5} & \frac{17}{5} & \frac{9}{5} & 1 \end{array}\right]$$

Multiply row 3 by $\frac{30}{34}$ and subtract from row 2, giving

$$\left(0-\frac{30}{34}\times 0\right),\left(-5-\frac{30}{34}\times 0\right),\left(6-\frac{30}{34}\times\frac{34}{5}\right),\left(3-\frac{30}{34}\times\frac{17}{5}\right),\left(1-\frac{30}{34}\times\frac{9}{5}\right),$$
$$\left(0-\frac{30}{34}\times 1\right)=\left(0,-5,0,0,-\frac{20}{34},-\frac{30}{34}\right)$$

Multiply row 3 by $\frac{5}{34}$ and subtract from row 1, giving

$$\left(1-\frac{5}{34}\times 0\right),\left(-3-\frac{5}{34}\times 0\right),\left(1-\frac{5}{34}\times\frac{34}{5}\right),\left(1-\frac{5}{34}\times\frac{17}{5}\right),\left(0-\frac{5}{34}\times\frac{9}{5}\right),$$
$$\left(0-\frac{5}{34}\times 1\right)=(1,-3,0,\frac{1}{2},-\frac{9}{34},-\frac{5}{34})$$

$$\mathbf{A}_{aug,Equiv}=\left[\begin{array}{ccc|ccc} 1 & -3 & 0 & \frac{1}{2} & -\frac{9}{34} & -\frac{5}{34} \\ 0 & -5 & 0 & 0 & -\frac{20}{34} & -\frac{30}{34} \\ 0 & 0 & \frac{34}{5} & \frac{17}{5} & \frac{9}{5} & 1 \end{array}\right]$$

Multiply row 2 by $\frac{3}{5}$ and subtract from row 1, giving

$$\left(1-\frac{3}{5}\times 0\right),\left(-3-\frac{3}{5}\times(-5)\right),\left(0-\frac{3}{5}\times 0\right),\left(\frac{1}{2}-\frac{3}{5}\times 0\right),\left(-\frac{9}{34}+\frac{3}{5}\times\frac{20}{34}\right),$$
$$\left(-\frac{5}{34}+\frac{3}{5}\times\frac{30}{34}\right)=\left(1,0,0,\frac{1}{2},\frac{3}{34},\frac{13}{34}\right)$$

$$\mathbf{A}_{aug,Equiv}=\left[\begin{array}{ccc|ccc} 1 & 0 & 0 & \frac{1}{2} & \frac{3}{34} & \frac{13}{34} \\ 0 & -5 & 0 & 0 & -\frac{20}{34} & -\frac{30}{34} \\ 0 & 0 & \frac{34}{5} & \frac{17}{5} & \frac{9}{5} & 1 \end{array}\right]$$

Divide row 2 by –5 and row 3 by $\frac{34}{5}$, giving

$$\mathbf{A}_{aug,Equiv}=\left[\begin{array}{ccc|ccc} 1 & 0 & 0 & \frac{1}{2} & \frac{3}{34} & \frac{13}{34} \\ 0 & 1 & 0 & 0 & \frac{4}{34} & \frac{6}{34} \\ 0 & 0 & 1 & \frac{1}{2} & \frac{9}{34} & \frac{5}{34} \end{array}\right]$$

Thus,

$$\mathbf{A}^{-1} = \begin{bmatrix} \frac{1}{2} & \frac{3}{34} & \frac{13}{34} \\ 0 & \frac{4}{34} & \frac{6}{34} \\ \frac{1}{2} & \frac{9}{34} & \frac{5}{34} \end{bmatrix}$$

It is left as a student exercise to show that $\mathbf{AA}^{-1} = \mathbf{I}$.

3.8 The Eigenvalue Problem

One application of the eigenvalue problem is in resonant circuits. Consider the LC network shown in Figure 3.3. Using the constituent relations for voltage across an inductor $\left(v = L\frac{di}{dt}\right)$ and current through a capacitor $\left(i = C\frac{dv}{dt}\right)$, the governing differential equations describing the two node voltages v_1 and v_2 are

$$\frac{d^2 v_1}{dt^2} = -\left(\frac{1}{L_1 C_1}\right) v_1 + \left(\frac{1}{L_1 C_1}\right) v_2 \tag{3.17}$$

$$\frac{d^2 v_2}{dt^2} = \left(\frac{1}{L_1 C_2}\right) v_1 - \left(\frac{1}{L_1 C_2} + \frac{1}{L_2 C_2}\right) v_2 \tag{3.18}$$

We wish to determine the modes of oscillation such that both voltages oscillate at the same frequency. To obtain such a solution, set

$$v_1 = K_1 e^{j\omega t} \tag{3.19}$$

$$v_2 = K_2 e^{j\omega t} \tag{3.20}$$

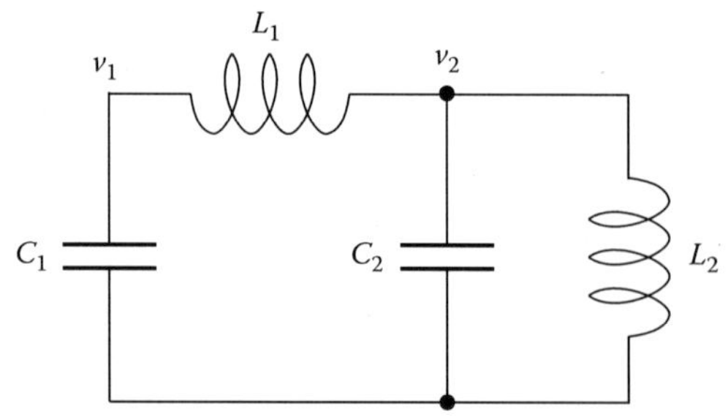

Figure 3.3 LC circuit.

where K_1 and K_2 are constants to be determined. Substituting Equations (3.19) and (3.20) into Equations (3.17) and (3.18) gives

$$\left(\frac{1}{L_1C_1} - \omega^2\right)K_1 - \frac{1}{L_1C_1}K_2 = 0 \tag{3.21}$$

$$-\frac{1}{L_1C_2}K_1 + \left(\frac{1}{L_1C_2} + \frac{1}{L_2C_2} - \omega^2\right)K_2 = 0 \tag{3.22}$$

Equations (3.21) and (3.22) are two homogeneous linear algebraic equations in two unknowns. Linear algebra tells us that the only way for two homogeneous linear algebraic equations in two unknowns to have a nontrivial solution is for the determinant of the coefficient matrix to be zero. Thus,

$$\begin{vmatrix} \left(\frac{1}{L_1C_1} - \omega^2\right) & -\frac{1}{L_1C_1} \\ -\frac{1}{L_1C_2} & \left(\frac{1}{L_1C_2} + \frac{1}{L_2C_2} - \omega^2\right) \end{vmatrix} = 0 \tag{3.23}$$

Now, let $\omega^2 = \lambda$ and also let

$$\mathbf{A} = \begin{bmatrix} \frac{1}{L_1C_1} & -\frac{1}{L_1C_1} \\ -\frac{1}{L_1C_2} & \frac{1}{L_1C_2} + \frac{1}{L_2C_2} \end{bmatrix}$$

Rewriting Equation (3.23) in terms of λ and the individual elements a_{ij} of **A** gives

$$\lambda^2 - (a_{11} + a_{22})\,\lambda + (a_{11}\,a_{22} - a_{12}\,a_{21}) = 0 \tag{3.24}$$

The solution of Equation (3.24) gives the eigenvalues λ_1 and λ_2 of matrix **A**, which represent the square of the two natural frequencies for this system. The ratio of the amplitudes of the oscillation of the two voltages can be obtained by substituting the values of λ into Equation (3.21) or (3.22), which gives

$$\frac{K_2}{K_1} = -(a_{11} - \lambda_1)/a_{12} = 1 - L_1C_1\lambda_1$$

for the first mode, and

$$\frac{K_2}{K_1} = -(a_{11} - \lambda_2)/a_{12} = 1 - L_1C_1\lambda_2$$

for the second mode.

The eigenvector $\mathbf{V}_1$ associated with λ_1 is

$$\begin{bmatrix} K_1 \\ -K_1(a_{11}-\lambda_1)/a_{12} \end{bmatrix}$$

and the eigenvector $\mathbf{V}_2$ associated with λ_2 is

$$\begin{bmatrix} K_1 \\ -K_1(a_{11}-\lambda_2)/a_{12} \end{bmatrix}$$

Since K_1 is arbitrary, we can select $K_1 = 1$, and thus

$$\mathbf{V}_1 = \begin{bmatrix} 1 \\ -(a_{11}-\lambda_1)/a_{12} \end{bmatrix} \tag{3.25}$$

and

$$\mathbf{V}_2 = \begin{bmatrix} 1 \\ -(a_{11}-\lambda_2)/a_{12} \end{bmatrix} \tag{3.26}$$

If $\mathbf{V}$ is an eigenvector of a matrix $\mathbf{A}$ corresponding to an eigenvalue λ, then so is $b\mathbf{V}$, where b is a nonzero constant [1].

MATLAB has a built-in function named `eig` that finds the eigenvalues of a square matrix. MATLAB's description of the function follows:

```
E = EIG(X) is a vector containing the eigenvalues of a square matrix X.
[V,D] = EIG(X) produces a diagonal matrix D of eigenvalues and a
full matrix V whose columns are the corresponding eigenvectors so
that X*V = V*D.
```

For this problem, the matrix $\mathbf{A}$ represents `X`. Thus, running

```
[V, D] = eig(A)
```

gives the eigenvectors associated with λ_1 and λ_2. `V(:,1)` corresponds to λ_1, and `V(:,2)` corresponds to λ_2.

Example 3.7

Suppose in Figure 3.3 the following parameters were given:

$$L_1 = 15\text{ mH},\ L_2 = 25\text{ mH},\ C_1 = 1\ \mu\text{F},\ C_2 = 33\ \mu\text{F}$$

We wish to create a MATLAB script that will determine

1. the eigenvalues of the system by Equations (3.21) and (3.22) by MATLAB's eig function.
2. the eigenfunctions by both Equations (3.21) and (3.22) and MATLAB's [V,D] output.

The program follows.

```
% Example_3_7.m: Eigenvalues and eigenvectors.
% L = eig(A) is a vector containing the eigenvalues of a
% square matrix A.
% [M,D] = eig(A) produces a diagonal matrix D of
% eigenvalues and a full matrix M whose columns are the
% corresponding eigenvectors such that A*L = M*D.
% Units are in SI units.
clear; clc;
L1=15e-3; L2=25e-3; % henries
C1=1e-6; C2=33e-6;  % farads
A(1,1)=1/(L1*C1);
A(1,2)=-1/(L1*C1);
A(2,1)=-1/(L1*C2);
A(2,2)=1/(L1*C2) + 1/(L2*C2);
% Solve for eigenvalues and eigenvectors using derivation
% in Eqn 3.25:
% lambda^2-(A(1,1)+A(2,2))
%       *lambda+(A(1,1)*A(2,2)-A(1,2)*A(2,1))=0
% Solve for lambda using quadratic formula:
b=-(A(1,1)+A(2,2)); c=A(1,1)*A(2,2)-A(1,2)*A(2,1);
lambda1=(-b+sqrt(b^2-4*c))/2;
lambda2=(-b-sqrt(b^2-4*c))/2;
% From Eqns 3.26 and 3.27:
eigenvector1=[1;-(A(1,1)-lambda1)/A(1,2)];
eigenvector2=[1;-(A(1,1)-lambda2)/A(1,2)];
fprintf('Eigenvalues solved via Equation 3.25: ');
fprintf('lambda1=%.0f  lambda2=%.0f\n',lambda1,lambda2);
fprintf('Eigenvectors solved via Equation 3.26 ');
fprintf('and 3.27:\n');
eigenvector1
eigenvector2
% Solve for eigenvalues and eigenvectors using MATLAB's
% eig function. Calling eig and returning result to a
% scalar will give the eigenvalues.
L=eig(A);
fprintf('Eigenvalues via MATLAB eig function: ');
fprintf('L(1)=%.0f  L(2)=%.0f\n',L(1),L(2));
% Calling eig and returning result to two variables will
% give the eigenvectors and a diagonal matrix of the
% eigenvalues.
[V D] = eig(A);
```

```
fprintf('Eigenvectors via MATLAB eig function:\n');
V1=V(:,1)
V2=V(:,2)
D
```

The following results were generated by MATLAB:

```
Eigenvalues solved via Equation 3.25: lambda1 = 68723140
lambda2 = 1175850
Eigenvectors solved via Equation 3.26 and 3.27:
eigenvector1 =
    1.0000
   -0.0308
eigenvector2 =
    1.0000
    0.9824
Eigenvalues via MATLAB eig function: L(1) = 68723140 L(2) =
1175850
Eigenvectors via MATLAB eig function:
V1 =
   0.9995
  -0.0308
V2 =
   0.7134
   0.7008
D =
  1.0e+007 *
    6.8723         0
         0    0.1176
```

Examining the results, it can be seen that `lambda1 = D(1,1)` and `lambda2 = D(2,2)`. Also, `eigenvector1` is a scalar multiple of `V1` and `eigenvector2` is a scalar multiple of `V2`.

Exercises

Exercise 3.1

Use Gauss elimination to solve the following systems of equations:

a.
$$\begin{aligned} 2x_1 + 3x_2 - x_3 &= 20 \\ 4x_1 - x_2 + 3x_3 &= -14 \\ x_1 + 5x_2 + x_3 &= 21 \end{aligned}$$

b.
$$\begin{aligned} 4x_1 + 8x_2 + x_3 &= 8 \\ -2x_1 - 3x_2 + 2x_3 &= 14 \\ x_1 + 3x_2 + 4x_3 &= 30 \end{aligned}$$

c.
$$\begin{aligned} 2x_1 + 3x_2 + x_3 - x_4 &= 1 \\ 5x_1 - 2x_2 + 5x_3 - 4x_4 &= 5 \\ x_1 - 2x_2 + 3x_3 - 3x_4 &= 3 \\ 3x_1 + 8x_2 - x_3 + x_4 &= -1 \end{aligned}$$

Projects

Project 3.1

For the circuit of Figure 3.1, solve for the five unknown currents instead of the three unknown voltages. Solve algebraically by using Equations (3.3), (3.4), and (3.5) and by using Kirchhoff's voltage law (KVL) to write two additional equations. KVL states that the sum of the voltage drops around any loop in the circuit must be zero. Write KVL equations for these two circuit loops: $V_1 \rightarrow R_1 \rightarrow R_2 \rightarrow R_4 \rightarrow R_5 \rightarrow V_2$ and $R_3 \rightarrow R_4 \rightarrow R_2$. You should wind up with a system of five equations and five unknowns. Solve with MATLAB using the inverse matrix technique and confirm that your answer matches the results found in Example 3.3.

Project 3.2

Figure P3.2 shows a resistive circuit known as a "ladder network."

1. Using Ohm's law and Kirchhoff's current law, write a system of equations for the second-order and third-order networks of Figures P3.2a and P3.2b. In addition, write the equations for a fourth-order ladder network.
2. You should see a pattern emerging from your solutions in part 1. Use this pattern to write the matrix for a eighth-order ladder network. Solve for all circuit voltages using MATLAB for $V_{ref} = 5\text{V}$ and the following resistor values:

$$R_{11} = 2200\,\Omega,\ R_{12} = 2200\,\Omega$$
$$R_{21} = 1200\,\Omega,\ R_{22} = 6800\,\Omega$$
$$R_{31} = 3900\,\Omega,\ R_{32} = 2200\,\Omega$$
$$R_{41} = 3300\,\Omega,\ R_{42} = 5700\,\Omega$$
$$R_{51} = 1800\,\Omega,\ R_{52} = 5100\,\Omega$$
$$R_{61} = 4700\,\Omega,\ R_{62} = 3900\,\Omega$$
$$R_{71} = 5700\,\Omega,\ R_{72} = 6800\,\Omega$$
$$R_{81} = 1200\,\Omega,\ R_{82} = 2700\,\Omega$$

3. Write a MATLAB program to solve this problem automatically for arbitrary n and R_0 (as shown in Figure P3.2c) under the following conditions:

$$R_0 = R_{11} = R_{21} = R_{31} = \cdots = R_{(n-1)} = R_{n1}$$
$$2R_0 = R_{12} = R_{22} = R_{32} = \cdots = R_{(n-1)2}$$

Find solutions for the following two cases:

$$n = 16,\quad R_0 = 1000\ \Omega,\quad V_{ref} = 10$$
$$n = 24,\quad R_0 = 100\ \Omega,\quad V_{ref} = 1$$

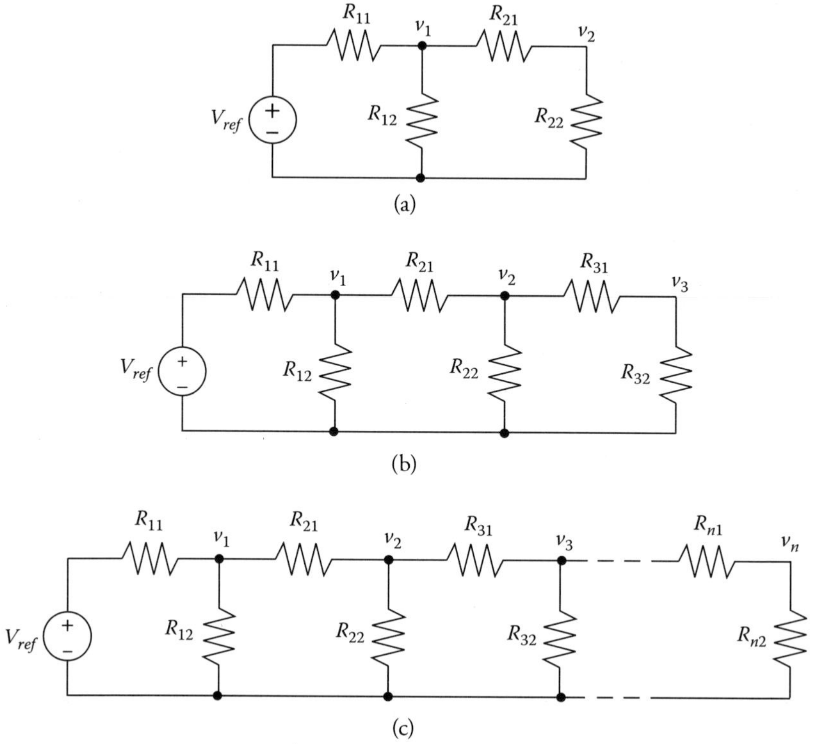

Figure P3.2 (a) Second-order resistor ladder network. (b) Third-order resistor ladder network. (c) An *n*th-order resistor ladder network.

Project 3.3

One very important application of the eigenvalue problem is in the theory of mechanical vibrations. Consider the system of two masses (m_1 and m_2) and three springs (with spring constants k_1, k_2, and k_3) shown in Figure P3.3.

The governing differential equations describing the motion of the two masses are

$$m_1 \ddot{x}_1 = k_2 (x_2 - x_1) - k_1 x_1 \tag{P3.3a}$$

$$m_2 \ddot{x}_2 = -k_2 (x_2 - x_1) - k_3 x_2 \tag{P3.3b}$$

Using MATLAB's `eig` function, determine the modes of oscillation such that each mass undergoes harmonic motion at the same frequency. Use the following values:

$m_1 = m_2 = 1500$ kg, $k_1 = 3250$ N/m, $k_2 = 3500$ N/m, $k_3 = 3000$ N/m

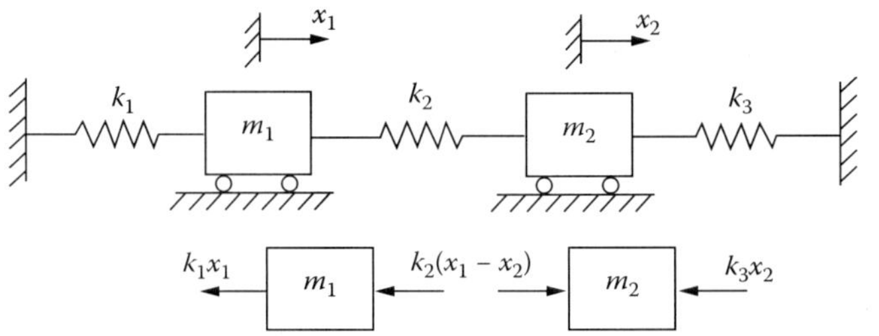

Figure P3.3 Mechanical vibration problem with two degrees of freedom.

Project 3.4

Suppose a manufacturer wishes to purchase a piece of equipment that costs \$40,000. He plans to borrow the money from a bank and pay off the loan in 10 years in 120 equal payments. The annual interest rate is 6%. Each month, the interest charged will be on the unpaid balance of the loan. He wishes to determine what his monthly payment will be. This problem can be solved by a system of linear equations.

Let x_j be the amount in the jth payment that goes toward paying off the principal. Then, the equation describing the jth payment is

$$j\text{th payment} = M = x_j + \left(P - \sum_{n=1}^{n=j-1} x_n \right) I \tag{P3.4a}$$

where

M = the monthly payment
P = the amount borrowed
I = the monthly interest rate = one-twelfth of the annual interest rate

The total number of unknowns is 121 (120 x_j values and M).

Applying Equation (P3.4a) to each month gives 120 equations. The 121st equation is

$$P = \sum_{n=1}^{n=120} x_n \tag{P3.4b}$$

Develop a MATLAB program that will:

1. Ask the user to enter from the keyboard the amount of the loan P, the annual interest rate I, and the time period Y (in years).
2. Set up the system of linear equations, using $A_{n,m}$ as the coefficient matrix of the system of linear equations. The n represents the equation number, and m represents the coefficient of x_m in that equation. Set $x_{121} = M$.

3. Solve the system of linear equations in MATLAB.
4. Print out a table consisting of four columns. The first column should be the month number, the second column the monthly payment, the third column the amount of the monthly payment that goes toward paying off the principal, and the fourth column the interest payment for that month.

Project 3.5

The `tic` and `toc` commands in MATLAB allow you to measure the execution time for a given series of commands. The `tic` and `toc` behave as a stopwatch; `tic` starts the stopwatch, and `toc` stops it and prints the elapsed time. An example usage is

```
tic;
a = factorial(25);
toc;
```

Running this script will compute 25! and then print the total execution time:

```
Elapsed time is 0.005509 seconds.
```

Of course, the time that you see will depend on the speed of your computer.

1. Write a program in MATLAB that creates a random $n \times n$ matrix **A** where each element is a random integer between $-E_{\max}$ and $E_{\max}$. Use MATLAB's `rand` and `round` functions to accomplish this. To learn how to use these functions, type **`help rand`** and **`help round`** into the MATLAB Command window. Initially, assume that n = 100 and $E_{\max} = 100$.
2. Also, create a $1 \times n$ column vector **C** with random elements, using the same values for n and $E_{\max}$ above.
3. Solve the equation **AX** = **C** for **X** in two ways: (a) by finding $\mathbf{A}^{-1}$ (with `inv`) and multiplying it by **C** and (b) by using Gauss elimination (the MATLAB '\' operator). Use `tic` and `toc` to measure the amount of time it takes for each method. Do the results make sense?
4. Rerun your program 10 times and obtain an average execution time for the two solution methods. Also find average execution times for the following values of n: 3, 10, 30, 300, 1000. Plot the execution times versus n on log-log axes.

Reference

1. Kreyszig, E., *Advanced Engineering Mathematics*, 8th ed., Wiley, New York, 1999.

Chapter 4

Roots of Algebraic and Transcendental Equations

4.1 Introduction

In the analysis of various engineering problems, we often are faced with a need to find roots of equations whose solution is not easily found analytically. Typical examples include *n*th degree polynomials and transcendental equations containing trigonometric functions, exponentials, or logarithms. In this chapter, we review several methods for solving such equations numerically with mathematical techniques of varying complexity and accuracy. Also included is a section on the `fzero` function of MATLAB®, which may be used to obtain the roots of equations of the type mentioned previously.

4.2 The Search Method

The equation whose roots are to be determined should be put into the following standard form:

$$f(x) = 0 \tag{4.1}$$

We proceed as follows: First, a search is made to obtain intervals in which real roots lie. This is accomplished by subdividing the x domain into N equal subdivisions, giving

$$x_1, x_2, x_3, \ldots x_{N+1} \quad \text{and} \quad x_{i+1} = x_i + \Delta x$$

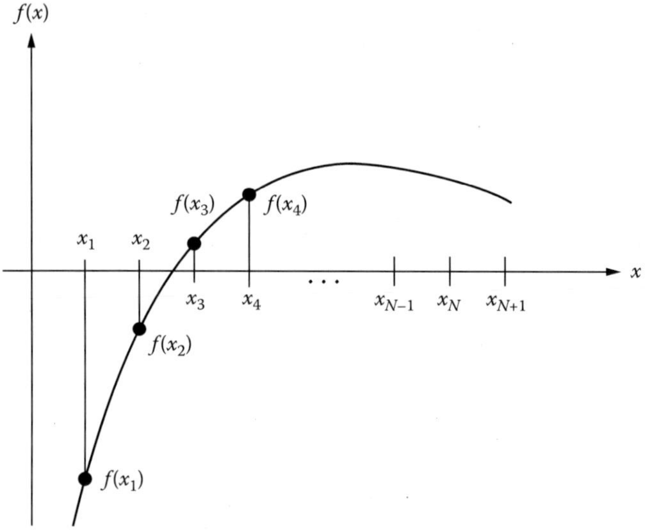

Figure 4.1 Selecting the interval in which a root lies. In this case, $f(x_2)f(x_3) < 0$, and thus the root lies between x_2 and x_3.

Then, locate where $f(x)$ changes sign (see Figure 4.1). This occurs when the signs of two consecutive values of $f(x)$ are different, that is,

$$f(x_i)f(x_{i+1}) < 0$$

The sign change usually indicates that a real root has been passed. However, it may also indicate a discontinuity in the function. (Example: tan x is discontinuous at $x = \pi/2$.)

Once the intervals in which the roots lie have been established, we can use several different methods for obtaining the real roots.

4.3 Bisection Method

Suppose it has been established that a root lies between x_i and x_{i+1}. Then, cut the interval in half (see Figure 4.2), and thus

$$x_{i+1/2} = x_i + \frac{\Delta x}{2}$$

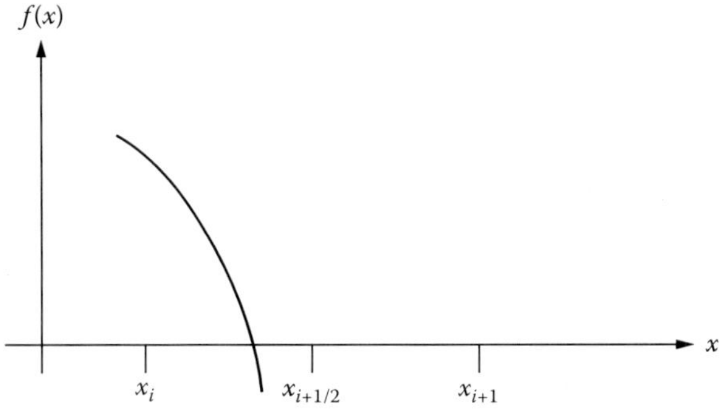

Figure 4.2 Selecting the interval containing the root in the bisection method.

Now compute $f(x_i)f(x_{i+\frac{1}{2}})$:

Case 1: If $f(x_i)f(x_{i+\frac{1}{2}})<0$, then the root lies between x_i and $x_{i+\frac{1}{2}}$.

Case 2: If $f(x_i)f(x_{i+\frac{1}{2}})>0$, then the root lies between $x_{i+\frac{1}{2}}$ and x_{i+1}.

Case 3: If $f(x_i)f(x_{i+\frac{1}{2}})=0$, then x_i or $x_{i+\frac{1}{2}}$ is a real root.

For cases 1 and 2, select the interval containing the root and repeat the process. Continue repeating the process, say r times, then $(\Delta x)_f = \dfrac{\Delta x}{2^r}$, where Δx is the initial size of the interval containing the root before the bisection process and $(\Delta x)_f$ is the size of the interval containing the root after r bisections. If $(\Delta x)_f$ is sufficiently small, then a very good approximation for the root is anywhere within the last bisected interval, say the midpoint of the interval.

Example: For 20 bisections,

$$(\Delta x)_f = \frac{\Delta x}{2^{20}} \approx \Delta x \times 1.0\times10^{-6}$$

Program method:

$$\text{Set} \quad x_A = x_i$$

$$x_B = x_{i+1}$$

$$x_C = \frac{1}{2}(x_A + x_B)$$

If $f(x_A)f(x_C) < 0$ (indicating that the root lies between x_A and x_C),

$$\text{Then set} \quad x_B = x_C$$

$$x_C = \frac{1}{2}(x_A + x_B)$$

and repeat the process.

Otherwise, if $f(x_A)f(x_C) > 0$ (indicating that the root lies between x_B and x_C),

$$\text{Then set} \quad x_A = x_C$$

$$x_C = \frac{1}{2}(x_A + x_B)$$

and repeat the process.

If $f(x_A)f(x_C) = 0$, then either x_A or x_C is a root.

4.4 Newton-Raphson Method

The Newton-Raphson method uses the tangent to the curve $f(x) = 0$ to estimate the root.

We need to obtain an expression for $f'(x)$ and make an initial guess for the root, say x_1 (see Figure 4.3). $f'(x_1)$ gives the slope of the tangent to the curve at x_1.

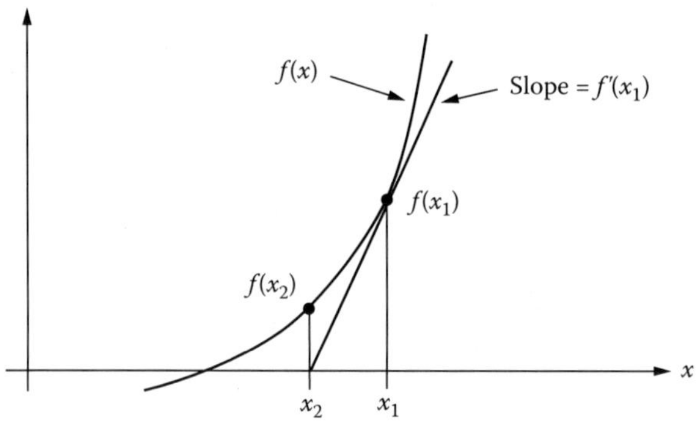

Figure 4.3 Predicting root in the Newton-Raphson method.

On the tangent to the curve,

$$\frac{f(x_1)-f(x_2)}{x_1-x_2}=f'(x_1) \tag{4.2}$$

Our next guess (or iteration) for the root is obtained by setting $f(x_2) = 0$ and solving for x_2, that is,

$$x_2 = x_1 - \frac{f(x_1)}{f'(x_1)} \tag{4.3}$$

Check if $|f(x_2)| < \varepsilon$, where ε is the error tolerance.

If true, then quit. x_2 is the root, so print x_2.

If not true, then set $x_1 = x_2$ and repeat the process.

Continue repeating the process until $|f(x_n)| < \varepsilon$, where n is the number of iterations.

An alternate condition for convergence is

$$\left|\frac{f(x_1)}{f'(x_1)}\right| < \varepsilon \tag{4.4}$$

Usually, ε should be a very small number, such as 10^{-4}, but it can be either larger or smaller depending on how close you wish to get to the real root. You can always test the accuracy of the obtained root by substituting the obtained root into the function $f(x)$ to see if it is sufficiently close to zero.

The Newton-Raphson method is widely used for its rapid convergence. However, there are cases where convergence will not occur. This can happen if

a. $f'(x)$ changes sign near the root.
b. The initial guess for the root is too far from the true root.

If we combine the Newton-Raphson method with the search method for obtaining a small interval in which the real root lies, convergence is generally not a problem.

4.5 MATLAB's `fzero` and `roots` Functions

MATLAB has built-in functions to determine the real roots of a function of one variable, such as a transcendental equation or an nth-degree polynomial. The `fzero` function is used for transcendental equations, and the `roots` function is used for polynomial equations. First, we discuss the `fzero` function.

4.5.1 The `fzero` Function

To get started, click in the Command window and type in

```
>> help fzero
```

This gives several different description, the first two are presented here.

```
FZERO Single-variable nonlinear zero finding.
    X = FZERO(FUN,X0) tries to find a zero of the function FUN
    near X0,if X0 is a scalar. It first finds an interval
    containing X0 where the function values of the interval
    endpoints differ in sign, then searches that interval for
    a zero. FUN is a function handle. FUN accepts real scalar
    input X and returns a real scalar function value F,
    evaluated at X. The value X returned by FZERO is near a
    point where FUN changes sign (if FUN is continuous), or
    NaN if the search fails.

    X = FZERO(FUN,X0), where X0 is a vector of length 2,
    assumes X0 is a finite interval where the sign of
    FUN(X0(1)) differs from the sign ofFUN(X0(2)). An error
    occurs if this is not true. Calling FZERO with a finite
    interval guarantees FZERO will return a value near a point
    where FUN changes sign.
```

As described, `fzero` has several different usages depending on whether you have a single initial guess of `X0` (i.e., `X0` is a scalar) or if you have a known interval for the zero (i.e., `X0` is a vector of length 2). The first usage is appropriate if you have some idea of where the root lies. The second usage is more appropriate when there is more than one root, and all roots need to be obtained. The second usage should be used in combination with the search method described previously.

The first usage of `fzero` function is

```
X = FZERO(FUN,X0)
```

`FUN` is *function handle* for the function to be solved and can be the name of a function file (with the *.m* extension) or can be an anonymous function (as described in Section 2.8). `X0` is the initial guess for the root, and `X` is the solution calculated by MATLAB. Thus, suppose the name of the function file whose root is to be obtained is *myfun.m,* and our guess for the root is 3.0. Then, we would write

```
X = fzero('myfun',3.0)
```

An alternative and equivalent way to run the command is

`X = fzero(@myfun, 3.0)` (no single quotation marks needed)

If no root is found, `fzero` returns `NaN` (not a number).

In the second usage of `fzero`, `X0` is a vector of length 2 that defines an interval over which `FUN` changes sign, that is, the value of `FUN` at `X0(1)` is opposite in sign to the value at `X0(2)`. MATLAB gives an error if this condition is not met.

In some instances, we would like to find the zero of a function of two arguments, say `X` and `P`, where `P` is a parameter and is fixed. To solve with `fzero`, `P` must be defined in the calling program. For example, suppose `myfun` is defined in an M-file as a function of two arguments:

```
function f = myfun(X,P)
f = cos(P*X);
```

The `fzero` statement would need to be invoked as follows:

```
P = 1000;
root = fzero(@(X) myfun(X,P), X0)
```

where `root` is the zero of function `myfun` when `P = 1000`. Note that `P` needs to be defined *before* the `fzero` function is called.

An alternative to adding parameter `P` as an argument to `myfun` is to use MATLAB's `global` statement to define parameter `P` in function `myfun` as an externally assigned variable. The `global` statement needs to be used in both the calling program and the function `myfun`.

Example:
Calling program:

```
global P;
P = 1000;
X0 = 10.0;
root = fzero(@myfun, X0);
-------------------------------------------------------
```

The file *myfun.m*:

```
function f = myfun(x)
global P;
f = cos(P*x);
-------------------------------------------------------
```

Examples of both methods follow.

Example 4.1: Using the `fzero` function to Find the First Root of a Transcendental Function

In Section 2.17, the governing equation for the voltage $v(t)$ of a parallel RLC circuit was derived. For the case when $\left(\frac{1}{2RC}\right)^2 < \frac{1}{LC}$, the system is underdamped, and the solution for $v(t)$ has the form

$$v(t) = \exp\left(-\frac{1}{2RC}t\right)\left\{A\cos\left(\sqrt{\frac{1}{LC}-\left(\frac{1}{2RC}\right)^2}\,t\right)+B\sin\left(\sqrt{\frac{1}{LC}-\left(\frac{1}{2RC}\right)^2}\,t\right)\right\} \tag{4.5}$$

Determine the the smallest time when $v(t)$ is zero, that is, find the first zero crossing of $v(t)$ on the t axis. Assume the following parameters:

$$R = 100\,\Omega,\ \ L = 10^{-3}\,\text{H},\ \ C = 10^{-6}\,\text{F},\ \ A = 6.0\,\text{V},\ \ B = -9.0\,\text{V}$$

$$0 \le t \le 0.5 \text{ msec}$$

```
% Example_4_1.m
% This script determines the initial zero crossing of the
% underdamped response of a parallel RLC circuit.  The
% underdamped response is:
% v(t)=exp(-t/(2RC))*(A*cos(sqrt(1/LC-(1/2RC)^2)t)
%                  + B*sin(sqrt(1/LC-(1/2RC)^2)t))
% The circuit component values and initial conditions
% are:
% R=100 ohms; L=1.0e-3 henry; C=1.0e-6 farads;
% A= 6.0 volt, B=-9.0 volt
% Solve over the interval 0 <= t <= 0.5e-3 sec
clear; clc;
R=100; L=1.0e-3; C=1.0e-6;  A=6.0; B=-9;
fprintf('Example 4.1: Find first zero crossing of ');
fprintf('underdamped RLC circuit\n');
tmin=0.0; tmax=0.5e-3;
% split up timespan into 100 intervals:
N=100;
dt=(tmax-tmin)/N;
% First, calculate t and v(t) at each timestep
for n=1:N+1
    t(n)  = tmin+(n-1)*dt;
    v(n)  = func_RLC(t(n),A,B,R,L,C);
    fprintf('    %10.4e        %10.3f \n',t(n),v(n));
end
plot(t,v), xlabel('t'), ylabel('v'),
title('v vs t for a RLC circuit'), grid;
% Next, use the search method to find the first timestep
% where the sign of v(t) changes. When found, use fzero
% to solve.
for n=1:N
```

```
    sign = v(n)*v(n+1);
    if sign <= 0.0
        root_interval(1)=t(n);
        root_interval(2)=t(n+1);
        % Solve for the zero of the multi-argument
        % function func_RLC.m by invoking func_RLC as an
        % anonymous function of one variable.
        root = fzero(@(t) func_RLC(t,A,B,R,L,C), ...
            root_interval);
        break;
    end
end
fprintf('\n\n');
if n < N
    fprintf('First zero crossing is at t=%10.4e s\n',...
        root);
else
    fprintf('No roots lie within  %g <= t <= %g s\n',...
        tmin,tmax);
end
% Check solution. Putting root into func_RLC should
% produce zero.
v = func_RLC(root,A,B,R,L,C);
fprintf('v=%8.6e \n',v);
------------------------------------------------------------------------
% func_RLC.m
% This function works with Example_4_1.m
function v=func_RLC(t,A,B,R,L,C)
arg1=1/(2*R*C);
arg3=sqrt(1/(L*C)-1/(2*R*C)^2);
% Equation (4.5):
v=exp(-arg1*t)*(A*cos(arg3*t)+B*sin(arg3*t));
------------------------------------------------------------------------
```

PROGRAM RESULTS

```
First zero crossing is at t = 1.8831e-005 s
```

We can modify Example 4.1 and use the `global` statement to bring the parameters into the function. To do this,

1. Add the following global statement immediately after the `clear; clc;` statements in the calling program and immediately after the function statement in the function program:

   ```
   global R L C A B;
   ```

2. Replace the function statement:

   ```
   function v = func_RLC(t,A,B,R,L,C)
   ```

with

```
function v = func_RLC(t)
```

3. Replace the following statement in the calling program:

```
v(n) = func_RLC(t(n),A,B,R,L,C);
```

with

```
v(n) = func_RLC(t(n));
```

4. Replace the following statement in the calling program:

```
root = fzero(@(t) func_RLC(t,A,B,R,L,C), root_inteval);
```

with

```
root = fzero('func_RLC',root_inteval);
```

Run each program and check to see if both programs give the same answer.

4.5.2 The `roots` Function

MATLAB has a function to obtain the roots of a polynomial. The function is `roots`. To obtain the usage of the function, in the Command Window type

```
>> help roots
```

This gives

```
ROOTS Find polynomial roots.
    ROOTS(C) computes the roots of the polynomial whose
    coefficients are the elements of the vector C. If C has N+1
    components, the polynomial is C(1)*X^N +... + C(N)*X + C(N+1).
```

Thus, to find the roots of the polynomial $Ax^4 + Bx^3 + Cx^2 + Dx + E = 0$, run `roots([A B C D E])`. The roots function will give both real and imaginary roots of the polynomial.

Some additional useful MATLAB functions are

`poly(V)`	Finds the coefficients of the polynomial whose roots are V
`real(X)`	Gives the real part of X
`imag(X)`	Gives the imaginary part of X

Example 4.2: Using `roots` to Find the Zeros of a Polynomial

```
% Example_4_2.m
% This program determines the roots of a polynomial using
% the built in function 'roots'.
% The first polynomial is: f=x^3-4.7*x^2-35.1*x+85.176.
% The roots of this polynomial are all real.
% The second polynomial is: f=x^3-9*x^2+23*x-65. The
% roots of this polynomial are both real and complex.
% Complex roots must be complex conjugates.
% To obtain more info on complex numbers in MATLAB, run
% "help complex" in the Command Window.
clear; clc;
% Define coefficients of first polynomial (real roots)
C(1)=1.0;  C(2)=-4.7; C(3)=-35.1; C(4)=85.176;
fprintf('The first polynomial coefficients are:\n');
C
fprintf('The roots are: \n');
V=roots(C)
fprintf('The recalculated coefficients of the ');
fprintf('polynomial whose roots are V are:\n');
C_recalc=poly(V)
fprintf('\n\n');
% Define coefficients of second polynomial (real and
% complex roots)
D(1)=1.0; D(2)=-9.0; D(3)=23.0; D(4)=-65.0;
fprintf('The second polynomial coefficients are:\n');
D
fprintf('The roots are: \n');
W=roots(D)
fprintf('The real and imaginary parts of the ');
fprintf('roots are:\n');
re=real(W)
im=imag(W)
fprintf('The recalculated coefficients of the ');
fprintf('polynomial whose roots are W are:\n');
W_recalc=poly(W)
```

Projects

Project 4.1

The current-voltage relationship of a semiconductor PN diode can be written as follows:

$$i_D = I_S\left(e^{\frac{q}{kT}v_D} - 1\right) \tag{P4.1a}$$

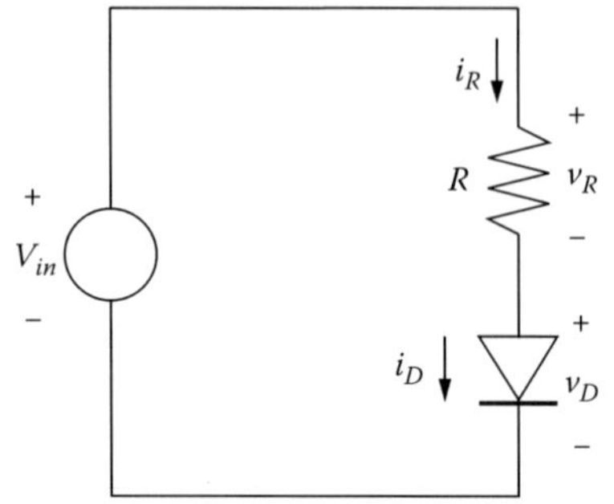

Figure P4.1 Diode-resistor circuit.

where i_D and v_D are the diode current and voltage, respectively, as defined in Figure P4.1; I_S is a constant (with units of amperes), which is determined by the semiconductor doping concentrations and the device geometry; $q = 1.6 \times 10^{-19}$ coulomb is the unit electric charge; $k = 1.38 \times 10^{-23}$ joule/kelvin is the Boltzmann constant; and T is absolute temperature (in kelvin).

We would like to determine the current and voltage through the diode for this circuit. Using Kirchhoff's voltage law, we know that the sum of the voltage drops around the circuit must sum to zero:

$$V_{in} - v_R - v_D = 0 \tag{P4.1b}$$

Applying Ohm's law for the current through the resistor $v_R = i_R R$ and observing that the resistor current equals the diode current $i_R = i_D$, we can rewrite Equation (P4.1b) as

$$V_{in} - I_S\left(e^{\frac{q}{kT}v_D} - 1\right)R - v_D = 0 \tag{P4.1c}$$

Let

$$f(v_D) = V_{in} - I_S\left(e^{\frac{q}{kT}v_D} - 1\right)R - v_D$$

1. Create a MATLAB function for $f(v_D)$ and plot for the interval $0 \le v_D \le 0.8$ V for 10 mV steps (80 subdivisions on the v_D domain).
2. Use the search method to obtain a small interval within which the root of Equation (P4.1c) lies.
3. Use MATLAB's `fzero` function to obtain a more accurate value for the root. Use the following parameters:

$$T = 300\text{K},\ I_S = 10^{-14}\text{A},\ V_{in} = 5\text{V},\ R = 1000\,\Omega.$$

Project 4.2

We wish to determine the DC transfer characteristic for the diode circuit of Figure P4.1. We will consider V_{in} as a parameter, where $5\text{V} \le V_{in} \le 12\text{V}$ in steps of 1 V. We wish to find the value of v_D for all values of V_{in}.

Write a MATLAB program that will find the roots of $f(v_d) = 0$, where

$$f(v_D) = V_{in} - I_S\left(e^{\frac{q}{kT}v_D} - 1\right)R - v_D$$

Your program should

1. Use a global statements to bring values of V_{in} into the function $f(v_D)$.
2. Take $0.2 \le v_D \le 0.8$ V with 60 subdivisions on the v_D domain.
3. Use the search method to find a small interval in which the root of $f(v_D) = 0$ lies.
4. Use the MATLAB's `fzero` function to obtain a more accurate value for the root.
5. Construct a table consisting of all values of V_{in} and the corresponding roots of $f(v_D) = 0$.
6. If you did Project 4.1, confirm that your program returns the same result as in Project 4.1 when $V_{in} = 5$ V.

Project 4.3

Repeat Project 4.2, but this time do not use global statements. Instead, modify your $f(v_d)$ function to include the argument V_{in}. You will also need to modify the `fzero` statement appropriately to use a function with multiple arguments.

Project 4.4

We wish to consider the *settling time* (described in the following) of the inductor current i_L in the RLC circuit of Section 2.17 and Project 2.9. The resistance R_{crit} that makes the circuit critically damped is given by

$$R_{crit} = \sqrt{\frac{L}{4C}}$$

For $R > R_{crit}$, the governing equation describing i_L is

$$i_L = \exp\left(-\frac{1}{2RC}t\right)\left\{A\cos\left(\sqrt{\frac{1}{LC} - \left(\frac{1}{2RC}\right)^2}\,t\right) + B\sin\left(\sqrt{\frac{1}{LC} - \left(\frac{1}{2RC}\right)^2}\,t\right)\right\}$$

The coefficients A and B are determined by the initial conditions and the component values. The solutions for A and B are

$$A = i_L(0)$$

$$B = \frac{1}{\sqrt{\frac{1}{LC} - \left(\frac{1}{2RC}\right)^2}} \times \left(\frac{v(0)}{L} + \frac{i_L(0)}{2RC}\right)$$

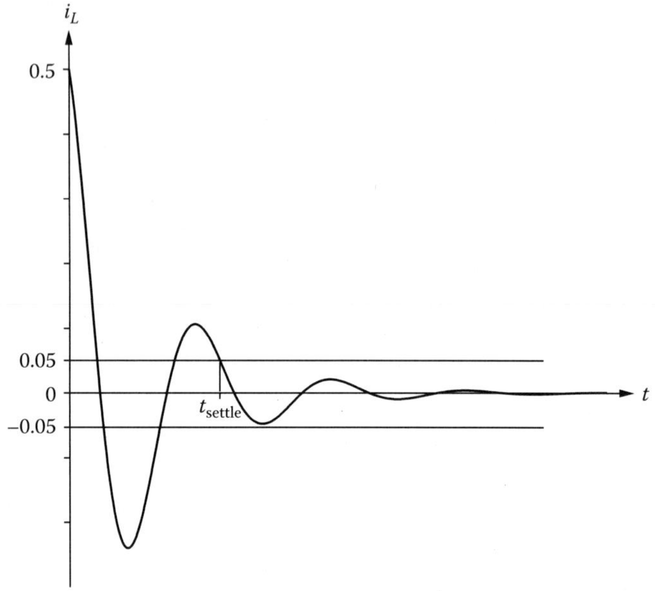

Figure P4.4 The settling time t_{settle} is defined as the time it takes for i_L to reach and stay within some error band of its final value. This problem uses an error band of ±10%, but error bands of ±5% or ±2% are also common.

The settling time of a waveform is the time t_{settle} that it takes the waveform (i_L) to reach within a percentage of some specified value and stay within that range (see Figure P4.4). For this problem, we will take the settling time for $i_L(t)$ to be within ±10% of the initial value $i_L(0)$ and stay within that range. Write a MATLAB program that determines the settling time for the following circuit parameters:

$$R = 4R_{crit},\ \ L = 1.0\,\text{mH},\ \ C = 1.0\,\mu\text{F},\ \ i_L(0) = 0.25\,\text{A},\ \ v(0) = 6\,\text{V},\ \ 0 \le t \le 1000\,\mu\,\text{s}$$

1. Create a plot of $i_L(t)$ versus t. On the same plot, create the lines $0.1i_L(0)$ and $-0.1i_L(0)$.
2. Use the search method and MATLAB's `fzero` function to determine the settling time of $i_L(t)$. Hint: Use $|i_L(t)|$ and the $0.1i_L(0)$ line to find the maximum root, thus determining the settling time.

Project 4.5

An n-channel metal-oxide-semiconductor field-effect transistor (MOSFET) is shown in Figure P4.5a. The MOSFET has three terminals: *gate, source,* and *drain.* (Actually, MOSFETs also have a fourth *bulk* terminal, which we do not discuss here.) In MOSFET circuits, we are usually concerned with the drain current i_D as

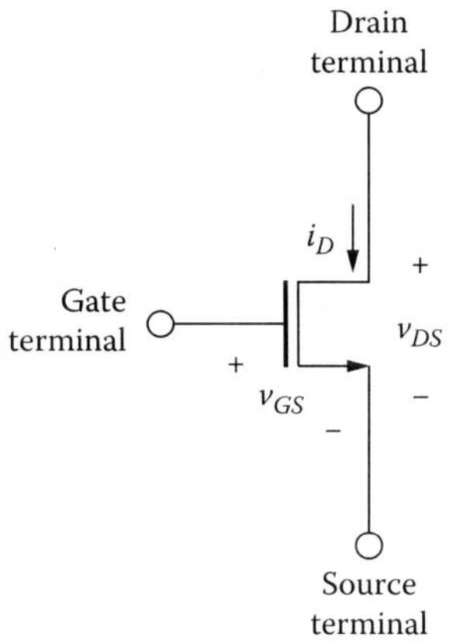

(a)

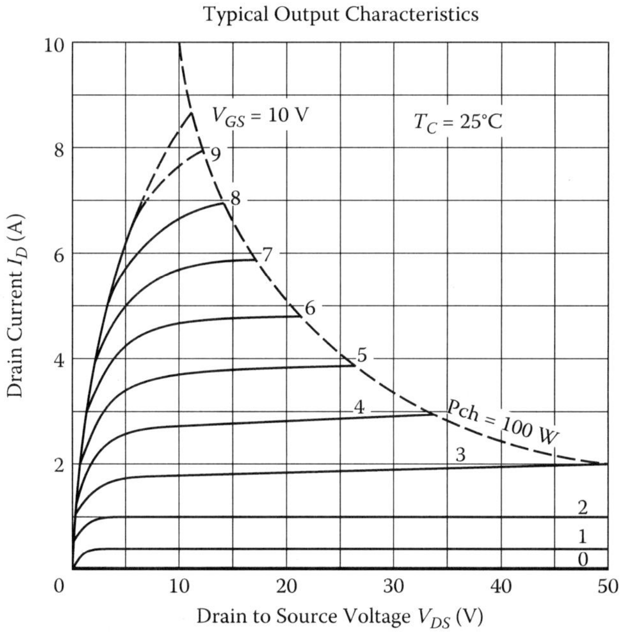

(b)

Figure P4.5 (a) An n-channel MOS transistor and its defined terminal parameters. (b) Terminal characteristics of the 2SK1056 power MOSFET. (Courtesy of Renesas Electronics Corporation.)

a function of the terminal voltages. A common mathematical model for the drain current i_D for an n-channel MOSFET [1] is as follows:

$$i_D = \begin{cases} 0 & \text{for} \quad v_{GS} \le V_{th} \\ K\left[2(v_{GS} - V_{th})v_{DS} - v_{DS}^2\right](1-\lambda v_{DS}) & \text{for} \quad v_{GS} > V_{th} \text{ and } v_{DS} \le (v_{GS} - V_{th}) \\ K(v_{GS} - V_{th})^2(1-\lambda v_{DS}) & \text{for} \quad v_{GS} > V_{th} \text{ and } v_{DS} > (v_{GS} - V_{th}) \end{cases} \tag{P4.5a}$$

where i_D is defined in Figure P4.5a; v_{GS} and v_{DS} are the transistor gate-to-source and drain-to-source voltages, respectively; V_{th} is the transistor "threshold voltage"; and K and λ are constants that are dependent on silicon doping levels, electron mobility, and device geometry. Figure P4.5b shows a plot of typical i_D as a function of v_{DS} (for various fixed values of v_{GS}) for the 2SK1056 power MOSFET.

1. Create a MATLAB function `id_powerfet` that takes two arguments `vds` and `vgs` and computes the MOSFET current `id` as defined by Equation (P4.5a). Take

$$V_{th} = 0.2\,\text{V}, \quad K = 0.2, \quad \lambda = 0.01$$

2. Plot i_D as a function of v_{DS} for $0 \le v_{DS} \le 50\,\text{V}$ for values of $v_{GS} = 1, 2, 3, 4, 5, 6, 7,$ and 8 V. Your plot should look similar (but not identical) to the one in Figure P4.5b.
3. Because the 2SK1056 is rated for a maximum of 100 W, Figure P4.5b does not show values of i_D under conditions where the total device power $P = i_D \times v_{DS}$ exceeds 100 W. Modify your function definition for `id_powerfet` to check the device power and return `NaN` (not a number) if the power exceeds 100 W. Rerun your plot and confirm that it now resembles Figure P4.5b.
4. Use the `fzero` function to find the value of v_{GS} when v_{DS} = 5 V and i_D = 2 A. Hint: For this problem, you will need to solve `id_powerfet` as a function of v_{GS} with v_{DS} and i_D as fixed parameters.

Project 4.6

The simplest digital logic gate is the *inverter* (Figure P4.6a), which converts a Boolean "true" into "false" and vice versa. In electronics, we often represent a logical true as a high voltage (e.g., +5 V) and false as a low voltage (e.g., 0 V). Thus, from an electronic standpoint, an inverter is a circuit that accepts a +5 V input and outputs 0 V and accepts a 0 V input and outputs +5 V. A simple circuit that implements these requirements is the resistor-MOSFET circuit of Figure P4.6b and is a form of *resistor-transistor logic* (RTL). In this case, an n-channel MOSFET is loaded with a 2-kΩ resistor, V_{DD} is the power supply voltage (typically 5 V), v_{in} is the input (and is equal to v_{GS}), and v_{out} is the output (and is equal to v_{DS}).

Using Kirchhoff's voltage law, we can write an equation for the output voltage loop:

$$V_{DD} - v_R - v_{DS} = 0 \tag{P4.6a}$$

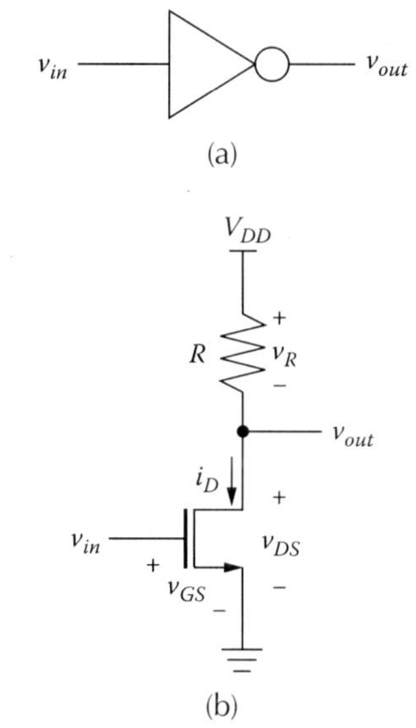

Figure P4.6 (a) Logic inverter. (b) RTL inverter circuit using an n-channel MOS transistor.

By Ohm's law,

$$v_R = i_D R \tag{P4.6b}$$

Substituting Equation (P4.6b) into Equation (P4.6a) gives

$$V_{DD} - i_D R - v_{DS} = 0 \tag{P4.6c}$$

where i_D is determined by Equation (P4.5a).

Create a MATLAB program that uses MATLAB's `fzero` function to determine the roots of Equation (P4.6c). Use the following n-channel MOSFET parameters: V_{DD} = 5 V, V_{th} = 0.7 V, K = 0.0005, and λ = 0.05. Take $0 \le v_{DS} \le 5$ V in steps of 0.1 V and $0 \le v_{GS} \le 5$ V in steps of 0.1 V. In actuality, a *range* of voltages is considered a valid "low" or a valid "high" signal. For the RTL inverter described here, assume that the range 0–1 V constitutes a valid low and 4–5 V constitutes a valid high.

1. Create a table of v_{out} versus v_{in} (corresponding to v_{DS} vs. v_{GS}).
2. Plot v_{out} versus v_{in}
3. Does the circuit described here behave like an inverter; that is, does a high input produce a low output and vice versa?
4. The inverter *noise margin* is defined as the amount of noise allowed on a valid input such that the output remains valid. For example, if v_{in} raised above the legal range for a low, say to 1.1 V, does the output remain a valid high? Find the *highest* low v_{in} that still produces a valid high v_{out}. Also, find the *lowest* high v_{in} that still produces a valid low v_{out}. Print these values to the screen.

Project 4.7

The RTL logic family of Project 4.6 was typically used in the 1950s when transistors were expensive (and packaged individually) and resistors were cheap. When integrated circuits were invented in the 1960s, the opposite became true: transistors became very cheap, and resistors became comparatively expensive (because they are inefficient to implement on a chip).

Figure P4.7a shows a *complementary MOSFET* (CMOS) inverter. In this case, the resistor is replaced by a p-channel MOSFET. We can mathematically model

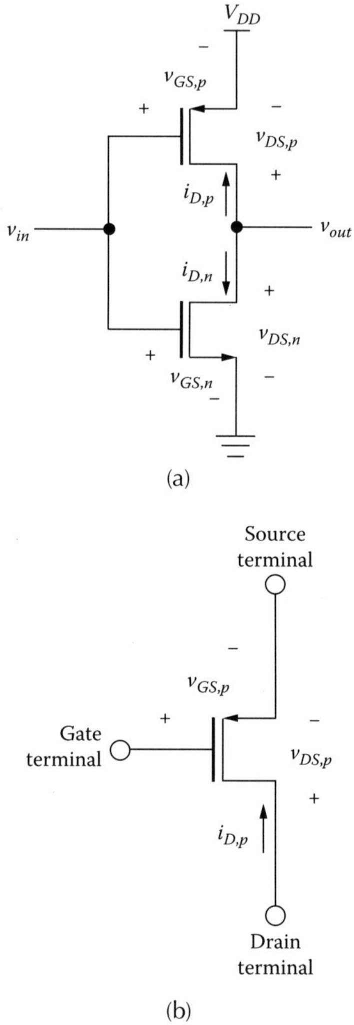

Figure P4.7 (a) CMOS inverter circuit. (b) A p-channel MOS transistor and its defined terminal parameters.

the p-channel MOSFET similarly to the n-channel MOSFET of Project 4.5; that is, the p-channel drain current $i_{D,P}$ is given by

$$i_{D,p} = \begin{cases} 0 & \text{for} \quad v_{GS,p} \geq V_{th,p} \\ -K_p\left[2(v_{GS,p} - V_{th,p})v_{DS,p} - v_{DS,p}^2\right](1-\lambda_p v_{DS,p}) & \text{for} \quad v_{GS,p} < V_{th,p} \text{ and } v_{DS,p} \geq (v_{GS,p} - V_{th,p}) \\ -K_p(v_{GS,p} - V_{th,p})^2(1-\lambda_p v_{DS,p}) & \text{for} \quad v_{GS,p} < V_{th,p} \text{ and } v_{DS,p} < (v_{GS,p} - V_{th,p}) \end{cases} \tag{P4.7a}$$

where $v_{GS,p}$, $v_{DS,p}$, and $i_{D,p}$ are as defined in Figure P4.7b. Note that the p-channel model mentioned is similar to the n-channel model of Equation (P 4.5a) except for some sign changes. In addition, for a given integrated circuit technology, the values of V_{th}, K, and λ will be different for p- versus n-channel MOSFETs (and thus will be denoted with p and n subscripts, respectively). Kirchhoff's voltage law is used to relate the voltages in the output side of the circuit:

$$v_{DS,n} = v_{out} \tag{P4.7b}$$

$$v_{DS,p} = v_{out} - V_{DD} \tag{P4.7c}$$

Similarly, on the input side:

$$v_{GS,n} = v_{in} \tag{P4.7d}$$

$$v_{GS,p} = v_{in} - V_{DD} \tag{P4.7e}$$

We can also apply Kirchhoff's current law at the output node:

$$i_{D,n} + i_{D,p} = 0 \tag{P4.7f}$$

where the n-channel source current $i_{D,n}$ is defined as

$$i_{D,n} = \begin{cases} 0 & \text{for} \quad v_{GS,n} \leq V_{th,n} \\ K_n\left(2(v_{GS,n} - V_{th,n})v_{DS,n} - v_{DS,n}^2\right)(1+\lambda_n v_{DS,n}) & \text{for} \quad v_{GS,n} > V_{th,n} \text{ and } v_{DS,n} \leq (v_{GS,n} - V_{th,n}) \\ K_n(v_{GS,n} - V_{th,n})^2(1+\lambda_n v_{DS\,n}) & \text{for} \quad v_{GS,n} > V_{th,n} \text{ and } v_{DS,n} > (v_{GS,n} - V_{th,n}) \end{cases} \tag{P4.7g}$$

1. Create a MATLAB program using the `fzero` function to obtain the roots of Equation (P4.7f) by applying equations (P4.7a) and (P4.7g). Take V_{DD} = 5V, $V_{th,n}$ = 0.7 V, $V_{th,p}$ = −0.8 V, K_n = 0.0005, K_p = 0.00015, λ_n = 0.05, and λ_p = 0.1. Assume $0 \leq v_{out} \leq 5$ V in steps of 0.1 V and $0 \leq v_{in} \leq 5$ V in steps of 0.1 V.

2. Create a table of v_{out} versus v_{in}.
3. Plot v_{out} versus v_{in}.
4. Does the circuit described here behave like an inverter? That is, does a high input produce a low output and vice versa?

Reference

1. A.S. Sedra and K.C. Smith, *Microelectronic Circuits*, 3rd ed., Saunders College, Philadelphia, 1989.

Chapter 5

Numerical Integration

5.1 Introduction

In this chapter, we derive Simpson's rule for approximating the solution of definite integrals. We then demonstrate usage of the built-in MATLAB® functions `quad` and `dblquad` for evaluating definite integrals. Finally, we apply these functions to solve some common problems in electromagnetic field theory.

5.2 Numerical Integration and Simpson's Rule

We want to evaluate the integral I where

$$I = \int_{A}^{B} f(x)\,dx \tag{5.1}$$

The steps for calculating I numerically are as follows:

- Subdivide the x axis from $x = A$ to $x = B$ into N subdivisions, where N is an even integer.
- Simpson's rule consists of connecting groups of three points on the curve $f(x)$ by second-degree polynomials (parabolas) and summing the areas under the parabolas to obtain the approximate area under the curve (see Figure 5.1).

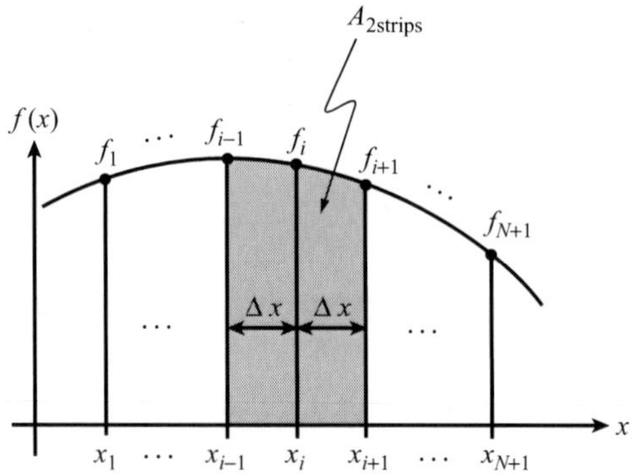

Figure 5.1 Arbitrary three points on the curve *f*(*x*).

We proceed by first expanding $f(x)$ in a Taylor series about x_i using three terms, that is,

$$f(x) = a(x - x_i)^2 + b(x - x_i) + c \tag{5.2}$$

where a, b, and c are constants to be determined.

Then, the area under two adjacent strips $A_{2\text{strips}}$ is computed by integrating $f(x)$ between x_{i-1} and x_{i+1}:

$$A_{2\text{ strips}} = \int_{x_{i-1}}^{x_{i+1}} f(x)\,dx = \int_{x_i-\Delta x}^{x_i+\Delta x} [a(x - x_i)^2 + b(x - x_i) + c]\,dx \tag{5.3}$$

Let $\xi = x - x_i$

Then,

$$d\xi = dx$$

When $x = x_i - \Delta x$, $\xi = -\Delta x$, and when $x = x_i + \Delta x$, $\xi = \Delta x$.

Making these substitutions into Equation (5.3) gives

$$\begin{aligned} A_{2\text{ strips}} &= \int_{x_{i-1}}^{x_{i+1}} f(x)\,dx \\ &= \int_{-\Delta x}^{\Delta x} \left[a\xi^2 + b\xi + c\right] d\xi \\ &= \frac{a\xi^3}{3} + \frac{b\xi^2}{2} + c\xi \Big|_{-\Delta x}^{\Delta x} \\ &= \frac{a}{3}(\Delta x)^3 - \frac{a}{3}(-\Delta x)^3 + \frac{b}{2}(\Delta x)^2 - \frac{b}{2}(-\Delta x)^2 + c(\Delta x) - c(-\Delta x) \end{aligned}$$

Thus,

$$A_{2\text{ strips}} = \frac{2a}{3}(\Delta x)^3 + 2c\,\Delta x$$

Now, define $f_i = f(x_i)$. Solving Equation (5.2) for f_i, f_{i+1}, and f_{i-1} gives

$$f(x_i) = f_i = c$$

$$f(x_{i+1}) = f_{i+1} = a(\Delta x)^2 + b\,\Delta x + c$$

$$f(x_{i-1}) = f_{i-1} = a(-\Delta x)^2 + b(-\Delta x) + c$$

Adding the last two equations gives $f_{i+1} + f_{i-1} = 2a\,\Delta x^2 + 2c$.
Solving for a gives

$$a = \frac{1}{2\Delta x^2}[f_{i+1} + f_{i-1} - 2f_i]$$

Then,

$$A_{2\text{ strips}} = \frac{2}{3} \times \frac{1}{2\Delta x^2}[f_{i+1} + f_{i-1} - 2f_i](\Delta x^3) + 2f_i\Delta x \;= \frac{\Delta x}{3}[f_{i+1} + f_{i-1} - 2f_i + 6f_i]$$

or

$$A_{2\text{ strips}} = \frac{\Delta x}{3}[f_{i-1} + 4f_i + f_{i+1}] \tag{5.4}$$

To obtain an approximation for the integral I, we need to sum all the two-strip areas under the curve from $x = A$ to $x = B$ (see Figure 5.2), that is,

$$A_1 = \frac{\Delta x}{3}[f_1 + 4f_2 + f_3]$$

$$A_2 = \frac{\Delta x}{3}[f_3 + 4f_4 + f_5]$$

$$A_3 = \frac{\Delta x}{3}[f_5 + 4f_6 + f_7]$$

$$\vdots$$

$$A_{N/2} = \frac{\Delta x}{3}[f_{N-1} + 4f_N + f_{N+1}]$$

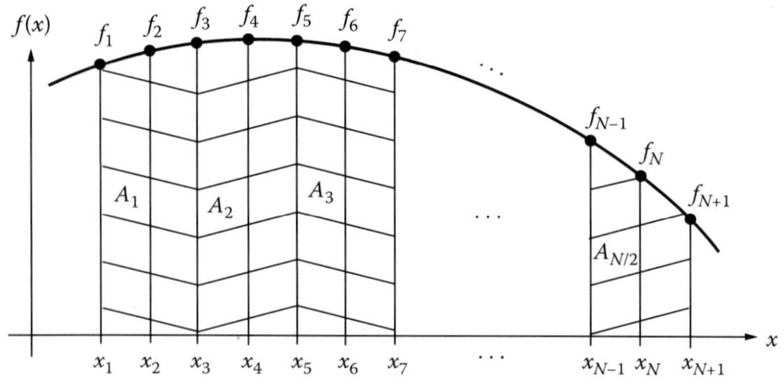

Figure 5.2 Integration areas for Simpson's rule.

Thus,

$$I = \int_{x_1=A}^{x_{N+1}=B} f(x)\,dx = \frac{\Delta x}{3}[f_1 + 4f_2 + 2f_3 + 4f_4 + 2f_5 + \cdots + 4f_N + f_{N+1}] \quad (5.5)$$

This is Simpson's rule for integration.

Example 5.1

Solve by Simpson's rule:

$$I = \int_0^{10} (x^3 + 3.2x^2 - 3.4x + 20.2)\,dx$$

```
% Example_5_1.m
% This program calculates an integral by Simpson's Rule
% The integrand is: x^3+3.2*x^2-3.4*x+20.2
% The limits of integration are from 0-10.
clear; clc;
A=0; B=10;
N=100; dx=(B-A)/N;
% Compute values of x and f at each point:
x = A:dx:B;
f = x.^3 + 3.2*x.^2 - 3.4*x + 20.2;
% Use two separate loops to sum up the even and odd terms
% of Simpson's Rule. Also, exclude endpoints in the loop.
sum_even=0.0;
for i=2:2:N
    sum_even=sum_even+f(i);
end
```

```
sum_odd=0.0;
for i=3:2:N-1
    sum_odd=sum_odd+f(i);
end
% Calculate integral as per Equation 5.5
I = dx/3 * (f(1) + 4*sum_even + 2*sum_odd + f(N+1));
% Display results
fprintf('Integrand: x^3 + 3.2*x^2 - 3.4*x + 20.2 \n');
fprintf('Integration limits: %.1f to %.1f \n',A,B);
fprintf('I = %10.4f \n', I);
--------------------------------------------------------------
```

PROGRAM RESULTS

```
Integrand: x^3 + 3.2*x^2 - 3.4*x + 20.2
Integration limits: 0.0 to 10.0
I = 3598.6667
```

5.3 Improper Integrals

An integral is improper if the integrand approaches infinity at either of the endpoints. In many cases, the integration will still result in a finite solution.

Example 5.2

$$I = \int_0^1 \frac{\log(1+x)}{x} dx \tag{5.6}$$

This integral is improper since both the numerator and denominator are zero at the lower limit ($x = 0$). The exact value of I can be obtained by residue theory in complex variables and in this case evaluates to $I = \dfrac{\pi^2}{12} = 0.822467$.

Let

$$I = \int_0^1 \frac{\log(1+x)}{x} dx = I_1 + I_2$$

where

$$I_1 = \int_\varepsilon^1 \frac{\log(1+x)}{x} dx$$

and

$$I_2 = \int_0^\varepsilon \frac{\log(1+x)}{x} dx$$

where $\varepsilon << 1$. To evaluate I_2, expand $\log(1 + x)$ in a Taylor series about $x = 0$, giving

$$\log(1+x) = x - \frac{1}{2}x^2 + \frac{1}{3}x^3 - \frac{1}{4}x^4 + \frac{1}{5}x^5 - \cdots + \cdots$$

then

$$\frac{\log(1+x)}{x} = 1 - \frac{1}{2}x + \frac{1}{3}x^2 - \frac{1}{4}x^3 + \frac{1}{5}x^4 - \cdots + \cdots$$

$$I_2 = \int_0^{\varepsilon} \left[1 - \frac{1}{2}x + \frac{1}{3}x^2 - \frac{1}{4}x^3 + \frac{1}{5}x^4 - \frac{1}{6}x^5 + \frac{1}{7}x^6 - \cdots + \cdots\right] dx$$

$$I_2 = \varepsilon - \frac{1}{4}\varepsilon^2 + \frac{1}{9}\varepsilon^3 - \frac{1}{16}\varepsilon^4 + \frac{1}{25}\varepsilon^5 - \frac{1}{36}\varepsilon^6 + \frac{1}{49}\varepsilon^7 - \cdots + \cdots \quad (5.7)$$

Evaluate I_1 by Simpson's rule and evaluate I_2 by Equation (5.7). The following program illustrates the method:

```
% Example_5_2.m
% This program evaluates the improper integral:
% log(1+x)/x The limits of integration are from 0 to 1.
% The integrand is undefined (0/0)at x=0.  Thus, the
% integral is broken up into 2 parts: I1 and I2.
% I1 is evaluated from epsilon to 1.
% I2 is expanded in a Taylor Series and evaluated from 0
% to epsilon.
clear; clc;
epsilon = 0.0001;
A = 0;  B = 1;
N = 100; dx = (B-epsilon)/N;
% Evaluate I1.  First, evaluate log(1+x)/x for each value
% of x over the interval [epsilon,1].
x = epsilon:dx:B;
f = log(1+x) ./ x;
% Next, calculate the even and odd terms for Simpson's
% Rule.
sumeven=0.0;
for i=2:2:N
    sumeven=sumeven+f(i);
end
sumodd=0.0;
for i=3:2:N-1
    sumodd=sumodd+f(i);
end
% As per Equation (5.5), I1 is the weighted sum of the
% even and odd terms, plus the end terms.
```

```
I1 = dx/3 * (f(1) + 4*sumeven + 2*sumodd + f(N+1));
fprintf('Integrand = log(1+x)/x \n');
fprintf('I1 limits of integration are ');
fprintf('from %.4f to %.4f\n',epsilon,B);
fprintf('I2 limits of integration are ');
fprintf('from %.4f to %.4f\n',A,epsilon);
fprintf('I1 =%15.6f \n',I1);
% Calculate I2 via first 4 terms of Taylor series
% expansion.
I2 = epsilon - 1/4*epsilon^2 + 1/9*epsilon^3 ...
    - 1/16*epsilon^4;
fprintf('I2 =%15.6f \n',I2);
I=I1+I2;
fprintf('I=I1+I2 =%10.6f \n',I);
I_exact=0.822467;
fprintf('I_exact =%10.6f \n',I_exact);
----------------------------------------------------------------------
```

PROGRAM RESULTS

```
Integrand = log(1+x)/x
I1 limits of integration are from 0.0001 to 1.0000
I2 limits of integration are from 0.0000 to 0.0001
I1 =          0.822367
I2 =          0.000100
I = I1+I2 = 0.822467
I_exact =    0.822467
```

As we see, the method works quite well.

5.4 MATLAB's `quad` Function

The MATLAB function for evaluating an integral is `quad`. A description of the function can be obtained by typing **`help quad`** in the Command window (excerpted in the following):

```
Q = QUAD(FUN,A,B) tries to approximate the integral of scalar-
valued function FUN from A to B to within an error of 1.e-6
using recursive adaptive Simpson quadrature. FUN is a function
handle. The function Y = FUN(X) should accept a vector argument
X and return a vector result Y, the integrand evaluated at each
element of X.

Q = QUAD(FUN,A,B,TOL) uses an absolute error tolerance of TOL
instead of the default, which is 1.e-6. Larger values of TOL
result in fewer function evaluations and faster computation,
but less accurate results. The QUAD function in MATLAB 5.3 used
a less reliable algorithm and a default tolerance of 1.e-3.
```

Thus, the quad function takes as arguments a function handle FUN that defines the integrand in a *.m* file and the limits of integration. Alternatively. if the integrand is not very large and can be expressed in a single line, then you can define the integrand within your script with an anonymous or an inline function (see Examples 5.4 and 5.5). If the integrand involves very small numbers or very large numbers, you might wish to change the default tolerance by adding a third argument to quad (as shown in the second usage description). The quad function is able to evaluate certain improper integrals (see Exercises 5.2d, 5.2e, and 5.2f).

Example 5.3

We now repeat Example 5.1, but this time we use MATLAB's quad function to do the integration. The integral I in Example 5.1 is

$$I = \int_0^{10} (x^3 + 3.2x^2 - 3.4x + 20.2)dx$$

The program follows:

```
% Example_5_3.m
% This program evaluates the integral of the function
% 'f1' between A and B by MATLAB's quad function. Since
% the function 'f1' is just a single line, we can use the
% anonymous form of the function.
clear; clc;
f1=@(x) (x.^3+3.2*x.^2-3.4*x+20.2);
A=0.0;  B=10.0;
I = quad(f1,A,B);
fprintf('Integration of f1 over [%.0f,%.0f] ',A,B);
fprintf('by MATLAB''s quad function:\n');
fprintf('f1 = x^3 + 3.2*x^2 - 3.4*x + 20.2 \n');
fprintf('integral = %10.4f \n', I);
-----------------------------------------------------------------
```

PROGRAM RESULTS

```
Integration of f1 over [0,10] by MATLAB's quad function:
f1 = x^3 + 3.2*x^2 - 3.4*x + 20.2
integral = 3598.6667
```

We see that the results are the same as those obtained in Example 5.1.

Example 5.4

$$\text{Evaluate: } \int_0^1 \frac{t}{t^3 + t + 1} dt$$

```
% Example_5_4.m
% This program evaluates the integral of function "f2"
% between A and B by MATLAB's quad function. The
% integrand can be expressed in a single line and thus we
% can use the anonymous form of the function.
clear; clc;
A=0.0; B=1.0;
f2 = @(t) t ./ (t.^3 +t + 1.0);
I2 = quad(f2,A,B);
fprintf('Integration of f2 over [%.0f,%.0f] ',A,B);
fprintf('by MATLAB''s quad function:\n');
fprintf('f2 = t/(t^3 + t + 1) \n');
fprintf('integral=%f \n',I2);
------------------------------------------------------------------
```

PROGRAM RESULTS

```
Integration of f2 over [0,1] by MATLAB's quad function:
f2 = t/(t^3 + t + 1)
integral = 0.260068
```

Let us repeat Example 5.2, in which we evaluated the improper integral described by Equation (5.6), but this time we evaluate the integral using MATLAB's `quad` function with limits from 0 to 1. Recall that the function $\log(1 + x)/x$ is undefined at $x = 0$. In addition, we use the inline method for specifying the function.

Example 5.5

```
% Example_5_5.m
% This program evaluates the improper integral log(1+x)/x
% with limits from 0 to 1 using quad.
clear; clc;
A=0; B=1;
fprintf('This program uses the quad function to\n');
fprintf('evaluate the integral of log(1+x)/x from ');
fprintf('%.0f to %.0f.\n', A, B);
I = quad(inline('log(1+x)./x'), A, B);
fprintf('I = %10.6f \n', I);
------------------------------------------------------------------
```

This program produces the following result:

```
This program uses the quad function to evaluate
the integral of log(1+x)/x from 0 to 1.
I = 0.822467
```

This answer is the same as shown in Example 5.2.

5.5 The Electric Field

Electric field problems often involve integration, and before we proceed, we review some basic concepts about electromagnetic fields.

We begin by assuming that a point charge of Q coulombs is located at the coordinates (x_p, y_p, z_p) in free space. We denote the location of Q by the vector $\vec{\mathbf{r}}_p$

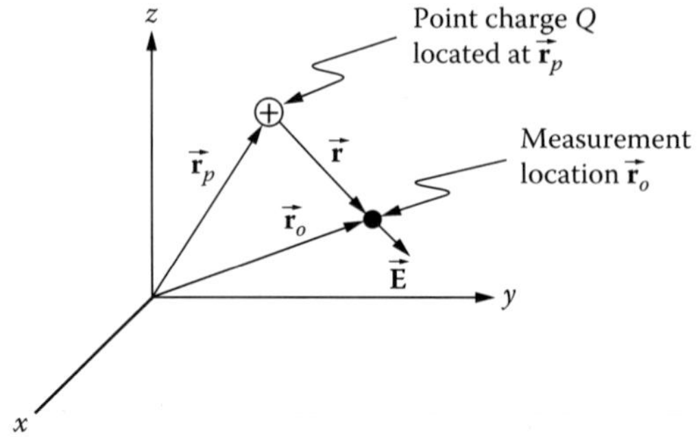

Figure 5.3 The electric field $\vec{\mathbf{E}}$ at observation point $\vec{\mathbf{r}}_o$ due to a point charge located at $\vec{\mathbf{r}}_p$.

(see Figure 5.3). The electric field $\vec{\mathbf{E}}$ at the observation point $\vec{\mathbf{r}}_o$ (corresponding to the coordinates (x_o, y_o, z_o)) due to the charge at $\vec{\mathbf{r}}_p$ is defined as

$$\vec{\mathbf{E}} = \frac{Q}{4\pi\varepsilon_o |\vec{\mathbf{r}}|^2}\hat{\mathbf{e}}_r \tag{5.8}$$

where ε_o is the permittivity of free space (8.85×10^{-12} farad/m), $\vec{\mathbf{r}}$ is the vector from the point charge to the point of measurement, $\hat{\mathbf{e}}_r$ is the unit vector in the $\vec{\mathbf{r}}$ direction, and the resulting $\vec{\mathbf{E}}$ is in volts/meter. From Figure 5.3, we can observe the vector sum $\vec{\mathbf{r}}_o = \vec{\mathbf{r}}_p + \vec{\mathbf{r}}$, and thus $\vec{\mathbf{r}} = \vec{\mathbf{r}}_o - \vec{\mathbf{r}}_p$. Then, Equation (5.8) becomes

$$\vec{\mathbf{E}} = \frac{Q}{4\pi\varepsilon_o \left|\vec{\mathbf{r}}_o - \vec{\mathbf{r}}_p\right|^2}\frac{\vec{\mathbf{r}}_o - \vec{\mathbf{r}}_p}{\left|\vec{\mathbf{r}}_o - \vec{\mathbf{r}}_p\right|} \tag{5.9}$$

where we have applied the definition of the unit vector $\hat{\mathbf{e}}_r = \dfrac{\vec{\mathbf{r}}}{|\vec{\mathbf{r}}|}$.

We now break down $\vec{\mathbf{r}}_o$ and $\vec{\mathbf{r}}_p$ into their *x*, *y*, and *z* components so that we can express them vectorially in Cartesian coordinates as $\vec{\mathbf{r}}_o = x_o\hat{\mathbf{e}}_x + y_o\hat{\mathbf{e}}_y + z_o\hat{\mathbf{e}}_z$ and $\vec{\mathbf{r}}_p = x_p\hat{\mathbf{e}}_x + y_p\hat{\mathbf{e}}_y + z_p\hat{\mathbf{e}}_z$, where $\hat{\mathbf{e}}_x$, $\hat{\mathbf{e}}_y$, and $\hat{\mathbf{e}}_z$ are unit vectors in the *x*, *y*, and *z* directions, respectively. Then, $\left|\vec{\mathbf{r}}_o - \vec{\mathbf{r}}_p\right| = \sqrt{(x_o - x_p)^2 + (y_o - y_p)^2 + (z_o - z_p)^2}$, and Equation (5.8) becomes

$$\vec{\mathbf{E}} = \frac{Q}{4\pi\varepsilon_o}\frac{(x_o - x_p)\mathbf{e}_x + (y_o - y_p)\mathbf{e}_y + (z_o - z_p)\mathbf{e}_z}{\left((x_o - x_p)^2 + (y_o - y_p)^2 + (z_o - z_p)^2\right)^{3/2}} \tag{5.10}$$

Thus, Equation (5.10) gives the electric field at the location (x_o, y_o, z_o) due to a point charge of magnitude Q located at (x_p, y_p, z_p).

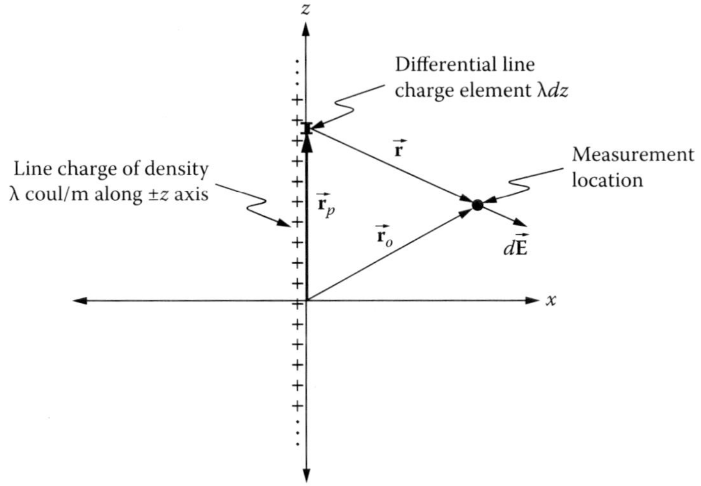

Figure 5.4 The differential electric field $d\vec{E}_r$ at observation point $\vec{r}_o$ due to a differential line charge element λdz located along the z axis.

We now wish to calculate the electric field due to a line of point charges extending along the z-axis from $-\infty$ to ∞ (see Figure 5.4). We shall assume that the charges are evenly spaced along the line with a *linear charge density* represented by the symbol λ with units coulomb/meter. We can rewrite Equation (5.10) in differential form to obtain an expression for $d\vec{\mathbf{E}}$ in terms of the differential quantity $dQ = \lambda dz_p$, where dz_p represents an infinitesimal segment of the line charge in the z direction:

$$d\vec{\mathbf{E}} = \frac{\lambda dz_p}{4\pi\varepsilon_o} \frac{(x_o - x_p)\mathbf{e}_x + (y_o - y_p)\mathbf{e}_y + (z_o - z_p)\mathbf{e}_z}{\left((x_o - x_p)^2 + (y_o - y_p)^2 + (z_o - z_p)^2\right)^{3/2}} \tag{5.11}$$

Separating the individual directional components of Equation (5.11) and integrating from $-\infty$ to $+\infty$ gives

$$E_x = \int_{-\infty}^{\infty} \frac{\lambda dz_p}{4\pi\varepsilon_o} \frac{x_o - x_p}{\left((x_o - x_p)^2 + (y_o - y_p)^2 + (z_o - z_p)^2\right)^{3/2}} \tag{5.12}$$

$$E_y = \int_{-\infty}^{\infty} \frac{\lambda dz_p}{4\pi\varepsilon_o} \frac{y_o - y_p}{\left((x_o - x_p)^2 + (y_o - y_p)^2 + (z_o - z_p)^2\right)^{3/2}} \tag{5.13}$$

$$E_z = \int_{-\infty}^{\infty} \frac{\lambda dz_p}{4\pi\varepsilon_o} \frac{z_o - z_p}{\left((x_o - x_p)^2 + (y_o - y_p)^2 + (z_o - z_p)^2\right)^{3/2}} \tag{5.14}$$

Example 5.6

Given a line charge located along the z axis with density $\lambda = 2\times10^{-9}$ coul/m, calculate the electric field at the location $(x_o, y_o, z_o) = (0.005, 0, 0)$.

```
% Example_5_6.m
% This program uses the quad function to evaluate the
% integrals of equations (5.12), (5.13) and (5.14) to
% find Ex, Ey and Ez. The following parameters are used
% in the integration: lambda=2e-9 coul/m, xo=5e-3, yo=0
% and zo=0.
% Assume that 10 is a good approximation for infinity.
clc; clear;
global xo yo zo lambda epsilon0;
lambda=2e-9; epsilon0=8.85e-12;
xo=5e-3; yo=0; zo=0;
Ex = quad(@linecharge_Ex,-10,10);
Ey = quad(@linecharge_Ey,-10,10);
Ez = quad(@linecharge_Ez,-10,10);
fprintf('E-field due to a line charge ');
fprintf('at [%5.3f,%5.3f,%5.3f]:\n', xo,yo,zo);
fprintf('[Ex,Ey,Ez] = [%10.4e,%5.2f,%5.2f] V/m\n',...
    Ex,Ey,Ez);
-----------------------------------------------------------------

% linecharge_Ex.m: Function to calculate Ex at (xo,yo,zo)
% for a line charge on the z axis
function Ex = linecharge_Ex(zp)
global xo yo zo lambda epsilon0;
Ex = lambda/(4*pi*epsilon0) * xo ...
    ./ (xo.^2 + yo.^2 + (zo-zp).^2).^1.5;
-----------------------------------------------------------------

% linecharge_Ey.m: Function to calculate Ey at (xo,yo,zo)
% for a line charge on the z axis
function Ey = linecharge_Ey(zp)
global xo yo zo lambda epsilon0;
Ey = lambda/(4*pi*epsilon0) * yo ...
    ./ (xo.^2 + yo.^2 + (zo-zp).^2).^1.5;
-----------------------------------------------------------------

% linecharge_Ez.m: Function to calculate Ez at (xo,yo,zo)
% for a line charge on the z axis
function Ez = linecharge_Ez(zp)
global xo yo zo lambda epsilon0;
Ez = lambda/(4*pi*epsilon0) * (zo-zp) ...
    ./ (xo.^2 + yo.^2 + (zo-zp).^2).^1.5;
-----------------------------------------------------------------
```

PROGRAM RESULTS

```
E-field due to a line charge at [0.005,0.000,0.000]:
[Ex,Ey,Ez] = [7.1934e+003, 0.00, 0.00] V/m
```

5.6 The quiver Plot

A quiver plot is a two-dimensional plot of a vector function that uses small arrows to represent the local vector magnitude and direction. For example, a quiver plot can be used to show an electric or magnetic field (i.e., the output from the vector function) as a function of position (i.e., the input to the vector function). The MATLAB command is `quiver(X,Y,U,V)`. To see the syntax, run **`help quiver`** in the Command window:

```
QUIVER(X,Y,U,V) plots velocity vectors as arrows with components (u,v)
at the points (x,y). The matrices X,Y,U,V must all be the same size
and contain corresponding position and velocity components (X and Y
can also be vectors to specify a uniform grid). QUIVER automatically
scales the arrows to fit within the grid.
```

Before we can use the `quiver` function, we need to establish an `(X,Y)` grid of observation points, and the simplest way to accomplish this is to use MATLAB's `meshgrid` function. The `meshgrid` command is invoked as follows:

```
[X,Y] = meshgrid(x,y)
```

where `x` and `y` are vectors of values over which to create the grid. The following example creates a grid over the area $-2 \leq x \leq 2$ and $-2 \leq y \leq 2$ with a step size of 1 by using the `meshgrid` command. The grid that is created will consist of two arrays of 25 *x-y* coordinates (one array of *x* coordinates and a second array of *y* coordinates).

Example 5.7

```
% Example_5_7.m: example usage of meshgrid()
fprintf('This printout is from meshgrid():\n');
x = -2:1:2;
y = -2:1:2;
[X Y] = meshgrid(x,y)
------------------------------------------------------------------------
```

PROGRAM RESULTS

```
This printout is from meshgrid():
X =
    -2      -1      0       1       2
    -2      -1      0       1       2
    -2      -1      0       1       2
    -2      -1      0       1       2
    -2      -1      0       1       2
```

```
Y =
    -2    -2    -2    -2    -2
    -1    -1    -1    -1    -1
     0     0     0     0     0
     1     1     1     1     1
     2     2     2     2     2
```

Thus, `meshgrid` is a very compact way of generating the coordinate sets. As can be seen, the number of elements in the grid will equal the number of elements in `x` times the number of elements in y. For each grid point, there is an `X` element and a `Y` element.

Example 5.8

To demonstrate the `quiver` plot, we will calculate the electric field on the *x-z* plane resulting from the line charge along the *z* axis of Example 5.6.

```
% Example_5_8.m
% This program plots the electric field on the X-Z plane
% for a line charge located on the Z axis and extending
% to infinity in both Z directions. The calculation is
% made over the interval xo = [-.01,.01] m and zo =
% [-.01,.01] m with a step size of 0.002 m.  This example
% reuses the functions already defined in Example 5.6.
clc; clear;
global xo yo zo lambda epsilon0;
lambda=2e-9; epsilon0=8.85e-12;
% for measurements on the X-Z plane, yo will always be 0:
yo=0;
% First create a grid of X-Z locations for which
% calculate the electric field
[X,Z]=meshgrid(-10e-3:2e-3:10e-3,-10e-3:2e-3:10e-3);
% Calculate the E-field at each X-Z location, and store
% the result in the matrices Ex and Ez
for i=1:length(X(:,1))
    for j=1:length(Z(1,:))
        xo=X(i,j);
        zo=Z(i,j);
        % NOTE: don't calculate the field when situated
        % ON the line charge because it will be infinity.
        % Instead, use the value "NaN" (which will cause
        % no point to be printed on the quiver plot).
        if xo==0
            Ex(i,j)=NaN;
            Ez(i,j)=NaN;
        else
            Ex(i,j)=quad(@linecharge_Ex,-10,10);
            Ez(i,j)=quad(@linecharge_Ez,-10,10);
        end
    end
end
% Plot the electric field
```

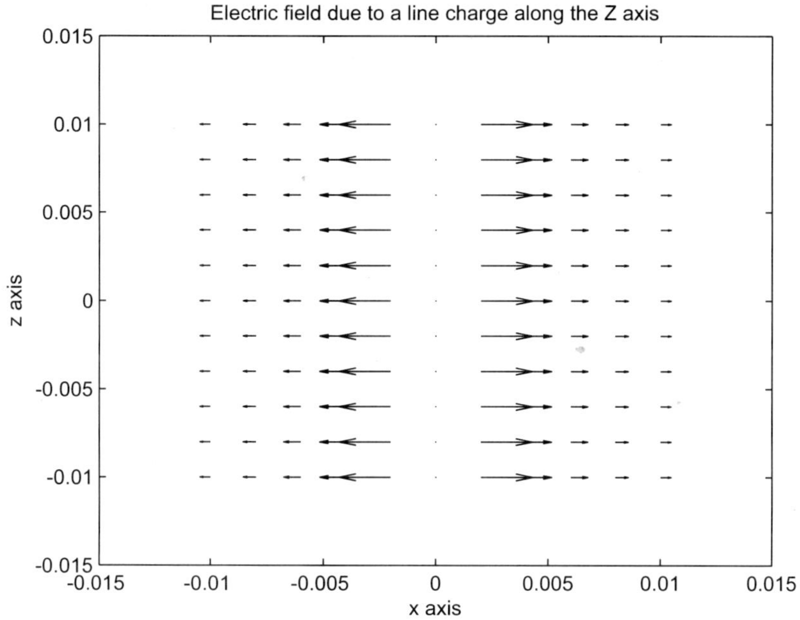

Figure 5.5 Vector plot of the electric field in the *x-z* plane due to a line charge along the *z* axis.

```
quiver(X,Z,Ex,Ez);
title('E-field due to a line charge along the Z axis');
xlabel('x axis');
ylabel('z axis');

---------------------------------------------------------------
```

Figure 5.5 shows the resulting quiver plot.

5.7 MATLAB's `dblquad` Function

The MATLAB function for numerically evaluating a double integral is `dblquad`. A description of the function can be obtained by typing **`help dblquad`** in the Command window:

```
Q = DBLQUAD(FUN,XMIN,XMAX,YMIN,YMAX) evaluates the double integral
of FUN(X,Y) over the rectangle XMIN <= X <= XMAX, YMIN <= Y <=
YMAX. FUN is a function handle. The function Z = FUN(X,Y) should
accept a vector X and a scalar Y and return a vector Z of values
of the integrand.
```

```
Non-square regions can be handled by setting the integrand
to zero outside of the region of interest. For example, the
volume of a hemisphere of radius R can be determined by the
dblquad function by setting -R <= x <= R and 0 <= y <= R and
setting z = 0 for points (x, y) that lie outside the circle of
radius R around the origin.
```

The usage of `dblquad` is similar to `quad`, except

- `FUN` must be a function of two variables (instead of one): a vector of values in the x direction and a single value in the y direction.
- There must be two sets of integration limits (one for the x direction, and one for the y direction).

Example 5.9

Calculate the surface area and volume of a hemisphere with radius of 1 m.

To find the surface area, we define a differential area element $dA = R^2 \sin\phi d\theta d\phi$ (as shown in Figure 5.6) and then double integrate over the intervals $\phi = [0, \pi/2]$ and $\theta = [0, 2\pi]$ using `dblquad`. To find the volume,

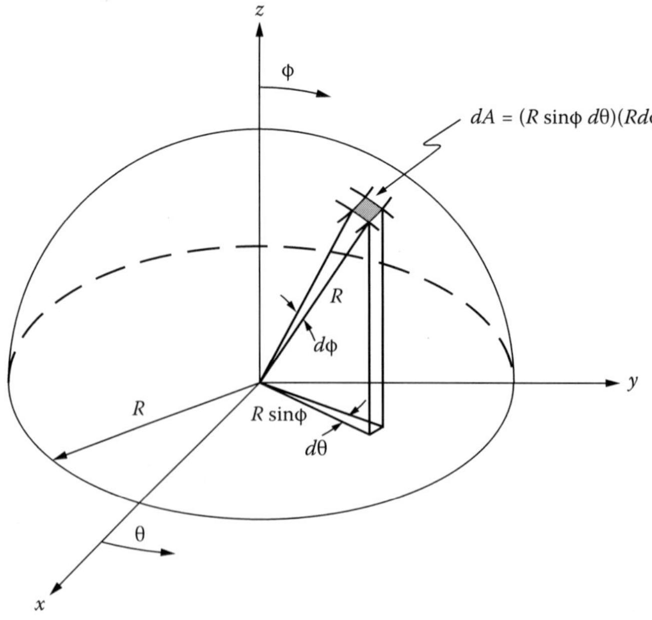

Figure 5.6 To find the surface area of a hemisphere, we define a differential surface element *dA* and then do a double integration over *dϕ* and *dθ*.

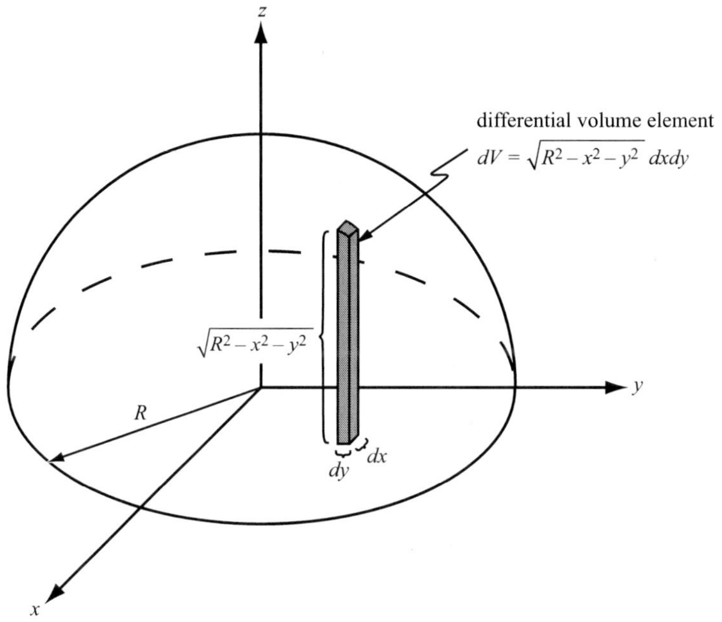

Figure 5.7 To find the volume of a hemisphere, we define a differential volume element *dV* and then do a double integration over *dx* and *dy*.

we define a differential volume element $dV = \sqrt{R^2 - x^2 - y^2}dxdy$ (as shown in Figure 5.7) and double integrate over the intervals $x = [-R,R]$ and $y = [-R,R]$.

```
% Example_5_9.m
% This program calculates the surface area and volume of
% a hemisphere (with radius=1) using dblquad.  The exact
% values from formulae are also calculated.
clear; clc;
global R;
R = 1;
% calculate surface area
SA = dblquad('hemisphere_dA',0,pi/2,0,2*pi);
SA_exact = 2*pi*R^2;
% calculate volume
V = dblquad('hemisphere_dV',-R,R,-R,R);
V_exact = 2/3*pi*R^3;
% print results
fprintf('Surface area SA of a hemisphere of ');
fprintf('radius %.4f m\n',R);
fprintf('SA by DBLQUAD = %.4f m^2\n',SA);
fprintf('SA exact      = %.4f m^2\n',SA_exact);
fprintf('Volume V of a hemisphere of radius %.4f m\n',R);
```

```
fprintf('V by DBLQUAD   = %.4f m^3\n',V);
fprintf('V exact        = %.4f m^3\n',V_exact);
-------------------------------------------------------------

% hemisphere_dA.m: This function defines the integrand
% for determining the surface area of a hemisphere and is
% used in MATLAB's dblquad function.
function [ dA ] = hemisphere_dA( phi, theta )
global R;
dA = R^2 * sin(phi);
-------------------------------------------------------------

% hemisphere_dV.m: This function defines the integrand
% z(x,y) for determining the volume of a hemisphere and
% is used in MATLABís dblquad function. From analytical
% geometry, the equation of a sphere is X^2 + Y^2 + Z^2 =
% R^2. Thus, dV=Z*dX*dY, where Z=sqrt(R^2-X^2-Y^2). Note
% that the hemisphere is only defined for (X,Y) points
% which lie within a circle of radius R around the
% origin, the region that is the projection of the
% hemisphere onto the X-Y plane. An 'if' statement is
% used to set Z = 0 for (X,Y) points outside the circle
% of radius R. Note: X is a vector and Y is a scalar.
function Z = hemisphere_dV(X,Y)
global R;
for i=1:length(X)
    if X(i)^2 + Y^2 <= R^2
        Z(i) = sqrt(R^2 - X(i)^2 - Y^2);
    else
        Z(i) = 0;
    end
end
-------------------------------------------------------------
```

PROGRAM RESULTS

```
Surface area SA of a hemisphere of radius 1.0000 m
SA by DBLQUAD = 6.2832 m^2
SA exact      = 6.2832 m^2
Volume V of a hemisphere of radius 1.0000 m
V by DBLQUAD  = 2.0944 m^3
V exact       = 2.0944 m^3
```

Exercises

Exercise 5.1

Use a Taylor series expansion of $\log(1 + x)$ about $x = 0$ to show that

$$\log(1+x) = x - \frac{1}{2}x^2 + \frac{1}{3}x^3 - \frac{1}{4}x^4 + \frac{1}{5}x^5 - \cdots + \cdots$$

Exercise 5.2

Use MATLAB's `quad` function to evaluate the following integrals; note that integrals d, e, and f are improper integrals:

a. $I = \int_0^3 \frac{dx}{5e^{3x} + 2e^{-3x}}$

b. $I = \int_{-\pi/2}^{\pi/2} \frac{\sin x \, dx}{\sqrt{1 - 4\sin^2 x}}$

c. $I = \int_0^{\pi} (\sinh x - \cos x)\, dx$

d. $I = \int_0^1 \frac{3e^x \, dx}{\sqrt{1 - x^2}}$

e. $I = \int_0^1 \frac{\log x \, dx}{(1 - x)}$

f. $I = \int_0^1 \frac{\log x \, dx}{(1 - x^2)}$

Projects

Project 5.1

For the line charge of Example 5.8, calculate and plot (using `quiver`) the electric field in the *x-y* plane (instead of the *x-z* plane) for the interval $-50 \le x \le 50$ mm and $-50 \le y \le 50$ mm with a step size of 10 mm. Remember *not* to calculate the field at the location of the line charge.

Project 5.2

We now modify the line charge of Example 5.8 to be of a finite length $\ell = 0.02$ m along the *z* axis, starting at $z = -0.01$ m and ending at $z = +0.01$ m. Assume $\lambda = 2 \times 10^{-9}$ coul/m.

1. Calculate and plot (using `quiver`) the magnitude of the electric field for the interval $-0.05 \le x \le 0.05$ m and $-0.05 \le z \le 0.05$ m with a step size of 0.01 m.

2. Print to the screen every fourth value of x_0, z_0, and the corresponding values of E_x, E_z, and the magnitude of $\vec{\mathbf{E}}$.
3. Now, assume that the total charge of the line segment $Q = \lambda \ell = 0.04 \times 10^{-9}$ coul is concentrated as a point charge at the origin. Calculate the magnitude of the electric field for this point charge over the same interval as previously using Equation (5.8). Note that because Q is a point charge, you can use Equation (5.8) directly, and no integration is required.
4. Calculate the percentage error in using the point charge method in the values of E_x and E_z at each point as calculated in parts 1 and 3. Use the following formula for calculating the percentage error in E_x and a similar formula for calculating the percentage error in E_z.

$$\% \text{ error in } E_x = \frac{\left| E_{x,1} - E_{x,2} \right|}{E_{x,1}} \times 100$$

where

$$E_{x,1} = E_x \text{ calculated in part 1.}$$

$$E_{x,2} = E_x \text{ calculated in part 3.}$$

Print to the screen every fourth value of x_o, z_o, and the corresponding values of the percentage error in the values of E_x and E_z.
5. At what distance from the origin is the percentage error in using the point charge method less than 5%? In many cases, if we are far enough away from the charge, we can avoid integrating over its geometry and instead just treat it as a point charge, thereby making our calculations much easier. This is called the *far-field approximation.*

Project 5.3

A positive *surface charge density* of magnitude $\sigma = 4 \times 10^{-12}$ coul/m^2 extends infinitely in the *x-y* plane as shown in Figure P5.3a. Using a method similar to what was described in Section 5.4 (show your work), define a differential charge element $dQ = \sigma\, dy\, dx$ and then find the resulting electric field by integrating over the sheet of charge for $x_p = [-\infty, \infty]$, $y_p = [-\infty, \infty]$, and $z_p = 0$:

$$E_x = \int_{-\infty}^{\infty}\int_{-\infty}^{\infty} \frac{\sigma dy_p dx_p}{4\pi\varepsilon_o} \frac{x - x_p}{\left((x_o - x_p)^2 + (y_o - y_p)^2 + (z_o - z_p)^2\right)^{3/2}} \tag{P5.3a}$$

$$E_y = \int_{-\infty}^{\infty}\int_{-\infty}^{\infty} \frac{\sigma dy_p dx_p}{4\pi\varepsilon_o} \frac{y - y_p}{\left((x_o - x_p)^2 + (y_o - y_p)^2 + (z_o - z_p)^2\right)^{3/2}} \tag{P5.3b}$$

$$E_z = \int_{-\infty}^{\infty}\int_{-\infty}^{\infty} \frac{\sigma dy_p dx_p}{4\pi\varepsilon_o} \frac{z - z_p}{\left((x_o - x_p)^2 + (y_o - y_p)^2 + (z_o - z_p)^2\right)^{3/2}} \tag{P5.3c}$$

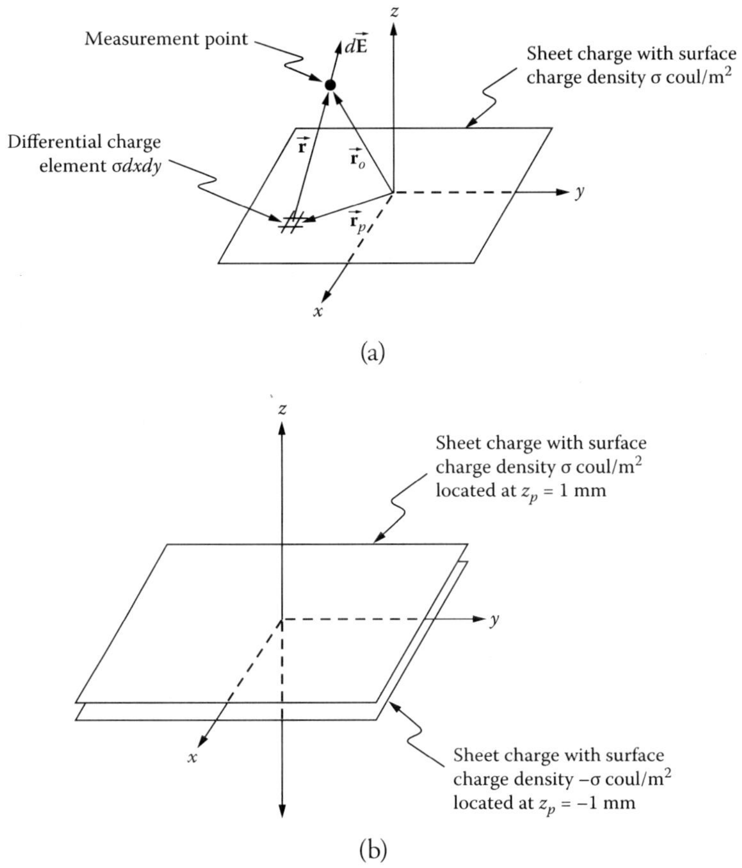

Figure P5.3 (a) The differential electric field $d\vec{E}$ at observation point $\vec{r}_o$ due to a differential sheet charge element *σdxdy* located on the x-y plane. (b) Two parallel and oppositely charged sheet charges located on the planes $z_p = +1\text{mm}$ and $z_p = -1\text{mm}$.

1. Write a MATLAB program using the `dblquad` function to calculate E_x, E_y, and E_z at the following points:

   $x_o, y_o, z_o = [0, 0, 2 \times 10^{-3}]$ (above the plate)

   $x_o, y_o, z_o = [\ 30 \times 10^{-3}, -5 \times 10^{-3}, 12 \times 10^{-3}\ ]$ (below the plate)

   Assume that 10 is a good enough approximation for infinity. Note that by symmetry, the *x* and *y* components of the field should integrate to zero (or close to it). Confirm this result.
2. Now, assume that there are two sheet charges in the planes parallel to the *x*-*y* plane: the first sheet located at $z_p = +1$ mm with surface charge density $\sigma = 4 \times 10^{-12}$ coul/m^2 and the second sheet located at $z_p = -1$ mm and oppositely charged with surface charge density $\sigma = -4 \times 10^{-12}$ coul/m^2 (see Figure P5.3b). Find the electric field via superposition by calculating the electric field

separately for each sheet and then adding them together. Find E_x, E_y, and E_z for the these three points:

$x_o, y_o, z_o = [0, 0, 2 \times 10^{-3}]$ (above the plates)

$x_o, y_o, z_o = [10 \times 10^{-3}, 0, -0.5 \times 10^{-3}]$ (between the plates)

$x_o, y_o, z_o = [\ 30 \times 10^{-3}, -5 \times 10^{-3}, 12 \times 10^{-3}\ ]$ (below the plates)

Print out the results. Do these results make sense?

Project 5.4

The Biot-Savart law relates electrical current to magnetic field (see Figure P5.4a) and is defined for current flow through wires as

$$d\vec{\mathbf{B}} = \frac{\mu_o}{4\pi} \frac{I d\vec{\ell} \times \mathbf{e}_r}{\left|\vec{\mathbf{r}}\right|^2} \tag{P5.4}$$

where $d\vec{\mathbf{B}}$ is the differential magnetic field (a vector), μ_o is the permeability of free space ($4\pi \times 10^{-7}$ henry/m), I is the current (in amperes), $d\vec{\ell}$ is a differential wire length with direction corresponding to the current flow, $\vec{\mathbf{r}}$ is the vector from the current element to the measurement point, $\hat{\mathbf{e}}_r$ is the unit vector in the $\vec{\mathbf{r}}$ direction, and $\times$ represents the vector cross product. In Figure P5.4a, we also define $\vec{\mathbf{r}}_p$ as the location of the current element and $\vec{\mathbf{r}}_o$ as the point of measurement such that $\vec{\mathbf{r}} = \vec{\mathbf{r}}_o - \vec{\mathbf{r}}_p$.

We wish to calculate the magnetic field for an infinite wire extending along the z axis and carrying a current of $I = 1$ mA in the $+z$ direction. Note that, in reality, an infinite-

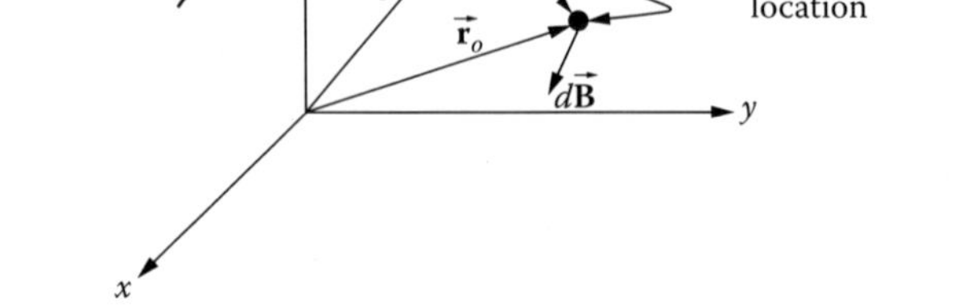

Figure P5.4a The differential magnetic field element $d\vec{\mathbf{B}}$ at observation point $\vec{\mathbf{r}}_o$ due to a differential wire element carrying current $Id\vec{\ell}$.

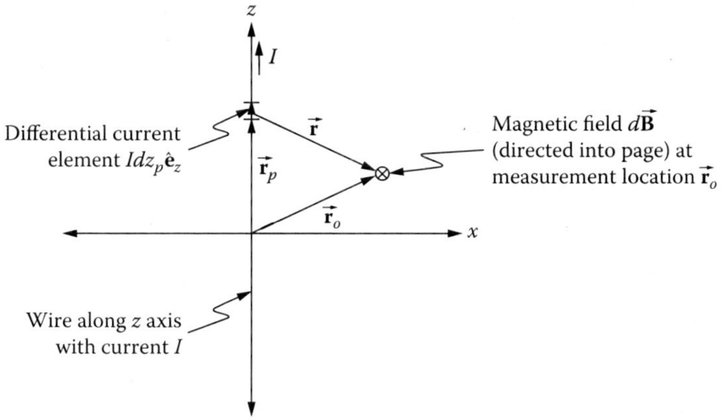

Figure P5.4b The magnetic field due to a wire along the *z* axis will have only *x* and *y* components.

length current-carrying wire is impossible because it violates conservation of charge. For now, it is sufficient to presume that the wire is connected to a current source at ±∞.

1. As shown in Figure P5.4b, for a wire in the z direction, $d\vec{\ell} = dz_p\hat{\mathbf{e}}_z$. Due to the cross product in Equation P5.4, if $d\vec{\ell}$ is z directed, then the resulting $d\vec{\mathbf{B}}$ will only have components in the x and y directions. Write two separate equations for dB_x and dB_y by writing $\hat{\mathbf{e}}_r$ in terms of its $\hat{\mathbf{e}}_x$, $\hat{\mathbf{e}}_y$, and $\hat{\mathbf{e}}_z$ components, computing the cross products between $d\vec{\ell}$ and $\hat{\mathbf{e}}_r$ and then separating the x and y components of $d\vec{\mathbf{B}}$ into separate equations. Hint: Derive $\hat{\mathbf{e}}_x$ and $\hat{\mathbf{e}}_y$ from $\hat{\mathbf{e}}_r$ using the method employed in Equation (5.10).
2. Write two MATLAB functions for dB_x and dB_y that compute the x- and y-directed magnetic fields in terms of a single argument z_p. Use global variables for the measurement position parameters x_o, y_o, and z_o. Use the `quad` function to integrate over the interval $z_p = [-\infty, \infty]$ and calculate the magnetic field at these points:

$$x, y, z = [1\times10^{-4}, 1\times10^{-4}, 0] \qquad \text{(first quadrant)}$$

$$x, y, z = [-1\times10^{-4}, 1\times10^{-4}, 0] \qquad \text{(second quadrant)}$$

$$x, y, z = [-1\times10^{-4}, -1\times10^{-4}, 0] \qquad \text{(third quadrant)}$$

$$x, y, z = [1\times10^{-4}, -1\times10^{-4}, 0] \qquad \text{(fourth quadrant)}$$

Assume that 10 is a sufficient approximation for infinity. Print out the results. Comment on any symmetry you find in these solutions.

3. Use the `meshgrid` function to create a set of points for $\vec{\mathbf{r}}_o$ where $-200 \le x_o \le 200$ mm, $-200 \le y_o \le 200$ mm, and $z_o = 0$. Use a step size

of 50 mm for both x_o and y_o. Compute the magnetic field B_x and B_y at each value of $\vec{\mathbf{r}}_o$ and plot with `quiver`. When iterating over your values for $\vec{\mathbf{r}}_o$, be sure to skip the point at the origin.

Project 5.5

Figure P5.5a shows a circular wire with radius R centered at the origin and carrying a current I. Using the Biot-Savart law from Equation (P5.4), we can write the differential magnetic field in terms of a differential current element $Id\vec{\ell} = IRd\theta_p\hat{\mathbf{e}}_\theta$, where $Rd\theta_p$ is the differential length (in cylindrical coordinates) of the current element at location $\vec{\mathbf{r}}_p$, and $\hat{\mathbf{e}}_\theta$ is the unit vector in the θ_p direction. In this type of problem with cylindrical symmetry, the simplest approach is to convert the cylindrical unit vectors into (constant) cartesian unit vectors but still perform the integration using the cylindrical variables. Figure P5.5b shows how $\vec{\mathbf{r}}_p$ and $\hat{\mathbf{e}}_\theta$ can be expressed in terms of their x and y components using the unit vectors $\hat{\mathbf{e}}_x$ and $\hat{\mathbf{e}}_y$:

$$\vec{\mathbf{r}}_p = \hat{\mathbf{e}}_x R\cos\theta_p + \hat{\mathbf{e}}_y R\sin\theta_p \tag{P5.5a}$$

$$\hat{\mathbf{e}}_\theta = -\hat{\mathbf{e}}_x \sin\theta_p + \hat{\mathbf{e}}_y \cos\theta_p \tag{P5.5b}$$

We can now rewrite Equation (P5.4) as

$$d\vec{\mathbf{B}} = \frac{\mu_o IR}{4\pi} d\theta_p \frac{(-\hat{\mathbf{e}}_x \sin\theta_p + \hat{\mathbf{e}}_y \cos\theta_p)\times(\hat{\mathbf{e}}_x(x_o - R\cos\theta_p) + \hat{\mathbf{e}}_y(y_o - R\sin\theta_p) + \hat{\mathbf{e}}_z(z_o - z_p))}{((x_o - R\cos\theta_p)^2 + (y_o - R\sin\theta_p)^2 + (z_o - z_p)^2)^{3/2}} \tag{P5.5c}$$

where μ_o is the permeability of free space ($4\pi\times 10^{-7}$ H/m).

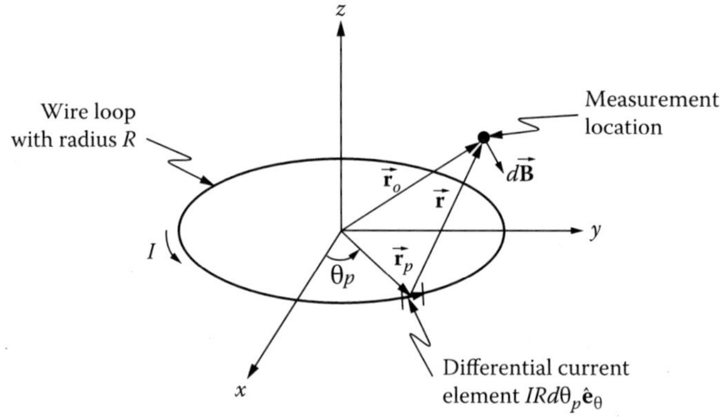

Figure P5.5a The differential magnetic field element $d\vec{\mathbf{B}}$ at observation point $\vec{\mathbf{r}}_o$ due to a wire loop located in the x-y plane.

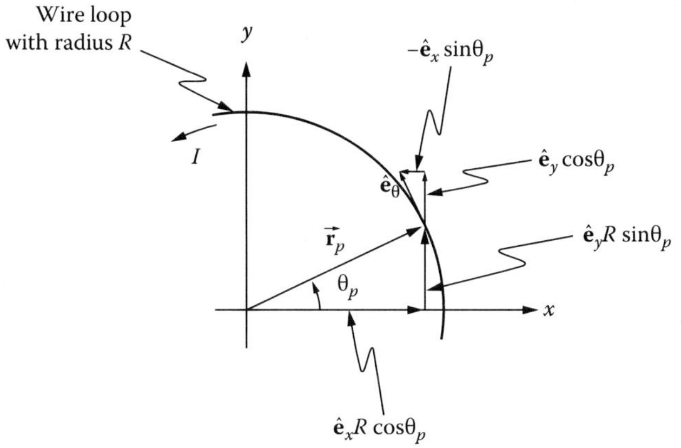

Figure P5.5b $\vec{\mathbf{r}}_p$ **and** $\hat{\mathbf{e}}_{\theta_p}$ **may be decomposed into their** ***x*** **and** ***y*** **components to solve for the magnetic field with MATLAB's `quad` function.**

1. Calculate the vector cross product in Equation (P5.5c) and split the result into three separate equations for the *x*, *y*, and *z* components of the differential magnetic field. Use the resulting expressions for dB_x, dB_y, and dB_z to write three MATLAB functions that take one argument (θ_p) and can be used with MATLAB's `quad` function to determine B_x, B_y, and B_z.
2. Use MATLAB's `meshgrid` function to create a set of points in the *x*-*z* plane for $-8 \le x_0 \le 8$ mm (with a step size of 1 mm) and $-2 \le z_0 \le 2$ mm (with a step size of 0.5 mm). Determine B_x and B_z at each point in the set (be sure to use the correct integration limits) and plot with `quiver`. Assume $R = 2.5$ mm, $I = 1$ mA.

Project 5.6

A *solenoid* is a coil of wire used to create a magnetic field to activate an actuator. Typical uses include electrical relays, electrically controlled water valves, and automotive starter gears. Figure P5.6a shows a solenoid with radius *R*, length *D*, turn count *N*, and current *I*.

We model the solenoid in MATLAB as a cylindrical sheet current with density $\vec{\mathbf{K}} = \dfrac{NI}{D}\hat{\mathbf{e}}_\theta$ A/m with the current density directed in the θ direction. The Biot-Savart law for a surface current is

$$d\vec{\mathbf{B}} = \frac{\mu_o}{4\pi}\frac{\vec{\mathbf{K}}dA \times \mathbf{e}_r}{\left|\vec{\mathbf{r}}\right|^2} \qquad \text{(P5.6a)}$$

where dA is a two-dimensional differential surface element, $\vec{\mathbf{r}}$ is the vector from the differential surface to the measurement point, $\hat{\mathbf{e}}_r$ is the unit vector in the $\vec{\mathbf{r}}$ direction, × represents the vector cross product, and μ_o is the permeability of free space ($4\pi \times 10^{-7}$ H/m). From Figure P5.6b, we see that in cylindrical coordinates,

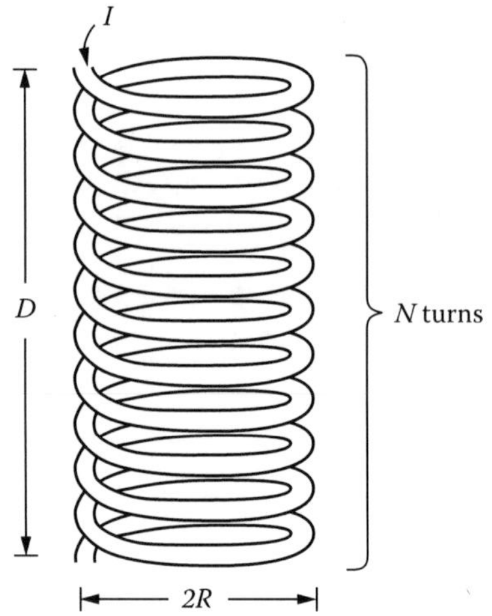

Figure P5.6a A solenoid consisting of *N* turns, radius *R*, length *D*, and current *I*.

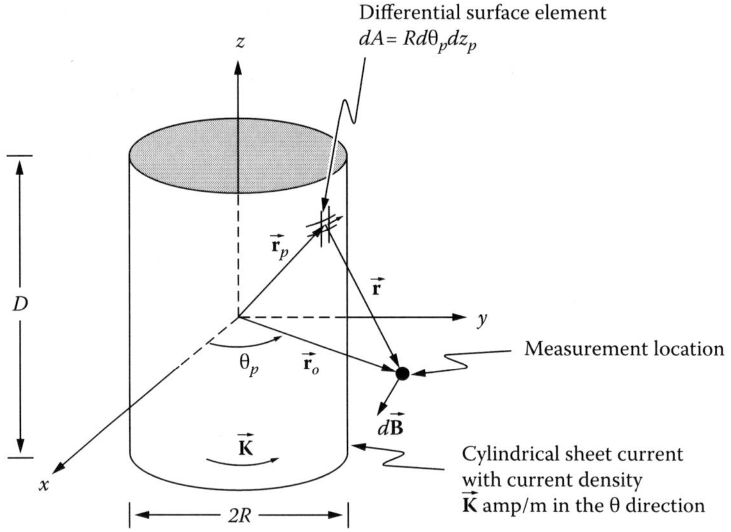

Figure P5.6b The solenoid can be modeled as a sheet current of magnitude *K* A/m.

$dA = Rd\,\theta_p dz_p$, where $\vec{\mathbf{r}}_p$ is the location of the differential surface (with cylindrical components r_p, θ_p, and z_p), and $\hat{\mathbf{e}}_\theta$ is the unit vector in the θ_p direction. We also define the observation point $\vec{\mathbf{r}}_o = x_o\hat{\mathbf{e}}_x + y_o\hat{\mathbf{e}}_y + z_o\hat{\mathbf{e}}_z$. From the geometry of the problem, we can write $\vec{\mathbf{K}}dA$ and $\vec{\mathbf{r}}$ in terms of Cartesian unit vectors:

$$\vec{\mathbf{K}}dA = \frac{NI}{D} Rd\,\theta_p dz_p \hat{\mathbf{e}}_\theta = \frac{NI}{D} Rd\theta_p dz_p(-\hat{\mathbf{e}}_x \sin\theta_p + \hat{\mathbf{e}}_y \cos\theta_p) \qquad \text{(P5.6b)}$$

$$\vec{\mathbf{r}} = \vec{\mathbf{r}}_o - \vec{\mathbf{r}}_p = \hat{\mathbf{e}}_x(x_o - R\cos\theta_p) + \hat{\mathbf{e}}_y(y_o - R\sin\theta_p) + \hat{\mathbf{e}}_z(z_o - z_p) \qquad \text{(P5.6c)}$$

Substituting back into Equation (P5.6a) gives

$$d\vec{\mathbf{B}} = \frac{\mu_o NIR}{4\pi D} d\,\theta_p dz_p \frac{(-\hat{\mathbf{e}}_x \sin\theta_p + \hat{\mathbf{e}}_y \cos\theta_p) \times \left(\hat{\mathbf{e}}_x(x_o - R\cos\theta_p) + \hat{\mathbf{e}}_y(y_o - R\sin\theta_p) + \hat{\mathbf{e}}_z(z_o - z_p)\right)}{\left((x_o - R\cos\theta_p)^2 + (y_o - R\sin\theta_p)^2 + (z_o - z_p)^2\right)^{3/2}}$$

(P5.6d)

1. Calculate the vector cross product in Equation (P5.6d) and split the result into three separate equations for the *x*, *y*, and *z* components of the differential magnetic field. Use the resulting expressions for dB_x, dB_y, and dB_z to write three MATLAB functions that take two arguments (θ_p and z_p) and compute the differential *B* field in the *x*, *y*, and *z* directions, respectively.
2. Assume that the solenoid is centered at the origin with radius $R = 2.5$ mm and $D = 15$ mm. Use `meshgrid` to create a three-dimensional point set `[X,Y,Z]` of measurement points for $\vec{\mathbf{r}}_o$. Note that `meshgrid` takes an optional third argument to create three-dimensional point sets (see `help meshgrid` for usage details). Use these limits for (x_o, y_o, z_o) : $-3 \le x_o \le 3$ mm (with a step size of 1.5 mm), $0 \le y_o \le 3$ (with a step size of 1.5 mm), and $-10 \le z_o \le 10$ mm (with a step size of 5 mm).
3. Use `dblquad` to calculate B_x, B_y, and B_z at each point in the set (be sure to use the correct integration limits). Assume: $N = 500$, $I = 1$ mA.
4. Create a three-dimensional quiver plot of your results using MATLAB's `quiver3` function (run `help quiver3` for usage details).

Chapter 6

Numerical Integration of Ordinary Differential Equations

6.1 Introduction

In this chapter, we examine several methods for solving ordinary differential equations (ODEs). ODEs can be broken up into two categories:

a. *Initial value problems* in which we know the necessary initial conditions, for example, the value of a circuit node voltage (or its slope) at $t = 0$;
b. *Boundary value problems* in which we know the value of the dependent variable at specific coordinates in the problem geometry, for example, the electric potential at both ends of a conductor.

For initial value problems, we examine several numerical integration methods, including the Euler method, the modified Euler method, the Runge-Kutta method, and the built-in `ode45` function of MATLAB. For boundary value problems, we employ implicit finite-difference methods that reduce ODEs to a system of linear algebraic equations, which turn out to be a tri-diagonal system that can be solved algebraically.

6.2 The Initial Value Problem

In an initial value problem, the values of the dependent variable and the necessary derivatives are known at the point at which the integration begins. We begin with a first-order differential equation of the general form such that the derivative is a known function of x and y, and the initial condition, $y(0) = Y_I$, is known:

$$\frac{dy}{dx} = f(x, y)$$
$$y(0) = Y_I \tag{6.1}$$

There are several techniques for solving this type of problem, including Euler's method, which is simple but not used very much; the modified Euler method; the Runge-Kutta method; and others. Each technique has pros and cons with respect to simplicity, accuracy, and computational efficiency.

6.3 The Euler Algorithm

The general approach to solving differential equations numerically is to subdivide the x domain into N subdivisions giving $x_1, x_2, x_3, \ldots x_{N+1}$, and then "march" in the x direction over the interval while calculating $y_2, y_3, y_3, \ldots, y_{N+1}$. Note y_1 is

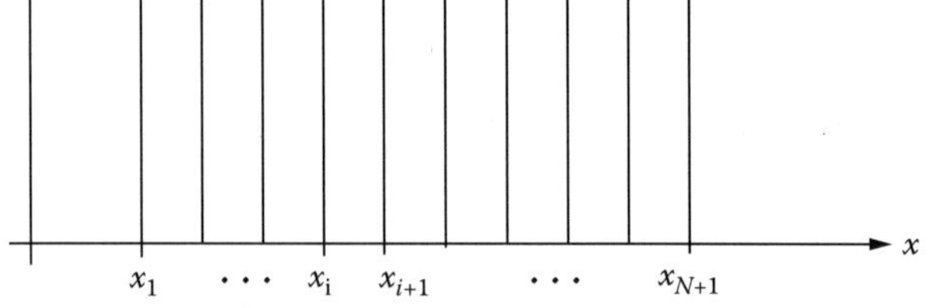

Figure 6.1 To solve a first-order differential equation $y' = f(x, y)$, we divide the interval of interest into N subdivisions and then estimate the next value of y by using an approximation based on a Taylor series around the known point.

specified and is equal to the initial condition Y_I (see Figure 6.1). A Taylor series expansion about an arbitrary point x_i gives

$$y(x) = y(x_i) + \frac{y'(x_i)}{1!}(x - x_i) + \frac{y''(x_i)}{2!}(x - x_i)^2 + \cdots \tag{6.2}$$

If we use only the first two terms of the series, we can approximate the value for $y(x_{i+1})$ (which we denote as y_{i+1}) as

$$\begin{aligned} y_{i+1} &\approx y(x_i) + \frac{y'(x_i)}{1}(x_{i+1} - x_i) \\ &\approx y_i + y_i' h \end{aligned} \tag{6.3}$$

where $h = x_{i+1} - x_i$, which is defined as the *step size*, and y_i' is the slope of the curve of $y(x)$ at x_i. Substituting Equation (6.1) into (6.3), we obtain

$$y_{i+1} = y_i + h\,f(x_i, y_i) \tag{6.4}$$

As can be seen for the configuration shown in Figure 6.2, the prediction of y_{i+1} by Euler's method overshoots the true value of y_{i+1}. Thus, starting with $i = 1$, we obtain

$$y_2 = y_1 + h\,f(x_1, y_1) = Y_I + h\,f(x_1, Y_I)$$

Similarly, y_3 can be determined by substituting $i = 2$ into Equation (6.4):

$$y_3 = y_2 + h\,f(x_2, y_2)$$

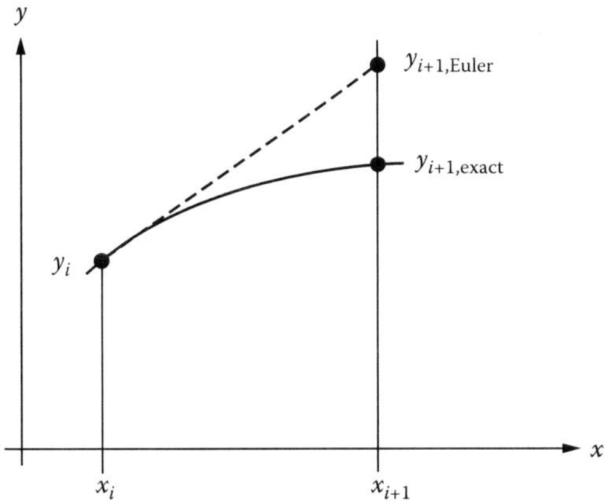

Figure 6.2 In the Euler method, we use a first-order Taylor series approximation (i.e., a straight line) to approximate the next value of *y*.

The process is continued, obtaining $y_4, y_5, y_6, \ldots, y_{N+1}$. The Euler method is an example of an *explicit* method because each new value for y_{i+1} depends solely on previous values of x and y.

6.4 Modified Euler Method with Predictor-Corrector Algorithm

The modified Euler method is a more accurate way for calculating the value of y_{i+1} than the simple linear approximation of the Euler method in the previous section. Again, we consider a differential equation of standard form $y' = f(x, y)$ with initial condition $y(0) = Y_I$, and again we subdivide the x domain into N subdivisions and march in the x direction. We saw that in the Euler method, taking $y_{i+1} = y_i + hy_i' = y_i + hf(x_i, y_i)$ overshoots the true value of y_{i+1} (as shown in Figure 6.2). Now, suppose we were able to determine $y'(x_{i+1})$, which would be the slope to the curve at x_{i+1}. If we were to predict y_{i+1} by using $y'(x_{i+1})$ in Equation 6.3, that is,

$$y_{i+1} = y_i + h\, y'_{i+1} = y_i + h\, f(x_{i+1}, y_{i+1}) \tag{6.5}$$

then we would undershoot the true value of y_{i+1}. This is shown in Figure 6.3. Here, we have constructed a tangent to the curve at y_{i+1} and drawn a parallel line passing

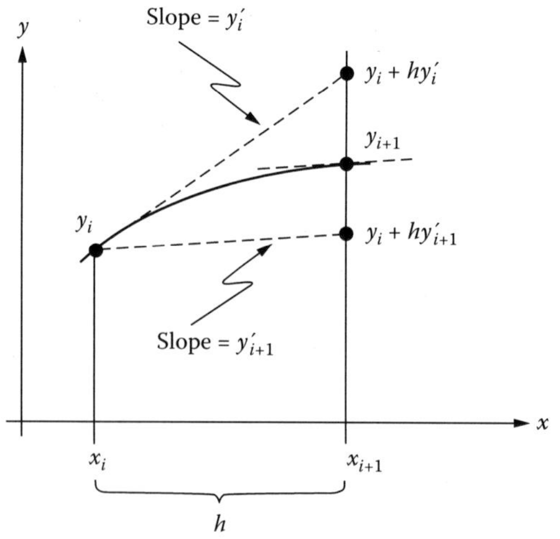

Figure 6.3 In the modified Euler method, we use the average of two straight-line approximations to predict y_{i+1}.

through point (x_i, y_i) to obtain the predicted value for y_{i+1}. Since using y_i' in Equation (6.3) overshoots the true value of y_{i+1} and using y_{i+1}' in Equation (6.3) undershoots the true value of y_{i+1}, we see that a better estimate for y_{i+1} would be obtained by using an average of the two derivatives in Equation (6.3), that is,

$$y_{i+1} = y_i + h\left(\frac{y_i' + y_{i+1}'}{2}\right) \tag{6.6}$$

Unfortunately, Equation (6.6) is no longer explicit because we do *not* know the value of y_{i+1}'. The use of Equation (6.6) in solving the differential Equation (6.1) is an example of an *implicit* method. However, we can approximate a value for y_{i+1}' by using the *predictor-corrector* method. To apply this method, we rewrite Equation (6.6) as follows:

$$y_{i+1}^C = y_i + h\left(\frac{y_i' + \left(y_{i+1}'\right)^P}{2}\right) \tag{6.7}$$

where the P superscript indicates the *predicted* value, and the C superscript indicates the *corrected* value. Equation (6.7) is called the *corrector equation* and can be used to iteratively calculate the value for y_{i+1}. Substituting Equation (6.1) into (6.7) gives

$$y_{i+1}^C = y_i + \frac{h}{2}\left(f(x_i, y_i) + f(x_{i+1}, y_{i+1}^P)\right) \tag{6.8}$$

The predictor-corrector technique proceeds as follows:

1. Use the Euler method to determine a first predicted value for y_{i+1}, called $y_{i+1}^{P_1}$, that is,

$$y_{i+1}^{P_1} = y_i + h\, f(x_i, y_i)$$

2. Calculate the first corrected value $y_{i+1}^{C_1}$ by using $y_{i+1}^{P_1}$ in Equation (6.8).
3. Use $y_{i+1}^{C_1}$ as the new predicted value $y_{i+1}^{P_2}$ in Equation (6.8).
4. Calculate a new corrected value $y_{i+1}^{C_2}$.
5. Repeat steps 3 and 4 until $\left|y_{i+1}^{C_{n+1}} - y_{i+1}^{C_n}\right| < \varepsilon$, where ε is an error tolerance that depends on the desired accuracy and is typically a fraction of a percent of the last corrected value, for example, $\varepsilon = 0.01\% \times y_{i+1}^{C_n}$.

Example 6.1

In this example, we find the exact solution of a first-order differential equation and then compare with the corresponding solutions found by the Euler and modified Euler methods.

A simple RC circuit is "driven" by a voltage source V_D as shown in Figure 6.4. Writing Kirchhoff's voltage law around the loop gives

$$V_D - v_R - v_C = 0 \tag{6.9}$$

Applying Ohm's law $(v_R = iR)$ and the constituent relation for capacitor current $\left(i = C\dfrac{dv_C}{dt}\right)$, we can rewrite Equation (6.9) as

$$V_D - RC\frac{dv_C}{dt} - v_C = 0$$

Rearranging gives

$$\frac{dv_C}{dt} + \frac{1}{\tau}v_C = \frac{V_D}{\tau} \tag{6.10}$$

where $\tau = RC$ is the *time constant* for the RC circuit. Equation (6.10) is a first-order differential equation of v_C with respect to time. We assume that at $t = 0$, the initial capacitor voltage is zero, and that the driving voltage is a ramp function, that is $V_D(t) = V_o t$. We first solve Equation (6.10) analytically so that we can have a basis for comparison with numerical solutions. We begin by guessing a particular solution $v_{C,P}$ having the same form as the driving function:

$$v_{C,P} = \alpha t + \beta \tag{6.11}$$

where α and β are constants to be determined. Substituting $v_{C,P}$ into Equation (6.10), we obtain

$$\frac{d}{dt}(\alpha t + \beta) + \frac{1}{\tau}(\alpha t + \beta) = \frac{V_o t}{\tau}$$

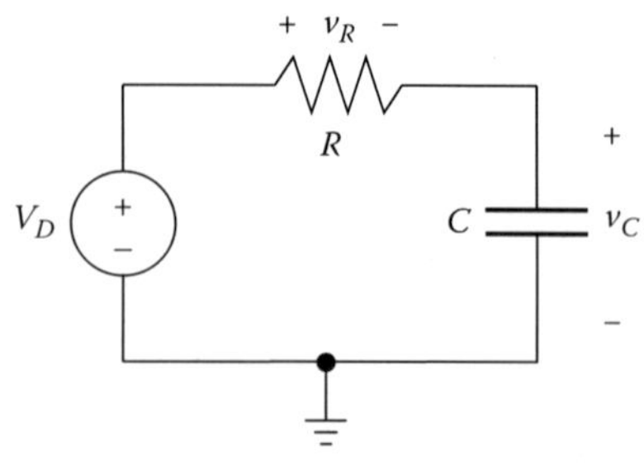

Figure 6.4 RC circuit.

which gives

$$\frac{\alpha t}{\tau} + \left(\alpha + \frac{\beta}{\tau}\right) = \frac{V_o t}{\tau} \tag{6.12}$$

Matching terms between the left and right sides of Equation (6.12), we see that $\alpha = V_o$ and $\beta = -V_o\tau$. Thus,

$$v_{C,P} = V_o t - V_o \tau$$

Next, we find the complementary solution, $v_{C,H}$, to the homogeneous equation, which is Equation (6.10) when the driving function is zero.

$$\frac{dv_{C,H}}{dt} + \frac{1}{\tau} v_{C,H} = 0 \tag{6.13}$$

Equation (6.13) is separable. Thus,

$$\frac{dv_{C,H}}{v_{C,H}} = -\frac{dt}{\tau} \rightarrow \ln v_{C,H} = -\frac{t}{\tau} + \ln\gamma \rightarrow v_{C,H} = \gamma e^{-t/\tau} \tag{6.14}$$

where γ is a constant to be determined. We now take the complete solution as the sum of the particular and homogeneous solutions:

$$\begin{aligned} v_C &= v_{C,P} + v_{C,H} \\ &= V_o t - V_o\tau + \gamma e^{-t/\tau} \end{aligned} \tag{6.15}$$

Applying the initial condition $v_C(0) = 0$ to Equation (6.15), we find that $\gamma = V_o\tau$. Thus, the complete solution for the ramp response of an RC circuit is

$$v_C(t) = V_o\left(t - \tau\left(1 - e^{-t/\tau}\right)\right) \tag{6.16}$$

We now solve Equation (6.10) numerically for the following parameter values: $R = 1$ kΩ, $C = 1$ μF, and $V_o = 10$ V. First, we rearrange the governing differential equation (6.10) into the form of Equation (6.1):

$$\frac{dv_C}{dt} = \frac{1}{\tau}(V_D - v_C) = \frac{1}{\tau}(V_o t - v_C) = f(t, v_C) \tag{6.17}$$

Next, we choose a time interval and time step. For the RC circuit, we know that the interesting transient behavior will occur within a few multiples of the time constant, and thus we arbitrarily choose an interval of $t = [\,0,\ 10\tau\,]$. We also divide the interval into 20 steps, and thus $h = \dfrac{10\tau}{20}$.

A MATLAB script that carries out the Euler method and the modified Euler method follows:

```
% Example_6_1.m
% Calculate ramp response of RC circuit via 3 methods:
% 1. exact solution
% 2. by Euler method
% 3. by modified Euler method
clc; clear;
% Circuit parameters:
R=1e3;       % ohms
C=1e-6;      % farads
tau = R*C;   % seconds
Vo = 10;     % volts
f = @(tm,Vc) (1/tau)*(Vo*tm-Vc); % Equation 6.17
% Parameters for Euler algorithm
interval = 10*tau;
steps = 20;
h = interval/steps;
% Create set of time points to calculate
t = 0:h:interval;
% Initial conditions
Vc_exact(1)=0;
Vc_euler(1)=0;
Vc_mod_euler(1)=0;
% Exact and Euler method: march in time
for i=1:length(t)-1
    % Apply Equation 6.16
    Vc_exact(i+1) = Vo*(t(i+1)-tau+tau*exp(-t(i+1)/tau));
    % Apply Equation 6.4
    Vc_euler(i+1) = Vc_euler(i) + h*f(t(i),Vc_euler(i));
end
% Modified Euler: apply corrector equation
tolerance = 1e-4; % .01 percent
for i=1:length(t)-1
    % use the Euler method to calculate an initial guess
    % for the predicted value
    Vc_predicted =  Vc_mod_euler(i) ...
        + h*f(t(i),Vc_mod_euler(i));
    % Repeatedly apply the corrector equation until the
    % predictor and corrector are equal (or within
    % tolerance)
    for j=1:50
        Vc_corrected = Vc_mod_euler(i) ...
            + (h/2)*(f(t(i),Vc_mod_euler(i)) ...
            + f(t(i+1),Vc_predicted));
        if abs(Vc_corrected-Vc_predicted)/Vc_predicted...
                < tolerance
            break;
        else
            Vc_predicted = Vc_corrected;
        end
    end
    % if we reached the iteration limit of 50, then print
    % warning:
    if j==50
```

```
        fprintf('Warning at step ');
        fprintf('%d: reached iteration limit\n',i);
    end
    Vc_mod_euler(i+1)=Vc_corrected;
end
% Plot results
subplot(1,2,1), plot(t,Vc_euler,'x',t,Vc_exact),
legend('Euler','Exact','Location','NorthWest');
title('Euler solution compared to exact');
xlabel('seconds'); ylabel('Vc (volts)');
text(0.006,0.005,sprintf('%d steps',steps));
subplot(1,2,2), plot(t,Vc_mod_euler,'x',t,Vc_exact),
legend('Modified Euler','Exact','Location','NorthWest');
title('Modified Euler solution compared to exact');
xlabel('seconds'), ylabel('Vc (volts)');
text(0.006,0.005,sprintf('%d steps',steps));
```

The resulting solutions for Example 6.1 are graphed in Figure 6.5. Note that for $N = 20$ subdivisions in the time domain, both the Euler and modified Euler solutions are almost indistinguishable from the exact solution.

Figure 6.6 shows the same example where we have increased the time step by reducing N to 6 (accomplished by changing `steps = 20` to `steps = 6` in the program). Note that in this case, the Euler solution deviates substantially from the exact solution and also oscillates above and below the exact solution. On the other hand, the solution for the modified Euler method remains accurate and stable even for small N. Ideally, we would like to reduce N to as small as possible (to reduce computation time), but at the same time we want to avoid numerical instability. Thus, the modified Euler method is a compromise that has some additional computational operations (due to the iterative predictor-corrector algorithm) but yet stays stable for large time steps.

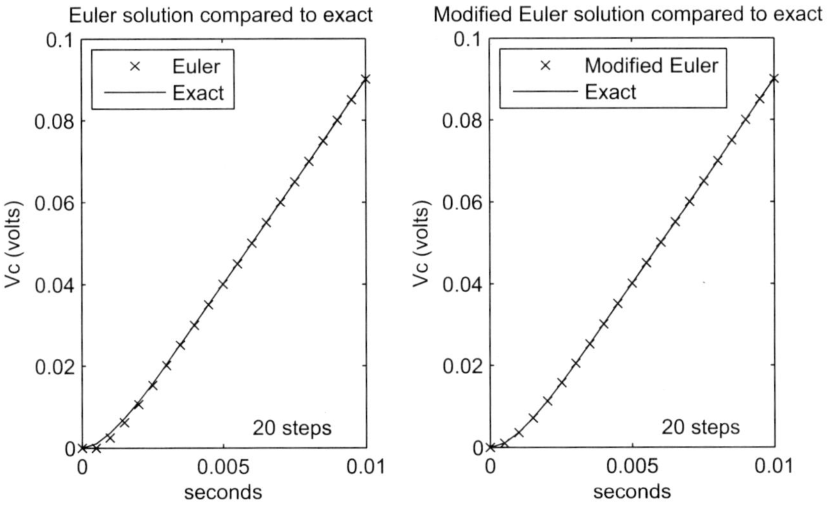

Figure 6.5 Plot of V_C versus t for RC circuit for 20 steps over the interval $0 \le t \le 10\tau$: (a) Euler and exact solutions; (b) modified Euler and exact solutions.

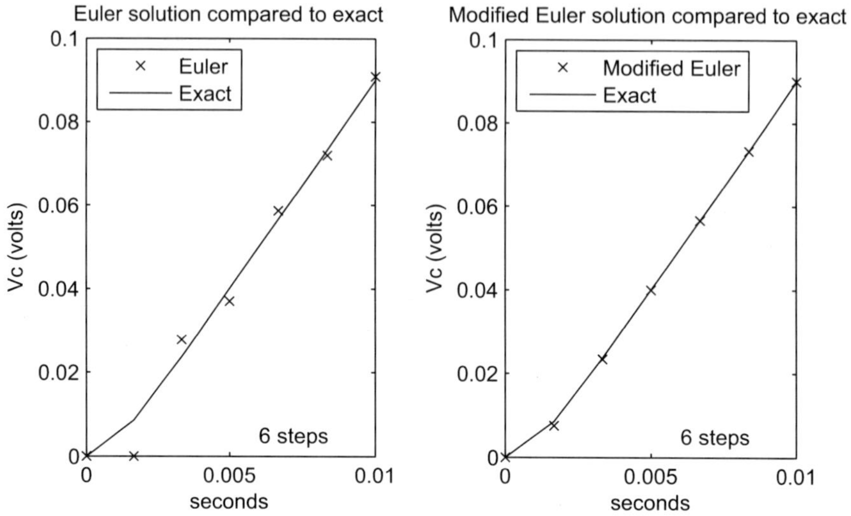

Figure 6.6 Plot of V_C versus t for RC circuit for six steps over the interval $0 \le t \le 10\tau$. (a) Euler and exact solutions. Note that the Euler solution oscillates. (b) Modified Euler and exact solutions. Note that the modified Euler method is stable even for a large step size.

6.5 Numerical Error for Euler Algorithms

Solutions to differential equations using the Euler and modified Euler algorithms are by definition an approximation to the exact solution because the derivations of these algorithms have their basis in a truncated Taylor series. If we wish to determine the accuracy of a particular numerical scheme, we can test it on a differential equation for which an exact solution is available. Unfortunately, in most cases, we do not know (or cannot solve for) the exact solution of the differential equation; this is usually why we resorted to a numerical method in the first place. However, in Example 6.1, we did derive the exact solution; thus, we can calculate the *global percentage error* $E_{i,\text{global}}$ for a given numerical algorithm at time step i as

$$E_{i,\text{global}} = \left| \frac{y_{i,\text{exact}} - y_{i,\text{numerical}}}{y_{i,\text{exact}}} \right| \tag{6.18}$$

An alternative measure of accuracy is the *local truncation error* (LTE), in which we calculate the higher-order terms of the Taylor series (or at least the first discarded term) and use it to decide whether we have chosen too large a time step. For example, in Equation (6.3), we discarded the second-order and higher terms in the Taylor series to derive the Euler method; thus, the LTE is

$$LTE_{\text{Euler}} = \frac{y_i''}{2}h^2 + \text{higher-order terms}$$

If we neglect the higher-order terms, then the truncation error is on the order of h^2, which is commonly written as $O(h^2)$. Qualitatively, this means that if we reduce the step size by a factor of two, then the LTE is reduced by approximately a factor of four, resulting in a more accurate solution.

In practice, the simplest method for choosing the step size is to start with some fraction of the fastest known parameter in the system. For example, when solving an RC circuit, start with a step size of 1/100 of the time constant, or $h = \frac{RC}{100}$. Then, double the step size and rerun the program. If the two solutions are identical, then the step size is sufficiently small, and if the program runs slowly, then you might consider redoubling your step size and comparing again to obtain a faster execution time without losing accuracy.

6.6 The Fourth-Order Runge-Kutta Method

The fourth-order Runge-Kutta method uses a weighted average of derivative estimates within the interval of interest to calculate a value for y_{i+1}. We again start with the first-order differential equation of Equation (6.1) with known initial conditions. In the modified Euler method, we used $y_{i+1} = y_i + \frac{h}{2}(y_i' + y_{i+1}')$. In the Runge-Kutta method, instead we use

$$y_{i+1} = y_i + \frac{h}{6}(k_1 + 2k_2 + 2k_3 + k_4) \tag{6.19}$$

where

$$k_1 = f(x_i, y_i) \qquad (\text{value of } y' \text{ at } x_i)$$

$$k_2 = f\left(x_i + \frac{h}{2}, y_i + \frac{h}{2}k_1\right) \qquad \left(\text{estimate of } y' \text{ at } x_i + \frac{h}{2}\right)$$

$$k_3 = f\left(x_i + \frac{h}{2}, y_i + \frac{h}{2}k_2\right) \qquad \left(\text{a second estimate of } y' \text{ at } x_i + \frac{h}{2}\right)$$

$$k_4 = f(x_i + h, y_i + hk_3) \qquad (\text{estimate of } y' \text{ at } x_{i+1})$$

Runge-Kutta is an explicit algorithm and thus is simple to compute with MATLAB.

Example 6.2

Solve the RC circuit of Example 6.1 using the Runge-Kutta method for N = 20 and N = 6 steps. Also, find the worst-case global error for each case. The MATLAB program follows:

```
% Example_6_2.m
% Calculate ramp response of RC circuit via two methods:
% 1. exact solution
% 2. Runge-Kutta method
clc; clear;
% circuit parameters
R=1e3;       % ohms
C=1e-6;      % farads
tau = R*C;   % seconds
Vo = 10;     % volts
f = @(tm,Vc) 1/tau*(Vo*tm-Vc);  % Equation 6.16
% parameters for Euler algorithm
interval = 10*tau;
steps = [20 6];
for j=1:length(steps)
    h = interval/steps(j);
    % create set of time points to calculate
    t = 0:h:interval;
    Vc_exact = zeros(length(t),1);
    Vc_RK = zeros(length(t),1);
    % initial conditions
    Vc_exact(1)=0;
    Vc_RK(1)=0;
    for i=1:length(t)-1
        % Calculate exact solution
        Vc_exact(i+1) = Vo ...
            * (t(i+1)-tau+tau*exp(-t(i+1)/tau));
        % Calculate Runge-Kutta solution
        k1=f(t(i),Vc_RK(i));
        k2=f(t(i)+h/2,Vc_RK(i)+h/2*k1);
        k3=f(t(i)+h/2,Vc_RK(i)+h/2*k2);
        k4=f(t(i+1),Vc_RK(i)+h*k3);
        Vc_RK(i+1)=Vc_RK(i)+h/6*(k1+2*k2+2*k3+k4);
    end
    % plot results
    subplot(1,length(steps),j)
    plot(t,Vc_RK,'x',t,Vc_exact),
    legend('Runge-Kutta','Exact','Location','NorthWest');
    title('Ramp Response for RC circuit');
    xlabel('seconds'), ylabel('Vc (volts)');
    text(0.005,0.005,sprintf('%d steps',steps(j)));
    % calculate global error
    global_error_RK = abs((Vc_exact -Vc_RK) ./ Vc_exact);
    fprintf('Worst case global percent error for ');
    fprintf('Runge-Kutta for %2d steps: %4.2f %%\n',...
        steps(j),100*max(global_error_RK));
end
------------------------------------------------------------
```

PROGRAM RESULTS

```
Worst case global percent error for Runge-Kutta for 20 steps: 0.23%
Worst case global percent error for Runge-Kutta for  6 steps: 9.73%
```

Note that the fewer the steps, the larger the corresponding global error. Results are plotted in Figure 6.7.

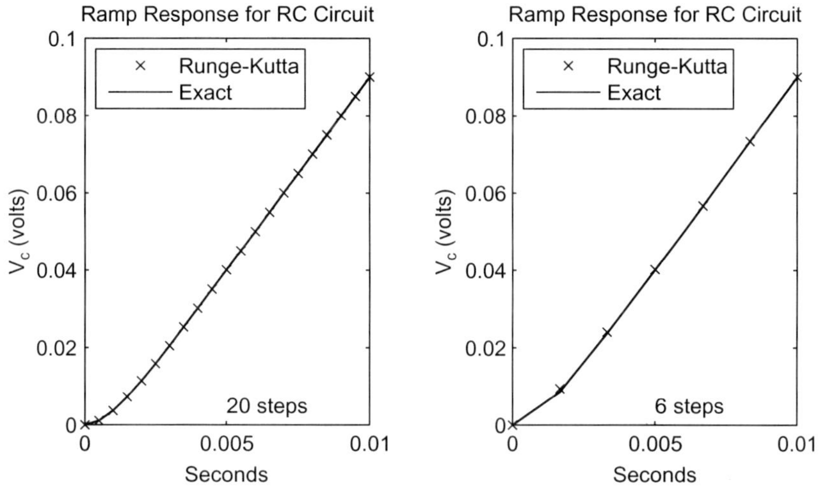

Figure 6.7 Plot of V_C versus t for RC circuit via Runge-Kutta method: (a) 20 steps; (b) 6 steps.

6.7 System of Two First-Order Differential Equations

Consider the following two first-order ODEs.

$$\begin{aligned} \frac{du}{dt} &= f(t,u,v); \qquad u(0) = u_0 \\ \frac{dv}{dt} &= g(t,u,v); \qquad v(0) = v_0 \end{aligned} \tag{6.20}$$

To solve a system of two first-order differential equations by the Runge-Kutta method, take

$$\begin{aligned} u_{i+1} &= u_i + \frac{h}{6}(k_1 + 2k_2 + 2k_3 + k_4) \\ v_{i+1} &= v_i + \frac{h}{6}(l_1 + 2l_2 + 2l_3 + l_4) \end{aligned} \tag{6.21}$$

where

$$
\begin{aligned}
k_1 &= f(t_i, u_i, v_i) && \text{(estimate of } u' \text{ at } t_i) \\
l_1 &= g(t_i, u_i, v_i) && \text{(estimate of } v' \text{ at } t_i) \\
k_2 &= f\left(t_i + \frac{h}{2},\, u_i + \frac{h}{2}k_1,\, v_i + \frac{h}{2}l_1\right) && \left(\text{first estimate of } u' \text{ at } t_i + \frac{h}{2}\right) \\
l_2 &= g\left(t_i + \frac{h}{2},\, u_i + \frac{h}{2}k_1,\, v_i + \frac{h}{2}l_1\right) && \left(\text{first estimate of } v' \text{ at } t_i + \frac{h}{2}\right) \\
k_3 &= f\left(t_i + \frac{h}{2},\, u_i + \frac{h}{2}k_2,\, v_i + \frac{h}{2}l_2\right) && \left(\text{second estimate of } u' \text{ at } t_i + \frac{h}{2}\right) \\
l_3 &= g\left(t_i + \frac{h}{2},\, u_i + \frac{h}{2}k_2,\, v_i + \frac{h}{2}l_2\right) && \left(\text{second estimate of } v' \text{ at } t_i + \frac{h}{2}\right) \\
k_4 &= f(t_i + h,\, u_i + hk_3,\, v_i + hl_3) && \text{(estimate of } u' \text{ at } t_i + h) \\
l_4 &= g(x_i + h,\, u_i + hk_3,\, v_i + hl_3) && \text{(estimate of } v' \text{ at } t_i + h)
\end{aligned}
\tag{6.22}
$$

and $h = \Delta t = t_{i+1} - t_i$.

Example 6.3

Solve the following system of first-order differential equations by the Runge-Kutta method over the interval $0 \le t \le 10$:

$$
\begin{aligned}
\frac{dr}{dt} &= 2re^{-0.1t} - 2ry = f(t,r,y) \\
\frac{dy}{dt} &= -y + ry = g(r,y)
\end{aligned}
\tag{6.23}
$$

Initial conditions: $r(0) = 1.0$, $y(0) = 3.0$.

```
% Example_6_3.m
% This program solves a system of 2 first order ordinary
% differential equations by the Runge-Kutta Method.
% First, define two functions to compute dr/dt and dy/dt:
rprime_func = @(t,r,y) 2.0*r*exp(-0.1*t) - 2.0*r*y;
yprime_func = @(r,y) -y + r*y;
% Open a file to write results:
fo=fopen('Example_6_3_output.txt','w');
fprintf(fo,'   t          r           y    \n');
fprintf(fo,'---------------------------\n');
% Define time interval and step size
tmax=10; steps=1000; h=tmax/steps;
% Initial conditions:
r(1)=1.0; y(1)=3.0; t(1)=0.0;
```

```
% Estimate of derivatives and marching in time.
for i=1:steps
    t(i+1)=i*h;
    K(1)=rprime_func(t(i),r(i),y(i));
    L(1)=yprime_func(r(i),y(i));
    K(2)=rprime_func(t(i)+h/2,r(i)+h/2*K(1),...
        y(i)+h/2*L(1));
    L(2)=yprime_func(r(i)+h/2*K(1),y(i)+h/2*L(1));
    K(3)=rprime_func(t(i)+h/2,r(i)+h/2*K(2),...
        y(i)+h/2*L(2));
    L(3)=yprime_func(r(i)+h/2*K(2),y(i)+h/2*L(2));
    K(4)=rprime_func(t(i)+h,r(i)+h*K(3),y(i)+h*L(3));
    L(4)=yprime_func(r(i)+h*K(3),y(i)+h*L(3));
    r(i+1)=r(i)+h/6*(K(1)+2*K(2)+2*K(3)+K(4));
    y(i+1)=y(i)+h/6*(L(1)+2*L(2)+2*L(3)+L(4));
    if mod(i-1,10)==0
       fprintf(fo,'%.2f %10.4f %10.4f\n',t(i),r(i),y(i));
    end
end
fclose(fo);
plot(t,r,t,y,'--'), xlabel('t'), ylabel('r,y');
grid, legend('r','y');
title('Runge-Kutta Solution For 2nd-Order System');
```

PROGRAM OUTPUT

The resulting MATLAB plot is shown in Figure 6.8.

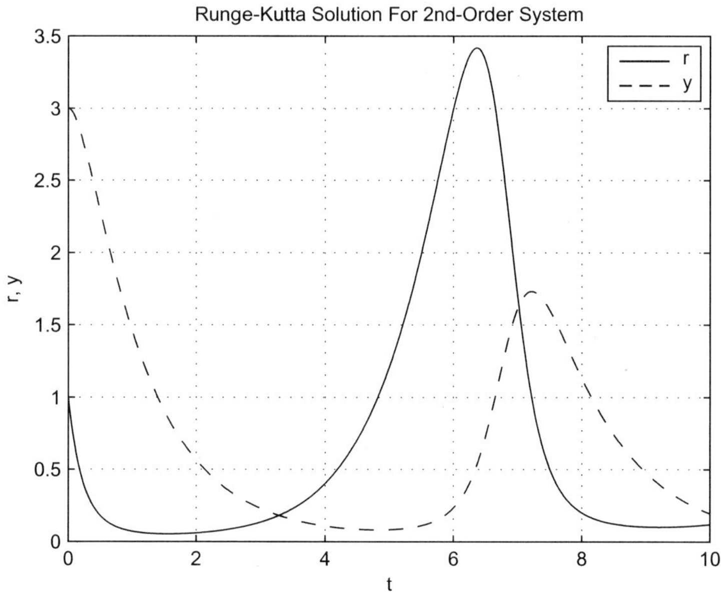

Figure 6.8 Solution of two first-order differential equations by the Runge-Kutta method.

6.8 A Single Second-Order Equation

For a single second-order ODE, the method of solution is to reduce the equation to a system of two first-order equations. Given the following second-order differential equation with initial conditions

$$u'' = \frac{d^2u}{dt^2} = f(t,u,u') \qquad\qquad (6.24)$$
$$u(0) = u_0 \quad \text{and} \quad u'(0) = u_0'$$

Let $u' = v$, then $u'' = \dfrac{dv}{dt} = v' = f(t,u,v)$. Also, $u' = g(t,u,v) = v$, giving

$$u' = v \qquad\qquad (6.25)$$
$$v' = f(t,u,v)$$

Thus, we have converted Equations (6.24) into two first-order differential equations of the same form as Equations (6.20); thus, the same solution techniques can be applied, that is,

$$k_1 = f(t_i, u_i, v_i) \qquad (v' \text{ at } t_i)$$

$$l_1 = u'(t_i) = v_i \qquad (u' \text{ at } t_i)$$

$$k_2 = f\left(t_i + \frac{h}{2},\, u_i + \frac{h}{2}l_1,\, v_i + \frac{h}{2}k_1\right) \qquad \left(\text{first estimate of } v' \text{ at } t_i + \frac{h}{2}\right)$$

$$l_2 = u'\left(t_i + \frac{h}{2}\right) = v_i + \frac{h}{2}k_1 \qquad \left(\text{first estimate of } u' \text{ at } t_i + \frac{h}{2}\right)$$

$$k_3 = f\left(t_i + \frac{h}{2},\, u_i + \frac{h}{2}l_2,\, v_i + \frac{h}{2}k_2\right) \qquad \left(\text{second estimate of } v' \text{ at } t_i + \frac{h}{2}\right)$$

$$l_3 = u'\left(t_i + \frac{h}{2}\right) = v_i + \frac{h}{2}k_2 \qquad \left(\text{second estimate of } u' \text{ at } t_i + \frac{h}{2}\right)$$

$$k_4 = f(t_i + h,\, u_i + h\,l_3,\, v_i + h\,k_3) \qquad (\text{estimate of } v' \text{ at } t_i + h)$$

$$l_4 = u'(t_i + h) = v_i + h\,k_3 \qquad (\text{estimate of } u' \text{ at } t_i + h)$$

The values of u and v at the next time step are given by

$$u_{i+1} = u_i + \frac{h}{6}\left(l_1 + 2l_2 + 2l_3 + l_4\right)$$

$$v_{i+1} = v_i + \frac{h}{6}\left(k_1 + 2k_2 + 2k_3 + k_4\right)$$

Example 6.4

We illustrate this method by applying it to the series RLC circuit of Appendix A. Equation (A.6) gives the capacitor voltage v_C (with no driving voltage) as

$$\frac{d^2v_C}{dt^2} + \frac{R}{L}\frac{dv_C}{dt} + \frac{1}{LC}v_C = 0$$

We wish to solve for v_C for the component values $R = 10\ \Omega$, $L = 1$ mH, $C = 2\ \mu$F, and initial conditions $v_C(0) = 10$ and $\frac{dv_C}{dt}(0) = \frac{6}{\sqrt{LC}}$.

We first reduce this single second-order differential equation into two first-order equations.

Let $\frac{dv_C}{dt} = v_2$. Then, the two coupled equations are

$$\frac{dv_C}{dt} = v_2$$

$$\frac{dv_2}{dt} = \frac{d^2v_C}{dt^2} = -\frac{1}{LC}v_C - \frac{R}{L}v_2$$

Assuming an underdamped system, the exact solution has the form

$$v_C = \exp\left(-\frac{R}{2L}t\right)\left\{\alpha\cos\left(\sqrt{\frac{1}{LC}-\left(\frac{R}{2L}\right)^2}\,t\right) + \beta\sin\left(\sqrt{\frac{1}{LC}-\left(\frac{R}{2L}\right)^2}\,t\right)\right\}$$

For the given initial conditions, $\alpha = 0$ and $\beta = \frac{\frac{dv_C}{dt}(0)}{\sqrt{\frac{1}{LC}-\left(\frac{R}{2L}\right)^2}}$.

The program follows:

```
% Example_6_4.m
% This program solves a single second order ordinary
% differential equation by the Runge-Kutta Method.  The
% differential equation describes the capacitor voltage
% in a series RLC circuit
clear; clc;
% Component values:
R=10; L=1.0e-3; C=2.0e-6;
% Initial conditions:
vc(1)=0; v2(1)=6* sqrt(1/(L*C));
% Define time interval and step size.  Since the natural
% frequency sqrt(1/LC) is 3559 Hz, choose a time interval
% to capture several oscillations. 3559 Hz has period of
% 281 usec, so choose 1000 usec for interval.
tmax=1000e-6; steps=100; h=tmax/steps;
t=0:h:tmax;
% Define v2' = f(t,x,y):
v2_prime = @(t,x,y) -(1/(L*C))*x - (R/L)*y;
% Do Runge-Kutta algorithm:
for i=1:steps
    K1=v2_prime(t(i), vc(i), v2(i));
    L1=v2(i);
    K2=v2_prime(t(i), vc(i)+h/2*L1, v2(i)+h/2*K1);
    L2=v2(i)+h/2*K1;
    K3=v2_prime(t(i), vc(i)+h/2*L2, v2(i)+h/2*K2);
    L3=v2(i)+h/2*K2;
    K4=v2_prime(t(i), vc(i)+h*L3, v2(i)+h*K3);
    L4=v2(i)+h*K3;
    vc(i+1)=vc(i)+h/6*(L1+2*L2+2*L3+L4);
    v2(i+1)=v2(i)+h/6*(K1+2*K2+2*K3+K4);
end
% Calculate exact solution
beta = v2(1) / sqrt( 1/(L*C) - (R/(2*L))^2);
vc_exact = exp(-R/(2*L) * t)* beta ...
    .* sin(sqrt( 1/(L*C) - (R/(2*L))^2)*t );
% Print results to screen.
fprintf('Runge-Kutta solution for a single ');
fprintf('second order ODE:\n\n');
fprintf('    t        R-K Sol''n   Exact Sol''n\n');
fprintf('-------------------------------------\n');
for i=1:10:steps+1  % just print every tenth step
    fprintf('%10.3e  %8.4f   %8.4f \n', ...
        t(i),vc(i), vc_exact(i));
end
% Plot results:
plot(t,vc_exact,t,vc,'x');
xlabel('t (seconds)'), ylabel('volts');
title('Capacitor voltage of series RLC circuit');
legend('Exact','Runge-Kutta');
```

A comparison of the Runge-Kutta solution with the exact solution is shown in Figure 6.9.

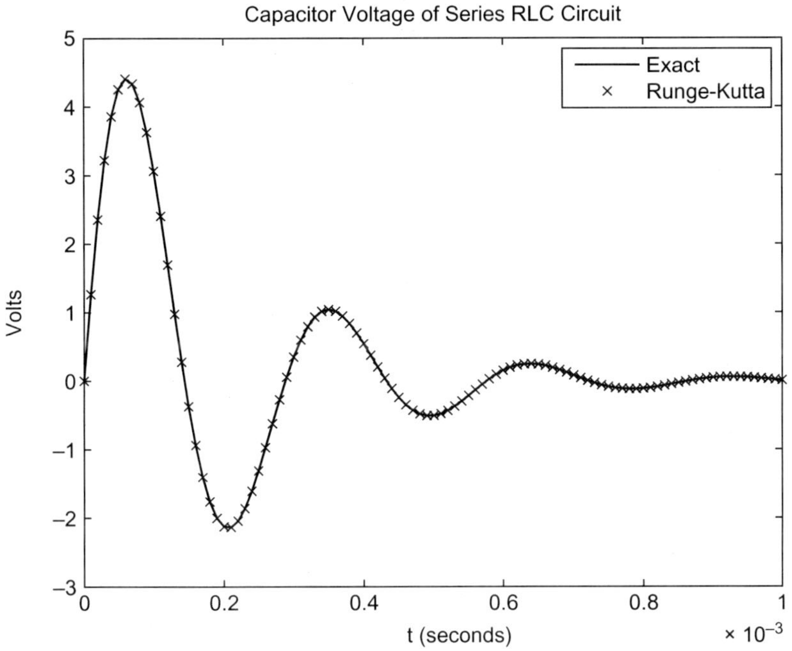

Figure 6.9 Solution of a single second-order differential equation by the Runge-Kutta method.

6.9 MATLAB's ODE Function

MATLAB has several built-in ODE functions that solve a system of first-order ODEs, including ode23 and ode45. In this chapter, we demonstrate ode45, which is based on fourth- and fifth-order Runge-Kutta methods. A description of the ode45 function follows (this description can be obtained by typing **help ode45** in the Command window):

```
ODE45 Solve non-stiff differential equations, medium order method.
    [TOUT,YOUT] = ODE45(ODEFUN,TSPAN,Y0) with TSPAN = [T0
    TFINAL] integrates the system of differential equations y' =
    f(t,y) from time T0 to TFINAL with initial conditions Y0.
    ODEFUN is a function handle. For a scalar T and a vector Y,
    ODEFUN(T,Y) must return a column vector corresponding to
    f(t,y). Each row in the solution array YOUT corresponds to
    a time returned in the column vector TOUT. To obtain
    solutions at specific times T0,T1,...,TFINAL (all
    increasing or all decreasing), use TSPAN = [T0 T1...
    TFINAL].
```

Thus, ode45 takes as arguments a handle to a function describing the differential equations (ODEFUN), a vector describing a time interval (TSPAN), and a vector describing the initial conditions (Y0). The function ODEFUN must take two arguments: a time t and a vector of values $y_1, y_2, \ldots, y_n$, to be passed to the differential equations. The system of n differential equations must be in standard form, that is, n equations of the form $y_n' = f(t, y_1, y_2, \ldots, y_n)$. ODEFUN must return a vector of derivatives of the form $y_1', y_2', \ldots, y_n'$. The time interval TSPAN is typically a two-element vector containing a start and end time; ode45 will automatically choose an appropriate time step (and might even vary the time step within the interval). ode45 will return two vectors: a list of timepoints TOUT and the solution YOUT at each timepoint. If you want to force ode45 to solve the system at specific timepoints, then you can explicitly specify the timepoints in TSPAN (instead of just the start and end timepoints).

Example 6.5

Solve the following system of three first-order differential equations using MATLAB's ode45 function:

$$y_1' = y_2 y_3 t$$

$$y_2' = -y_1 y_3$$

$$y_3' = -0.51 y_1 y_2$$

Initial conditions: $y_1(0) = 0$, $y_2(0) = 1.0$, and $y_3(t) = 1.0$.

```
% Example_6_5.m
% This program solves a system of 3 ordinary differential
% equations by using MATLAB's ode45 function.
% y1'=y2*y3*t, y2'=-y1*y3, y3'=-0.51*y1*y2
% y1(0)=0, y2(0)=1.0, y3(0)=1.0
clear; clc;
initial=[0.0 1.0 1.0];
tspan=0.0:0.1:10.0;
[t,Y]=ode45(@dydt3,tspan,initial);
y1=Y(:,1);
y2=Y(:,2);
y3=Y(:,3);
fid=fopen('output.txt','w');
fprintf(fid,'    t          y1          y2          y3    \n');
fprintf(fid,'-------------------------------------------\n');
for i=1:2:101
    fprintf(fid,'%6.2f  %8.4f  %8.4f  %8.4f \n', ...
        t(i),y1(i),y2(i),y3(i));
end
fclose(fid);
plot(t,y1,t,y2,'-.',t,y3,'--');
xlabel('t'), ylabel('y1,y2,y3');
title('(y1, y2, y3) vs. t'), grid;
```

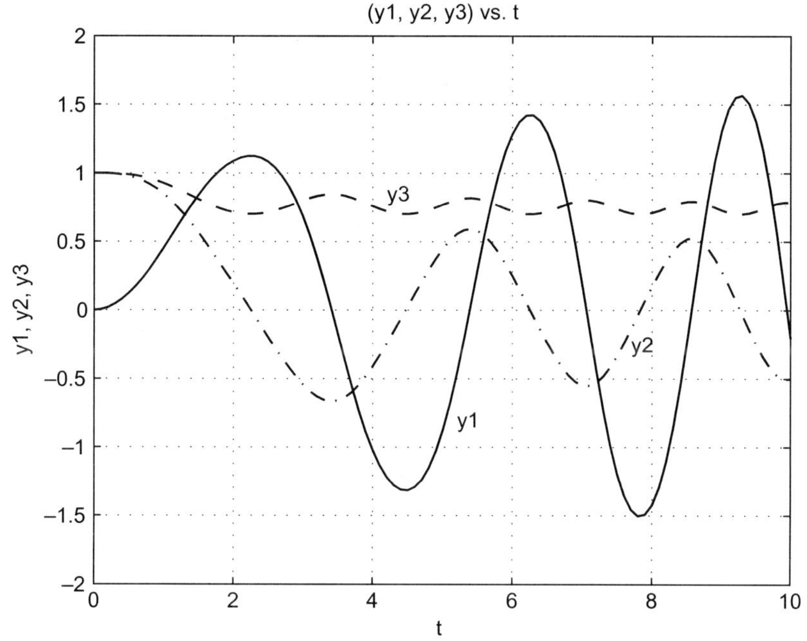

Figure 6.10 Solution of three differential equations by MATLAB's `ode45` function.

```
text(5.2,-0.8,'y1'), text(7.7,-0.25,'y2');
text(4.2,0.85,'y3');
```

```
--------------------------------------------------------------------------

% dydt3.m
% This function works with Example_6_5.m
% y1'=y2*y3*t, y2'=-y1*y3, y3'=-0.51*y1*y2
% y1=Y(1), y2=Y(2), y3=Y(3).
function Yprime=dydt3(t,Y)
Yprime=zeros(3,1);
Yprime(1)=Y(2)*Y(3)*t;
Yprime(2)=-Y(1)*Y(3);
Yprime(3)=-0.51*Y(1)*Y(2);
```

PROGRAM RESULTS

The calculated solutions for y_1, y_2, and y_3 are shown in Figure 6.10.

Example 6.6

Solve the parallel RLC circuit of Section 2.17 using MATLAB's `ode45` function. Assume $R = 50\,\Omega$, $L = 1\,\mu\text{H}$, $C = 10\,\text{nF}$, $v(0) = 3.3\,\text{V}$, $i_L(0) = 0\,\text{A}$. Plot the results for $0 \le t \le 4$ μsec.

```
% Example_6_6.m
% Solve a system of two first-order ordinary differential
% equations (Equations 2.6 and 2.7).
% Assume: y(1)=v and y(2)=iL
% Assume: R=50, L=1e-6, C=10e-9, v(t=0)=3.3, i(t=0)=0.
% Equation 2.6: yprime(2) = (1/L)*y(1)
% Equation 2.7: yprime(1) = -1/(R*C)*y(1) - (1/C)*y(2)
clear; clc;
initial=[3.3 0];
tspan=0:.01e-6:4e-6;
[ t,y ] = ode45('dydt_rlc',tspan,initial);
v = y(:,1);
iL = y(:,2);
fprintf('      t                  v            iL    \n');
fprintf('--------------------------------------\n');
% print every tenth value of v and iL
for i=1:10:length(t)
    fprintf(' %1.10f   %10.4f   %10.4f  \n', ...
        t(i),v(i),iL(i));
end
% Plot v and iL together.  Use plotyy() to create a
% second 'y' axis on the right side.  plotyy() returns
% graphics handles to the axes and lines so that their
% style can be adjusted.
[ axis,line1,line2 ] = plotyy(t,v,t,iL);
xlabel('t'), ylabel('v (volts)');
title('v and iL vs. t'), grid;
% set label for right 'y' axis
set(get(axis(2),'Ylabel'),'String','i_L (amps)');
% plot iL with a dashed line
set(line2,'LineStyle','--');
legend('v','i_L');

-------------------------------------------------------------

% dydt_rlc.m
% This function works with Example_6_6.m
% Assume: v=y(1) and iL=y(2)
function yprime = dydt_rlc(t,y)
yprime=zeros(2,1);
R=50; L=1e-6; C=10e-9;
yprime(1) = -1/(R*C)*y(1) - 1/C*y(2);
yprime(2) = (1/L)*y(1);
```

PROGRAM RESULTS

The results are plotted in Figure 6.11. Note the complementary nature of $v(t)$ and $i_L(t)$ such that when either is zero, the other is always near a maximum. This behavior demonstrates how the energy in the RLC circuit oscillates back and forth between the capacitor and inductor.

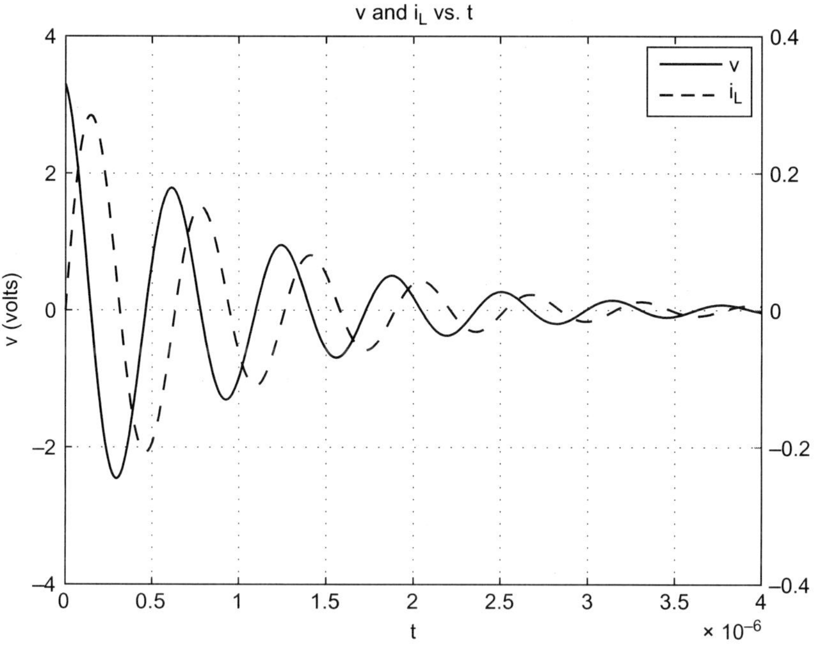

Figure 6.11 Solution of RLC circuit with the `ode45` function.

6.10 Boundary Value Problems

When an ODE involves boundary conditions instead of initial conditions, then we use a different approach to solve the problem. In a boundary value problem, we essentially need to "fit" a solution into the known boundary conditions as opposed to simply integrating from the initial conditions. An example of this type of problem is to determine the electric field between the plates of a capacitor with a known charge density between the plates and a fixed voltage across the plates. The fixed voltage is the boundary condition, and the solution may be found by numerically solving a second-order, nonhomogeneous ODE using *finite difference formulas*. With certain types of boundary conditions, the numerical method will reduce to solving a set of linear equations that fall into the category of a tri-diagonal matrix. The solution of a set of linear algebraic equations that are classified as a tri-diagonal system involves fewer calculations than the solution by the Gauss elimination method described in Chapter 3, which is important if the system of equations is large. The solution of a tri-diagonal system is discussed next.

6.11 Solution of a Tri-Diagonal System of Linear Equations

A *tri-diagonal* system of equations has the following form:

$$\begin{bmatrix} 1 & -a_1 & 0 & 0 & 0 \\ -b_2 & 1 & -a_2 & 0 & 0 \\ 0 & -b_3 & 1 & -a_3 & 0 \\ 0 & 0 & -b_4 & 1 & -a_4 \\ 0 & 0 & 0 & -b_5 & 1 \end{bmatrix} \begin{bmatrix} x_1 \\ x_2 \\ x_3 \\ x_4 \\ x_5 \end{bmatrix} = \begin{bmatrix} c_1 \\ c_2 \\ c_3 \\ c_4 \\ c_5 \end{bmatrix} \tag{6.26}$$

where a_i, b_i, and c_i are constant terms, and x_i are the unknowns. The term *tri-diagonal* refers to the fact that the elements of the coefficient matrix on the left side of Equation (6.26) is nonzero for the main diagonal and the diagonals immediately above and below the main diagonal. Aside from the three diagonals, the rest of the elements in the coefficient matrix are all zero. By multiplying out the matrices in Equation (6.26), the set of equations for this fifth-order system becomes

$$x_1 - a_1 x_2 = c_1 \tag{6.27}$$

$$-b_2 x_1 + x_2 - a_2 x_3 = c_2 \tag{6.28}$$

$$-b_3 x_2 + x_3 - a_3 x_4 = c_3 \tag{6.29}$$

$$-b_4 x_3 + x_4 - a_4 x_5 = c_4 \tag{6.30}$$

$$-b_5 x_4 + x_5 = c_5 \tag{6.31}$$

The general concept for solving a tri-diagonal system is as follows:

We can solve Equation (6.27) for x_1 and substitute the result into Equation (6.28), giving an equation involving only x_2 and x_3, which we designate as Equation (6.28′).

We can then solve Equation (6.28′) for the x_2 in terms of x_3 and substitute the result into Equation (6.29). This gives an equation only involving x_3 and x_4, which we designate as Equation (6.29′).

This process is continued until the last equation. When x_4 is substituted into Equation (6.31), an equation only involving x_5 is obtained, thus allowing us to solve algebraically for x_5.

Then, by back substitution, we can obtain all the other x_i values.

Method Summary for m equations

Arrange the set of equations into the general form

$$x_i = a_i x_{i+1} + b_i x_{i-1} + c_i \tag{6.32}$$

Note: for the first and last equations (corresponding to the upper-left and lower-right coefficients in the tri-diagonal matrix), $b_1 = 0$ and $a_m = 0$.

By the substitution procedure outlined, we can obtain a set of equations of the form

$$x_i = d_i + e_i x_{i+1} \tag{6.33}$$

where d_i and e_i are the coefficients for the "prime" equations. Note that $e_m = 0$.

Then,

$$\begin{aligned} x_m &= d_m \\ x_{m-1} &= d_{m-1} + e_{m-1} x_m \\ &\vdots \\ x_1 &= d_1 + e_1 x_2 \end{aligned} \tag{6.34}$$

If general expressions for d_i and e_i can be obtained, then we can solve the system for all x_i.

We start by rewriting Equation (6.33) to put the $(i-1)$th equation into the form

$$x_{i-1} = d_{i-1} + e_{i-1} x_i \tag{6.35}$$

Substituting Equation (6.35) in (6.32) gives

$$x_i = a_i x_{i+1} + b_i (d_{i-1} + e_{i-1} x_i) + c_i$$

Solving for x_i gives

$$x_i = \frac{(c_i + b_i d_{i-1})}{(1 - b_i e_{i-1})} + \frac{a_i x_{i+1}}{(1 - b_i e_{i-1})} \tag{6.36}$$

Matching terms between Equations (6.36) and (6.33), we obtain

$$\begin{aligned} d_i &= \frac{c_i + b_i d_{i-1}}{1 - b_i e_{i-1}} \\ e_i &= \frac{a_i}{1 - b_i e_{i-1}} \end{aligned} \tag{6.37}$$

which is valid for $i = 2, 3, \ldots, m$.

The very first equation in the system is already in the form $x_i = d_i + e_i x_{i-1}$; thus, matching terms between Equations (6.27) and (6.33), we obtain

$$\begin{aligned} d_1 &= c_1 \\ e_1 &= a_1 \end{aligned} \tag{6.38}$$

We can now successively apply Equation (6.37) to find $d_2, d_3, \ldots, d_m$ and $e_2, e_3, \ldots, e_m$.

Then, $x_m = d_m$, and by back substitution

$$\begin{aligned} x_{m-1} &= d_{m-1} + e_{m-1} x_m \\ x_{m-2} &= d_{m-2} + e_{m-2} x_{m-1} \\ &\vdots \\ x_1 &= d_1 + e_1 x_2 \end{aligned}$$

Example 6.7

Solve the following system of equations for all x_i:

$$\begin{array}{cccccccc} x_1 & +2x_2 & & & & & = & 7 \\ 4x_1 & +3x_2 & +14x_3 & & & & = & -9 \\ & 11x_2 & +x_3 & -6x_4 & & & = & 3 \\ & & -3x_3 & +2x_4 & +31x_5 & & = & 1 \\ & & & 4x_4 & +x_5 & -8x_6 & = & -19 \\ & & & & 20x_5 & +x_6 & = & 11 \end{array} \qquad \begin{array}{c} (6.39) \\ (6.40) \\ (6.41) \\ (6.42) \\ (6.43) \\ (6.44) \end{array}$$

First, we need to put the equations in the form of Equation (6.32), which is

$$x_i = a_i x_{i+1} + b_i x_{i-1} + c_i$$

This gives

$$x_1 = -2x_2 + 7$$

$$x_2 = -\frac{14}{3}x_3 - \frac{4}{3}x_1 - \frac{9}{3}$$

$$x_3 = 6x_4 - 11x_2 + 3$$

$$x_4 = -\frac{31}{2}x_5 + \frac{3}{2}x_3 + \frac{1}{2}$$

$$x_5 = 8x_6 - 4x_4 - 19$$

$$x_6 = -20x_5 + 11$$

We see that

$$a = \begin{bmatrix} -2 & -14/3 & 6 & -31/2 & 8 & 0 \end{bmatrix}$$

$$b = \begin{bmatrix} 0 & -4/3 & -11 & 3/2 & -4 & -20 \end{bmatrix}$$

$$c = \begin{bmatrix} 7 & -3 & 3 & 1/2 & -19 & 11 \end{bmatrix}$$

A MATLAB program to solve Equations (6.39)–(6.44) for all x_i follows:

```
% Example_6_7.m
% Example of solving a tri-diagonal system of equations
a = [-2   -14/3   6   -31/2   8     0];
b = [0    -4/3   -11   3/2   -4   -20];
c = [7     -3     3    1/2   -19   11];
m = length(a);
% Compute d and e coefficients:
d(1)=c(1);
e(1)=a(1);
for i=2:m
    d(i) = (c(i) + b(i)*d(i-1)) / (1 - b(i)*e(i-1));
    e(i) = a(i) / (1 - b(i)*e(i-1));
end
% Compute x:
x(m)=d(m);
for i=(m-1):-1:1
    x(i) = d(i) + e(i)*x(i+1);
end
% Display the solution:
x
```

PROGRAM RESULTS

```
x =
    37.3362 -15.1681 -8.0600 -29.6515 1.1653 -12.3051
```

Note that the example contains only arithmetic operations and no expensive matrix operations (e.g., solving by Gauss elimination or finding an inverse matrix). Thus, the algorithm will be extremely fast, even for systems with many equations (e.g., order of m = 1000 or more).

6.12 Difference Formulas

To solve a boundary value problem involving an ordinary, linear differential equation numerically, we need the difference formulas obtained by Taylor series expansion. This will enable us to reduce differential equations to a set of algebraic equations. As we saw in Section 6.3, we can expand $y = g(x)$ in a Taylor series expansion about point x_i, that is,

$$y(x) = y(x_i) + y'(x_i)(x_i - x) + \frac{y''(x_i)}{2!}(x_i - x)^2 + \frac{y'''(x_i)}{3!}(x_i - x)^3 + \cdots$$

We define the step size $h = x_i - x$, which gives

$$y(x_i + h) = y(x_i) + y'(x_i)h + \frac{y''(x_i)}{2!}h^2 + \frac{y'''(x_i)}{3!}h^3 + \cdots$$

Let $y(x_i + h) = y_{i+1}$ and $y(x_i) = y_i$, $y'(x_i) = y_i'$, and so on. Then, the Taylor series expansion equation can be written as

$$y_{i+1} = y_i + y_i' h + \frac{y_i'' h^2}{2!} + \frac{y_i''' h^3}{3!} + \cdots \tag{6.45}$$

We now rewrite Equation (6.45) for the point $x = x_i - h$, that is, the equidistant point on the other side of x_i. This gives

$$y(x_i - h) = y_{i-1} = y_i + y_i'(-h) + \frac{y_i''}{2!}(-h)^2 + \frac{y_i'''}{3!}(-h)^3 + \cdots$$

or

$$y_{i-1} = y_i - y_i' h + \frac{y_i'' h^2}{2!} - \frac{y_i''' h^3}{3!} + \cdots - \cdots \tag{6.46}$$

We use Equations (6.45) and (6.46) to derive several difference formulas. We start by using the first two terms of Equation (6.45):

$$y_{i+1} = y_i + y_i' h$$

Solving for y_i' gives

$$y_i' = \frac{y_{i+1} - y_i}{h} \tag{6.47}$$

This is the forward difference formula for y_i' with error of order h. Similarly, from Equation (6.46), using the first two terms in the expansion gives

$$y_i' = \frac{y_i - y_{i-1}}{h} \tag{6.48}$$

This is the backward difference formula for y_i' with error of order h.

Now, let us subtract Equation (6.46) from Equation (6.45) and keep the first three terms in each equation. This gives

$$y_{i+1} - y_{i-1} = 2y_i'h$$

Solving for y_i' gives

$$y_i' = \frac{y_{i+1} - y_{i-1}}{2h} \tag{6.49}$$

This is the central difference formula for y_i' with an error of order h^2 (the error is order h^2 because three terms in the Taylor series were used to obtain the formula). If we add Equations (6.45) and (6.46) and keep the first three terms in each equation, we obtain

$$y_{i+1} + y_{i-1} = 2y_i + y_i''h^2$$

Solving for y_i'' gives

$$y_i'' = \frac{y_{i+1} + y_{i-1} - 2y_i}{h^2} \tag{6.50}$$

This is the central difference formula for y_i'' with error of order h^2.

The four difference formulas derived are summarized in Table 6.1. We now show how they are applied to model a boundary value problem that leads to a tri-diagonal system of linear equations.

Table 6.1 Summary of Finite Difference Formulas for Boundary Value Problems

$y_i' = \frac{y_{i+1} - y_i}{h}$	First-order forward difference formula. Used for y' boundary condition at beginning of the domain.
$y_i' = \frac{y_i - y_{i-1}}{h}$	First-order backward difference formula. Used for y' boundary condition at end of the domain.
$y_i' = \frac{y_{i+1} - y_{i-1}}{2h}$	First-order central difference formula. Used for first-order differential equation at interior points.
$y_i'' = \frac{y_{i+1} + y_{i-1} - 2y_i}{h^2}$	Second-order central difference formula. Used for second-order differential equation at interior points.

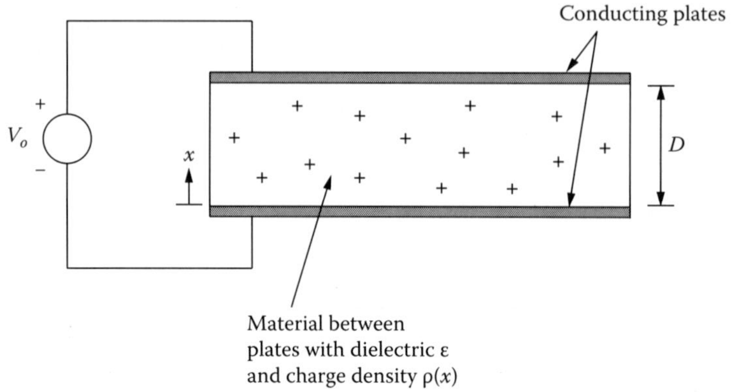

Figure 6.12 Parallel plate capacitor with plate separation of *D* meters and fixed charged density ρ(x) C/m³ between the plates.

6.13 One-Dimensional Plate Capacitor Problem

Figure 6.12 shows a parallel plate capacitor with constant applied voltage V_o and a fixed charge density ρ between the plates. For cases with planar symmetry such as the parallel plate capacitor for which the charge density only changes in the *x* direction (i.e., there is no *y* or *z* dependency), then Poisson's equation describing the electric potential Φ reduces to an ODE:

$$\frac{d^2\Phi(x)}{dx^2} = \frac{-\rho(x)}{\varepsilon} \tag{6.51}$$

where $\Phi(x)$ is the electric potential (in volts), $\rho(x)$ is the *x*-dependent charge density (in C/m³), and ε is the dielectric constant for the material between the plates.

Example 6.8

Solve for $\Phi(x)$ between the plates of the capacitor of Figure 6.12 with a plate separation of *D* meters, $\rho(x) = \rho_o(x - D)^2$, and boundary conditions $\Phi(0) = 0$ and $\Phi(D) = V_o$.

Substituting the expression for $\rho(x)$ into Equation (6.51), we obtain

$$\frac{d^2\Phi}{dx^2} = \frac{-\rho_o}{\varepsilon}(x - D)^2 = \frac{-\rho_o}{\varepsilon}(x^2 - 2Dx + D^2) \tag{6.52}$$

As we did for the RC circuit in this chapter, we solve Equation (6.52) using both classical and numerical techniques and then compare the solutions. We can solve this simple differential equation by integrating twice on both sides, giving

$$\Phi(x) = \frac{-\rho_o}{\varepsilon}\left(\frac{1}{12}x^4 - \frac{D}{3}x^3 + \frac{D^2}{2}x^2 + \alpha x + \beta\right) \tag{6.53}$$

where α and β are constants of integration that are determined by applying the boundary conditions. Applying the first boundary condition $\Phi(0) = 0$ gives

$$0 = \frac{-\rho_o}{\varepsilon}\left(\frac{1}{12}0^4 - \frac{D}{3}0^3 + \frac{D^2}{2}0^2 + \alpha 0 + \beta\right)$$

Thus, $\beta = 0$.

For the second boundary condition $\Phi(D) = V_o$, we get

$$V_o = \frac{-\rho_o}{\varepsilon}\left(\frac{1}{12}D^4 - \frac{D^3}{3}D^3 + \frac{D^2}{2}d^2 + \alpha D\right)$$

Solving for α gives

$$\alpha = \frac{-\varepsilon V_o}{D\rho_o} - \frac{D^3}{4}$$

Thus, the exact solution to Equation (6.52) is

$$\Phi(x) = \frac{-\rho_o}{\varepsilon}\left[\frac{1}{12}x^4 - \frac{D}{3}x^3 + \frac{D^2}{2}x^2 - \left(\frac{\varepsilon V_o}{D\rho_o} + \frac{D^3}{4}\right)x\right] \tag{6.54}$$

To solve Equation (6.52) numerically, we subdivide the region between the plates into N intervals and apply the finite difference formulas of Table 6.1. Dividing the region $0 \le x \le D$ into N intervals will result in $N + 1$ values for x and thus $N + 1$ values for Φ. Our goal is to determine the coefficients in an $(N + 1) \times (N + 1)$ tri-diagonal matrix.

We begin by applying the second-order central difference formula from Table 6.1 to Equation (6.52), giving

$$\Phi_i'' = \frac{\Phi_{i+1} + \Phi_{i-1} - 2\Phi_i}{h^2} = \frac{-\rho_o}{\varepsilon}\left(x_i^2 - 2Dx_i + D^2\right)$$

Solving for Φ_i gives

$$\Phi_i = \frac{1}{2}\Phi_{i+1} + \frac{1}{2}\Phi_{i-1} + \frac{\rho_o h^2}{2\varepsilon}\left(x_i^2 - 2Dx_i + D^2\right) \tag{6.55}$$

This equation is valid for $i = 2, 3, 4, \ldots, N$. Note that Equation (6.55) is in the same general form as Equation (6.32). We can identify the elements of a tri-diagonal matrix as

$$a_i = \frac{1}{2}, \quad b_i = \frac{1}{2}, \quad c_i = \frac{\rho_o h^2}{2\varepsilon}\left(x_i^2 - 2Dx_i + D^2\right)$$

We now use the boundary conditions to determine the values for the upper-left and lower-right corners of the coefficient matrix. First, we rewrite the boundary conditions as

$$\Phi(0) = 0 \quad \rightarrow \quad \Phi_1 = 0 \tag{6.56}$$

$$\Phi(D) = V_o \quad \rightarrow \quad \Phi_{N+1} = V_o \tag{6.57}$$

Equation (6.56) gives

$$a_1 = b_1 = c_1 = 0$$

Equation (6.57) gives

$$a_{N+1} = 0, \quad b_{N+1} = 0, \quad c_{N+1} = V_o$$

A MATLAB program to solve Equation (6.51) numerically follows:

```
% Example_6_8.m
% Find the electric potential between a parallel plate
% capacitor with fixed charge density between the plates
% and known boundary conditions.
clc; clear;
N=40;                    % step count
D=.0004;                 % plate separation (meters)
h=D/N;                   % step size
rho_o=1e4;               % coulomb/m^3
epsilon = 1.04e-12;      % dielectric between the plates
Vo=5;                    % voltage across plates
% First, calculate all values of x.  Also calculate
% the exact solution.
x = 0:h:D;
% Calculate exact solution (Equation 6.54)
phi_exact = (-rho_o/epsilon)* (x.^4/12 - (D/3)*x.^3 ...
    + (D^2/2)*x.^2 - ((epsilon*Vo/(D*rho_o))+(D^3/4))*x);
% Next, solve numerically using a tri-diagonal matrix.
% Define 'a', 'b', and 'c' vectors:
a = .5 * ones(1,N+1);
b = .5 * ones(1,N+1);
c = (rho_o*h^2/(2*epsilon))*( x.^2 - 2*D*x +D^2);
% Set boundary conditions for 'a', 'b', and 'c' vectors
a(1)=0; b(1)=0; c(1)=0;
a(N+1)=0; b(N+1)=0; c(N+1)=Vo;
% Solve tri-diagonal matrix by calculating "d" and
% "e" vectors
d(1)=c(1);
e(1)=a(1);
for i=2:N+1
    d(i) = (c(i) + b(i)*d(i-1)) / (1 - b(i)*e(i-1));
```

```
    e(i) = a(i) / (1 - b(i)*e(i-1));
end
% calculate phi based on d and e, also calculate
% global error
phi(N+1)=d(N+1);
for i=N:-1:1
    phi(i) = d(i) + e(i)*phi(i+1);
end
% Plot numerical and exact solutions for phi:
plot(x,phi,'x',x,phi_exact);
xlabel('{\it x} (meters)'), ylabel('\Phi (volts)');
grid;
legend('numerical solution','exact solution',...
    'Location','SouthEast');
% Find worst-case global error:
error = abs( (phi - phi_exact) ./ phi_exact );
fprintf('Max global error for %d steps: %5.3f%%\n',...
    N,100*max(error));
```

PROGRAM RESULTS

```
Maximum global error for 40 steps: 0.029%
```

The MATLAB plot of Φ as a function of x is shown in Figure 6.13.

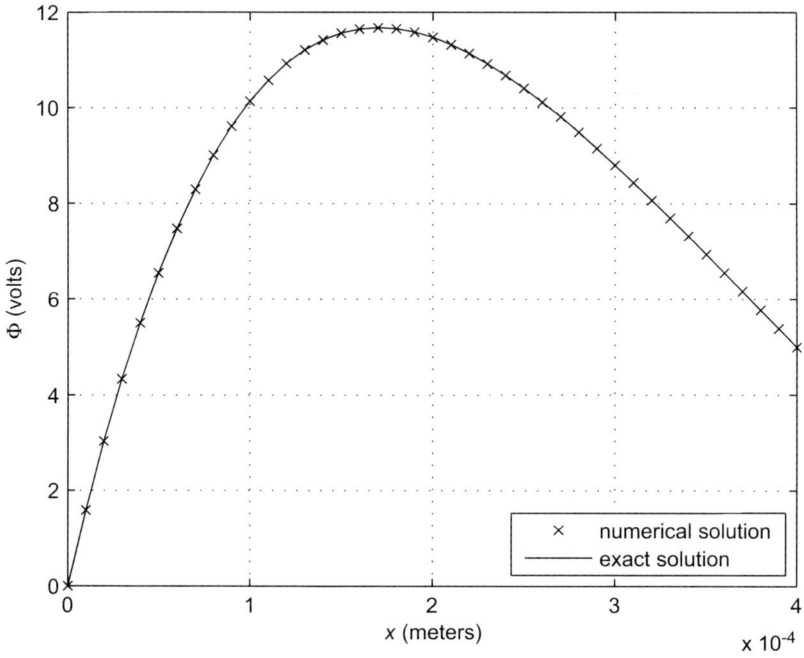

Figure 6.13 Plot of the electric potential $\Phi(x)$ between the plates, including exact solution and finite difference solution for N = 40.

Projects

Project 6.1

Solve the RC circuit of Figure 6.4 for v_C(t) where the driving voltage has the following form:

$$V_D(t) = \begin{cases} V_o \sin \omega t & t \geq 0 \\ 0 & t < 0 \end{cases}$$

Assume the initial condition $v_C(0) = 0$ and parameter values $R = 1$ kΩ, $C = 1$ μF, $\omega = 2000$ rad/sec, and $V_o = 10$ V.

1. Find the exact solution for $v_C(t)$ by assuming a particular solution of the form $v_{C,P}(t) = \alpha \sin \omega t + \beta \cos \omega t$ and using Equation (6.14) for the homogenous equation solution, which is $v_{C,H} = \gamma\ e^{-t/\tau}$. Solve for the constants by α, β, and γ by substituting back into the governing differential equation and applying the initial condition.
2. Use the Euler algorithm to solve numerically for $v_C(t)$. Solve over the interval t = [0, 5] ms with a time step of 0.1 ms.
3. Use the Modified Euler algorithm to solve numerically for $v_C(t)$ for the same interval as part 2.
4. On one graph plot $v_C(t)$ versus t obtained by both the Euler method and the exact solution. On a separate graph, plot $v_C(t)$ versus t obtained both by the modified Euler method and the exact solution.
5. Increase the step size in your numerical solutions until you start to see instability. What is a reasonable rule of thumb to ensure numerical stability in this first-order system with sinusoidal input?

Project 6.2

Figure P6.2a shows a third-order RLC circuit. To run a time-domain transient analysis, we transform the circuit into differential equations using the following method:

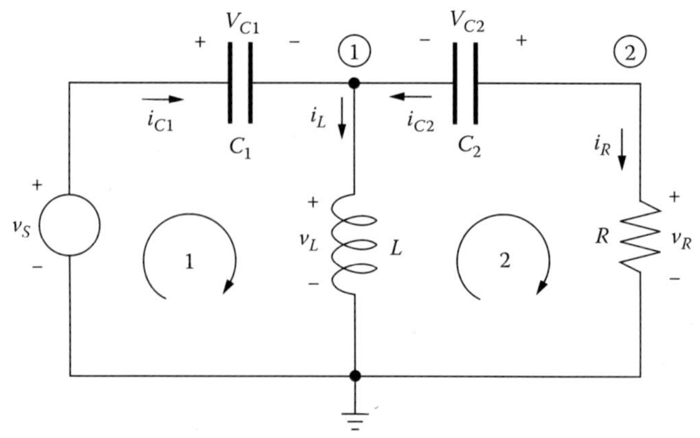

Figure P6.2a Third-order RLCC circuit containing two capacitors and an inductor.

First, write Kirchhoff's current law for each node in the circuit:

$$\text{at node 1: } i_{C1} + i_{C2} - i_L = 0 \tag{P6.2a}$$

$$\text{at node 2: } i_R + i_{C2} = 0 \tag{P6.2b}$$

Second, write Kirchhoff's voltage law for the two loops in the circuit:

$$\text{for loop 1: } v_S - v_{C1} - v_L = 0 \tag{P6.2c}$$

$$\text{for loop 2: } v_L + v_{C2} - v_R = 0 \tag{P6.2d}$$

Third, write the constituent relations for each circuit element:

$$\text{for } C_1\text{: } i_{C1} = C_1 v'_{C1} \tag{P6.2e}$$

$$\text{for } C_2\text{: } i_{C2} = C_2 v'_{C2} \tag{P6.2f}$$

$$\text{for } L\text{: } v_L = L i'_L \tag{P6.2g}$$

$$\text{for } R\text{: } v_R = i_R R \tag{P6.2h}$$

We choose the three voltages and currents with derivative terms (v_{C1}, v_{C2}, and i_L) as the *state variables* for this problem.

1. Rearrange equations (P6.2a)–(P6.2h) into the following standard form:

$$\frac{dv_{C1}}{dt} = f(v_{C1}, v_{C2}, i_L, v_S(t)) \tag{P6.2i}$$

$$\frac{dv_{C2}}{dt} = g(v_{C1}, v_{C2}, i_L, v_S(t)) \tag{P6.2j}$$

$$\frac{di_L}{dt} = h(v_{C1}, v_{C2}, i_L, v_S(t)) \tag{P6.2k}$$

where the functions *f*, *g* and *h* involve parameters C_1, C_2, *L*, and *R*.

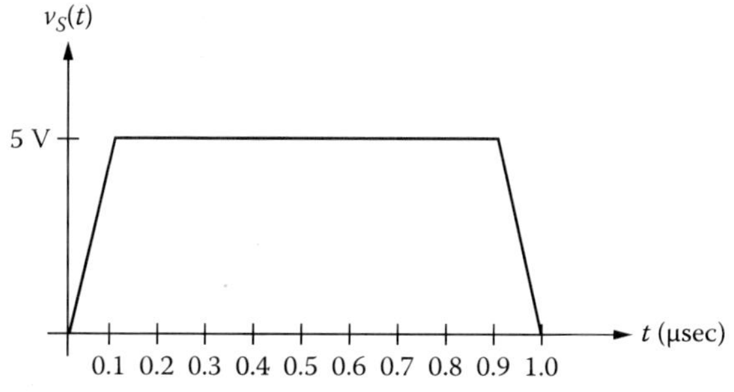

Figure P6.2b Input pulse for the RLCC circuit.

2. Solve Equations (P6.2i)–(P6.2k) with the Runge-Kutta algorithm for the following circuit parameters: $C_1 = 1\ \mu F$, $C_2 = 0.001\ \mu F$, $R = 100\ k\Omega$, $L = 0.01$ mH. Use a time interval of $0 \le t \le 10\,\mu s$ and a step size of 0.01 μs. Assume $v_s(t)$ is a 5-V pulse starting at time $t = 0$ with rise time of 0.1 μs, an "on" time of 0.8 μs, and fall time of 0.1 μs (as shown in Figure P6.2b). Initial conditions: $v_{C1}(0) = 0$, $v_{C2}(0) = 0$, and $i_L(0) = 0$.
3. Plot on separate graphs: $v_{C1}(t)$, $v_{C2}(t)$, $i_L(t)$ and $v_S(t)$ versus time.

Project 6.3

The *Sallen-Key* circuit (Figure P6.3) is commonly used to implement second-order (or higher) filters. Although there are several ways to model this circuit, we analyze it here directly in the time domain using differential equations. If we assume that the op amp is ideal, then $v_2 = v_{out}$ and $i_5 = 0$. Applying Kirchhoff's current law at the nodes labeled v_1 and v_2 and using the constituent relations for resistors ($v_R = i_R R$) and capacitors $\left(i_C = C\dfrac{dv_C}{dt}\right)$, we get

$$\text{At node } v_1:\ i_1 + i_2 + i_3 = 0 \quad \Rightarrow \quad \frac{v_{in} - v_1}{R_1} + \frac{v_2 - v_1}{R_2} + C_1\frac{d(v_{out} - v_1)}{dt} = 0$$

$$\text{At node } v_2:\ i_2 + i_4 = 0 \quad \Rightarrow \quad \frac{v_2 - v_1}{R_2} + C_2\frac{dv_2}{dt} = 0$$

Rearranging into a system of two first-order ODEs and setting $v_2 = v_{out}$, we get

$$\frac{dv_{out}}{dt} = \left(\frac{-1}{R_2C_2}\right)v_{out} + \left(\frac{1}{R_2C_2}\right)v_1 \tag{P6.3a}$$

$$\frac{dv_1}{dt} = \left(\frac{1}{R_2C_1} - \frac{1}{R_2C_2}\right)v_{out} + \left(\frac{1}{R_2C_2} - \frac{1}{R_1C_1} - \frac{1}{R_2C_1}\right)v_1 + \left(\frac{1}{R_1C_1}\right)v_{in} \tag{P6.3b}$$

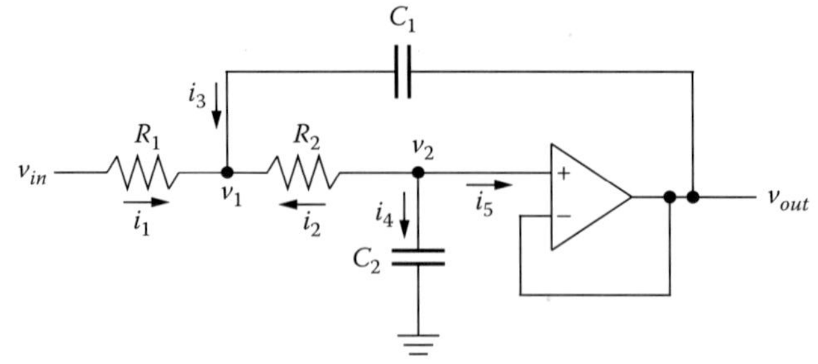

Figure P6.3 Sallen-Key circuit.

1. Solve for v_{out} and v_1 using MATLAB's `ode45` function. Assume that the input to the circuit v_{in} is a step voltage that changes from 0 V to 1 V at time $t = 0^+$. Assume the following values for the circuit elements: $R_1 = 5000\ \Omega$, $R_2 = 5000\ \Omega$, $C_1 = 2200$ pF, $C_2 = 1100$ pF. Use a time interval of t = [0, 100 μs] and assume $v_{out}(0) = v_1(0) = 0$.
2. Find the impulse response of the circuit by first creating a MATLAB function `pulse(t)` that returns the following values:

$$\texttt{pulse(t)} = \begin{cases} 10^6 & \text{for } 0 < t < 10^{-6} \\ 0 & \text{otherwise} \end{cases}$$

   Then, solve for v_{out} and v_1 using MATLAB's `ode45` function where v_i = `pulse(t)`. Use the same component values, time interval, and initial conditions as in part 1.
3. Plot the step response (from part 1) and the impulse response (from part 2) on the same set of axes. What relationship can you see between the two?
4. What is one advantage of the Sallen-Key circuit versus the ordinary second-order RLC circuit of Appendix A?

Problem 6.4

By cascading the Sallen-Key circuit, we can create higher-order filters. Figure P6.4 shows an example of a fourth-order filter.

Using Equations (P6.3a) and (P6.3b), write a system of four first-order differential equations to describe the fourth-order Sallen-Key circuit. Remember that v_{out} of the first stage will be equal to v_{in} of the second stage.

1. Solve for v_{out} using MATLAB's `ode45` function. Assume that the input to the circuit v_{in} is a step voltage that changes from 0 V to 1 V at time $t = 0^+$. Assume the following values for the circuit elements: $R_1 = R_2 = R_3 = R_4 = 5000\,\Omega$, $C_1 = 18000$ pF, $C_2 = 15000$ pF, $C_3 = 4.7$ μF, and $C_4 = 10$ pF. Use a time interval of t = [0, 0.005] sec and assume $v_o(0) = v_1(0) = v_2(0) = v_3(0) = 0$.
2. Plot v_{out} and v_{in} with respect to t on the same set of axes.

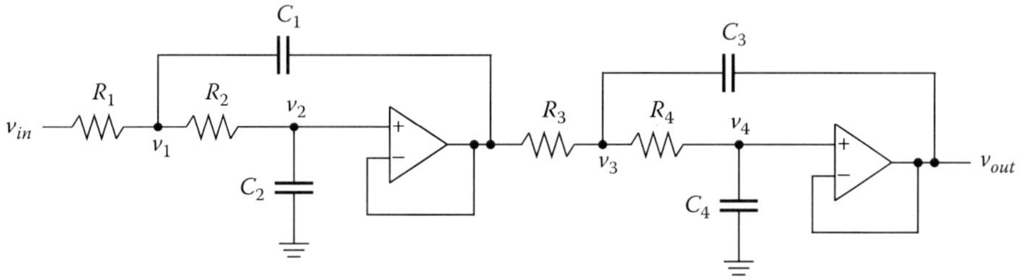

Figure P6.4 Fourth-order filter using cascaded Sallen-Key circuits.

Project 6.5

A common boundary value problem in electrical engineering is solving for the electric potential in the depletion region of a PN junction. PN junctions are formed by two adjacent regions of oppositely doped semiconductor (typically silicon) and are used to create electronic devices such as bipolar transistors, MOSFETs, (metal-oxide-semiconductor field-effect transistors) and JFETs (junction field-effect transistor). Here we will analyze the simplest device, the PN diode.

Figure P6.5a shows the circuit representation of a diode with applied voltage V_A and resulting current i_D. Figure P6.5b shows a physical representation of the diode as

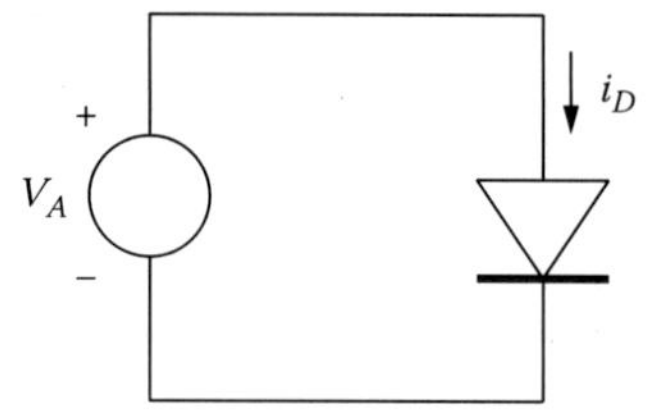

Figure P6.5a Diode circuit.

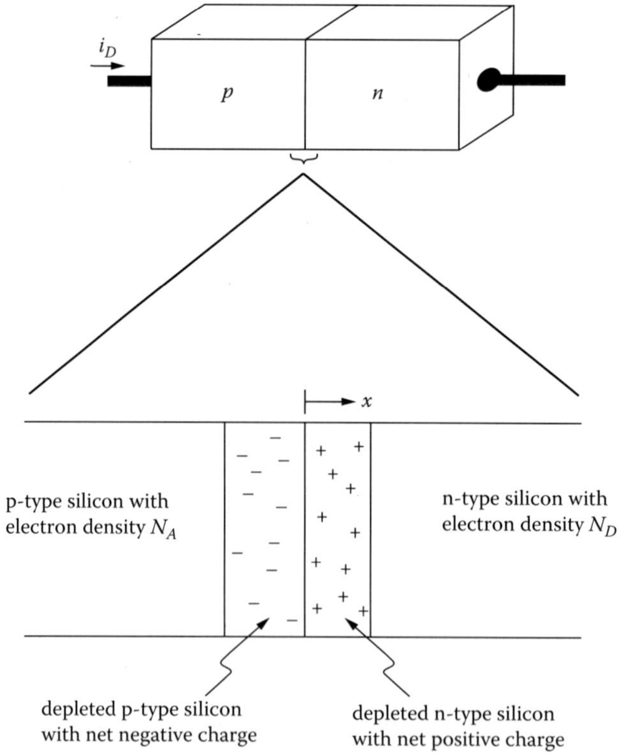

Figure P6.5b Close-up of the depletion region of a PN junction.

adjacent regions of *p-type* semiconductor (where current is primarily carried by mobile *holes* with density N_A carriers/cm^3) and *n-type* semiconductor (where current is primarily carried by mobile electrons with density N_D carriers/cm^3). In the area immediately surrounding the junction (shown in the figure detail), the mobile charge carriers of the (normally neutral) p-type and n-type regions will recombine, leaving a net fixed charge density layer around the junction called the *depletion region*. The charge density in the depletion region is dependant on the *doping profile,* and an example doping profile is shown in Figure P6.5c. In this figure, we have made two approximations: (a) that the silicon doping levels change abruptly from N_A to N_D at the junction (i.e. at $x = 0$), and (b) that the depletion region ends abruptly at $-x_P$ on the left side and at x_N on the right side. Thus, the charge densities can be approximated as straight lines:

$$\rho_P = -qN_A \qquad \text{for } -x_P < x < 0 \tag{P6.5a}$$

$$\rho_N = qN_D \qquad \text{for } 0 < x < x_N \tag{P6.5b}$$

where ρ_P and ρ_N are the charge densities in the p- and n-type regions respectively, and q is the unit electric charge (1.6×10^{-19} coulomb). (Note that the charge density on the P side of the depletion region is negative because it is depleted of positive carriers. Similarly, the N side will have a positive charge density.)

The governing equation for the voltage potential Φ in the p-type depletion region is

$$\frac{d^2\Phi}{dx^2} = \frac{qN_A}{\varepsilon} \tag{P6.5c}$$

and the governing equation for the voltage potential Φ in the n-type depletion region is

$$\frac{d^2\Phi}{dx^2} = -\frac{qN_D}{\varepsilon} \tag{P6.5d}$$

We set $x = 0$ at the exact point of the P-to-N transition and arbitrarily set the voltage potential $\Phi = 0$ V at $x = 0$; that is,

$$\Phi(0) = 0 \tag{P6.5e}$$

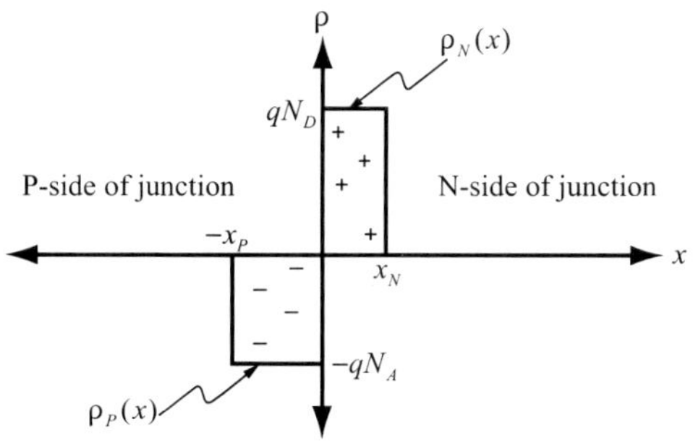

Figure P6.5c Charge densities $\rho_N(x)$ and $\rho_P(x)$ at the PN junction.

The second boundary condition is that the electric field must be zero in the neutral region outside the depletion region because there is no net charge in that region. Because $E = -\frac{d\Phi}{dx}$, this condition implies that

$$\Phi' = 0 \quad \text{at} \quad x = -x_P \tag{P6.5f}$$

$$\Phi' = 0 \quad \text{at} \quad x = x_N \tag{P6.5g}$$

Assume that we can model the PN junction as a parallel plate capacitor with the plates located at $x = x_N$ and $x = -x_P$. Use the technique demonstrated in Example 6.8 to calculate the electric potential in the depletion region. Assume the following parameters:

$$q = 1.6\times 10^{-19} \text{ coulomb},\ N_D = 10^{16} \text{ carriers/cm}^3,\ N_A = 0.3\times 10^{16},$$

$$x_N = 0.15\ \mu\text{m},\ x_P = 0.5\ \mu\text{m},\ \Delta x = 0.005\,\mu m,\ \varepsilon = 1.04\times 10^{-12} \text{ F/cm}.$$

1. Solve for Φ in the p-type region over the interval $-x_P \le x \le 0$ with the boundary conditions $\Phi'(-x_P) = 0$ and $\Phi(0) = 0$ and using the finite difference equations to define a tri-diagonal matrix and then solving the matrix problem.
2. Solve for Φ in the n-type region over the interval $0 \le x \le x_N$ with the boundary conditions $\Phi(0) = 0$ and $\Phi'(x_N) = 0$ using the same method as described in part 1.
3. Plot your results for both the p- and n-type regions on one graph over the interval $-x_P \le x \le x_N$.

Problem 6.6

For the PN junction in Problem 6.5, we arbitrarily set the ground point $\Phi = 0$ to be at the exact point of the P-to-N boundary. Suppose instead we set the ground point to be at the P-to-intrinsic boundary, that is, $\Phi(-x_P) = 0$. The problem (for the p-type region) becomes

$$\frac{d^2\Phi}{dx^2} = \frac{qN_A}{\varepsilon} \tag{P6.6a}$$

$$\Phi(-x_p) = 0 \tag{P6.6b}$$

$$\Phi'(-x_P) = 0 \tag{P6.6c}$$

For the n-type region,

$$\frac{d^2\Phi}{dx^2} = -\frac{qN_D}{\varepsilon} \tag{P6.6d}$$

At the intersection of the two regions, where $x = 0$,

$$\Phi(0^-) = \Phi(0^+) \tag{P6.6e}$$

and

$$\frac{d\Phi}{dx}(0^-) = \frac{d\Phi}{dx}(0^+) \tag{P6.6f}$$

1. Find an exact solution for Equations (P6.6a)–(P6.6f) by direct integration.
2. Find a numerical solution for Equations (P6.6a)–(P6.6f) using MATLAB's `ode45` function. Assume: $N_A = 0.3 \times 10^{16}$ carriers/cm³, $N_D = 10^{16}$ carriers/cm³, $\varepsilon = 1.04 \times 10^{-12}$ F/cm, $-x_P \leq x \leq x_N$, where $x_P = 0.5\ \mu\text{m}$, $x_N = 0.15\ \mu\text{m}$, and $\Delta x = 0.005\,\mu\text{m}$.
3. Plot your exact and `ode45` solutions on the same axes.
4. Find and print the global error in the `ode45` solution.

Problem 6.7

A *heat sink* is often attached to electronic components to dissipate excess heat generated by the device to prevent it from overheating (Figure P6.7a). A sketch of one heat sink fin is shown in Figure P6.7b, where the trapezoidal fin has a bottom width W_1, top width W_2, height L_1, and depth D, and the coordinates x and y are as drawn in the diagram. The temperature distribution in the fin is governed by a one-dimensional analysis of the heat equation in a solid. The analysis includes an empirical relation that involves the convective heat transfer coefficient h. This empirical relation is introduced to separate the heat conduction problem in the solid from the heat transfer problem in the surrounding fluid. The convective heat transfer coefficient h is determined by either experiment or analytical/numerical methods. The governing equation for the fin is

$$\frac{d}{dx}\left(A\frac{dT}{dx}\right) = \frac{hP}{k}(T - T_\infty) \tag{P6.7a}$$

Figure P6.7a Typical fin heat sink used to cool an electronic component such as a microprocessor.

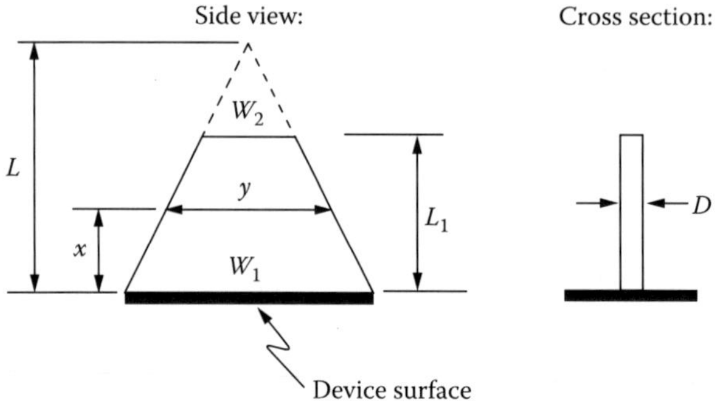

Figure P6.7b Side and cross-sectional views of a single fin of the heat sink with trapezoidal height L_1, bottom width W_1, top width W_2, and depth D. The trapezoid is formed from a truncated triangle of height L.

or

$$\frac{dA}{dx}\frac{dT}{dx} + A\frac{d^2T}{dx^2} = \frac{hP}{k}(T - T_\infty) \tag{P6.7b}$$

where T is the temperature in the fin at position x, T_∞ is the surrounding ambient air temperature, A is the fin cross-sectional area, h is the convective heat transfer coefficient, k is the thermal conductivity of the fin material, and P is its perimeter. We begin by writing equations for the area and perimeter in terms of the measurements of the fin:

$$A = yD$$

$$P = 2y + 2D$$

By the geometry of similar triangles, we can determine that $\frac{y}{W_1} = \frac{L-x}{L}$, and thus the area and perimeter as functions of x are

$$A(x) = \frac{W_1 D}{L}(L - x)$$

$$P(x) = \frac{2W_1 D}{L}(L - x) + 2D$$

The governing differential equation becomes

$$\frac{W_1 D}{L}(L - x)\frac{d^2T}{dx^2} - \frac{W_1 D}{L}\frac{dT}{dx} = \frac{h}{k}\left[\frac{2W_1}{L}(L - x) + 2D\right](T - T_\infty) \tag{P6.7c}$$

The first boundary condition is that at the surface of the device, the temperature T_W is known:

$$T(0) = T_W \tag{P6.7d}$$

To obtain the second boundary condition, we employ the concept of energy conservation, that is

Rate that Heat Leaves the Fin at ($x = L_1$) per Unit Surface Area by Conduction
= Rate that Heat Is Carried Away by Convection per Unit Surface Area

This statement can be written mathematically as

$$-k\frac{dT}{dx}(L_1) = h[T(L_1) - T_\infty] \tag{P6.7e}$$

We wish to solve this problem numerically using the finite difference method.

First, subdivide the x axis into N subdivisions, giving $x_1, x_2, x_3, \ldots x_{N+1}$. Take the temperature at x_i to be T_i. The finite difference formulas for $\frac{d^2T}{dx^2}$ and $\frac{dT}{dx}$ (see Table 6.1) are

$$\frac{d^2T}{dx^2}(x_i) = \frac{T_{i+1} + T_{i-1} - 2T_i}{\Delta x^2}$$

$$\frac{dT}{dx}(x_i) = \frac{T_{i+1} - T_i}{\Delta x}$$

The finite differential form of Equation (P6.7c) is

$$\frac{W_1 D}{L}(L - x_i)\left(\frac{T_{i+1} + T_{i-1} - 2T_i}{\Delta x^2}\right) - \frac{w_1 D}{L}\left(\frac{T_{i+1} - T_i}{\Delta x}\right) = \frac{h}{k}\left[\frac{2W_1}{L}(L - x_i) + 2D\right](T_i - T_\infty)$$

Solving for T_i gives

$$T_i = \left\{\frac{2W_1 D}{L}(L - x_i) - \frac{W_1 D}{L}\Delta x + \frac{h\Delta x^2}{k}\left(\frac{2W_1}{L}(L - x_i) + 2D\right)\right\}^{-1}$$

$$\times\left\{\left[\frac{W_1 D}{L}(L - x_i) - \frac{W_1 D}{L}\Delta x\right]T_{i+1} + \frac{W_1 D}{L}(L - x_i)T_{i-1} + \frac{h\Delta x^2}{k}\left[\frac{2W_1}{L}(L - x_i) + 2D\right]T_\infty\right\} \tag{P6.7f}$$

Equation (P6.7f) is valid for $i = 2, 3, \ldots, N$.

The finite difference form for Equation (P6.7e) is

$$-k\frac{T_{N+1} - T_N}{\Delta x} = h[T_{N+1} - T_\infty]$$

Solving for T_{N+1} gives

$$T_{N+1} = \frac{1}{1+\frac{h\Delta x}{k}}\left\{T_N + \frac{h\Delta x}{k}T_\infty\right\}$$

Also, $T_1 = T_W$.

All the heat transfer from the fin to the surrounding air passes through the base of the fin. Thus, the rate of heat loss Q through the fin is given by

$$Q = -\frac{kA_1}{\Delta x}(T_2 - T_1)$$

where A_1 is the cross-sectional area at the base of the fin, that is, at $x = 0+$.

Using the method described in Section 6.11 for a tri-diagonal system of equations, write a MATLAB program that will solve for the temperature distribution in the fin and the rate of heat loss through the fin. Use the following values:

$$T_W = 200°\text{C},\ T_\infty = 40°\text{C},\quad k = 204\ \text{W/m-K},\ h = 60\ \text{W/m}^2\text{-K},$$

$$N = 50,\ W_1 = 5\ \text{cm},\ L = 20\ \text{cm},\quad L_1 = 5\ \text{cm},\ D = 0.2\ \text{cm}$$

The output of your program should include the values of h, k, T_w, T_∞, Q; a table of T versus x at every 0.1 cm; and a plot of T versus x.

Chapter 7

Laplace Transforms

7.1 Introduction

Transform techniques involve applying a mathematical operation to the equations of a problem, solving in the (presumably easier) transform domain, and then taking the inverse transform to obtain an answer in the domain of interest. *Laplace transforms* are frequently used to solve ordinary and partial differential equations. The method reduces an ordinary differential equation to an algebraic equation, which can be manipulated to a form such that the inverse transform is easily obtained. In circuit theory, any circuit containing capacitors or inductors will contain at least one differential relationship, and a large circuit may contain many more. In Chapter 6, we solved circuits directly in the time domain by integrating the differential equations in MATLAB. We now describe the Laplace transform approach [1,2]; we convert the time-domain equations to the Laplace domain, solve algebraically, and then take the inverse transform back to the time domain to obtain the final answer. Sometimes, we do not even bother with the final step because the result in the Laplace domain is sufficient to fully solve the problem of interest.

7.2 Laplace Transform and Inverse Transform

Let $f(t)$ be a *causal* function such that it has some defined value for all $t \geq 0$ and is zero otherwise, that is, $f(t) = 0$ for $t < 0$. The unilateral Laplace transform is defined as

$$\mathcal{L}(f(t)) = F(s) = \int_0^{\infty} e^{-st} f(t)\, dt \tag{7.1}$$

$F(s)$ is called the *Laplace transform* of $f(t)$, and the symbol $\mathcal{L}$ is used to indicate the transform operation. By convention, we use lowercase letters for time domain functions and uppercase for their Laplace domain (or "s-domain") counterparts.

The *inverse Laplace transform* of $F(s)$ is defined to be the function $f(t)$ such that

$$\mathcal{L}^{-1}(F(s)) = f(t) \tag{7.2}$$

Tables have been created that contain both $f(t)$ and the corresponding $F(s)$ (see Table 7.1 at the end of this chapter). Often, we need to rearrange the transform to a form or several forms that are available in the table of Laplace transforms. We now derive the Laplace transform for some common functions.

7.2.1 Laplace Transform of the Unit Step

We define the unit step function $u(t)$ mathematically as

$$u(t) = \begin{cases} 1 & \text{for } t \geq 0 \\ 0 & \text{for } t < 0 \end{cases}$$

Then

$$\mathcal{L}(u(t)) = \int_0^\infty (1)e^{-st}\,dt$$

$$= -\frac{e^{-st}}{s}\Bigg|_0^\infty$$

$$= \frac{1}{s} \tag{7.3}$$

7.2.2 Exponential

Let

$$f(t) = e^{at}$$

where a is a constant. Then,

$$\mathcal{L}(e^{at}) = \int_0^\infty e^{at} e^{-st}\, dt$$

$$= \int_0^\infty e^{-(s-a)t}\, dt$$

$$= -\frac{e^{-(s-a)t}}{(s-a)}\bigg|_0^\infty$$

$$= \frac{1}{s-a} \tag{7.4}$$

7.2.3 Linearity

Let

$$f(t) = Ag(t) + Bh(t)$$

where $g(t)$ and $h(t)$ are functions, and A and B are constants. Then,

$$\mathcal{L}(A\,g(t) + B\,h(t)) = \int_0^\infty (Ag(t) + Bh(t))e^{-st}\, dt$$

$$= A\int_0^\infty g(t)e^{-st}\, dt + B\int_0^\infty h(t)e^{-st}\, dt$$

$$= A\mathcal{L}(g(t)) + B\mathcal{L}(h(t)) \tag{7.5}$$

Thus, the Laplace transform of a sum is equal to the sum of the transforms of the addends, and the Laplace transform of a scaled function is equal to the transform of the unscaled function multiplied by the scaling factor.

7.2.4 Time Delay

Let

$$f(t) = g(t - T)$$

where $f(t)$ is simply a time-delayed version of $g(t)$ with delay time T seconds (with T presumed always positive). Then,

$$\mathcal{L}(g(t-T)) = \int_{T}^{\infty} g(t-T)e^{-st}\,dt$$

where the bottom integration limit has been set to T because $g(t - T)$ is presumed to be zero for $t < T$. Then, let $\tau = t - T$ (and thus $d\tau = dt$). Then,

$$\mathcal{L}(g(t-T)) = \int_{0}^{\infty} g(\tau)e^{-s(\tau+T)}\,d\tau$$

$$= e^{-sT}\int_{0}^{\infty} g(\tau)e^{-s\tau}\,d\tau$$

$$= e^{-sT}G(s) \tag{7.6}$$

Thus, the Laplace transform of a delayed function is equal to the transform of the undelayed function multiplied by the delay factor e^{-sT}.

7.2.5 Complex Exponential

Let

$$f(t) = e^{j\omega t}$$

Then, applying Equation (7.4), we get

$$\mathcal{L}(e^{j\omega t}) = \frac{1}{s-j\omega}$$

$$= \frac{1}{s-j\omega} \times \frac{s+j\omega}{s+j\omega}$$

$$= \frac{s+j\omega}{s^2+\omega^2}$$

$$= \frac{s}{s^2+\omega^2} + j\frac{\omega}{s^2+\omega^2} \tag{7.7}$$

By applying the identity $e^{jx} = \cos x + j\sin x$, we also know

$$\begin{aligned}\mathcal{L}(e^{j\omega t}) &= \mathcal{L}(\cos\omega t + j\sin\omega t)\\ &= \mathcal{L}(\cos\omega t) + j\,\mathcal{L}(\sin\omega t)\end{aligned} \tag{7.8}$$

Equating the real and imaginary components of Equation (7.7) and Equation (7.8) gives the Laplace transforms for sine and cosine:

$$\mathcal{L}(cos\ \omega\ t) = \frac{s}{s^2+\omega^2} \tag{7.9}$$

$$\mathcal{L}(sin\ \omega\ t) = \frac{\omega}{s^2+\omega^2} \tag{7.10}$$

Generalizing to the case when the exponent has both real and imaginary parts,

$$\begin{aligned}\mathcal{L}(e^{(a+j\omega)t}) &= \frac{1}{s-(a+j\omega)}\\ &= \frac{1}{(s-a)-j\omega}\\ &= \frac{s-a}{(s-a)^2+\omega^2} + j\frac{\omega}{(s-a)^2+\omega^2}\\ &= \mathcal{L}(e^{at}\cos\omega t) + j\mathcal{L}(e^{at}\sin\omega t)\end{aligned}$$

We may observe from this that multiplication of the function $f(t) = e^{j\omega t}$ by e^{at} in the time domain produces an s shift in the Laplace domain. This may be generically stated as

$$\mathcal{L}(e^{at} f(t)) = F(s-a) \tag{7.11}$$

7.2.6 Powers of t

Let

$$f(t) = t^{n+1}$$

Then,

$$\mathcal{L}(t^{n+1}) = \int_0^\infty t^{n+1} e^{-st}\,dt$$

To solve, integrate by parts. Let $u = t^{n+1}$ and $dv = e^{-st}dt$. Then, $du = (n+1)t^n dt$ and $v = -\frac{e^{-st}}{s}$. Applying $\int udv = uv - \int vdu$, we get

$$\int_0^\infty t^{n+1}e^{-st}\,dt = -t^{n+1}\frac{e^{-st}}{s}\bigg|_{t=0}^{\infty} + \frac{n+1}{s}\int_0^\infty t^n e^{-st}\,dt = \frac{n+1}{s}\mathfrak{L}(t^n) \tag{7.12}$$

From Equation (7.12), we can see that

$$\mathfrak{L}(t^n) = \frac{n}{s}\mathfrak{L}(t^{n-1})$$

$$\mathfrak{L}(t^{n-1}) = \frac{n-1}{s}\mathfrak{L}(t^{n-2})$$

$$\vdots$$

$$\mathfrak{L}(t^1) = \frac{1}{s}\mathfrak{L}(t^0) = \frac{1}{s}\mathfrak{L}(1) = \frac{1}{s^2} \tag{7.13}$$

7.2.7 Delta Function

The *delta function* was formalized by physicist Paul Dirac and is defined as follows:

$$\delta(t) = \begin{cases} \infty & \text{for } t = 0 \\ 0 & \text{otherwise} \end{cases}$$

and

$$\int_0^\infty \delta(t)\,dt = 1$$

Although we cannot physically realize $\delta(\tau)$ in an actual circuit (though it is often approximated), it has many useful applications in circuit theory, and its Laplace transform is

$$\mathfrak{L}(\delta(t)) = \int_0^\infty \delta(t)e^{-st} = e^{-st}\Big|_0^\infty = 1$$

Example 7.1

Find the Laplace transform of the pulse $p(t)$ as shown in Figure 7.1, where A is the amplitude, T_1 is the turn-on time, and T_2 is the turn-off time.

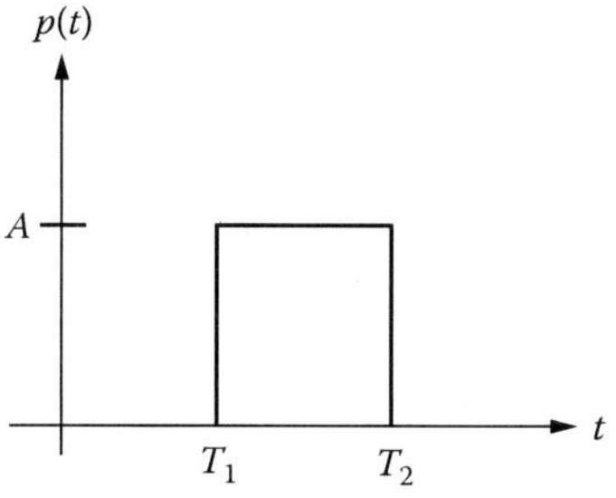

Figure 7.1 Pulse with amplitude A, turn-on time T_1, and turn-off time T_2.

We can express the pulse mathematically as the sum of two delayed unit steps with amplitude A:

$$p(t) = Au(t - T_1) - Au(t - T_2)$$

We know from Equation (7.3) that the Laplace transform of the unit step is $\frac{1}{s}$. Also, from Equation (7.5), the transform of a sum is simply the sum of the transforms. In addition, from Equation (7.6), the transform of a time-delayed function is simply e^{-sT} times the transform of the undelayed function. Thus, the transform of the pulse is

$$P(s) = (A)(e^{-sT_1})\left(\frac{1}{s}\right) - (A)(e^{-sT_2})\left(\frac{1}{s}\right)$$

$$= \frac{A}{s}(e^{-sT_1} - e^{-sT_2}) \tag{7.14}$$

Example 7.2

Find the inverse Laplace transform of the following function:

$$F(s) = \frac{1 - e^{-sT}}{s^2} + \frac{2\pi T^2 e^{-sT}}{T^2 s^2 + 4\pi^2} \tag{7.15}$$

We start by decomposing the first term of Equation (7.15):

$$\frac{1 - e^{-sT}}{s^2} = \frac{1}{s^2} - e^{-sT}\frac{1}{s^2} \tag{7.16}$$

We know from Equation (7.13) that $\mathcal{L}(t) = \frac{1}{s^2}$ and from Equation (7.6) that multiplication by e^{-sT} in the Laplace domain corresponds to delay

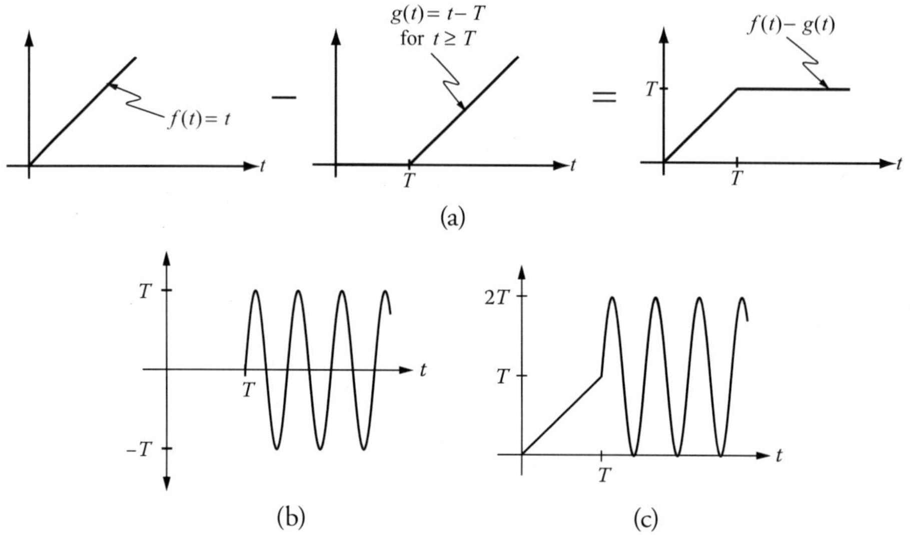

Figure 7.2 Example of inverse Laplace transform. (a) The inverse transform of $\frac{1}{s^2} - e^{-sT}\frac{1}{s^2}$ is the subtraction of a ramp and a time-delayed ramp. (b) The inverse transform of $Te^{-sT}\frac{\omega}{s^2+\omega^2}$ is a time-delayed sine wave. (c) The complete inverse transform is the sum of the graphs in (a) and (b).

in the time domain. Thus, the inverse transform of Equation (7.16) is the subtraction of a ramp $(f(t) = t)$ and a time-delayed ramp and is shown graphically in Figure 7.2a.

For the second term of Equation (2.15), we rearrange as follows:

$$\frac{2\pi T^2 e^{-sT}}{(Ts)^2 + 4\pi^2} = Te^{-sT}\frac{2\pi T}{T^2 s^2 + (2\pi)^2}$$

$$= Te^{-sT}\frac{\frac{2\pi}{T}}{s^2 + \left(\frac{2\pi}{T}\right)^2}$$

$$= Te^{-sT}\frac{\omega}{s^2 + \omega^2} \tag{7.17}$$

By inspection, Equation (7.17) corresponds to a time-delayed sine wave of amplitude T and frequency $\omega = \frac{2\pi}{T}$ and is illustrated in Figure 7.2b. The complete inverse transform is shown in Figure 7.2c.

7.3 Transforms of Derivatives

Let

$$f'(t) = \frac{df(t)}{dt}$$

Then,

$$\mathcal{L}(f') = \int_0^\infty \frac{df}{dt} e^{-st}\, dt = \int_0^\infty e^{-st}\, df$$

Integrating by parts, let $dv = df$ and $u = e^{-st}$. Then, $v = f$ and $du = -se^{-st}dt$. Applying $\int udv = uv - \int vdu$, we get

$$\int_0^\infty e^{-st}\, df = fe^{-st}\Big|_{t=0}^{\infty} + s\int_0^\infty fe^{-st}\, dt = -f(0) + s\mathcal{L}(f) \qquad (7.18)$$

Thus, the Laplace transform of a derivative is the transform of the original function multiplied by s and minus the value of the function at time $t = 0$ (i.e., less the initial condition).

Similarly, for the second derivative,

$$\mathcal{L}(f'') = \int_0^\infty f''(t) e^{-st}\, dt$$

$$\mathcal{L}(f'') = \int_0^\infty \frac{df'}{dt} e^{-st}\, dt = \int_0^\infty e^{-st}\, df'$$

Let $dv = df'$ and $u = e^{-st}$. Then, $v = f'$ and $du = -se^{-st}dt$. Integrating by parts, we get

$$\int_0^\infty f'' e^{-st}\, dt = f' e^{-st}\Big|_{t=0}^{\infty} + s\int_0^\infty f' e^{-st}\, dt$$

$$= -f'(0) + s\mathcal{L}(f')$$

$$= -f'(0) - s\, f(0) + s^2\mathcal{L}(f) \qquad (7.19)$$

By Equations (7.18) and (7.19), we can see the pattern for the Laplace transform of the nth derivative, that is:

$$\mathcal{L}(f^{(n)}) = s^n\mathcal{L}(f) - s^{n-1} f(0) - s^{n-2} f'(0) - \cdots - f^{(n)}(0) \qquad (7.20)$$

7.4 Ordinary Differential Equations, Initial Value Problem

Consider the differential equation arising from the parallel RLC circuit of Appendix A in Equation (A.7). The governing differential equation for the inductor current i is

$$i'' + \frac{1}{RC}i' + \frac{1}{LC}i = \frac{I_o(t)}{LC} \tag{7.21}$$

where L is the inductance (in henries), R is the resistance (in ohms), C is the capacitance (in farads), and I_o is the driving current.

We also assume the initial conditions to be

$$i(0) = \alpha \quad \text{and} \quad i'(0) = \beta$$

First, we convert this equation into the following general form: Let $y(t) = i(t)$, $p = \frac{1}{RC}$, $q = \frac{1}{LC}$ and $f(t) = \frac{I_o(t)}{LC}$. Then, Equation (7.20) becomes

$$y'' + py' + qy = f(t) \tag{7.22}$$

The Laplace transform of each of the terms in Equation (7.22) is as follows:

$$\mathfrak{L}(y'') = s^2Y(s) - \alpha s - \beta$$

$$\mathfrak{L}(py') = p(sY(s) - \alpha)$$

$$\mathfrak{L}(qy) = qY(s)$$

$$\mathfrak{L}(f) = F(s)$$

Thus, Equation (7.22) becomes

$$s^2Y(s) - \alpha s - \beta + p(sY(s) - \alpha) + qY(s) = F(s)$$

$$\rightarrow \quad Y(s) = \frac{(s+p)\alpha + \beta + F(s)}{s^2 + ps + q}$$

Let

$$H(s) = \frac{1}{s^2 + ps + q}$$

Then,

$$Y(s) = [(s+p)\alpha + \beta]H(s) + F(s)H(s) \tag{7.23}$$

By doing a partial fraction expansion of Equation (7.23) and using Laplace transform tables, we can obtain $y(t)$ by finding inverse transform of $Y(s)$, that is, $\mathcal{L}^{-1}(Y(s)) = y(t)$.

Example 7.3

Given the following differential equation (no damping and an exponentially decaying driving function), determine the solution for $y(t)$:

$$y'' + y = 5e^{-t}$$

$$y(0) = 2, \quad y'(0) = 0 \tag{7.24}$$

This problem fits the general form of Equation (7.22), with $p = 0$, $q = 1$, and $f = 5e^{-t}$. Thus,

$$Y(s) = (2s)H(s) + F(s)H(s)$$

where

$$H(s) = \frac{1}{s^2+1} \quad \text{and} \quad F(s) = \mathcal{L}(5e^{-t}) = \frac{5}{s+1}$$

Thus,

$$Y(s) = \frac{2s}{s^2+1} + \frac{5}{(s+1)(s^2+1)} \tag{7.25}$$

For the second term of Equation (7.25), we need to decompose by the method of partial fractions:

$$\frac{5}{(s+1)(s^2+1)} = \frac{A}{s+1} + \frac{Bs+C}{s^2+1}$$

$$= \frac{A(s^2+1) + (Bs+C)(s+1)}{(s+1)(s^2+1)}$$

Matching terms in the numerator,

$$A + B = 0, \quad C + B = 0, \quad A + C = 5$$

$$\rightarrow \quad A = \frac{5}{2}, \quad B = -\frac{5}{2}, \quad C = \frac{5}{2}$$

Thus,

$$\frac{5}{(s+1)(s^2-1)} = \frac{5}{2(s+1)} - \frac{5}{2}\frac{(s-1)}{(s^2+1)}$$

and substituting back into Equation (7.25), we get

$$Y(s) = \frac{2s}{(s^2+1)} + \frac{5}{2(s+1)} - \frac{5s}{2(s^2+1)} + \frac{5}{2(s^2+1)}$$

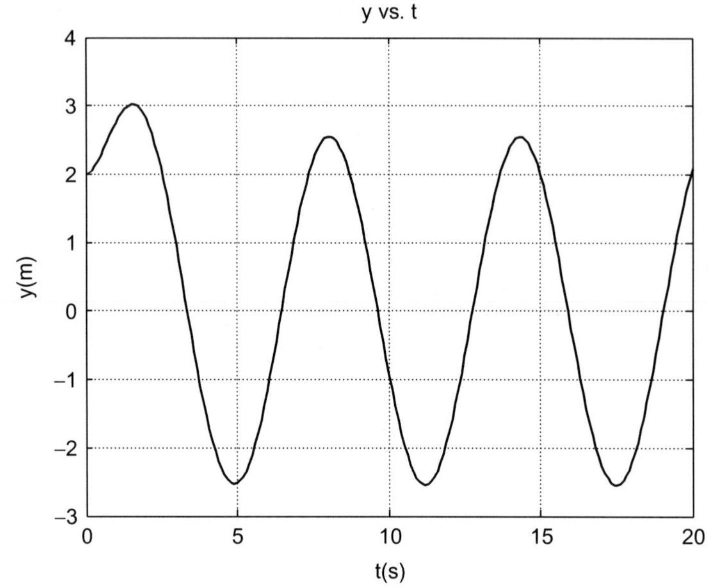

Figure 7.3 Plot of *y* versus *t* for Example 7.3.

From Table 7.1, we observe

$$\mathcal{L}^{-1}\left(\frac{s}{s^2+1}\right)=\cos t$$

$$\mathcal{L}^{-1}\left(\frac{1}{s^2+1}\right)=\sin t$$

$$\mathcal{L}^{-1}\left(\frac{1}{s+1}\right)=e^{-t}$$

Therefore, by applying inverse transforms, the solution to Equation (7.24) is

$$y(t)=-\frac{1}{2}\cos t+\frac{5}{2}\sin t+\frac{5}{2}e^{-t}$$

A plot of y versus t is shown in Figure 7.3.

Example 7.4

Determine the solution of the following differential equation:

$$y''+3y'+2y=5\sin 2t$$

$$y(0)=1,\quad y'(0)=-4 \tag{7.26}$$

Using the same form as Equation (7.22),

$$p = 3$$

$$q = 2$$

$$f(t) = 5\sin 2t = 10\frac{\sin 2t}{2}$$

In the Laplace domain,

$$H(s) = \frac{1}{s^2 + 3s + 2} = \frac{1}{(s+2)(s+1)}$$

$$F(s) = 10\mathcal{L}\left(\frac{\sin 2t}{2}\right) = \frac{10}{s^2 + 4}$$

Thus,

$$\begin{aligned} Y(s) &= \left[(s+3)(1) - 4\right]H(s) + F(s)H(s) \\ &= \frac{s}{(s+2)(s+1)} - \frac{1}{(s+2)(s+1)} + \frac{10}{(s^2+4)(s+2)(s+1)} \end{aligned} \quad (7.27)$$

We now make use of the MATLAB function `residue` function, which can be used to solve partial fraction expansions. The `residue` function takes two arguments that are arrays containing the coefficients of the numerator and denominator polynomials to be expanded. It then returns the numerator coefficients (the "residues"), the denominator roots (the "poles"), and any nonfractional term (which will always be zero in the usual case where the denominator is of higher order than the numerator).

To solve with `residue`, we rewrite the first term of Equation (7.27) in polynomial form:

$$\frac{s}{(s+2)(s+1)} = \frac{s}{s^2 + 3s + 2} \quad (7.28)$$

By the use of partial fractions, we can determine that

$$\frac{s}{(s+2)(s+1)} = \frac{2}{s+2} - \frac{1}{s+1}$$

Now, let us use MATLAB's `residue` to reduce the right-hand side of Equation (7.28) to the sum of two fractions. In the numerator of the right-hand side of Equation (7.28), we see that the first polynomial term (for s^1) has a coefficient of 1, and the second term (for s^0) has a coefficient of 0. This is expressed in MATLAB as `[1 0]`. Similarly, the denominator polynomial has an s^2 coefficient of 1, an s^1 coefficient of 3, and an s^0 coefficient of 2, which is expressed as `[1 3 2]`. Then, in MATLAB we run

```
>> [r, p, k] = residue([1 0],[1 3 2])

r =
      2
     -1
p =
     -2
     -1
k =
     []
```

This result shows that the residues are 2 and –1, and their respective poles are –2 and –1, giving

$$\frac{s}{s^2+3s+2}=\frac{2}{(s+2)}-\frac{1}{(s+1)} \tag{7.29}$$

which is the same that was obtained by the use of partial fractions.

For the second term in Equation (7.27), we run `residue([-1],[1 3 2])` to obtain

$$\begin{aligned}\frac{-1}{(s+2)(s+1)}&=\frac{-1}{s^2+3s+2}\\&=\frac{1}{(s+2)}-\frac{1}{(s+1)}\end{aligned} \tag{7.30}$$

For the third term in Equation (7.27), we first rewrite as a polynomial:

$$\frac{10}{(s^2+4)(s+2)(s+1)}=\frac{10}{s^4+3s^2+6s^2+12s+8}$$

Then, in MATLAB we obtain

```
>> [r, p, k] = residue([10],[1 3 6 12 8])
r =
   -0.3750 + 0.1250i
   -0.3750 - 0.1250i
   -1.2500
    2.0000
p =
    0.0000 + 2.0000i
    0.0000 - 2.0000i
   -2.0000
   -1.0000
k =
      []
```

Thus, the residues are at $-0.375 \pm 0.125j$, -1.25, and 2. The corresponding poles are at $\pm 2j$, -2, and -1. Thus,

$$\frac{10}{(s^2+4)(s+2)(s+1)} = \frac{10}{s^4+3s^2+6s^2+12s+8}$$
$$= \frac{-0.375+0.125j}{(s-2j)} + \frac{-0.375-0.125j}{(s+2j)}$$
$$- \frac{1.25}{(s+2)} + \frac{2}{(s+1)} \tag{7.31}$$

The final answer is the sum of the inverse transforms of Equations (7.29), (7.30), and (7.31). From Table 7.1,

$$\mathcal{L}^{-1}\left(\frac{1}{s+2}\right) = e^{-2t}$$

$$\mathcal{L}^{-1}\left(\frac{1}{s+1}\right) = e^{-t}$$

$$\mathcal{L}^{-1}\left(\frac{1}{s-2j}\right) = e^{2jt}$$

$$\mathcal{L}^{-1}\left(\frac{1}{s+2j}\right) = e^{-2jt}$$

Collecting all the terms in $Y(s)$ and applying these inverse transforms gives the complete solution for Equation (7.26):

$$y(t) = \mathcal{L}^{-1}(Y(s)) = 1.75e^{-2t} - 0.375e^{2jt} - 0.375e^{-2jt} + 0.125je^{2jt} - 0.125je^{-2jt}$$

Applying the identities $e^{j\omega t} + e^{-j\omega t} = 2\cos\omega t$ and $e^{j\omega t} - e^{-j\omega t} = 2j\sin\omega t$, we obtain

$$y(t) = 1.75e^{-2t} - 0.75\cos 2t - 0.25\sin 2t \tag{7.32}$$

It is illustrative to compare the Laplace-obtained solution with a direct solution of Equation (7.26) obtained via MATLAB's `ode45` function. The program follows, and the output is shown in Figure 7.4:

```
% Example_7_4.m: This program solves Equation 7.26 by
% converting it into a system of two differential
% equations and solving with ode45.
% Let v=y', Y=[y v], and Y'=[y' v'].
% Y(1)=y, Y(2)=v, Y'(1)=Y(2), Y'(2)=5*sin 2t-3Y(2)-2Y(1)
% Initial conditions: y(0)=1.0, y'(0)=v(0)=-4.0
clear; clc;
% Define initial conditions:
Y0=[1.0 -4.0];
% Define time interval to solve:
dt=0.1; Tstop=10; Tspan=0.0:dt:Tstop;
% solve the ODE directly with ode45:
[t,Yode45]=ode45('dydt',Tspan,Y0);
% compute the solution found via Laplace Transforms
```

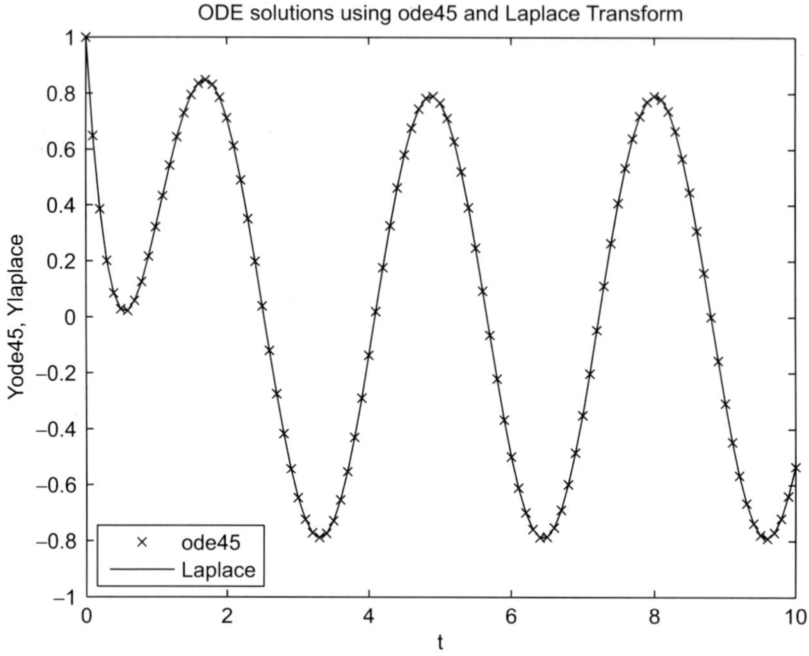

Figure 7.4 Comparison between solution obtained by Laplace transforms and MATLAB's `ode45` for Example 7.4.

```
%(Equation 7.32):
Ylaplace = 1.75*exp(-2*Tspan) ...
    - 0.75*cos(2*Tspan) - 0.25*sin(2*Tspan);
plot(t,Yode45(:,1),'x',Tspan,Ylaplace),
axis([0 Tstop -1 1]);
xlabel('t') ,ylabel('Yode45, Ylaplace');
title('ODE solutions using ode45 and Laplace Transform');
legend('ode45','Laplace','Location','SouthWest');
------------------------------------------------------------
% dydt: this function works with Example 7.4.
function Yprime=dydt(t,Y)
Yprime=zeros(2,1);
Yprime(1)=Y(2);
Yprime(2)=5*sin(2*t)-3.0*Y(2)-2.0*Y(1);
```

Example 7.5

Determine the solution of the following differential equation:

$$y'' + 3y' + 2y = \begin{cases} 5t, & \text{for } t < 2 \\ 0, & \text{for } t \ge 2 \end{cases} \tag{7.33}$$

$$y(0) = 1,\ y'(0) = 0$$

Applying the standard form of Equation (7.22), let $p = 3$, $q = 2$, and

$$f(t) = \begin{cases} 5t, & \text{for } t < 2 \\ 0, & \text{for } t \geq 2 \end{cases}$$

We begin by writing $f(t)$ into a form that is recognizably transformable, that is, in terms of the unit step function:

$$\begin{aligned} r(t) &= 5t\left(u(t) - u(t-2)\right) \\ &= 5t\,u(t) - 5t\,u(t-2) \end{aligned} \tag{7.34}$$

The first term in Equation (7.34) is easily transformable $\left(\mathcal{L}(5t\,u(t)) = \frac{5}{s^2}\right)$, but the second is less recognizably so. However, for the second term, let $5t = 5(t - 2 + 2)$. Then,

$$\begin{aligned} f(t) &= 5t\,u(t) - 5(t-2+2)u(t-2) \\ &= 5t\,u(t) - 5(t-2)u(t-2) - 5(2)u(t-2) \end{aligned}$$

Then,

$$\begin{aligned} F(s) &= \mathcal{L}\left(5t\,u(t) - 5(t-2)u(t-2) - 10u(t-2)\right) \\ &= \frac{5}{s^2} - e^{-2s}\frac{5}{s^2} - e^{-2s}\frac{10}{s} \end{aligned}$$

Thus,

$$Y(s) = [(s+3)(1)]H(s) + \left[\frac{5}{s^2} - e^{-2s}\left(\frac{5}{s^2} + \frac{10}{s}\right)\right]H(s)$$

$$H(s) = \frac{1}{s^2 + 3s + 2} = \frac{1}{(s+2)(s+1)}$$

$$\begin{aligned} Y(s) = \frac{s}{(s+2)(s+1)} + \frac{3}{(s+2)(s+1)} + \frac{5}{s^2(s+2)(s+1)} \\ - \frac{5e^{-2s}}{s^2(s+2)(s+1)} - \frac{10e^{-2s}}{s(s+2)(s+1)} \end{aligned}$$

Let $Y(s) = Y_1 + Y_2 + Y_3 + Y_4 + Y_5$, where

$$Y_1 = \frac{s}{(s+2)(s+1)}$$

$$Y_2 = \frac{3}{(s+2)(s+1)}$$

$$Y_3 = \frac{5}{s^2(s+2)(s+1)}$$

$$Y_4 = -\frac{5e^{-2s}}{s^2(s+2)(s+1)}$$

$$Y_5 = -\frac{10e^{-2s}}{s(s+2)(s+1)}$$

By partial fraction expansion via MATLAB's `residue` function, we can determine that

$$\mathcal{L}^{-1}(Y_1) = 2e^{-2t} - e^{-t}$$

$$\mathcal{L}^{-1}(Y_2) = -3e^{-2t} + 3e^{-t}$$

$$\mathcal{L}^{-1}(Y_3) = \frac{5}{2}t - \frac{15}{4} - \frac{5}{4}e^{-2t} + 5e^{-t}$$

$$\mathcal{L}^{-1}(Y_4) = -\left\{\frac{5}{2}t - t - \frac{15}{4} - \frac{5}{4}e^{4}e^{-2t} + 5e^{2}e^{-t}\right\}u(t-2)$$

$$\mathcal{L}^{-1}(Y_5) = -10\left\{\frac{1}{2} + \frac{1}{2}e^{4}e^{-2t} - e^{2}e^{-t}\right\}u(t-2)$$

Summing these five terms gives

$$y(t) = \begin{cases} \dfrac{5}{2}t - \dfrac{15}{4} - \dfrac{9}{4}e^{-2t} + 7e^{-t}, & \text{for } t<2 \\ -\left(\dfrac{9}{4} + \dfrac{15}{4}e^{4}\right)e^{-2t} + (7+5e^{2})e^{-t}, & \text{for } t \geq 2 \end{cases} \tag{7.35}$$

This problem can also be solved numerically by the use of the `ode45` function in MATLAB. The MATLAB program used to solve this problem follows:

```
% Example_7_5.m: This program solves Equation 7.33 by
% converting it into a system of two differential
% equations and solving with ode45.
% Let v=y', Y=[y v], and Y'=[y' v'].
% Y(1)=y, Y(2)=v, Y'(1)=Y(2).
% Y'(2)=5*t-3Y(2)-2Y(1)   for t < 2
% Y'(2)=-3Y(2)-2Y(1)      for t >= 2
% Initial conditions: y(0)=1, y'(0)=0
clear; clc;
% Define initial conditions:
Y0=[1.0 0.0];
% Define time interval to solve:
dt=0.1; Tstop=4; Tspan=0:dt:Tstop;
% Solve the ODE directly with ode45:
[t,Yode45]=ode45('dydt2',Tspan,Y0);
% Compute the solution found via Laplace Transforms
% (Equation 7.35)
for i=1:length(Tspan)
    if Tspan(i) < 2
        Ylaplace(i)=2.5*Tspan(i)- 15/4 - ...
            9/4*exp(-2*Tspan(i))+7*exp(-Tspan(i));
    else
```

```
        Ylaplace(i)= -(9/4+15/4*exp(4)) ...
             * exp(-2*Tspan(i)) ...
             +(7+5*exp(2))*exp(-Tspan(i));
    end
end
plot(t,Yode45(:,1),'x',Tspan,Ylaplace),
title('ODE solutions using ode45 and Laplace Transform');
legend('ode45','Laplace');
------------------------------------------------------------

% dydt2: This function works with Example 7.5.
% Y(1)=y, Y(2)=v
% Y1'=Y(2), Y2'=5*t-3Y2-2Y1, if t >2, Y2'=-3Y2-2Y1, if t >= 2
function Yprime=dydt2(t,Y)
Yprime=zeros(2,1);
Yprime(1)=Y(2);
if t < 2
    Yprime(2)=5*t-3.0*Y(2)-2.0*Y(1);
else
    Yprime(2)=-3.0*Y(2)-2.0*Y(1);
end
```

A comparison of the ode45 and the Laplace transform solution is shown in Figure 7.5.

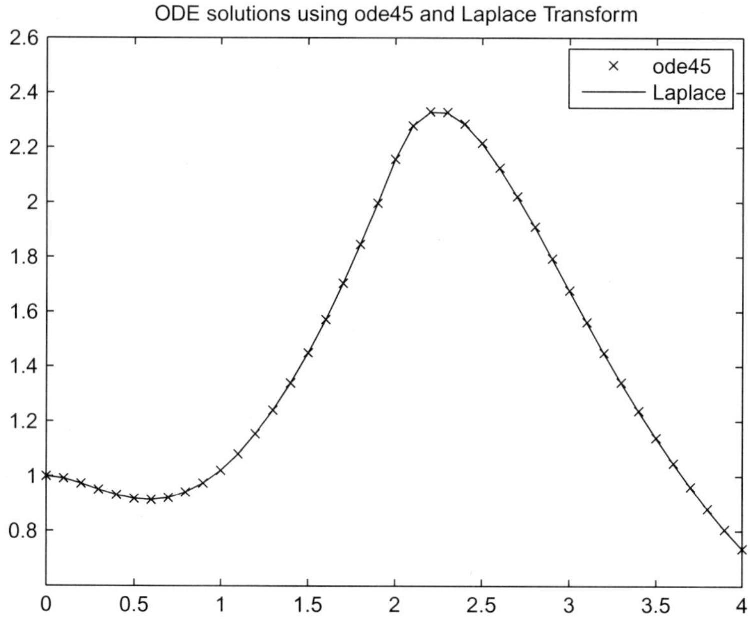

Figure 7.5 Comparison between solution obtained by Laplace transforms and MATLAB's ode45 for Example 7.5.

7.5 Convolution

Given two functions $f(t)$ and $g(t)$ with known transforms $F(s)$ and $G(s)$, respectively, then the inverse transform of the product $F(s)G(s)$ is the convolution integral

$$\mathcal{L}^{-1}(F(s)G(s)) = \int_0^t f(\tau)g(t-\tau)d\tau = \int_0^t g(\tau)f(t-\tau)d\tau \tag{7.36}$$

Proof:

$$\begin{aligned} F(s)G(s) &= \left(\int_0^\infty f(p)e^{-ps}\,dp\right)\left(\int_0^\infty g(\tau)e^{-\tau s}\,d\tau\right) \\ &= \int_0^\infty g(\tau)\left\{\int_0^\infty f(p)e^{-(p+\tau)s}\,dp\right\}d\tau \end{aligned} \tag{7.37}$$

Let $t = p + \tau$. Then, when $p = 0$, $t = \tau$ and when $p = \infty$, then $t = \infty$. Also, $dp = dt$. Then,

$$\begin{aligned} F(s)G(s) &= \int_0^\infty g(\tau)\left\{\int_\tau^\infty f(t-\tau)e^{-ts}\,dt\right\}d\tau \\ &= \iint_R g(\tau)f(t-\tau)e^{-ts}\,dt\,d\tau \end{aligned} \tag{7.38}$$

where R is the region below the line $t = \tau$ as shown in Figure 7.6.

The integration order of the multiple integral as written in Equation (7.38) is to integrate with respect to t first, then with respect to τ. In this case, the order of

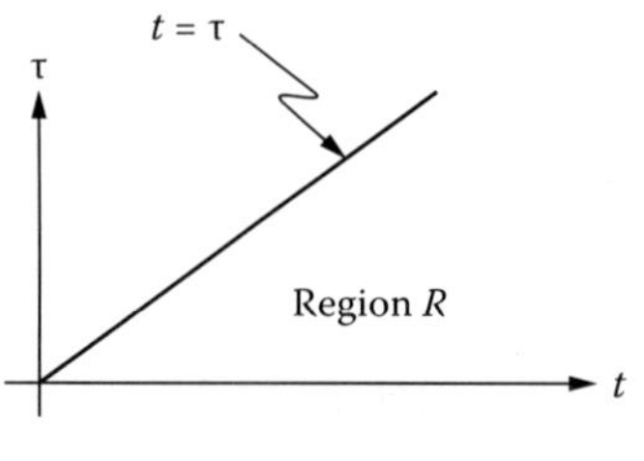

Figure 7.6 Integration region for convolution in the (τ, t) plane.

integration does not matter, so we can integrate with respect to τ first, then with respect to t. This gives

$$F(s)G(s) = \iint_R g(\tau)f(t-\tau)e^{-st}\,dt\,d\tau$$

$$= \int_0^\infty e^{-st}\left\{\int_0^t g(\tau)f(t-\tau)\,d\tau\right\}dt$$

$$= \mathfrak{L}\left(\int_0^t g(\tau)f(t-\tau)\,d\tau\right)$$

Thus,

$$\mathfrak{L}^{-1}(F(s)G(s)) = \int_0^t g(\tau)f(t-\tau)\,d\tau \tag{7.39}$$

Alternatively, we can reverse the roles of f and g, giving

$$\mathfrak{L}^{-1}(F(s)G(s)) = \int_0^t g(t-\tau)f(\tau)\,d\tau$$

Convolution is denoted by the "*" operator; thus,

$$\mathfrak{L}^{-1}\big(F(s)G(s)\big) = f(t)*g(t) = g(t)*f(t)$$

Example 7.6

We illustrate the Laplace transform of the convolution function by studying the waveforms of Figure 7.7a where we have two pulses $f(t)$ and $g(t)$:

$$f(t) = \begin{cases} \alpha & \text{for } 0 \le t < T_1 \\ 0 & \text{otherwise} \end{cases}$$

$$g(t) = \begin{cases} \beta & \text{for } T_2 \le t < T_3 \\ 0 & \text{otherwise} \end{cases}$$

Figure 7.7b shows the convolution operation where we take the mirror image $f(\tau - t)$ of $f(t)$ and slide it along the t axis (by varying τ) while

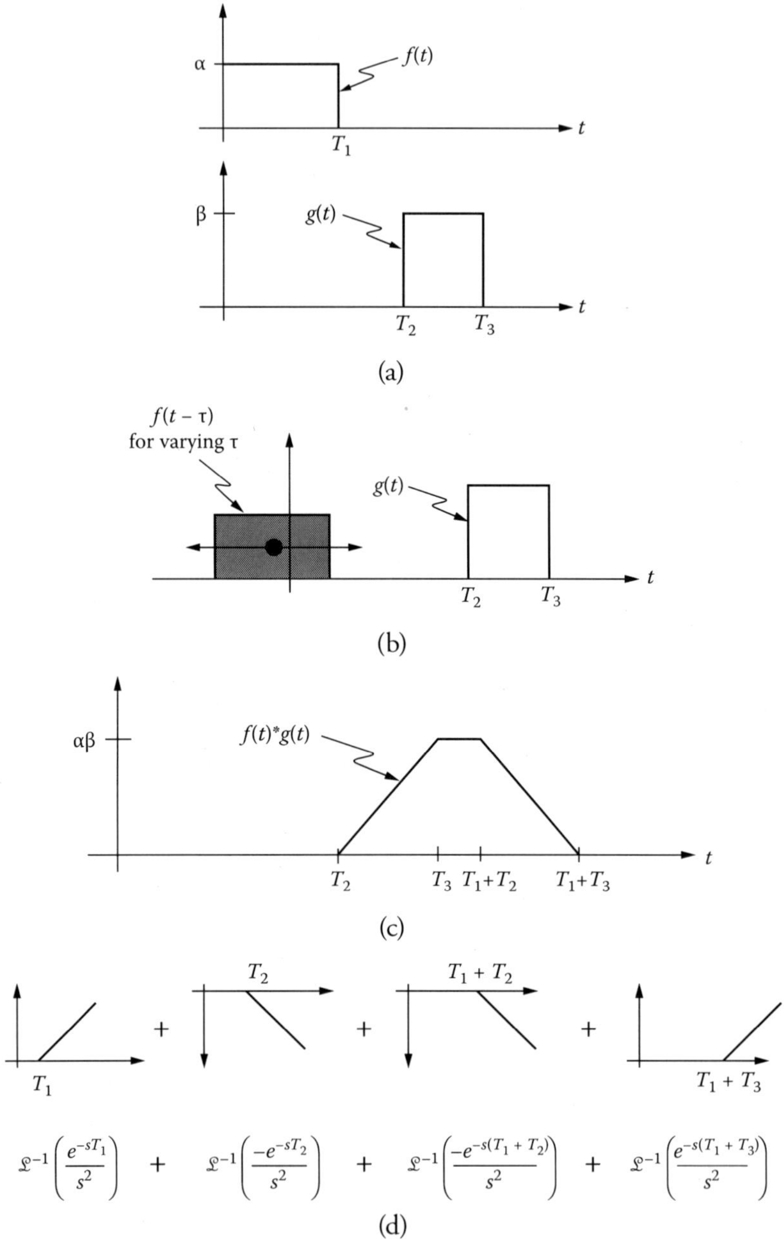

Figure 7.7 Graphical representation of convolution. (a) The pulse waveforms *f*(*t*) and *g*(*t*). (b) We perform the convolution graphically by taking the mirror image of *f*(*t*), sliding it on the *t* axis, and integrating with *g*(*t*). (c) The result of graphically convolving *f*(*t*)g*(*t*) is a trapezoidal waveform. (d) The identical solution is obtained by taking the inverse transform of *F*(*s*)*G*(*s*).**

integrating the two functions. The result of the convolution $f(t)*g(t)$ is the trapezoidal waveform shown in Figure 7.7c:

$$f(t)*g(t)=\begin{cases}\dfrac{\alpha\beta}{(T_3-T_2)}(t-T_2) & \text{for } T_2\le t<T_3\\ \alpha\beta & \text{for } T_3\le t<(T_1+T_2)\\ \dfrac{-\alpha\beta}{(T_3-T_2)}(t-T_1-T_3) & \text{for } (T_1+T_2)\le t<(T_1+T_3)\\ 0 & \text{otherwise}\end{cases} \tag{7.40}$$

We now calculate the Laplace transforms of $f(t)$ and $g(t)$, multiply them in the s domain, and then inverse transform to obtain the identical answer. We previously calculated the transform of a pulse in Equation (7.14). Thus,

$$F(s)=\frac{\alpha}{s}(1-e^{-sT_1})$$

$$G(s)=\frac{\beta}{s}(e^{-sT_2}-e^{-sT_3})$$

Multiplying,

$$F(s)G(s)=\frac{\alpha\beta}{s^2}\left(e^{-sT_2}-e^{-sT_3}-e^{-s(T_1+T_2)}+e^{-s(T_1+T_3)}\right) \tag{7.41}$$

By inspection, the inverse transform of Equation (7.41) consists of the sum of four time-delayed ramp functions and is shown graphically in Figure 7.7d. The sum of the four ramps equals the same trapezoid as in Figure 7.7c.

7.6 Laplace Transforms Applied to Circuits

In circuit theory, capacitors and inductors have constituent relations that particularly lend themselves to analysis in the Laplace domain. Starting with the capacitor,

$$i_C=C\frac{dv_C}{dt}$$

where i_C is the capacitor current, v_C is the capacitor voltage, and C is the capacitor value (in farads). Applying Equation (7.18), we can rewrite this equation in the Laplace domain as

$$I_C(s)=C\left(sV_C(s)-v_C(0)\right)$$

If we neglect for the moment the initial condition, this becomes

$$V_C(s)=I_C(s)\frac{1}{Cs} \tag{7.42}$$

Note that Equation (7.42) resembles Ohm's law $(v = iR)$, and we thus define the *complex impedance* Z_C of a capacitor to be

$$Z_C(s) = \frac{1}{Cs} \tag{7.43}$$

By similar analysis with the constituent relation for inductors $v_L = L\frac{di_L}{dt}$, the complex impedance Z_L of an inductor L (neglecting initial conditions) is shown to be

$$Z_L(s) = Ls \tag{7.44}$$

Finally, for resistors, the Laplace transform of Ohm's law implies

$$Z_R(s) = R \tag{7.45}$$

Because we have previously proven that Laplace transforms are linear, we can now solve complicated linear circuits directly in the Laplace domain by using the same algebraic techniques used to solve the input/output relationships for resistor-only circuits. For example, the parallel RLC circuit as redrawn in Figure 7.8 with input current $I_o(s)$, output voltage $V_c(s)$, and complex impedances can be solved with one equation:

$$V_C(s) = I_o(s)\left(Z_R(s) \,||\, Z_C(s) \,||\, Z_L(s)\right)$$

where the parallel operator (||) indicates the calculation for resistors (or impedances) in parallel. Then,

$$\frac{V_C(s)}{I_o(s)} = \frac{1}{\frac{1}{Z_R} + \frac{1}{Z_C} + \frac{1}{Z_L}}$$

$$= \frac{1}{\frac{1}{R} + Cs + \frac{1}{Ls}}$$

$$= \frac{1}{C} \times \frac{s}{s^2 + \frac{1}{RC}s + \frac{1}{LC}} \tag{7.46}$$

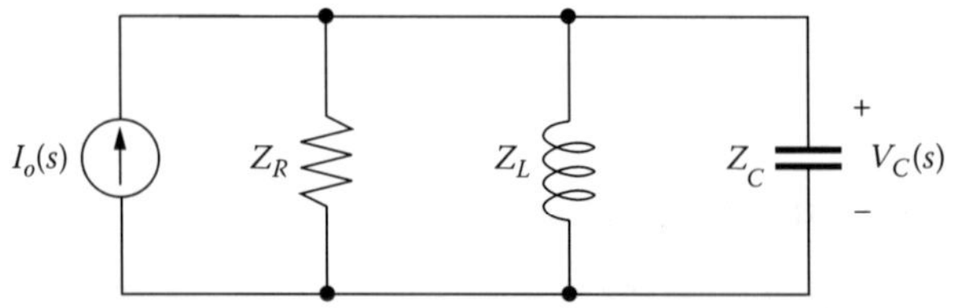

Figure 7.8 RLC circuit using impedances.

We also define

$$H(s) = \frac{V_C(s)}{I_o(s)} \tag{7.47}$$

as the *transfer function* of the circuit, that is, the ratio of the output variable (in this case V_C) to the input driving function (in this case I_o).

Let us now assume a sinusoidal form for $i_o(t)$ such that

$$i_o(t) = C\,e^{j\omega t}$$

where $e^{j\omega t}$ $(= \cos\omega t + j\sin\omega t)$ is a sum of sines and cosines of frequency ω. For convenience, we have also added a constant factor of C to simplify the math as we progress. Then,

$$I_o(s) = C\frac{1}{s - j\omega}$$

and

$$\begin{aligned} V_C(s) &= H(s)I_o(s) \\ &= \frac{s}{(s+s_1)(s+s_2)(s-j\omega)} \end{aligned} \tag{7.48}$$

where s_1 and s_2 are the zeros of the denominator of Equation (7.46) and are calculated from R, L, and C. We also assume for this analysis that s_1 and s_2 are real. Rearranging Equation (7.48) by partial fractions, we get

$$V_C(s) = \frac{\dfrac{s_1}{(s_1+s_2)(s_1-j\omega)}}{s+s_1} + \frac{\dfrac{s_2}{(s_2+s_1)(s_2-j\omega)}}{s+s_2} + \frac{\dfrac{j\omega}{(j\omega+s_1)(j\omega+s_2)}}{s-j\omega}$$

By inverse transform, we get

$$v_C(t) = \frac{s_1}{(s_1+s_2)(s_1-j\omega)}e^{-s_1t} + \frac{s_2}{(s_2+s_1)(s_2-j\omega)}e^{-s_2t} + H(j\omega)e^{j\omega t} \tag{7.49}$$

Although Equation (7.49) looks complicated, note that the first two terms contain negative exponentials and thus in the *steady state* ($t \to \infty$), this equation reduces to

$$\lim_{t\to\infty} v_c(t) = H(j\omega)e^{j\omega t} \tag{7.50}$$

The meaning of Equation (7.50) is that for any sinusoidal input (of frequency ω) to the circuit, we can calculate the value of the steady-state output (also of frequency ω) by calculating $H(j\omega)$. This derivation can be generalized for determining the *frequency response* of any linear circuit by finding the transfer function $H(s)$ analytically and then letting $s = j\omega$ to find its frequency-dependent behavior.

Frequency response is traditionally plotted as two graphs showing the magnitude $|H(j\omega)|$ and phase $\angle H(j\omega)$, both versus frequency. The magnitude plot is typically on log-log axes, and the phase plot is typically on semilog axes (linear phase vs. log frequency). Together, the plots are referred to as a *Bode plot*.

Example 7.7

Let

$$H(s) = \frac{1000}{s + 1000}$$

Plot the magnitude and phase of $H(j\omega)$ over the interval $\omega = [1\times10^{-1}, 1\times10^{6}]$ rad/sec. The solution is shown in Figure 7.9.

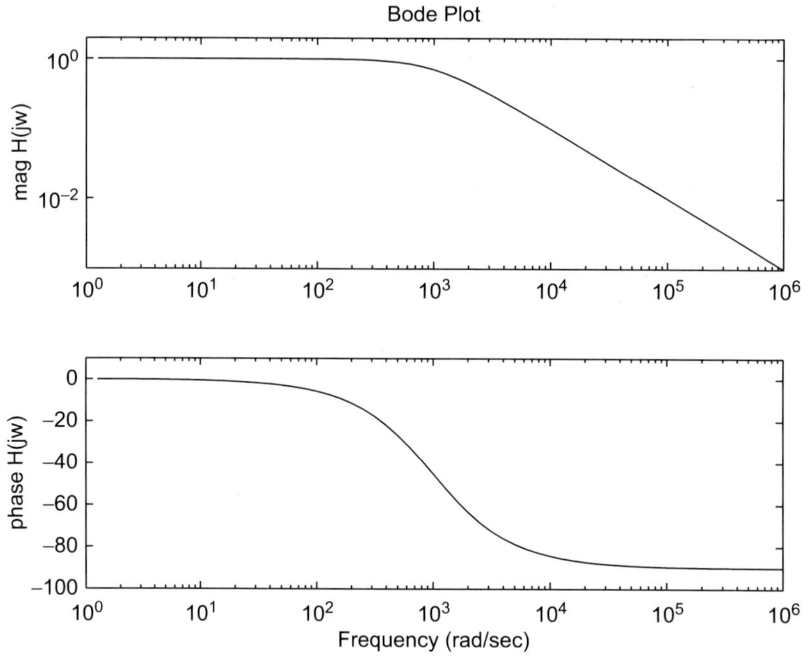

Figure 7.9 Bode plot for $H(j\omega) = \dfrac{1000}{j\omega + 1000}$.

```
% Example_7_7.m: Plot magnitude and phase of
% H(jw)= 1000/(s+1000) for w=[1e-1,1e6].
% First, create a logarithmic point set for the frequency
% range from 1 to 1e6 rad/sec with ten points in each
% decade.
for k=1:60
    w(k)=10^(k/10);
end
% Compute the magnitude for H(jw)
H_mag = abs( 1000 ./ (j*w + 1000) );
% Compute the phase for H(jw), and convert to degrees
H_phase = (180/pi) * angle( 1000 ./ (j*w + 1000) );
% Plot magnitude on log-log axes
subplot(2,1,1);
loglog(w,H_mag);
axis([10^0 10^6 10^-3 2*10^0]);
ylabel('mag H(jw)');
title('Bode Plot');
% Plot phase on log-linear axes
subplot(2,1,2);
semilogx(w,H_phase);
axis([10^0 10^6 -100 10]);
xlabel('Frequency (rad/sec)');
ylabel('phase H(jw)');
```

7.7 Impulse Response

In Section 7.2.7, we discussed the delta function and its properties. What happens if we use a delta function as the input to a circuit with known transfer function $H(s)$? In Equation (7.47), we defined $H(s)$ as the ratio of the circuit output to the circuit input. If we assume that the input is a delta function, then

$$\begin{aligned} V_C(s) &= H(s)I_o(s) \\ &= H(s)(1) \end{aligned} \tag{7.51}$$

where we have assumed $i_o(t) = \delta(t)$ with corresponding Laplace transform of unity. If we inverse transform Equation (7.51), we get

$$v_C(t) = h(t)$$

In other words, if the circuit input is a delta function, then the circuit output is simply the inverse transform of the transfer function $h(t)$, also known as the *impulse response*. Conversely, if we can accurately calculate (or measure) the impulse response $h(t)$ of a circuit, then we can obtain the transfer function $H(s)$ and thus predict the circuit behavior for *any* arbitrary input waveform. This concept is illustrated in Example 7.8.

Example 7.8

A circuit has an impulse response of

$$h(t) = 10e^{-2t}\cos 10t$$

What is the unit step response $r(t)$ of the circuit?

Transforming $h(t)$ into $H(s)$, we obtain

$$H(s) = 10\left(\frac{s+2}{(s+2)^2+100}\right)$$

where we have applied Equations (7.9) and (7.11) to determine the Laplace transform. To obtain the step response, we first multiply $H(s)$ by the unit step transform $\frac{1}{s}$ to obtain $R(s)$:

$$R(s) = 10\left(\frac{s+2}{(s+2)^2+100}\right)\left(\frac{1}{s}\right)$$

We now calculate the inverse transform as follows:

$$\begin{aligned}
r(t) &= \mathfrak{L}^{-1}\{R(s)\} \\
&= 10\,\mathfrak{L}^{-1}\left\{\frac{s+2}{s^3+4s^2+104s}\right\} \\
&= 10\,\mathfrak{L}^{-1}\left\{\frac{-0.0096-0.0481j}{s+(2-10j)}+\frac{-0.0096-0.0481j}{s+(2+10j)}+\frac{0.0192}{s}\right\} \\
&\quad \times(\text{calculated using residue}) \\
&= 10(-0.0096e^{-2t+10jt}+0.0481je^{-2t+10jt}-0.0096e^{-2t-10jt} \\
&\quad -0.0481je^{-2t-10jt}+0.0192u(t)) \\
&= 1.92e^{-2t}(-e^{-2t}\cos 10t - 5e^{-2t}\sin 10t + u(t))
\end{aligned}$$

Exercises

Exercise 7.1 Determine $\mathfrak{L}(\sin^2 \omega t)$.

Exercise 7.2 Determine $\mathfrak{L}(e^{2t}\cos t)$.

Exercise 7.3 Determine $\mathfrak{L}(e^{-3t}\sin 2t)$

Exercise 7.4 Determine the Laplace transform of the function shown graphically in Figure E7.4.

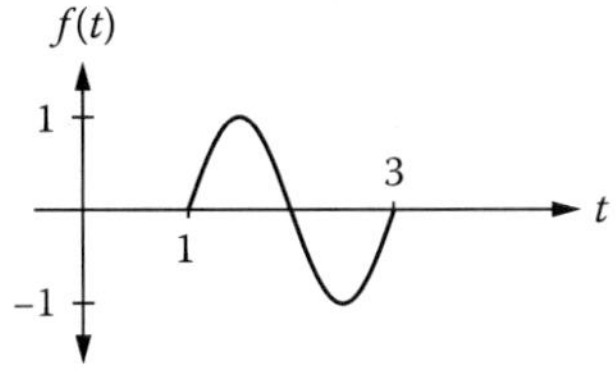

Figure E7.4 *f*(*t*) **consists of one cycle of a sine wave over the interval** $1 \le t \le 3$ **sec.**

Exercise 7.5 Determine $\mathcal{L}^{-1}\left(\dfrac{2s+1}{(s^2+9)(s-2)}\right)$.

Exercise 7.6 Determine $\mathcal{L}^{-1}\left(\dfrac{1}{(s^2+5s+6)}\right)$.

Exercise 7.7 Determine $\mathcal{L}^{-1}\left(\dfrac{1}{(s+1)(s^2+3s+2)}\right)$ by convolution in the time domain.

Exercise 7.8 Solve the following differential equation by Laplace transforms:

$$y'' + 3y' - 2y = 3e^{-t}, \quad y(0) = 1, \quad y'(0) = 2$$

Projects

Project 7.1

Figure P7.1 shows a series RLC circuit driven by an input voltage $v_i(t)$ and three defined output voltages $v_R(t)$, $v_L(t)$, and $v_C(t)$.

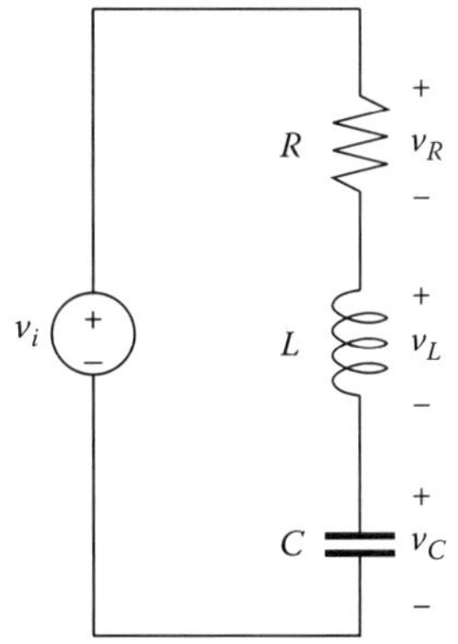

Figure P7.1 Series RLC circuit.

1. Solve the circuit using complex impedances to find the three transfer functions $H_R(s)=\frac{V_R(s)}{V_i(s)}$, $H_L(s)=\frac{V_L(s)}{V_i(s)}$, and $H_C(s)=\frac{V_C(s)}{V_i(s)}$. Put the transfer functions in the following standard form:

$$H(s)=\frac{K_1s^2+K_2s+K_3}{s^2+K_4s+K_5}$$

where the constants K_1 through K_5 are real. Note that the five constants are scaled such that the highest-order term in the denominator should have no constant.
2. Create the Bode plots for $H_R(j\omega)$, $H_L(j\omega)$, and $H_C(j\omega)$. Use these component values: R = 1 kΩ, L = 0.1 mH, and C = 0.1 μF. Plot over the range $\omega=[1,\ 1\times10^{10}]$ rad/sec.
3. The three transfer functions represent three types of filters: *high-pass*, *low-pass*, and *bandpass*. Which transfer function corresponds to which filter type?

Project 7.2

A *common emitter amplifier* is shown in Figure P7.2a with input voltage v_{in} and output voltage v_{out}. In these types of single-transistor circuits, the voltages of interest ride atop DC components V_{BIAS} and V_{OFFSET}, which are used to *bias* the transistor into its linear (i.e., amplification) mode. Figure P7.2b shows the small-signal *hybrid-pi* model of the bipolar transistor [3]. In the small-signal model, the DC components (V_{CC}, V_{BIAS}, and V_{OFFSET}) are ignored, and we can use Kirchhoff's

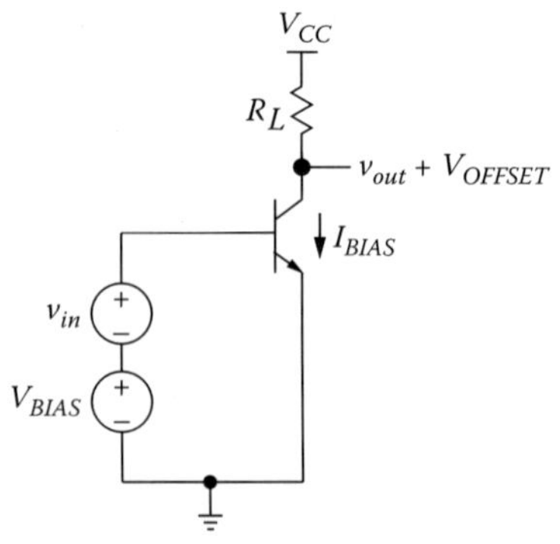

Figure P7.2a Common emitter amplifier. V_{BIAS} is the nonvarying ("DC") component of the input, which is adjusted to obtain the desired operating point (I_{BIAS}) of the transistor. V_{OFFSET} is the DC component of the output. The voltages of interest are the varying components of the input v_{in} and the output v_{out}.

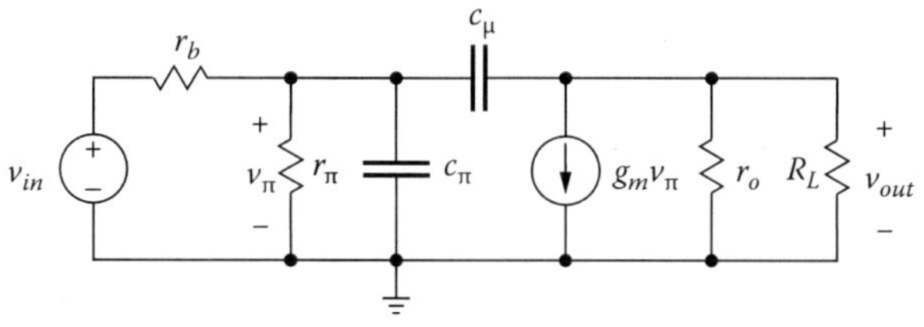

Figure P7.2b Small-signal model of the common emitter amplifier. r_b is the series base resistance, r_π is the small-signal base-emitter resistance, g_m is the transconductance (the transistor "gain"), r_o is the small-signal collector-emitter resistance, and c_π and c_μ are the base-emitter and collector-emitter capacitances, respectively. R_L is the load resistance of the amplifier.

current law to solve for the transfer function in terms of complex impedances. Writing KCL equations at nodes v_π and v_{out} gives

$$\frac{(v_{in}-v_\pi)}{r_b}-\frac{v_\pi}{r_\pi \,||\, \dfrac{1}{c_\pi s}}+\frac{(v_{out}-v_\pi)}{\dfrac{1}{c_\mu s}}=0 \qquad \text{(P7.2a)}$$

$$\frac{(v_{out}-v_\pi)}{\dfrac{1}{c_\mu s}}+g_m v_\pi+\frac{v_{out}}{r_o \,||\, R_L}=0 \qquad \text{(P7.2b)}$$

where v_π is the small-signal base-emitter voltage; r_π is the small-signal base-emitter resistance; r_b is the base resistance; c_π and c_μ are the base-emitter and collector-emitter capacitances, respectively; r_o is the small-signal collector-emitter resistance; g_m is the small-signal transconductance; and R_L is the load resistance. Solving these equations gives the transfer function of the system:

$$H(s)=\frac{v_{out}}{v_{in}}=\frac{\dfrac{1}{r_b}\left(c_\mu s-g_m\right)}{c_\pi c_\mu s^2+\left(\dfrac{c_\pi}{r_o \,||\, R_L}+\dfrac{c_\mu}{r_o \,||\, R_L \,||\, r_b \,||\, r_\pi \,||\, \dfrac{1}{g_m}}\right)s+\dfrac{1}{(r_b \,||\, r_\pi)(r_o \,||\, R_L)}} \qquad \text{(P7.2c)}$$

If we assume that the transistor is model 2N3904, we can obtain numerical values for the circuit parameters from the manufacturer data sheet for this component [4]. These are summarized in Table P7.2. We also assume that V_{BIAS} is adjusted to obtain a transistor collector current (I_{BIAS}) of 1 mA, and that $R_L = 5\ \text{k}\Omega$. Because the 2N3904 is a discrete device (and not part of an integrated circuit), we also assume a small base resistance $r_b = 25\ \Omega$. Also, assume that $g_m = \dfrac{I_o}{V_T}$, where $V_T = \dfrac{kT}{q} = 0.026\ \text{mV}$.

Table P7.2 Parameters for 2N3904 NPN transistor

Transistor Parameter	*Typical Value*
h_{FE} (= β)	125
C_{obo} (= c_μ)	3 pF
C_{ibo} (= c_π)	4 pF
h_{ie} (= r_π)	4 kΩ
h_{oe} (= $1/r_o$)	10 μmho

1. Create the Bode plot for the transfer function of Equation (P7.2a) using the parameters in Table P7.2. Plot over the frequency interval $\omega = [1\times 10^5, 1\times 10^{11}]$ rad/sec.
2. A common trick for hand analysis of this circuit is to use the *Miller approximation;* we assume alternative values for c_μ and c_π as follows:

$$c'_\mu = 0$$

$$c'_\pi = c_\pi + \left(g_m(r_o \,||\, R_L) + 1\right)c_\mu$$

   Substitute these approximated values for c_μ and c_π into Equation (P7.2a) and find the approximate transfer function $H_{\text{Miller}}(s)$.
3. Plot $H_{\text{Miller}}(s)$ on the same set of axes that you already used to plot $H(s)$. Under what circumstances is the Miller approximation reasonable to use?

References

1. Churchill, R.V., *Operational Mathematics*, 2nd ed., McGraw-Hill, New York, 1958.
2. Kreyszig, E., *Advanced Engineering Mathematics*, 8th ed., Wiley, New York, 1999.
3. Sedra, A.S., and Smith, K.C., *Microelectronic Circuits,* 3rd ed., Saunders College, Philadelphia, 1991.
4. 2N3904/MMBT3904/PZT3904 NPN general purpose amplifier, Fairchild Semiconductor data sheet, http://www.fairchildsemi.com, 2011.

Table 7.1 Common Laplace Transforms

	$f(t)$	$F(s)$
1	Unit step: 1	$\frac{1}{s}$
2	Ramp: t	$\frac{1}{s^2}$
3	Power of t: $\frac{t^{n-1}}{(n-1)!}$	$\frac{1}{s^n}$ $(n=1,2,\ldots)$
4	Derivative: $\frac{df(t)}{dt}$	$sF(s)-f(0)$
5	Time delay: $f(t-T)$	$e^{-sT}F(s)$
6	Exponential: $e^{at}f(t)$	$F(s-a)$
7	Convolution: $f(t)*g(t)$	$F(s)G(s)$
8	Delta function: $\delta(t)$	1
9	$\frac{1}{\sqrt{\pi t}}$	$\frac{1}{\sqrt{s}}$
10	$2\sqrt{\frac{t}{\pi}}$	$s^{-\frac{3}{2}}$
11	$\frac{2^n t^{n-1/2}}{1\times3\times5\times\ldots\times(2n-1)\sqrt{\pi}}$	$s^{-\left(n+\frac{1}{2}\right)}$ $(n=1,2,\ldots)$
12	e^{at}	$\frac{1}{s-a}$
13	te^{at}	$\frac{1}{(s-a)^2}$
14	$\frac{1}{(n-1)!}t^{n-1}e^{at}$	$\frac{1}{(s-a)^n}$ $(n=1,2,\ldots)$
15	$t^{k-1}e^{at}$	$\frac{\Gamma(k)}{(s-a)^k}$ $(k>0)$

(continued)

Table 7.1 Common Laplace Transforms (Continued)

	$f(t)$	$F(s)$
16	$\frac{1}{(a-b)}(e^{at}-e^{bt})$	$\frac{1}{(s-a)(s-b)}$ $(a \neq b)$
17	$\frac{1}{(a-b)}(ae^{at}-be^{bt})$	$\frac{s}{(s-a)(s-b)}$ $(a \neq b)$
18	$-\frac{(b-a)e^{at}+(c-a)e^{bt}+(a-b)e^{ct}}{(a-b)(b-c)(c-a)}$	$\frac{1}{(s-a)(s-b)(s-c)}$
19	$\frac{1}{a}\sin at$	$\frac{1}{s^2+a^2}$
20	$\cos at$	$\frac{s}{s^2+a^2}$
21	$\frac{1}{a}\sinh at$	$\frac{1}{s^2-a^2}$
22	$\cosh at$	$\frac{s}{s^2-a^2}$
23	$\frac{1}{a^2}(1-\cos at)$	$\frac{1}{s(s^2+a^2)}$
24	$\frac{1}{a^3}(at-\sin at)$	$\frac{1}{s^2(s^2+a^2)}$
25	$\frac{1}{2a^3}(\sin at - at\cos at)$	$\frac{1}{(s^2+a^2)^2}$
26	$\frac{t}{2a}\sin at$	$\frac{s}{(s^2+a^2)^2}$
27	$\frac{1}{2a}(\sin at + at\cos at)$	$\frac{s^2}{(s^2+a^2)^2}$
28	$t\cos at$	$\frac{s^2-a^2}{(s^2+a^2)^2}$

Table 7.1 Common Laplace Transforms (Continued)

	$f(t)$	$F(s)$
29	$\frac{\cos at - \cos bt}{b^2 - a^2}$	$\frac{s}{(s^2+a^2)(s^2+b^2)}$ $(a^2 \neq b^2)$
30	$\frac{1}{b}e^{at}\sin bt$	$\frac{1}{(s-a)^2+b^2}$
31	$e^{at}\cos bt$	$\frac{s-a}{(s-a)^2+b^2}$
32	$e^{-at} - e^{\frac{at}{2}}\left(\cos\frac{at\sqrt{3}}{2} - \sqrt{3}\sin\frac{at\sqrt{3}}{2}\right)$	$\frac{3a^2}{s^3+a^3}$
33	$\sin at \cosh at - \cos at \sinh at$	$\frac{4a^3}{s^4+4a^4}$
34	$\frac{1}{2a^2}\sin at \sinh at$	$\frac{s}{s^4+4a^4}$
35	$\frac{1}{2a^3}(\sinh at - \sin at)$	$\frac{1}{s^4-a^4}$
36	$\frac{1}{2a^2}(\cosh at - \cos at)$	$\frac{s}{s^4-a^4}$
37	$(1+a^2t^2)\sin at - at\cos at$	$\frac{8a^3s^2}{(s^2+a^2)^3}$
38	$L_n(t) = \frac{e^t}{n!}\frac{d^n}{dt^n}(t^n e^{-t})$	$\frac{1}{s}\left(\frac{s-1}{s}\right)^n$
39	$\frac{1}{\sqrt{\pi t}}e^{at}(1+2at)$	$\frac{s}{(s-a)^{\frac{3}{2}}}$
40	$\frac{1}{2\sqrt{\pi t^3}}(e^{bt} - e^{at})$	$\sqrt{s-a} - \sqrt{s-b}$

(continued)

Table 7.1 Common Laplace Transforms (Continued)

	$f(t)$	$F(s)$
41	$\frac{1}{\sqrt{\pi t}} - ae^{a^2 t}\,\mathrm{erfc}(a\sqrt{t})$	$\frac{1}{\sqrt{s}+a}$
42	$\frac{1}{\sqrt{\pi t}} + ae^{a^2 t}\,\mathrm{erfc}(a\sqrt{t})$	$\frac{\sqrt{s}}{s-a^2}$
43	$\frac{1}{a}e^{a^2 t}\,\mathrm{erf}(a\sqrt{t})$	$\frac{1}{\sqrt{s}(s-a^2)}$
44	$e^{a^2 t}\,\mathrm{erfc}(a\sqrt{t})$	$\frac{1}{\sqrt{s}(\sqrt{s}+a)}$
45	$\frac{1}{\sqrt{b-a}}e^{-at}\,\mathrm{erf}(\sqrt{b-a}\sqrt{t})$	$\frac{1}{(s+a)\sqrt{s+b}}$
46	$e^{a^2 t}\left[\frac{b}{a}\mathrm{erf}(a\sqrt{t})-1\right]$	$\frac{b^2-a^2}{\sqrt{s}(s-a^2)(\sqrt{s}+b)}$
47	$J_0(at)$	$\frac{1}{\sqrt{s^2+a^2}}$
48	$J_0(2\sqrt{kt})$	$\frac{1}{s}e^{-k/s}$
49	$\frac{1}{\sqrt{\pi t}}\cos 2\sqrt{kt}$	$\frac{1}{\sqrt{s}}e^{-k/s}$
50	$\frac{1}{\sqrt{\pi t}}\cosh 2\sqrt{kt}$	$\frac{1}{\sqrt{s}}e^{k/s}$
51	$\frac{1}{\sqrt{\pi k}}\sin 2\sqrt{kt}$	$\frac{1}{s^{3/2}}e^{-k/s}$
52	$\frac{1}{\sqrt{\pi k}}\sinh 2\sqrt{kt}$	$\frac{1}{s^{3/2}}e^{k/s}$
53	$\frac{k}{2\sqrt{\pi t^3}}\exp\left(-\frac{k^2}{4t}\right)$	$e^{-k\sqrt{s}}\ (k>0)$

Table 7.1 Common Laplace Transforms (Continued)

	$f(t)$	$F(s)$
54	$\operatorname{erfc}\left(\frac{k}{2\sqrt{t}}\right)$	$\frac{1}{s}e^{-k\sqrt{s}}\ (k \geq 0)$
55	$\frac{1}{\sqrt{\pi t}}\exp\left(-\frac{k^2}{4t}\right)$	$\frac{1}{\sqrt{s}}e^{-k\sqrt{s}}\ (k \geq 0)$
56	$2\sqrt{\frac{t}{\pi}}\exp\left(-\frac{k^2}{4t}\right) - k\operatorname{erfc}\left(\frac{k}{2\sqrt{t}}\right)$	$s^{-3/2}e^{-k\sqrt{s}}\ (k \geq 0)$
57	$-e^{ak}e^{a^2t}\operatorname{erfc}\left(a\sqrt{t} + \frac{k}{2\sqrt{t}}\right) + \operatorname{erfc}\left(\frac{k}{2\sqrt{t}}\right)$	$\frac{ae^{-k\sqrt{s}}}{s(a+\sqrt{s})}\ (k \geq 0)$
58	$e^{ak}e^{a^2t}\operatorname{erfc}\left(a\sqrt{t} + \frac{k}{2\sqrt{t}}\right)$	$\frac{e^{-k\sqrt{s}}}{\sqrt{s}(a+\sqrt{s})}\ (k \geq 0)$
59	$\frac{1}{t}(e^{bt} - e^{at})$	$\log\frac{s-a}{s-b}$
60	$\frac{2}{t}(1-\cos at)$	$\log\frac{s^2+a^2}{s^2}$
61	$\frac{2}{t}(1-\cosh at)$	$\log\frac{s^2-a^2}{s^2}$
62	$\frac{1}{t}\sin kt$	$\tan^{-1}\frac{k}{s}$

Chapter 8

Fourier Transforms and Signal Processing

8.1 Introduction

In electronic circuits, we are often presented with voltage and currents that represent signals that carry meaningful information. Examples include

- audio, including hi-fi and voice
- video, including television and surveillance
- telemetry from temperature sensors, strain gauges, medical instrumentation, power meters, and the like
- radar, loran, and GPS signals for detection and guidance systems on aircraft and ships
- modulated signals as AM, FM, VHF, UHF, CDMA (code division multiple access), GSM (Groupe spéciale mobile), and Wi-Fi for broadcast and point-to-point transmission of audio, video, voice, and data

There are countless reasons for processing signals. For audio and video, we might want to filter out noise or reduce bandwidth. For telemetry signals, we may want to examine the data from multiple sensors to achieve a goal such as predicting the

Table 8.1 Example Signals and Their Corresponding Frequency Ranges

Signal Type	*Frequency Range*
Speech	200 to 3200 Hz
High-fidelity audio (range of human ear)	20 to 20,000 Hz
AM radio	535 to 1705 kHz (North America) or 526.5 to 1606.5 kHz (Europe)
FM radio	87.5 to 108.0 MHz
802.11b Wi-Fi networking	2.401 to 2.473 GHz
White noise	0 to ∞ Hz
A above middle C on the piano	440 Hz (fundamental) 880 Hz, 1320 Hz, 1760 Hz, … (harmonics)

weather, reducing an automobile's fuel consumption, or interpreting sensor data from an electrocardiogram. In the case of communication systems, we can use modulation to multiplex audio or video signals (from radio or TV stations) onto high-frequency carriers, thereby allowing multiple signals to be carried over a common medium (e.g., a coaxial cable or optical fiber) or through the airwaves. In addition, we typically want to account for the link loss and intersymbol interference (ISI) introduced by the channel.

The primary mathematical tool used in signal processing is the *Fourier transform*. This transform provides a method for describing a signal in terms of its frequency components (i.e., in the "frequency domain") instead of in the more familiar and tangible "time domain." Table 8.1 lists several types of signals and their corresponding frequency ranges (i.e., the range of frequency components that *might* be present in the waveforms). For the rest of this chapter, we use audio signals in our examples because they are likely to be familiar to most readers. However, all of the techniques introduced in this chapter are applicable to signals of any frequency range.

Figure 8.1 shows an example waveform for some of the signals of Table 8.1. In general, the "sharpness" of the shape of each signal corresponds to its high-frequency components, and the more jagged the signal, the higher the frequency range. Thus, over a 25-msec interval, the high-fidelity audio signal shown in Figure 8.1b is more jagged than the speech signal in Figure 8.1a. Periodic signals (e.g., the musical note shown in Figure 8.1c) consist primarily of a single *fundamental* frequency plus smaller *harmonic* components that cause the waveform to deviate from a precise sinusoidal shape.

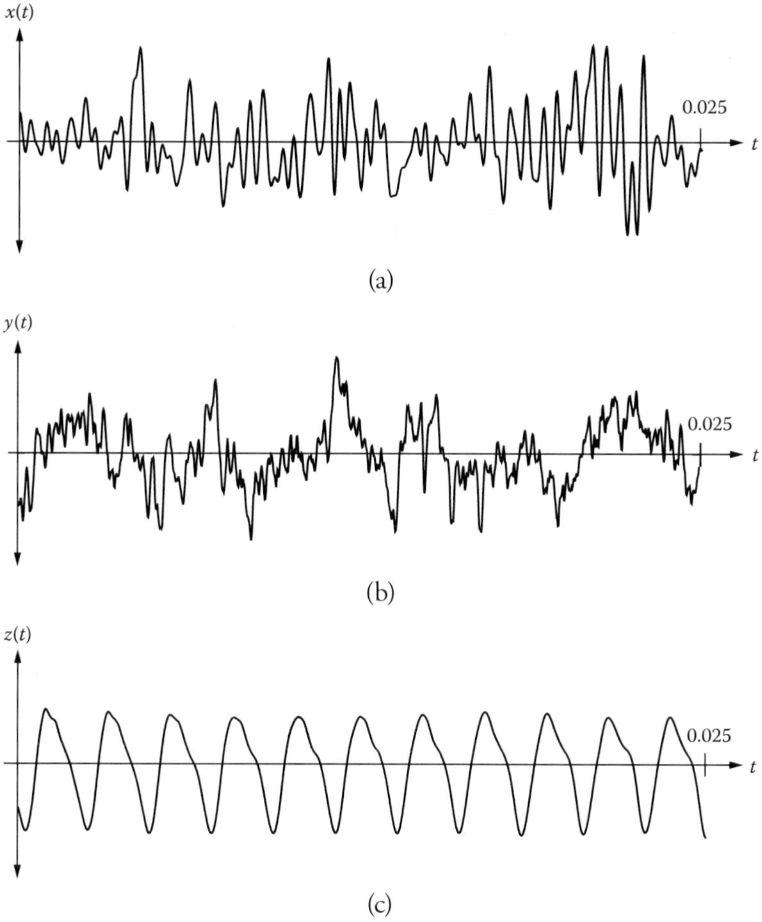

Figure 8.1 Example of band-limited waveforms: (a) speech; (b) high-fidelity audio; (c) A above middle C on the piano.

8.2 Mathematical Description of Periodic Signals: Fourier Series

We begin with a signal $x(t)$, which might represent audible sound that has been converted to a varying voltage using a *transducer* (e.g., a microphone). If $x(t)$ is periodic as shown in Figure 8.1c as a sustained A note on a piano, then Fourier theory tells us that the waveform may be expressed as a weighted sum of pure sinusoids:

$$x(t) = A_0 + \sum_{n=1,2,3,\ldots} A_n \cos(2\pi \cdot nf_o \cdot t) + \sum_{n=1,2,3,\ldots} B_n \sin(2\pi \cdot nf_o \cdot t) \qquad (8.1)$$

The frequencies nf_o in the second and third terms represent all possible sine and cosine components of $x(t)$. The $n = 1$ component is the *fundamental* frequency f_o, and components where $n > 1$ are called the *harmonics*. The factors A_n and B_n are called the *Fourier coefficients,* and A_0 is the "DC" component of $x(t)$. We can determine A_0, A_n, and B_n mathematically by multiplying $x(t)$ by each possible frequency component and then integrating over one period of $x(t)$. For example, to find the Fourier coefficient for the mth cosine term, we multiply both sides of Equation (8.1) by $\cos(2\pi m f_o t)$ and integrate over the interval $-\frac{T}{2} \le t \le \frac{T}{2}$, where $T = \frac{1}{f_o}$ is the time period for one cycle of the periodic waveform:

$$\int_{-T/2}^{T/2} x(t)\cos(2\pi m f_o t)\,dt$$

$$= \int_{-T/2}^{T/2} \left[A_0 + \sum A_n \cos(2\pi n f_o t) + \sum B_n \sin(2\pi n f_o t)\right]\cos(2\pi m f_o t)\,dt \quad (8.2)$$

Because sine and cosine are *orthogonal* functions, all of the terms on the right side of Equation (8.2) will integrate out to zero except for the cosine-cosine terms when $m = n$, that is,

$$\int_{-T/2}^{T/2} \cos(2\pi m f_o t)\cos(2\pi n f_o t)dt = \frac{T}{2}, \quad m = n$$

$$\int_{-T/2}^{T/2} \cos(2\pi m f_o t)\cos(2\pi n f_o t)dt = 0, \quad m \ne n \quad (8.3)$$

$$\int_{-T/2}^{T/2} \cos(2\pi m f_o t)\sin(2\pi n f_o t)dt = 0, \quad \text{all } m,n$$

Therefore, the integration operation will "filter" out all components of $x(t)$ except for the frequency where $m = n$. Applying Equation (8.3) to Equation (8.2) gives

$$A_n = \frac{2}{T}\int_{-T/2}^{T/2} x(t)\cos\left(2\pi n f_o t\right)dt$$

$$B_n = \frac{2}{T}\int_{-T/2}^{T/2} x(t)\sin\left(2\pi n f_o t\right)dt \quad (8.4)$$

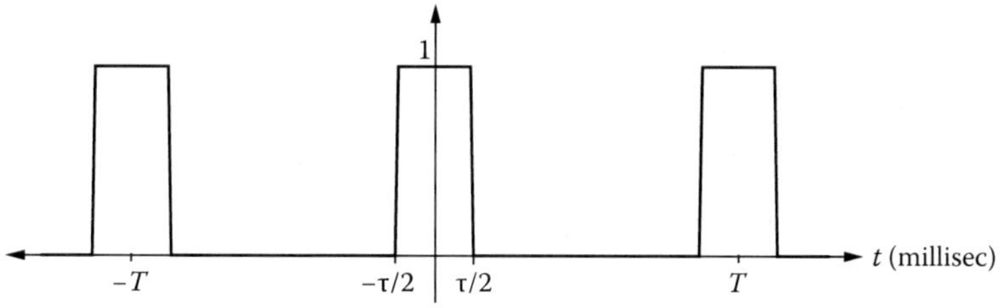

Figure 8.2 A pulse train with "on" time of τ and period *T*.

To calculate the DC coefficient A_0, we integrate Equation (8.3) for $m = 0$ to obtain

$$A_0 = \frac{1}{T}\int_{-T/2}^{T/2} x(t)\,dt \tag{8.5}$$

Example 8.1

Find the Fourier series for the periodic pulse train shown in Figure 8.2 with period T, frequency $f_o = \frac{1}{T}$, "on" time of τ, and "off" time of $T - \tau$.

By centering $x(t)$ on the y axis, we ensure that $x(t)$ is an even function. Thus, by symmetry, all of the odd terms in Equation (8.1) (i.e., the sine terms) will be zero. We begin by finding the DC term (for $n = 0$) by applying Equation (8.5) and integrating $x(t)$ over one cycle:

$$A_0 = \frac{1}{T}\int_{-\tau/2}^{\tau/2} 1 \cdot dt$$

$$= \frac{\tau}{T}$$

For the higher-order terms:

$$A_n = \frac{2}{T}\int_{-\tau/2}^{\tau/2} 1 \cdot \cos(2\pi n f_o t)\,dt$$

$$= \frac{2}{T}\left.\frac{\sin(2\pi n f_o t)}{2\pi n f_o}\right|_{-\tau/2}^{\tau/2}$$

$$= \frac{2}{\pi n}\sin(\pi n f_o \tau)$$

Thus, the solution for the first few terms of the Fourier series for the pulse train is

$$x(t) = \frac{\tau}{T} + \frac{2}{\pi}\sin\left(\frac{\pi\tau}{T}\right)\sin\left(2\pi f_o t\right) + \frac{1}{\pi}\sin\left(\frac{2\pi\tau}{T}\right)\sin\left(4\pi f_o t\right)$$

$$+\frac{2}{3\pi}\sin\left(\frac{3\pi\tau}{T}\right)\sin\left(6\pi f_o t\right) + \cdots$$

The following MATLAB program calculates the Fourier coefficients for the pulse train where $T = 1$ ms and $\tau = 0.25$ ms and then reconstructs the pulse train based on the Fourier coefficients.

```
% Example_8_1.m
% Compute the Fourier series for a pulse train.
T=1e-3;         % pulse period
fo=1/T;         % frequency of pulse train in Hz
tau=0.25e-3; % "on" time of a single pulse
n=1:10;         % we will compute the first 10 coefficients
% compute the DC coefficient:
A0 = tau/T;
% compute coefficients 1 thru n
for i=1:length(n)
    An(i) = (2/(pi *n(i))) * sin(pi*n(i)*fo*tau);
end
% Plot the coefficients:
subplot(2,1,1);
stem([0 fo*n],[A0 An]);
xlabel('Hz'); ylabel('Fourier coefficients');
axis([-200 10200 -.2 .6]);
% Use the Fourier coefficients to reconstitute the pulse
% train over the interval -1.5 < t < 1.5 millisec with n
% coefficients
t=-1.5e-3:1e-6:1.5e-3;
waveform = zeros(1,length(t));
% Add in the DC coefficient
waveform = waveform + A0;
% Add in signal components for 1 thru nth coefficients
for i=1:length(n)
    waveform = waveform + An(i) * cos(2*pi*n(i)*fo*t);
end
subplot(2,1,2);
plot(t*1000,waveform);
xlabel('t (millisec)'); ylabel('reconstituted x(t)');
-----------------------------------------------------------------
```

The first 10 calculated Fourier coefficients are shown in Figure 8.3a, and the reconstituted pulse using the 10 coefficients is shown in Figure 8.3b.

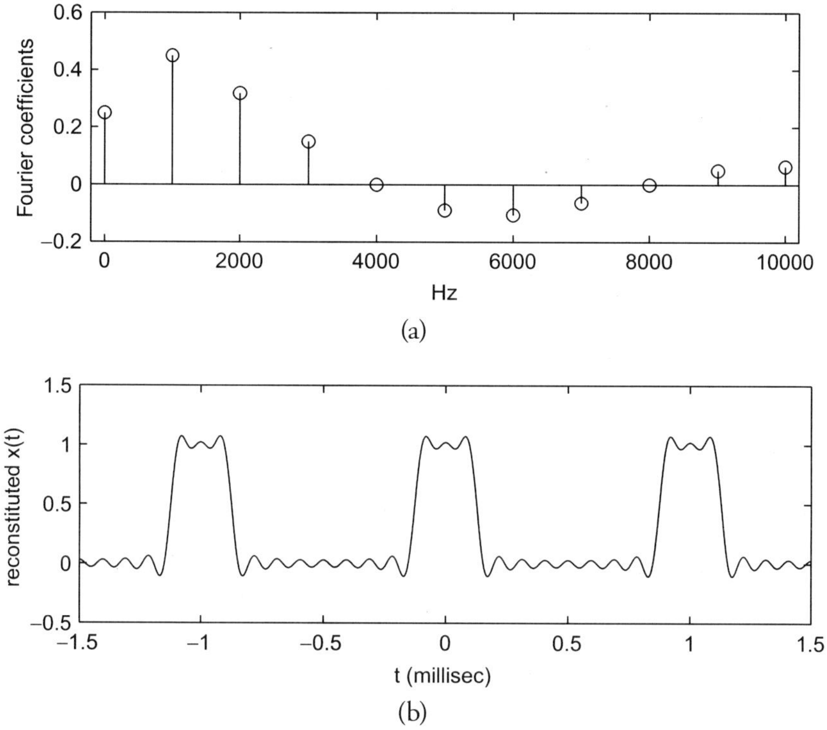

Figure 8.3 (a) Fourier coefficients for the pulse train of Figure 8.2 for $T = 1$ msec and $\tau = 0.25$ msec. (b) Pulse train reconstituted using the first 10 Fourier coefficients. Note that the missing higher-order terms cause the reconstituted waveform to be inaccurate, especially at the sharp transitions.

8.3 Complex Exponential Fourier Series and Fourier Transforms

Generally, a Fourier series may be comprised of the weighted sum of *any* set of orthogonal functions. Although sines and cosines are a common choice due to their familiarity, the preferred choice from a mathematical perspective is the set of complex exponential functions:

$$x(t) = \sum_{n=-\infty}^{\infty} C_n e^{j2\pi n f_o t} \tag{8.6}$$

Knowing the identities $\cos x = \dfrac{e^{jx} + e^{-jx}}{2}$ and $\sin x = \dfrac{e^{jx} - e^{-jx}}{2j}$, it can be proven that Equation (8.6) is equivalent to Equation (8.1) where $C_n = \dfrac{A_n - jB_n}{2}$, $C_{-n} = \dfrac{A_n + jB_n}{2}$, and $C_0 = A_0$. Multiplying an exponential by its complex conjugate and then integrating over one period implies equivalent orthogonality relations:

$$\int_{-T/2}^{T/2} e^{j2\pi m f_o t} e^{-j2\pi n f_o t} dt = \begin{cases} T, & m = n \\ 0, & m \neq n \end{cases} \tag{8.7}$$

Integrating both sides of Equation (8.6) over one period and applying Equation (8.7) gives an expression for the complex exponential Fourier coefficients for any periodic $x(t)$:

$$C_n = \frac{1}{T} \int_{-T/2}^{T/2} x(t) e^{-j2\pi n f_o t} \, dt \tag{8.8}$$

We now make two modifications to Equation (8.8). First, we normalize the Fourier coefficients by moving the $\dfrac{1}{T}$ factor from the right side to the left. Then, we define $X(f)$ as a function to represent the normalized Fourier coefficients. Equation (8.8) becomes

$$X(nf_o) = TC_n = \int_{-T/2}^{T/2} x(t) e^{-j2\pi n f_o t} \, dt \tag{8.9}$$

Next, we replace nf_o with the variable f (for frequency) and let $T \to \infty$, thereby implying that $x(t)$ becomes an *aperiodic* signal. Then, the integration limits in Equation (8.9) become infinity, and $X(f)$ becomes a continuous function:

$$X(f) = \int_{-\infty}^{\infty} x(t) e^{-j2\pi f t} \, dt \tag{8.10}$$

Equation (8.10) is the definition of the *Fourier transform* of the time-domain signal $x(t)$.

Example 8.2

Plot the normalized complex exponential Fourier coefficients for the pulse train shown in Figure 8.2. Assume $\tau = 0.25$ msec and generate three plots for $T = 1$, 2, and 10 msec.

As for Example 8.1, the DC component is $C_0 = \frac{\tau}{T}$. For the $n \neq 0$ terms,

$$C_n = \frac{1}{T}\int_{-\tau/2}^{\tau/2} 1 \cdot e^{-j2\pi n f_o t}\, dt$$

$$= \frac{1}{T}\frac{e^{-j2\pi n f_o t}}{-j2\pi n f_o}\Bigg|_{-\tau/2}^{\tau/2}$$

$$= \frac{e^{-j\pi n f_o \tau} - e^{j\pi n f_o \tau}}{-j2\pi n}$$

$$= \frac{\sin \pi n f_o \tau}{\pi n}$$

A program that computes and plots the coefficients follows:

```
% Example_8_2.m
% Compute normalized exponential Fourier series
% coefficients for a pulse train
tau = 0.25e-3;             % "on" time of a single pulse
T = [ 1e-3 2e-3 10e-3 ]; % pulse train periods
fo = 1 ./ T;               % frequency of pulse train in Hz
n = -150:150;
for i=1:length(T)
    Cn(i,:) = ( 1 ./ (pi*n) ) .* sin(pi*n*fo(i)*tau);
    % Find the "zero" entry in n and compute it
    % separately (because it has a different formula than
    % the rest):
    zeroeth_element = find(n==0);
    Cn(i,zeroeth_element) = tau/T(i);
    % Normalize the coefficients:
    Cn_normalized(i,:) = Cn(i,:) .* T(i);
end
% find reasonable limits for axes so that all 3 plots
% have the same min/max
x_axis_limits = [ -3.8/tau 3.8/tau];
y_axis_limits = [ 1.5*min(Cn_normalized(1,:)) ...
    1.25*max(Cn_normalized(1,:)) ];
% Plot separately for each value of T:
subplot(3,1,1);
stem( n*fo(1), Cn_normalized(1,:) );
ylabel({'Fourier coefficients';'for T=1 ms'});
axis([x_axis_limits y_axis_limits]);
title('Exponential Fourier Series for Pulse');
subplot(3,1,2);
stem( n*fo(2), Cn_normalized(2,:) );
axis([x_axis_limits y_axis_limits]);
ylabel({'Fourier coefficients';'for T=2 ms'});
subplot(3,1,3);
plot( n*fo(3), Cn_normalized(3,:) );
axis([x_axis_limits y_axis_limits]);
ylabel({'Fourier coefficients';'for T=10 ms'});
xlabel('f (Hz)');
```

Figure 8.4 shows the three sets of Fourier coefficients computed in Example 8.2 for pulse periods of $T = 1$, 2, and 10 msec. Note that by keeping the pulse width constant and increasing the pulse period, the Fourier coefficients get closer and closer together. When $T = 10$ msec, they are so close together that we have plotted them as a continuous function. In the limit $T \to \infty$, Figure 8.4c corresponds to the Fourier transform of the pulse.

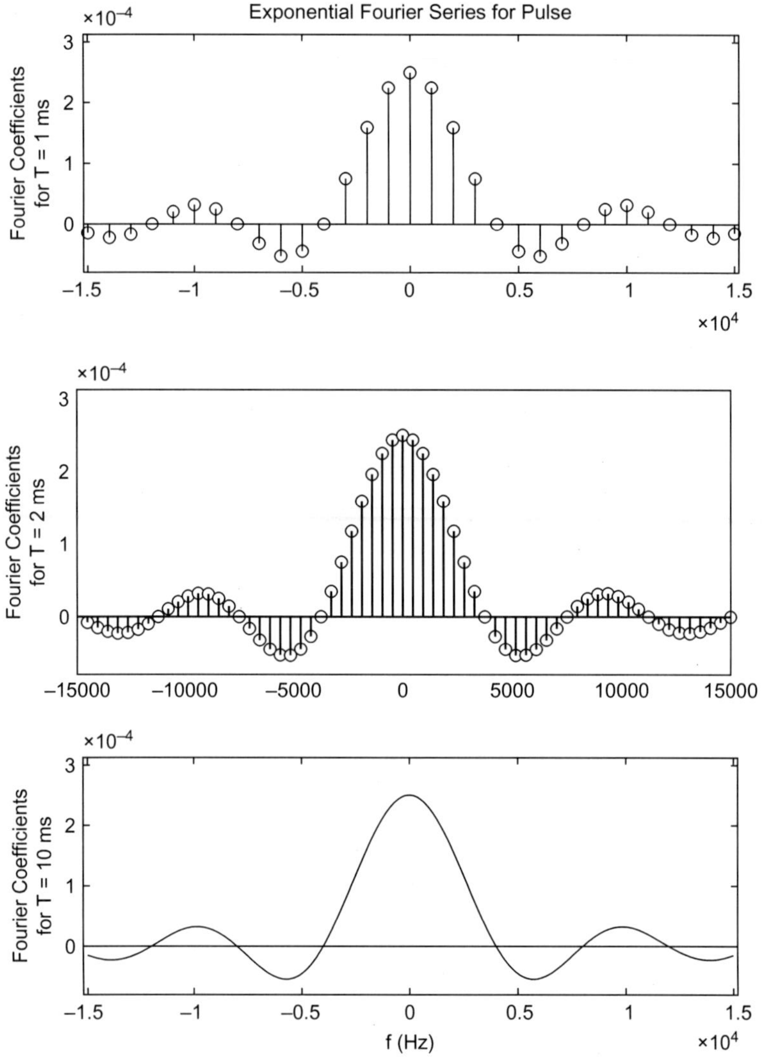

Figure 8.4 Plot of the Fourier series coefficients for a pulse train with 0.25 msec on time and (a) period of 1 msec, (b) period of 2 msec, and (c) period of 10 msec. For the last case, the coefficients are so close together that they are plotted as a continuous function.

8.4 Properties of Fourier Transforms

Qualitatively, the Fourier transform is a description of the frequency makeup of $x(t)$. Figure 8.5 shows the three signals of Figure 8.1 transformed into the frequency domain. Note that when describing their properties, the actual shapes of the Fourier transforms are in general unimportant (and in this case we have drawn them as rounded rectangles). For the moment, we are more interested in their beginning and endpoints. Note that the transforms are always symmetric around the y axis because we always assume that $x(t)$ originates from an actual waveform that is realizable and real (and thus has no imaginary component). Nevertheless,

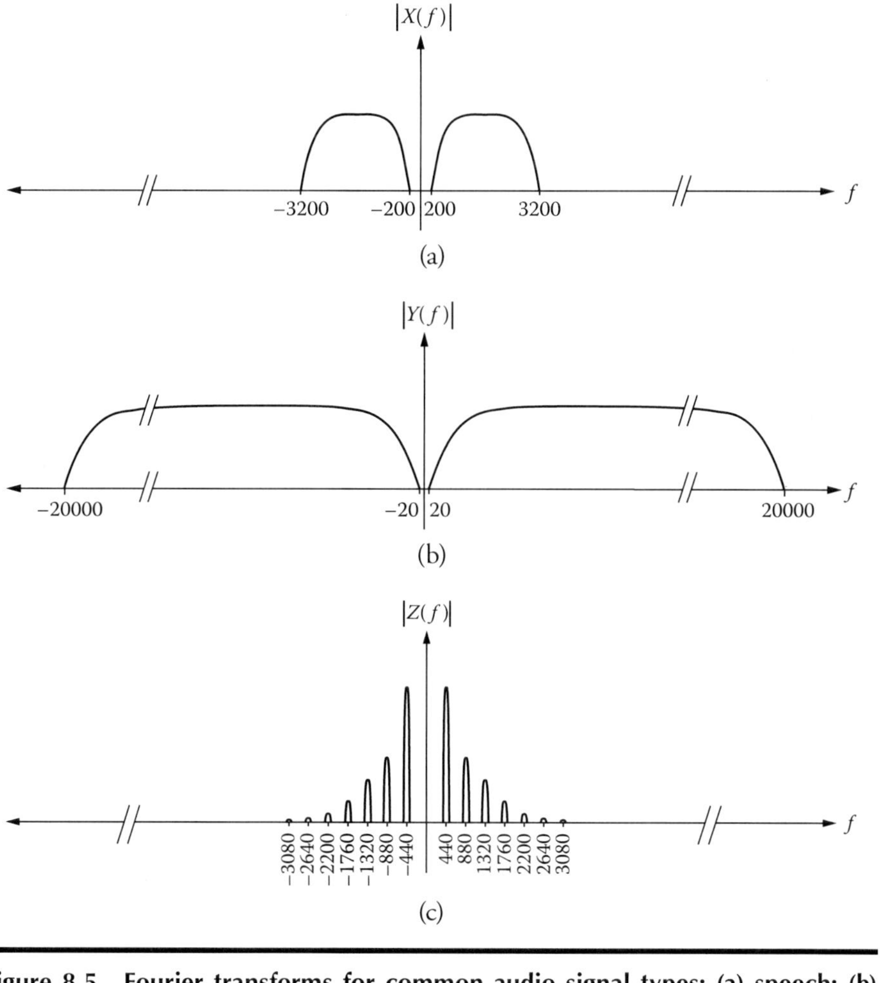

Figure 8.5 Fourier transforms for common audio signal types: (a) speech; (b) high-fidelity audio; (c) A above middle C on the piano.

Fourier transforms *do* have an imaginary component, and in Figure 8.5, we have only plotted the magnitude (and not the phase). The idea of a signal having complex or "negative frequency" may appear confusing, but it is simply an artifact of our using the complex exponential as the orthogonal function. When necessary, we can always change a complex frequency back to a real frequency by applying the identity $e^{jx} = \cos x + j\sin x$; in the meantime, we can take advantage of the simplified math that comes from "bundling" the sines and cosines together into one exponential term.

Mathematically, the Fourier transform may be considered a subset of the *bilateral Laplace transform* where $s = j2\pi f$ [1]. It does not provide as complete an analysis as the Laplace transform (e.g., it cannot be used to predict system stability), but its simplicity allows convenient insight into signal behavior. As with any transform technique, we can transform from one domain to the other at will to take advantage of the conveniences of each.

We can derive the *inverse Fourier transform* by substituting the denormalized Fourier transform $\frac{X(f)}{T}$ back into Equation (8.6) to obtain

$$x(t) = \frac{1}{T}\sum_{n=-\infty}^{\infty} X(nf_o)e^{j2\pi nf_o t}$$

$$= \sum_{n=-\infty}^{\infty} X(nf_o)e^{j2\pi nf_o t}\frac{nf_o}{n} \tag{8.11}$$

Letting $nf_o \rightarrow f$ and $\frac{f}{n} \rightarrow df$, in the limit the sum becomes an integral:

$$x(t) = \int_{-\infty}^{\infty} X(f)e^{j2\pi f t}\,df \tag{8.12}$$

Equation (8.12) is the definition of the inverse Fourier transform of $X(f)$.

Some important Fourier transform pairs are summarized in Table 8.2. Note that the similarity of the forward and inverse Fourier transforms (Equations (8.10) and (8.12) only differ by the sign of the exponential) leads to the *duality* property in which each entry in Table 8.2 can be considered a reversible pair (hence the bidirectional arrow for each entry in the table). For example, given that a pulse (of width 2τ) in the time domain transforms to $\frac{\sin 2\pi f\tau}{\pi f}$ in the frequency domain, we can also infer that a "pulse" in the frequency domain (of width $2F_o$) transforms to $\frac{\sin 2\pi F_o t}{\pi t}$ in the time domain.

Table 8.2 Common Fourier Transform Pairs

Property	*Time Domain x(t)*	↔	*Frequency Domain X(f)*
Linearity	$x(t) = Ay(t) + Bz(t)$	↔	$X(f) = AY(f) + BZ(f)$
Duality	$X(t)$	↔	$x(-f)$
Impulse	$x(t) = \delta(t)$	↔	$X(f) = 1$
Cosine	$x(t) = \cos 2\pi f_o t$	↔	$X(f) = \dfrac{\delta(f - f_o) + \delta(f + f_o)}{2}$
Sine	$x(t) = \sin 2\pi f_o t$	↔	$X(f) = \dfrac{\delta(f - f_o) - \delta(f + f_o)}{2j}$
Pulse	$x(t) = \begin{cases} 1 & \lvert t \rvert \le \tau \\ 0 & \text{otherwise} \end{cases}$	↔	$X(f) = \dfrac{\sin 2\pi f \tau}{\pi f}$
Ideal low-pass filter	$x(t) = \dfrac{\sin 2\pi f_o t}{\pi t}$	↔	$X(f) = \begin{cases} 1 & \lvert f \rvert \le f_o \\ 0 & \text{otherwise} \end{cases}$
Convolution/ multiplication	$y(t) = x(t) * h(t)$	↔	$Y(f) = X(f)H(f)$
Causal decaying exponential	$y(t) = u(t)e^{-\alpha t}$	↔	$Y(f) = \dfrac{1}{j2\pi f + \alpha}$
Causal decaying cosine	$y(t) = u(t)e^{-at}\cos 2\pi f_o t$	↔	$Y(f) = \dfrac{(j2\pi f + a)}{(j2\pi f + a)^2 + (2\pi f_o)^2}$
Causal decaying sine	$y(t) = u(t)e^{-at}\sin 2\pi f_o t$	↔	$Y(f) = \dfrac{2\pi f_o}{(j2\pi f + a)^2 + (2\pi f_o)^2}$

8.5 Filters

Filtering is the application of a frequency-dependent function on a waveform. The various types of filters are classified and characterized by the shape of their frequency response in the Fourier domain and are summarized in Table 8.3. For example, a *low-pass* filter has a Fourier transform that has a value of one at low frequencies and a value of

Table 8.3 Frequency Reponse for Common Filter Types

Low-pass:	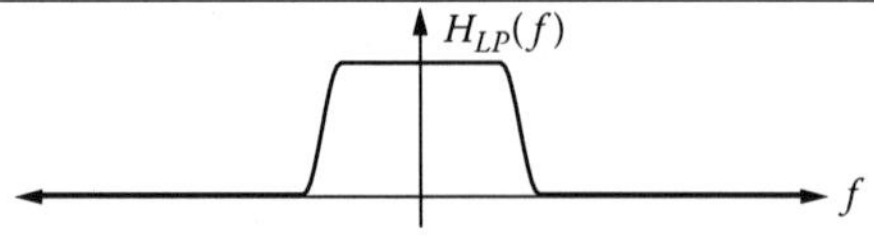
High-pass:	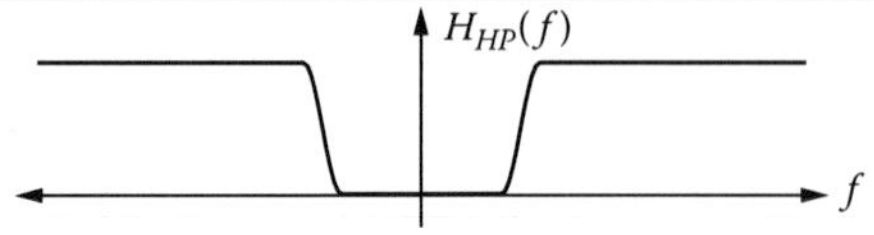
Bandpass:	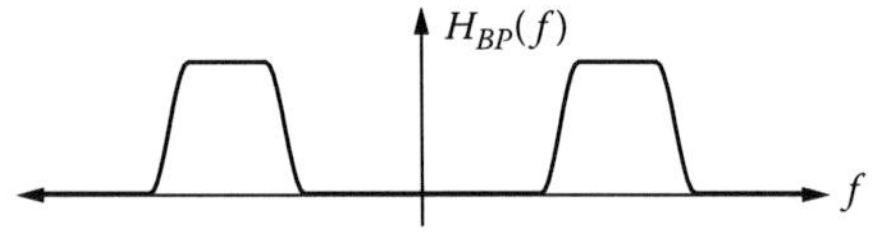
Band reject:	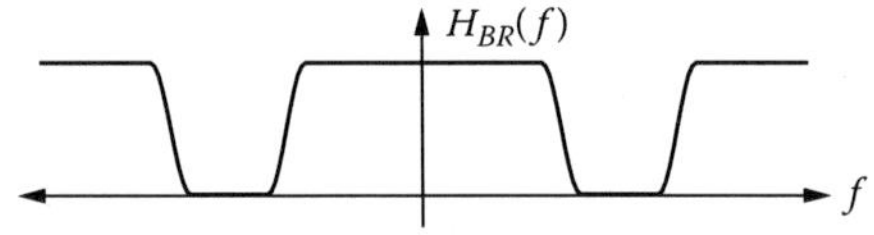
Equalizer:	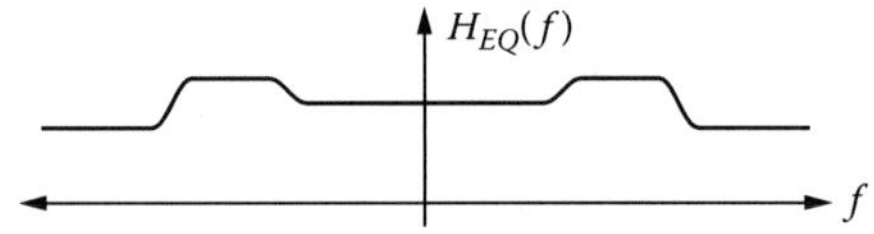

zero (or nearly zero) at high frequencies. In this case, the low-frequency region is called the *passband* because signals are passed through the filter unchanged, and the high-frequency region is called the *stopband* because signals in this region are stopped by the filter. Conversely, a *high-pass* filter has the stopband at low frequencies and the passband at high frequencies. In a *bandpass* filter, the passband has both a low and a high limit. A *band reject* (opposite of bandpass) has a low and high limit on the stopband. An *equalizer* has multiple passbands of varying magnitudes and is typically used to compensate for nonlinear frequency behavior in an amplifier or communication channel.

Figure 8.6a shows an example of an ideal low-pass filter with cutoff frequency f_o and corresponding frequency response $H_I(f)$ (where the I subscript denotes "ideal"). If we apply this filter to a waveform with Fourier transform $X(f)$ containing frequencies within the range $f_1 < |f| < f_2$, then the filter output is the product $H_I(f)X(f)$, and all frequencies greater than f_o are removed.

Unfortunately, there is a fundamental problem with this ideal "brick wall" filter in the frequency domain. We know from Table 8.2 that multiplication in the frequency domain corresponds to convolution in the time domain. If we examine $H_I(f)$ in the time domain, we see that the corresponding function $h_I(t) = \dfrac{\sin 2\pi f_o t}{\pi t}$ extends infinitely for all $\pm t$. Thus, to convolve $x(t)$ with $h_I(t)$, we need to know *all* values of $x(t)$,

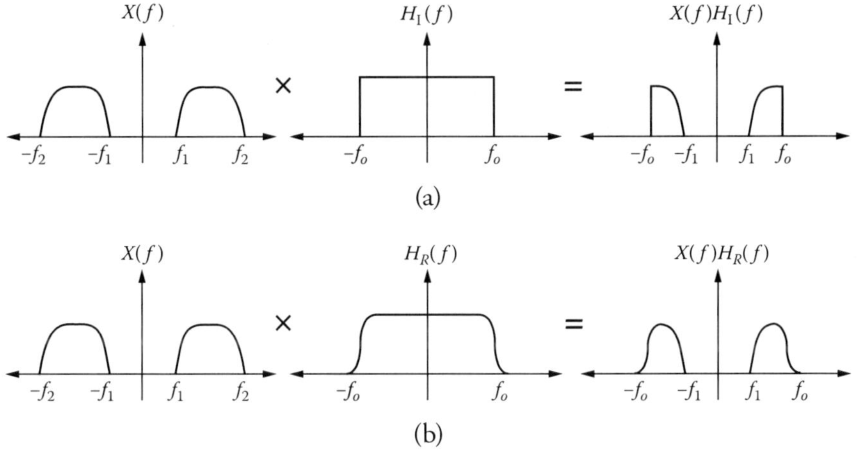

Figure 8.6 (a) An ideal "brick wall" low-pass filter with cutoff frequency f_o. (b) A realizable low-pass filter necessarily has a smooth transition band.

including those for $t < 0$. A filter that depends on values for $t < 0$ is called a *noncausal* filter and is impossible to implement, both with numerical algorithms and real circuit components.

Given that we cannot implement an ideal filter, there are various alternative approaches that can be used instead. One approach is to apply a *window function* to $h_I(t)$ to make it causal, and the simplest window function is to multiply $\frac{\sin 2\pi f_o t}{\pi t}$ by a rectangular window to truncate the infinite tails of $h_I(t)$, thus forcing it to be causal. Another approach is to use a known realizable filter characteristic such as the *Butterworth* or *Chebyshev* responses. In either case, the net result is to remove the discontinuity in the frequency response at f_o. The corresponding $H_R(f)$ (where the R means "realizable") is a smooth filter that can actually be implemented. This is shown in Figure 8.6b, where $H_R(f)$ now has curved edges, and the resulting filtered output also has similar edges.

8.6 Discrete-Time Representation of Continuous-Time Signals

In *digital signal processing* (and in MATLAB), we represent a continuous-time signal as a sequence of numbers by the process of *sampling*. Figure 8.7a shows a typical continuous-time signal $x(t)$ (with the time argument denoted by parentheses) and its discrete-time counterpart $x[n]$ (where the discrete argument is denoted with square brackets). We derive $x[n]$ from $x(t)$ by extracting the values of $x(t)$ at an evenly spaced

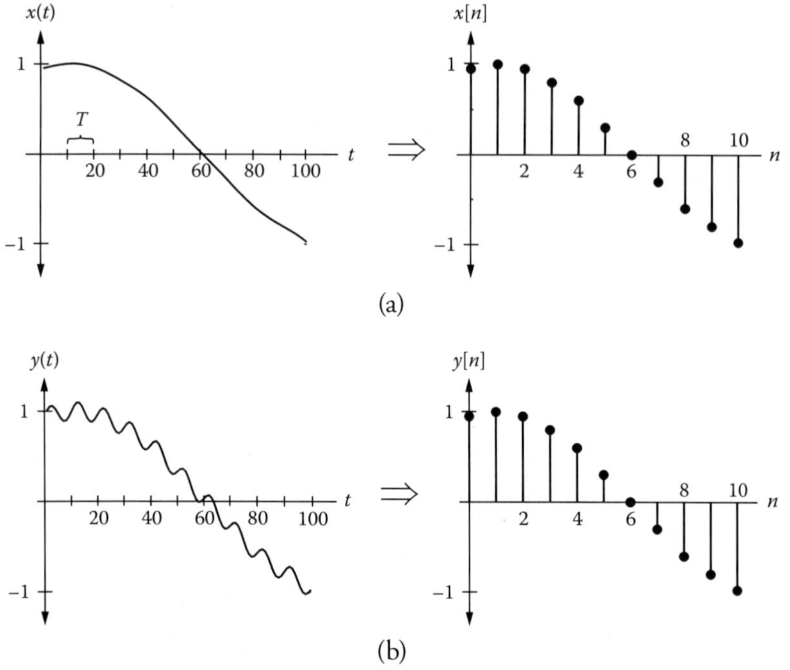

Figure 8.7 (a) A typical continuous-time signal *x*(*t*) and its corresponding discrete-time signal *x*[*n*], which is derived by sampling *x*(*t*) every *T* seconds. (b) If *y*(*t*) has an additional high-frequency component with a period of an exact fraction of *T*, then that component is invisible in the corresponding *y*[*n*].

interval of size T, called the *sampling time* (or equivalently at a *sampling rate* $f_S = \frac{1}{T}$). Mathematically, we convert from continuous to discrete time with the formula

$$x[n] = x(nT) \tag{8.13}$$

where n is an integer. Note that a discrete signal $x[n]$ does not inherently carry any time information but rather is just a series of values for x indexed by the dimensionless integer n. Thus, once we sample a continuous-time signal, it is important to remember the sample time T if we ever wish to convert the discrete version back to continuous time.

We must also take care to choose an appropriate sample rate. Figure 8.7b shows what can happen if we choose T too large. The corresponding discrete signal $y[n]$ is missing the high-frequency sine component (with frequency of exactly $\frac{1}{T}$) that "rides" atop $y(t)$. Thus, sampling a continuous-time signal does not guarantee uniqueness in the discrete domain, as evidenced in Figure 8.7 by the fact that $x[n]$ and $y[n]$ are identical. The *sampling theorem* states that to fully describe a continuous-time signal discretely, we must choose a sampling rate that is at least twice as fast as the highest-frequency component of the original signal. In practice, we usually choose a sampling rate that is slightly higher than the minimum required to account for circuit imperfections and component variations. For example, in audio CDs, which can reproduce frequencies up to 20,000 Hz, the sampling rate is 44,100 samples/sec (instead of the minimum value of 40,000 samples/sec).

There are many motivations for converting continuous-time signals to discrete time, but our immediate reason is so we can use a digital computer to carry out the signal processing with a program like MATLAB.

8.7 Fourier Transforms of Discrete-Time Signals

The *continuous-time* Fourier transform (which we now refer to as the CFT) introduced in Section 8.3 can be extended to discrete-time systems as the *discrete-time Fourier transform* (DTFT) $X(\phi)$ and is defined as

$$X(\phi) = \sum_{n=-\infty}^{\infty} x[n]e^{-j2\pi n\phi} \tag{8.14}$$

The corresponding inverse DTFT is calculated by

$$x[n] = \int_{-1/2}^{1/2} X(\phi)e^{j2\pi n\phi}\,d\phi \tag{8.15}$$

Note that the DTFT in Equation (8.14) is defined as a summation (instead of an integral) due to the discrete nature of $x[n]$. In addition, because $x[n]$ is dimensionless, the corresponding $X(\phi)$ is also dimensionless. Equation (8.14) is periodic in ϕ due to the $e^{-j2\pi n\phi}$ term; thus, it is sufficient to examine $X(\phi)$ over the range $-\frac{1}{2} \le \phi \le \frac{1}{2}$ instead of over all frequencies, as for the CFT. If $x[n]$ was derived by sampling a continuous-time signal $x(t)$ at a sampling rate f_S, then ϕ corresponds to the frequency range $-\frac{f_S}{2} \le f \le \frac{f_S}{2}$, which corresponds to the range of useful frequencies with respect to the sampling theorem.

It is important to realize that the DTFT is a continuous function and not a discrete one. As an example, suppose a 1000-Hz sine wave is sampled at 44100 samples/sec. This implies that the corresponding discrete version of the 1000-Hz sine wave will repeat every 44.1 samples, and the corresponding $X(\phi)$ will have nonzero components at $\phi = \pm\frac{1000}{44100}$, which is clearly not a whole number. If $x[n]$ contains a variety of frequency components, then they will all be represented in $X(\phi)$ at their corresponding ratio to f_S and will generate a continuous function.

Because Equation (8.14) is periodic with respect to ϕ, the values of $X(\phi)$ for $|\phi| > \frac{1}{2}$ are merely repeated copies of the values in the region $-\frac{1}{2} \le \phi \le \frac{1}{2}$. The implication of this is that we can treat $x[n]$ as a periodic function that can be represented by a Fourier series whose coefficients can be found by sampling $X(\phi)$. This is a reverse application of the same technique we used in Section 8.2 to derive the CFT as the "smear" of the Fourier coefficients of a periodic continuous-time waveform. Mathematically, the "unsmear" of the DTFT into its Fourier coefficients is called the *discrete Fourier transform* (DFT) and is defined as

$$X[k] = \sum_{n=0}^{N-1} x[n]e^{-j2\pi nk/N} \tag{8.16}$$

$$x[n] = \frac{1}{N}\sum_{k=0}^{N-1} X[k]e^{j2\pi nk/N} \tag{8.17}$$

where N is the number of points we used to sample $X(\phi)$. We have used the letter k to represent the index of the DFT in the dimensionless "discrete frequency" domain (corresponding to the physical frequencies 0 through f_S in steps of $\frac{1}{N-1}f_S$).

Note that whereas the DTFT uses the range $-\frac{1}{2} \le \phi \le \frac{1}{2}$ and is symmetric around the y axis, by convention the DFT uses the range $0 \le k \le N-1$ and thus is defined for $k \ge 0$, that is, in the right half plane. The reason for this is that a discrete waveform can only be symmetric around the y axis if it has an odd value of N, and the DFT is often calculated using an even value for N (usually a power of two). The implication (as we shall see in the example) is that the resulting DFT will be symmetric about $k = \frac{N-1}{2}$ instead of $k = 0$.

The preceding derivations may appear complicated and abstract, but there is a major advantage to using the DFT instead of the DTFT: The DFT can be computed using the *fast Fourier transform* (FFT) algorithm [2]. The FFT provides a computationally efficient way to calculate Equation (8.16) by using only integer additions and multiplications, thus enabling frequency-domain computations to be easily implemented with a low-cost *digital signal processor* (DSP). While the term FFT is often used interchangeably with DFT, in truth the FFT is simply one of several known methods that may be employed for computing the DFT.

MATLAB provides the `fft` function for calculating FFTs of discrete signals. Executing `X = fft(x)` will return the n-point FFT of the vector `x`, where n is the number of elements in `x`. Alternatively, you may explicitly specify the number of points in the FFT by adding a second argument to `fft`. Thus, running `X = fft(x,64)` will calculate a 64-point FFT on the vector `x`; if `x` has greater than 64 elements, then the extra elements will be discarded in the FFT calculation, and if `x` has fewer than 64 elements, then `x` will be automatically extended to 64 elements (by padding with zeros) prior to the FFT calculation. MATLAB also has a corresponding `ifft` function for computing the inverse DFT.

Example 8.3

Let $x(t)$ be the triangular waveform in Figure 8.8 with width 1 msec, height 1 V, and total waveform length of 4 msec. Assuming a sampling rate of 10 kilosamples/sec:

1. Calculate $|X(\phi)|$ (the DTFT magnitude) directly from its definition in Equation (8.14).
2. Calculate $|X[k]|$ (the DFT magnitude) directly from its definition in Equation (8.16).
3. Calculate $|X[k]|$ using MATLAB's `fft()` function.

```
% Example_8_3.m
% Calculate the DTFT and DFT for a triangular waveform.
% First, define x(t)
triangle_width = 1e-3;
triangle_height = 1;
T = 1e-4;
triangle_slope = triangle_height/(triangle_width/2);
fs = 1/T;
t = 0:T:4e-3;
n = t/T;
N = length(n);
% define discrete triangle waveform x[n]
x = zeros(1,N);
x(1:6) = 0:triangle_slope*T:triangle_height;
x(6:11) = 1:-triangle_slope*T:0;
% define phi for DTFT with arbitrary granularity of 200
% steps
phi=-.5:.005:.5;
% define k for DFT as same length as x[n]
k = 0:N-1;
% initialize DTFT and DFT vars
X_DTFT = zeros(1,length(phi));
X_DFT = zeros(1,length(k));
% calculate DTFT and DFT based on definitions (sum of
% complex exponentials)
for i=1:length(n)
    X_DTFT = X_DTFT + x(i)*exp(-j*2*pi*n(i)*phi);
    X_DFT = X_DFT + x(i)*exp(-j*2*pi*n(i)*k/N);
end
% Calculate 41-point FFT with MATLAB's fft() function
X_FFT = fft(x);
```

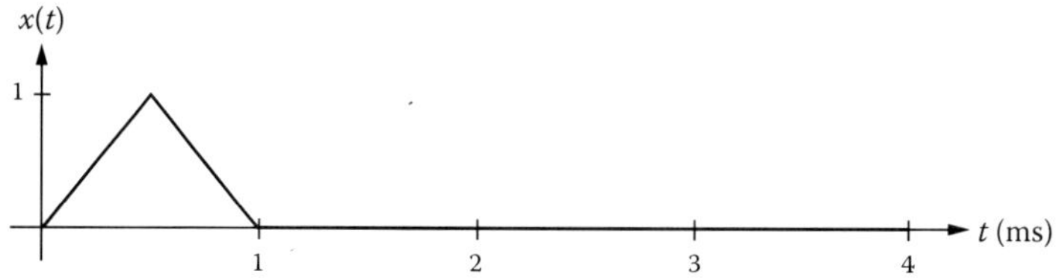

Figure 8.8 Triangular continuous-time waveform *x(t)*.

```
% plot results
subplot(4,1,1);
stem(n,x);
xlabel('n'); ylabel('x[n]');
subplot(4,1,2);
plot(phi,abs(X_DTFT));
xlabel('\phi'); ylabel('X(\phi) (DTFT)');
subplot(4,1,3);
stem(k, abs(X_DFT));
xlabel('k'); ylabel('X[k] (DFT)');
subplot(4,1,4);
% plot FFT horiz axis as proportion of sampling rate
stem(k/(N-1) * fs,abs(X_FFT));
xlabel('f = fs*(k/(N-1)) (Hz)'); ylabel('X[k] (FFT)');
-------------------------------------------------------------
```

Results are shown in Figure 8.9. Some observations are as follows:

- The discrete-time version of the triangle function is denoted $x[n]$ and is shown in Figure 8.9a.
- The DTFT of $x[n]$ is shown in Figure 8.9b and has the shape of $\frac{\sin^2 x}{x^2}$. This makes sense because a triangle waveform can be constructed by convolving two rectangular pulses, and thus in the frequency domain looks like the product of two $\frac{\sin x}{x}$ functions.
- The results for the DTFT (Figure 8.9b) and DFT (Figure 8.9c) are identically shaped, but the DFT plots the "negative" frequencies on the right half of the plot instead of the left. However, since the DFT is always symmetrical, we can simply discard the right half of the plot (or at least ignore it in our heads).
- The results for the sum-of-complex-exponentials DFT (Figure 8.9c) and the MATLAB-calculated FFT (Figure 8.9d) are identical, as expected. However, in Figure 8.9d, we chose to label the x axis in terms of $\frac{k}{N-1} f_S$ (in Hertz) instead of the abstract dimensionless k parameter, thus providing more context for the plot.

8.8 A Simple Discrete-Time Filter

As described in Section 8.3, a filter is a system in which the input/output relationship is some frequency-dependent function. In continuous-time filter design, an analog circuit containing capacitors, inductors, and amplifiers is typically used to implement the desired response. The filter is characterized by its frequency response $H(f)$ and corresponding impulse response $h(t)$, providing an input/output relationship determined by $Y(f) = H(f)X(f)$ in the frequency domain or $y(t) = h(t)*x(t)$ in the time domain (where the "*" indicates convolution). If $x(t)$ is the Dirac delta function $\delta(t)$, then $y(t) = h(t)$ because any function convolved with $\delta(t)$ is itself.

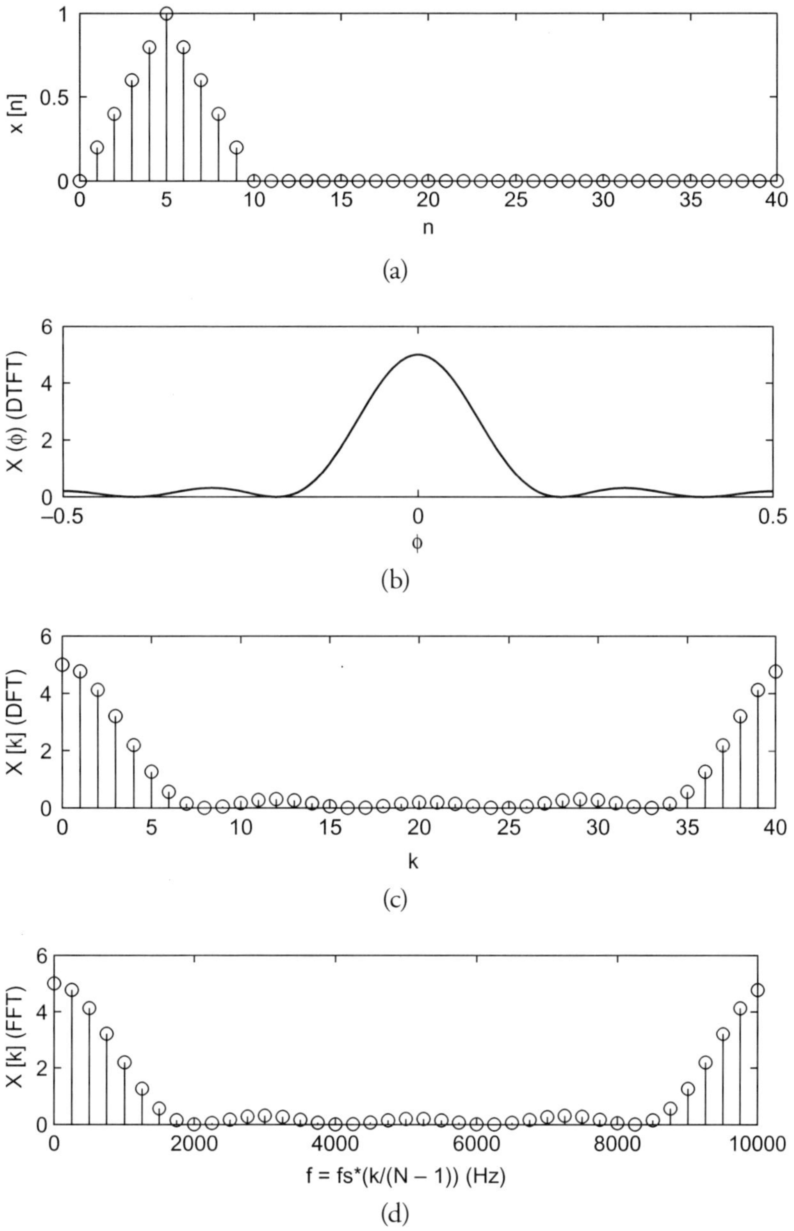

Figure 8.9 (a) Discrete-time version of the triangle waveform in Figure 8.8. (b) The DTFT magnitude $|X(\phi)|$. (c) The DFT magnitude $|X[k]|$. (d) The DFT as computed by MATLAB's `fft()` function. Note that in the last case, the frequency axis has been rescaled from 0 to f_s instead of zero to N.

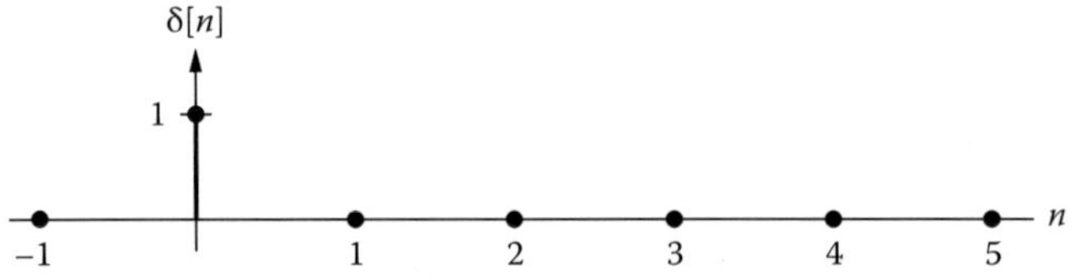

Figure 8.10 The discrete-time version of the delta function consists of a single sample of unity height at *n* = 0 and zeros elsewhere.

In continuous-time filters, $h(t)$ and $\delta(t)$ are largely a mathematical convenience because it is impossible to create a delta function exactly in the lab (though it is often approximated by a short pulse). On the other hand, in discrete-time systems, it *is* possible to represent the discrete delta function $\delta[n]$ accurately (also called the *unit sample* function or *Kronecker delta* function). The discrete delta function $\delta[n]$ is simply a sequence with a value of one at $n = 0$ and zero otherwise (see Figure 8.10) and thus is trivially implementable. In addition, *any* discrete sequence $x[n]$ can be expressed as a sum of delayed deltas. For example, the $x[n]$ shown in Figure 8.11a can be written mathematically as

$$x[n] = 0.5\delta[n] + 1.5\delta[n-1] + \delta[n-2] - 0.5\delta[n-3]$$

Therefore, if we can design a linear system with known behavior for $\delta[n]$ with a corresponding impulse response $h[n]$, then we can use that system to process any $x[n]$. In this case, we know the output precisely because $x[n]$ is just a weighted sum of delta functions.

This concept is illustrated by the system in Figure 8.11b, which implements the impulse response of Figure 8.11a. Conceptually, this system is built from amplifiers, an adder, and *delay elements* (denoted by “D” in the diagram) whose purpose is to store the value of a signal for exactly one “tick” of n. In practice, we use computer registers for the delay elements and computer arithmetic for the multiplication and addition. The system works as follows:

1. Initially, assume that all of the delay elements contain the value zero; thus, the output is zero
2. At “time” $n = 0$, the input delta function is one; thus, the summed output of the system is 0.5
3. At $n = 1$, the input returns to zero. However, the one from $n = 0$ is stored in the first delay element; thus, the summed output is 1.5
4. At $n = 2$, the input remains zero, and the one is shifted to the next delay element, causing the summed output to be 1.0.

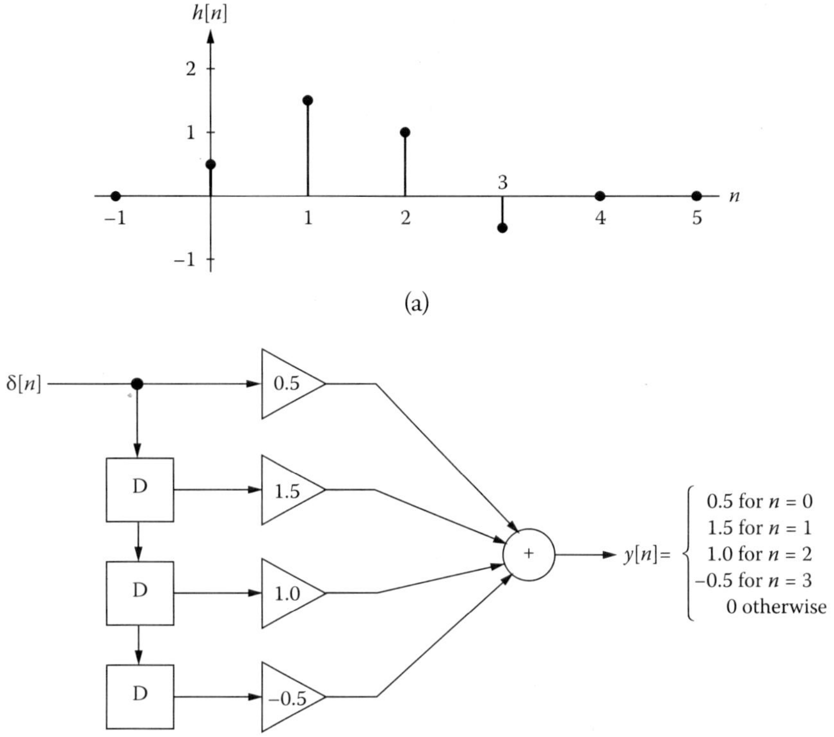

Figure 8.11 (a) Typical impulse response *h*[*n*] for a discrete-time filter. (b) A circuit to implement a filter with impulse response *h*[*n*] consists of three delay elements, four multipliers, and an adder.

5. At $n = 3$, the one gets shifted to the final delay element, and the summed output is −0.5.
6. Finally, for $n > 3$, all of the delay elements again contain zero and the output returns to zero.

Thus, the output sequence of this system with respect to n due to a delta function input will be { 0.5, 1.5, 1.0, −0.5 }, which corresponds to the same sequence as $h[n]$ in Figure 8.11a.

This type of filter is generalized in Figure 8.12 for N delay elements and is called an Nth-order (or equivalently an $N + 1$ "tap") *finite impulse response* (FIR) filter. Mathematically, this system calculates the convolution $y[n] = h[n]*x[n]$.

There are several methods for designing FIR filters [3], and the simplest method was described in Section 8.5: Begin with an ideal brick wall frequency response

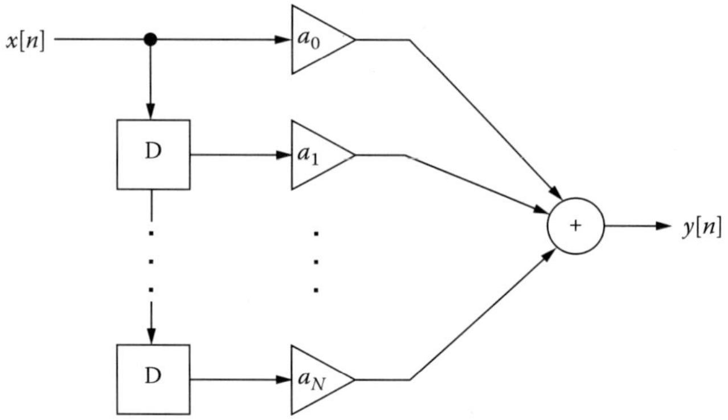

Figure 8.12 General circuit to implement an $N + 1$ tap FIR filter.

$H_I(f)$, convert $H_I(f)$ to the time domain to obtain a noncausal impulse response $h_I(t)$, then apply a window function to truncate the tails of $h_I(t)$, thus creating a realizable impulse response $h_R(t)$. We also shift $h_R(t)$ in time so that it begins at $t = 0$. Thus, for an ideal low-pass filter (shown in Figure 8.13a) with cutoff frequency f_o, the ideal impulse response is $h_I(t) = \dfrac{\sin 2\pi f_o t}{\pi t}$, and the corresponding realizable impulse response is

$$h_R(t) = \begin{cases} \dfrac{\sin 2\pi f_o\left(t - \frac{t_w}{2}\right)}{\pi\left(t - \frac{t_w}{2}\right)} & \text{for } t \le t_w \\ 0 & \text{otherwise} \end{cases} \tag{8.18}$$

where t_w is the width of the rectangular truncation window (see Figure 8.13b). To implement as a discrete-time filter with sampling rate f_S (and corresponding sampling time $T = \dfrac{1}{f_S}$), we convert $h_R(t)$ to $h_R[n]$ by applying $t = nT$; thus,

$$h_R[n] = \begin{cases} \dfrac{\sin 2\pi\phi_o\left(n - \frac{W}{2}\right)}{\pi\left(n - \frac{W}{2}\right)} & \text{for } n \le W \\ 0 & \text{otherwise} \end{cases}$$

where $\phi_o = f_o/f_S$ is the discrete-time filter cutoff frequency, and $W = t_w/T$ is the window width (see Figure 8.13c). Note that the number of taps in the FIR filter is $W + 1$, corresponding to W taps for $n = 1, 2, 3, \ldots, W$ plus one more at $n = 0$.

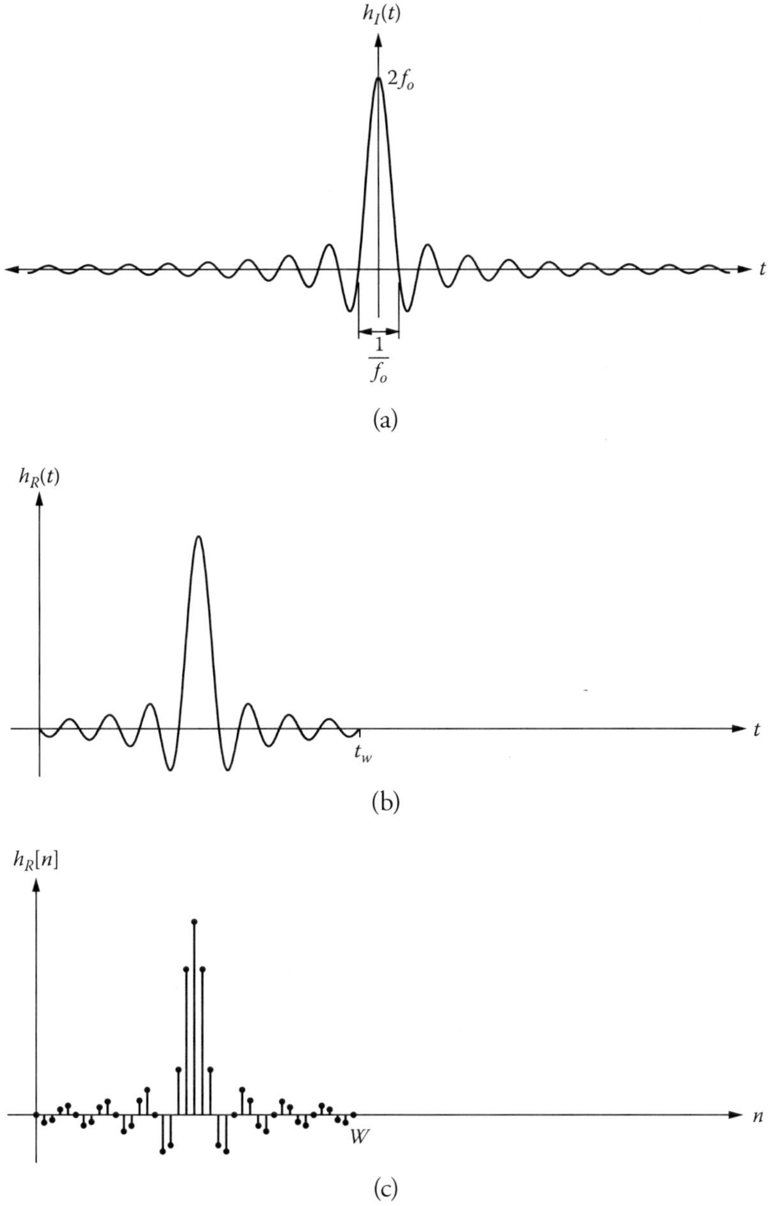

Figure 8.13 (a) Ideal impulse response $h_I(t)$ for an ideal low-pass filter. (b) By shifting and truncating $h_I(t)$, we obtain a realizable impulse response $h_R(t)$. (c) By sampling $h_R(t)$, we obtain $h_R[n]$, which can be implemented as a discrete-time FIR filter.

Example 8.4

Design a low-pass, discrete-time, rectangular-window FIR filter with cutoff frequency of $f_o = 1000$ Hz. Assume a sampling rate of $f_S = 40000$ samples/sec and use 401 taps.

A 401-tap filter implies that the impulse response should have a length of $W = 400T$. Thus, for a rectangular window, we create a realizable version of this filter by shifting $h_I(t)$ to the right by $200T$ and then truncating the tails for $t < 0$ and $t > 400T$ to obtain $h_R(t)$. The resulting realizable 401-point $h_R[n]$ is

$$h_R[n] = \begin{cases} \dfrac{\sin 2\pi \frac{f_o}{f_S}(n-200)}{\pi(n-200)} & \text{for } 0 \le n \le 400 \\ 0 & \text{otherwise} \end{cases}$$

Next, we create an input signal $x(t)$ to send into our filter. We want an input signal that contains components in both the passband and stopband; thus, we arbitrarily choose an $x(t)$ containing components at 500, 1500, and 3000 Hz. Thus,

$$x(t) = sin\ 2\pi 500t + sin\ 2\pi 1500t + sin\ 2\pi 3000t$$

In discrete time, the corresponding $x[n]$ is

$$x[n] = \sin\left(2\pi\frac{500}{44100}n\right) + \sin\left(2\pi\frac{1500}{44100}n\right) + \sin\left(2\pi\frac{3000}{44100}n\right)$$

A MATLAB program to implement this FIR filter follows:

```
% Example_8_4.m
% This example implements an FIR low-pass filter using a
% truncated sinc function (equivalent to an ideal filter
% with a rectangular window)
clc; clear;
% define sampling rate:
fs = 40000; T=1/fs;
% define cutoff frequency of low-pass filter:
fo = 1000;
% define frequencies of input signal x(t):
input_freqs = [ 500 1500 3000 ];
% define filter order (N):
taps = 401;   N = taps-1;
% Note: from this point forward, we will operate in the
% dimensionless discrete-time "n" domain.  First, we
% redefine the filter cutoff frequency in terms of the
% dimensionless Phi parameter of the DTFT:
phi_o = fo / fs;
% Define hr[n] as a shifted sinc function over 401 taps
for i=1:taps
    n = i-1;
    shifted_n = ( n - N/2 );
    hr(i) = sin(2 * pi * phi_o * shifted_n) ...
        / (pi * shifted_n);
    % Note: since sin(x)/x is singular for x=0, catch
```

```
    % this case and insert the appropriate limit value.
    % Otherwise, our hr[n] won't work because it will
    % have a single "NaN" value at the peak.
    if shifted_n==0
        hr(i) = 2*phi_o;
    end
end
% Run the filter for a long time so that we can be sure
% to reach the steady state.  Arbitrarily choose 20000
% samples.
max_n = fs/2;
n = 0:max_n;
% Define x[n]. First, rescale the input frequencies to be
% fractions of fs:
input_phis = input_freqs / fs;
x = zeros(1,length(n));
for i=1:length(input_phis)
    x = x + sin(2*pi*input_phis(i)*n);
end
% Shift x[n] to "turn on" at a time greater than the
% number of taps of the filter.  This is equivalent to
% setting the initial conditions of the filter to zero.
x_shifted = zeros(1,length(n));
x_shifted(taps:length(n)) = x(1:length(n)-N);
% Compute y[n] by simulating the delay circuit of Figure
% 8.12. This is equivalent to convolving x[n] with hr[n].
y = zeros(1,length(n));
for i=taps:length(n)
    for j=1:taps
        % calculate the value for each tap and add to the
        % running total
        y(i) = y(i) + hr(j)*x_shifted(i-j+1);
    end
end
% Convert the discrete signals hr[n], x[n], and y[n] to
% the time domain by rescaling the horizontal axis and
% connecting the dots.
interesting_interval = 1400*T;
subplot(3,1,1);
plot(T*n(1:taps), hr);
% rescale the axes to see the interesting parts:
axis([0 interesting_interval -.02 .06]);
ylabel('h_R(t)');
title('FIR filter w/ rectangular window, time domain');
subplot(3,1,2);
plot(T*n,x_shifted);
axis([0 interesting_interval -3 3]);
ylabel('x(t)');
subplot(3,1,3);
plot(T*n,y);
ylabel('y(t)'); xlabel('t (sec)');
axis([0 interesting_interval -1.5 1.5]);
figure;
% See how good our filter is by computing a 4096-point
% DFT of x[n] and y[n] and plotting on semilog axes.
% Rescale the horizontal axis to be in units of frequency
```

```
% instead of the dimensionless "k" parameter of the DFT.
fft_points = 4096;
scaled_freqs = 0:fs/(fft_points-1):fs;
interesting_freq = 6000;
subplot(3,1,1);
HR = fft(hr,fft_points);
semilogy(scaled_freqs,abs(HR));
ylabel('|H_R(f)|');
% rescale the axes to see the interesting parts:
axis([0 interesting_freq 1e-4 1e1]);
title('FIR filter w/ rectangular window, freq domain');
subplot(3,1,2);
% Calculate the fft on the end part of x[n] and y[n] so
% that we are sure that we are in the steady state
% portion.
x_end = x(end-fft_points+1:end);
X=fft(x_end);
semilogy(scaled_freqs,abs(X));
axis([0 interesting_freq 1e-1 1e4 ]);
ylabel('|X(f)|');
subplot(3,1,3);
y_end = y(end-fft_points+1:end);
Y=fft(y_end);
semilogy(scaled_freqs,abs(Y));
axis([0 interesting_freq 1e-1 1e4 ]);
ylabel('|Y(f)|');
xlabel('f (Hz)');
```

The time-domain signals $h_R(t)$, $x(t)$, and $y(t)$ for this filter are shown in Figure 8.14. Note that these plots transform the discrete-time signals back to continuous time by rescaling the horizontal axis by a factor of nT. In addition, although we calculated $y(t)$ for 0.5 sec, we only plotted the "interesting" part of the plot (for $t < 35$ ms). As expected, the multifrequency signal $x(t)$ is reduced by the filter to its low-frequency component at 500 Hz, as can be seen in the plot of $y(t)$.

In Figure 8.15, we show the frequency-domain results for the filter by running the `fft` function on $h_R(n)$, $x\{n\}$, and $y[n]$. In this case, we run a 4096-point FFT on all three signals. Then, these discrete-frequency DFT results are rescaled to the frequency domain and plotted on semilog axes for the interesting portion ($f < 6000$ Hz). Note the following:

- When viewed in the frequency domain, our truncated ideal impulse response causes ripples in both the passband and stopband and causes a nonzero stopband.
- The magnitude of the input signal $X(f)$ contains three identical components at 500, 1500, and 3000 Hz.
- The magnitude of the output signal $Y(f)$ contains the passband component at 500 Hz plus reduced (but nonzero) components at 1500 and 3000 Hz.

Depending on the application, this FIR filter may or may not be sufficient to provide the desired results. For example, in audio applications, the passband ripple

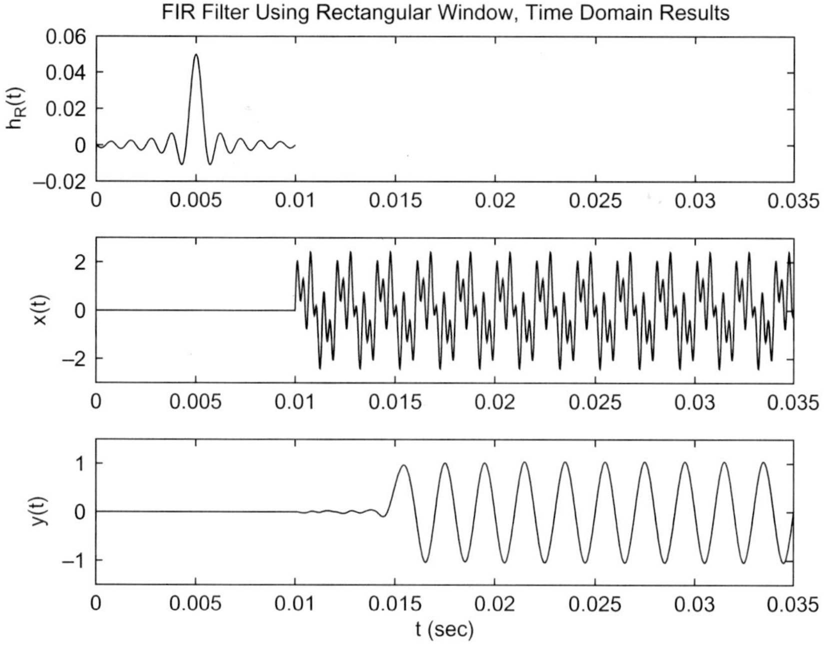

Figure 8.14 MATLAB-generated plot of an FIR filter and its input and output signals. By applying h_R(t) to $x(t)$, we obtain the resulting $y(t)$, which has the components above 1000 Hz filtered out.

may cause audible inaccuracies in the resulting filtered output. On the other hand, in other applications, a minimal transition region between passband and stopband (called the *transition band*) may be the most desirable, regardless of the ripple. One method for altering the filter frequency response is by applying different window functions to the ideal filter response. A comparison of windows is shown in Figure 8.16, which shows the ideal impulse response $h_I(n)$, three different windows $w[n]$, the corresponding realizable impulse response $h_R(n)$, and the resulting Fourier transform. The three examples shown are the rectangular window (also called a "boxcar"), which we have already discussed; a *Bartlett* window (a triangle); and a *Hamming* window, which has a cosine shape with an added DC component. The three windows are expressed mathematically as

$$\text{rectangular:} \quad w_R[n] = 1$$

$$\text{Bartlett:} \quad w_B[n] = \frac{2}{N}\left(\frac{N}{2} - \left|n - \frac{N}{2}\right|\right)$$

$$\text{Hamming:} \quad w_{\mathrm{H}}[n] = 0.56 - 0.46\cos\left(\frac{2\pi n}{N}\right)$$

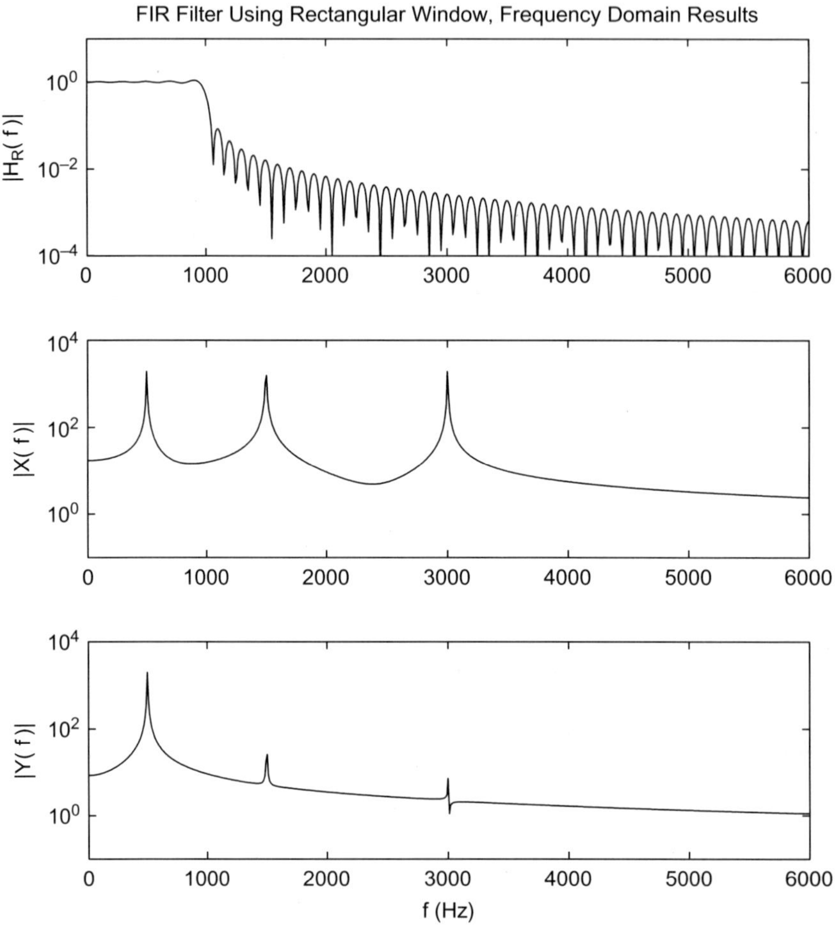

Figure 8.15 Fourier transforms of the signals of Figure 8.14 plotted on semilog axes. The top plot shows that the frequency response of the shifted and truncated ideal impulse response has ripple in the passband and stopband. The two rightmost peaks visible in $|X(f)|$ (middle plot) are substantially reduced in $|Y(f)|$ (bottom plot).

where $n = 0, 1, 2, \ldots, N$. The resulting frequency responses are all low pass, but with varying shapes. The rectangular window gives the most ripple in the passband and stopband but also has the sharpest transition band. The Bartlett window causes less ripple than the rectangular window but has a wider transition band. The Hamming window has the largest differential between the passband and stopband; that is, it has the largest drop between the passband and the first lobe of the stopband.

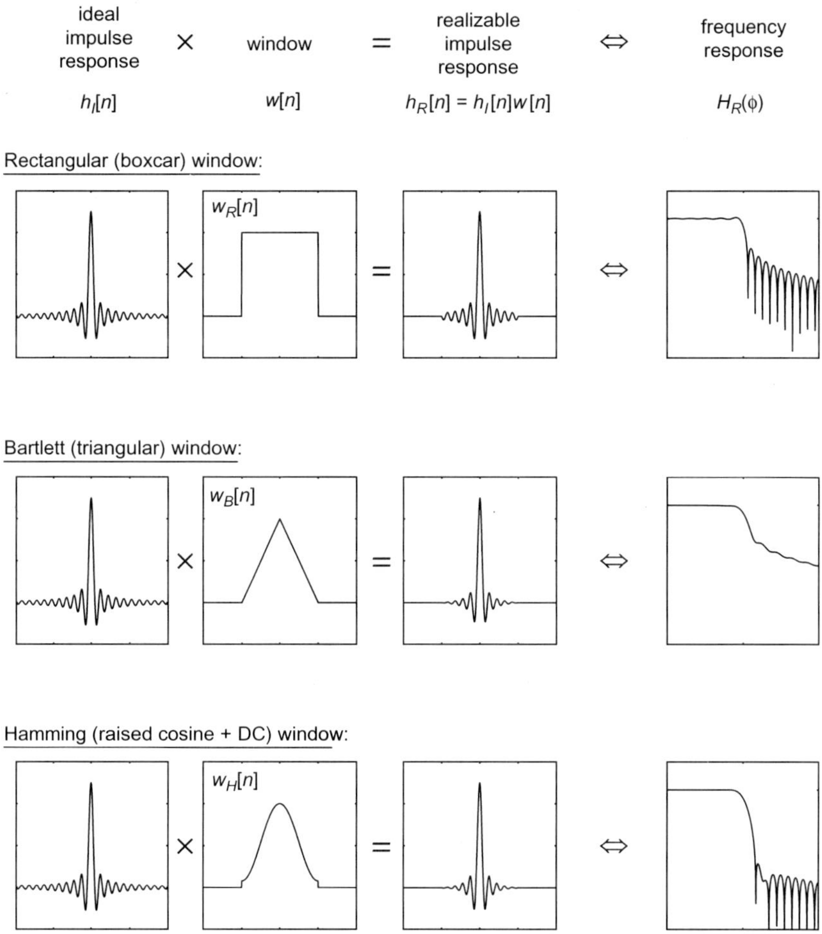

Figure 8.16 An example of some of the window functions $w[n]$ that may be applied to an ideal low-pass impulse response $h_I[n]$ to create a realizable impulse response $h_R[n]$ for use in an FIR filter. Note that to make the plots more readable, the discrete-time waveforms are drawn as continuous (by "connecting the dots"). The corresponding realizable DTFT frequency responses $H_R(\phi)$ are also shown.

Projects

Project 8.1

In telephony, *DTMF* (*dual-tone multifrequency*) is used to encode and transmit key presses from a local handset to a remote receiver over the telephone network. Figure P8.1 shows a simplified representation of a telephone keypad with seven switches and seven sinusoidal voltage sources. The switches are arranged such that on any key press, two switches for the corresponding row and column will close,

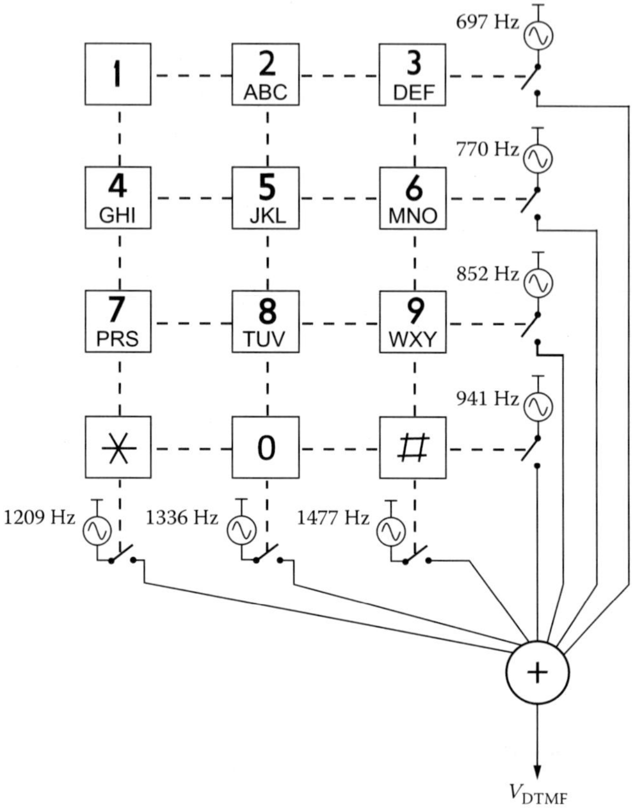

Figure P8.1 A telephone keypad consists of 12 buttons, 7 switches, 7 sine wave generators, and an adder.

thereby connecting two of the voltage sources to the adder on the lower right. The resulting output voltage V_{DTMF} will contain the sum of two distinct frequencies that are sent to the remote receiver. For example, the fact that "2" is in the top row and center column of the button array will cause signals of 697 Hz and 1336 Hz to be summed and sent to the remote receiver. On receiving the transmitted signal, the receiver can determine which button was pressed by determining the two unique frequencies in the received waveform.

1. Write a MATLAB function named *dtmf.m* that generates the appropriate DTMF tones for the numerals 0 through 9 (do not worry about the * and # buttons for now). Your function should take one argument (a number from 0 to 9) and generate a vector of the appropriate length containing the waveform. Assume the following parameters:

   Sampling rate: 8000 samples/sec
   Tone duration: 0.25 sec
   Maximum signal amplitude: 1

2. Use your DTMF function to create a single waveform that dials your own telephone number. You will need to run your function multiple times (for each digit in your phone number) and concatenate the results into a single vector.
3. Save the waveform to a file with MATLAB's `wavwrite()` command. The `wavwrite()` command can be run several ways (run **`help wavwrite`** for more information), but in the simplest case takes two arguments: a vector (presumed to be 8000 samples/sec) and a file name. Confirm that you can play the resulting WAV file through your computer speakers.
4. The waveform you generated does not generate a conforming DTMF sequence [4] because it does not contain the appropriate amount of silence between the individual tones. Modify your *dtmf.m* function to add 0.25 sec of silence at the end of each generated tone. Re-create your WAV file with the added silence between the tones. Try playing the resulting audio into your own telephone (by holding the handset up to your computer speaker) and see if you can get the generated tones to dial your phone. (Note that this will only work on landlines with a dial tone, not on a mobile phone.)

Project 8.2

Design a system to detect transmitted DTMF key presses. Assume that f_S = 8000 samples/sec. Proceed as follows:

1. Create 10 test signals $x_0(t)$ through $x_9(t)$ corresponding to the 10 numeric buttons on the DTMF keypad of Figure P8.1. Each signal should be 0.25 sec long and should contain the sum of two sine waves (each with an amplitude of one) corresponding to the row and column frequencies for each individual button. Concatenate all of your test signals together to obtain one long signal of 2.5 sec that contains all 10 simulated key presses in succession. (Alternatively, if you did Project 8.1, use the signal that you generated in that problem.)
2. Write a MATLAB program that does a 1024-point FFT on each successive set of 1024 elements in your input signal and detects the presence of any of the seven DTMF frequencies. Print your detection results to the screen for every FFT operation.
3. What happens when the FFT overlaps two key presses? Add 0.25 sec of silence in between each key press to avoid this problem and rerun your detection program to see if any erroneous entries are removed.
4. Reduce the size of your FFT window to 512, 256, 128, 64, and 32. What is the smallest window that you can use and still reliably detect all seven DTMF frequencies?

Project 8.3

Design a high-pass FIR filter with the following specifications:

f_S = 8000 samples/sec
f_o = 200 Hz
Taps = 201
Window: Bartlett (triangle)

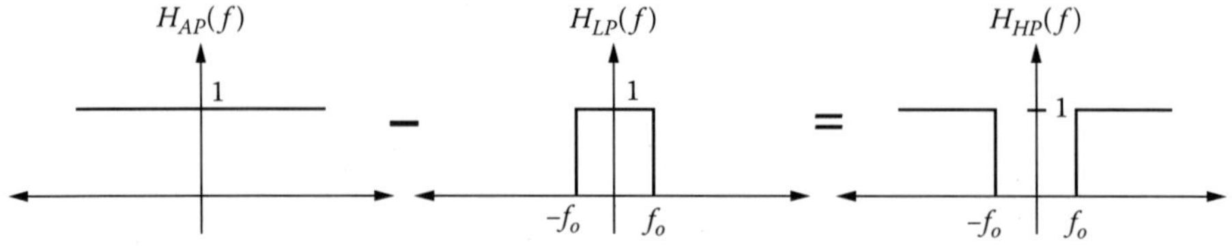

Figure P8.3 A high-pass frequency response $H_{HP}(f)$ can be constructed by subtracting a low-pass response $H_{LP}(f)$ from an all-pass response $H_{AP}(f)$.

Note that a high-pass filter can be decomposed into the difference of an *all-pass* filter and a low-pass filter (see Figure P8.3). An all-pass filter has a value of one for all frequencies.

1. Find the impulse response of an all-pass filter by explicitly calculating the inverse DTFT according to Equation (8.15) for values of $n = -2, -1, 0, 1, 2$. Does your solution make sense?
2. Calculate the ideal impulse response $h_I[n]$ for the high-pass filter by subtracting the corresponding low-pass impulse response from the all-pass impulse response.
3. Create a realizable high-pass impulse response $h_R[n]$ by multiplying the ideal response by a triangular window whose width is the number of taps and whose height is one.
4. Create a test input signal $x(t)$ containing sine waves at 60, 300, and 1000 Hz. Apply $x(t)$ to your high-pass impulse response and obtain the output $y(t)$ by simulating the FIR filter of Figure 8.12.
5. Perform a 1024-point FFT on $h_R(t)$, $x(t)$, and $y(t)$ and plot the magnitudes of the transforms on semilog axes (use a linear horizontal axis and log vertical axis). What frequency components make it through the high-pass filter?

Project 8.4

Design a bandpass FIR filter that detects keys from the second row of the DTMF keypad shown in Figure P8.1. Assume that $f_S = 8000$ samples/sec, and a filter with 401 taps. Follow this procedure:

1. First, create an ideal bandpass response in the frequency domain such that the passband is centered on 770 Hz and has a low cutoff frequency f_L and high cutoff frequency f_H. The frequencies f_L and f_H are determined by the necessity to reject the adjacent DTMF frequencies of 697 and 852 Hz.
2. Because Fourier transforms are linear, a bandpass response can be created by subtracting two low-pass responses. Decompose your bandpass response into a low-pass response with cutoff frequency f_H and a second low-pass response with cutoff frequency f_L. Create an ideal impulse response by subtracting the ideal impulse responses of the two low-pass filters.
3. Create a realizable impulse response by multiplying your ideal response by one of the windows in Figure 8.16. Explain which window you chose and why it is optimal for this application.

4. Create two test signals for your filter corresponding to the 2 and 5 buttons on the keypad and run them through your filter by simulating the FIR filter circuit of Figure 8.12. Plot the time-domain results and confirm in your filter output that your filter detects the 5 and not the 2.

Project 8.5

Use the technique employed in Example 8.2 and find the complex exponential Fourier coefficients for the triangular pulse of Figure P8.8.

Project 8.6

Rerun Example 8.4 for the low-pass FIR filter. Make the following changes to the filter parameters (one at a time) and comment qualitatively on the effect on the output plots.

1. Change the sampling rate f_S from 40,000 to 44,100 samples/sec.
2. Change the number of filter taps to 101.
3. Change the number of filter taps to 1601.
4. Change the three input frequencies to 200, 500, and 39,200 Hz.

References

1. Siebert, W.M., *Circuits, Signals, and Systems*, MIT Press, Cambridge, MA, 1986.
2. Cooley, J.W., and Tukey, J.W., An algorithm for the machine calculation of complex Fourier series, *Mathematics of Computation*, 19:297–301, 1965.
3. Oppenheim, A.V., and Schafer, R.W., *Digital Signal Processing*, Prentice-Hall, Englewood Cliffs, NJ, 1975.
4. Multifrequency push-button signal reception, ITU-T Recommendation Q.24, http://www.itu.int.

Chapter 9

Curve Fitting

9.1 Introduction

There are many occasions in engineering that require an experiment to determine the behavior of a particular phenomenon. The experiment may produce a set of data points that represents a relationship between the variables involved in the phenomenon. We may then wish to express this relationship analytically. A mathematical expression that describes the data is called an *approximating function*. There are two approaches to determining an approximating function:

1. The approximating function graphs as a smooth curve. In this case, the plotted curve will generally not pass through all the data points, but we seek to minimize the resulting error to get the best fit. A plot of the data on linear, semilog, or log-log coordinates can often suggest an appropriate form for the approximating function.
2. The approximating function passes through all data points (as described in Section 9.3). However, if there is some scatter in the data points, this approximating function may not be satisfactory.

9.2 Method of Least Squares

9.2.1 Best-Fit Straight Line

In the method of least squares, we seek to find the best-fit straight line given a set of n data points (x_1, y_1), $(x_2, y_2), \ldots, (x_n, y_n)$.

We wish to represent the approximating curve y_c as a straight line of the form

$$y_c = c_1 + c_2 x \tag{9.1}$$

where c_1 and c_2 are unknown constants to be determined. Let D be the sum of the square of the errors between the approximating line and the actual points. Then,

$$D = \sum_{i=1}^{n} [y_i - y_c(x_i)]^2 \tag{9.2}$$

$$= \sum_{i=1}^{n} [y_i - (c_1 + c_2 x_i)]^2 \tag{9.3}$$

$$= [y_1 - (c_1 + c_2 x_1)]^2 + [y_2 - (c_1 + c_2 x_2)]^2 + \cdots + [y_n - (c_1 + c_2 x_n)]^2 \tag{9.4}$$

To obtain the best-fit straight-line approximating function, minimize D by taking $\frac{\partial D}{\partial c_1} = 0$ and $\frac{\partial D}{\partial c_2} = 0$. Taking the partial derivative of Equation (9.3) with respect to c_1 gives

$$\frac{\partial D}{\partial c_1} = 0 = \sum_{i=1}^{n} 2[y_i - (c_1 + c_2 x_i)][-1]$$

$$0 = \sum_{i=1}^{n} y_i - c_2 \sum_{i=1}^{n} x_i - n c_1$$

or

$$n c_1 + \left(\sum_{i=1}^{n} x_i \right) c_2 = \sum_{i=1}^{n} y_i \tag{9.5}$$

Taking the partial derivative of Equation (9.3) with respect to c_2 gives

$$\frac{\partial D}{\partial c_2} = 0 = \sum_{i=1}^{n} 2[y_i - (c_1 + c_2 x_i)][-x_i]$$

$$0 = \sum_{i=1}^{n} x_1 y_i - c_1 \sum_{i=1}^{n} x_i - c_2 \sum_{i=1}^{n} x_i^2$$

or

$$\left(\sum_{i=1}^{n} x_i\right)c_1+\left(\sum_{i=1}^{n} x_i^2\right)c_2=\sum_{i=1}^{n} x_i y_i \tag{9.6}$$

Equations (9.5) and (9.6) describe a system of two algebraic equations in two unknowns that can be solved by the method of determinants (Cramer's rule):

$$c_1=\frac{\begin{vmatrix}\sum y_i & \sum x_i\\ \sum x_i y_i & \sum x_i^2\end{vmatrix}}{\begin{vmatrix} n & \sum x_i\\ \sum x_i & \sum x_i^2\end{vmatrix}}=\frac{\left(\sum y_i\right)\left(\sum x_i^2\right)-\left(\sum x_i\right)\left(\sum x_i y_i\right)}{n\sum x_i^2-\left(\sum x_i\right)\left(\sum x_i\right)} \tag{9.7}$$

$$c_2=\frac{\begin{vmatrix} n & \sum y_i\\ \sum x_i & \sum x_i y_i\end{vmatrix}}{\begin{vmatrix} n & \sum x_i\\ \sum x_i & \sum x_i^2\end{vmatrix}}=\frac{n\sum x_i y_i-\left(\sum x_i\right)\left(\sum y_i\right)}{n\sum x_i^2-\left(\sum x_i\right)\left(\sum x_i\right)} \tag{9.8}$$

9.2.2 Best-Fit mth-Degree Polynomial

We can generalize this approach for an mth-degree polynomial fit. In this case, take the approximating curve y_c to be

$$y_c=c_1+c_2x+c_3x^2+c_4x^3+\cdots+c_{m+1}x^m \tag{9.9}$$

where $m \leq n - 1$, and n is the number of data points.

The measured values are (x_i, y_i) for $i = 1, 2, \ldots, n$.

Let $y_{c,i} = y_c(x_i)$ be the approximated value of y_i at the point (x_i, y_i). Then,

$$D = \sum_{i=1}^{n} \left[y_i - y_{c,i} \right]^2 = \sum_{i=1}^{n} \left[y_i - \left(c_1 + c_2 x_i + c_3 x_i^2 + \cdots + c_{m+1} x_i^m \right) \right]^2$$

To minimize D, take

$$\frac{\partial D}{\partial c_1} = 0, \quad \frac{\partial D}{\partial c_2} = 0, \; \ldots, \quad \frac{\partial D}{\partial c_{m+1}} = 0$$

Then,

$$\frac{\partial D}{\partial c_1} = 0 = \sum_{i=1}^{n} 2\left[y_i - \left(c_1 + c_2 x_i + \cdots + c_{m+1} x_i^m \right) \right][-1]$$

$$\frac{\partial D}{\partial c_2} = 0 = \sum_{i=1}^{n} 2\left[y_i - \left(c_1 + c_2 x_i + \cdots + c_{m+1} x_i^m \right) \right][-x_i]$$

$$\frac{\partial D}{\partial c_3} = 0 = \sum_{i=1}^{n} 2\left[y_i - \left(c_1 + c_2 x_i + \cdots + c_{m+1} x_i^m \right) \right]\left[-x_i^2\right]$$

$$\vdots$$

$$\frac{\partial D}{\partial c_{m+1}} = 0 = \sum_{i=1}^{n} 2\left[y_i - \left(c_1 + c_2 x_i + \cdots + c_{m+1} x_i^m \right) \right]\left[-x_i^m\right]$$

This set of equations reduces to

$$\begin{aligned}
nc_1 + \left(\sum x_i\right) c_2 + \left(\sum x_i^2\right) c_3 + \cdots + \left(\sum x_i^m\right) c_{m+1} &= \sum y_i \\
\left(\sum x_i\right) c_1 + \left(\sum x_i^2\right) c_2 + \left(\sum x_i^3\right) c_3 + \cdots + \left(\sum x_i^{m+1}\right) c_{m+1} &= \sum x_i y_i \\
&\vdots \\
\left(\sum x_i^m\right) c_1 + \left(\sum x_i^{m+1}\right) c_2 + \left(\sum x_i^{m+2}\right) c_3 + \cdots + \left(\sum x_i^{2m}\right) c_{m+1} &= \sum x_i^m y_i
\end{aligned} \tag{9.10}$$

Equation (9.10) can be solved by Gauss elimination (as described in Chapter 3).

MATLAB uses mean square error (MSE) as a measure of the precision with which the fitted polynomial describes the data. MSE is defined by

$$\text{MSE} = \frac{1}{n}\sum_{i=1}^{n}(y_i - y_{c,i})^2 \tag{9.11}$$

where $y_{c,i} = y_c\,(y_i)$.

To obtain the best polynomial degree, run your program for several different m values and use the one with the lowest MSE.

9.3 Curve Fitting with the Exponential Function

Many systems (e.g., semiconductor devices) can be modeled with exponential functions. If your experimental data appears to fall into this category, it can be fitted with a function of the form

$$y_c = \alpha_1 e^{-\alpha_2 x} \tag{9.12}$$

where α_1 and α_2 are real constants.

Let us assume that a set of n measured data points (x_1, y_1), (x_2, y_2),…,(x_n, y_n) exists. Then, let $z_i = \ln y_i$ and $z_c = \ln y_c = \ln\alpha_1 - \alpha_2 x$ and let $c_1 = \ln\alpha_1$ and $c_2 = -\alpha_2$. Then, Equation (9.12) becomes linear in z_c, that is,

$$z_c = c_1 + c_2 x \tag{9.13}$$

For the data points (x_1, y_1), (x_2, y_2),…,(x_n, y_n), the new set of data points becomes (x_1, z_1), (x_2, z_2),…,(x_n, z_n).

As we derived in the previous section, the best-fit approximating straight-line curve by the method of least squares gives

$$c_1 = \frac{\left(\sum z_i\right)\left(\sum x_i^2\right) - \left(\sum x_i\right)\left(\sum x_i z_i\right)}{n\sum x_i^2 - \left(\sum x_i\right)^2} \tag{9.14}$$

and

$$c_2 = \frac{n\sum x_i z_i - \left(\sum x_i\right)\left(\sum z_i\right)}{n\sum x_i^2 - \left(\sum x_i\right)^2} \tag{9.15}$$

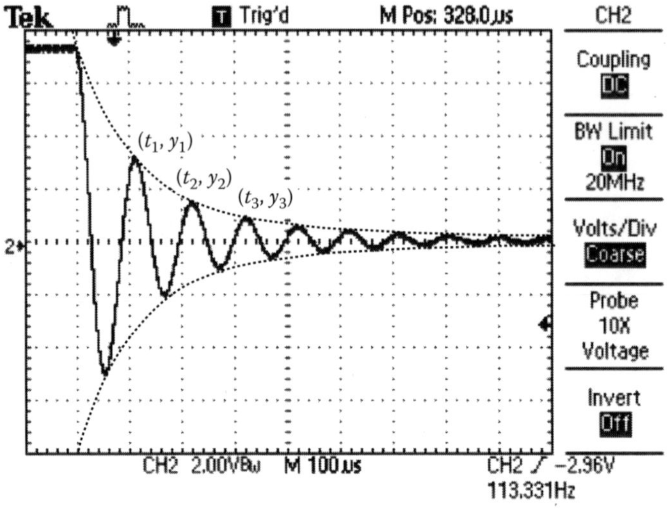

Figure 9.1 Oscilloscope screen shot of the step response of the capacitor voltage of a parallel RLC circuit. (With permission from Tektronix, Inc.)

Then, $\alpha_1 = \exp(c_1)$ and $\alpha_2 = -c_2$. The MSE can be determined by Equation 9.11.

This analysis can be used to determine the damping constant ζ in a parallel RLC circuit (as analyzed in Appendix A). This can be accomplished by examining the oscilloscope output of the step response (see Figure 9.1). The governing equation of the envelope of the response is of the form

$$y = y_0\, e^{-\zeta\omega_n t} \tag{9.16}$$

where

y = capacitor voltage

y_o = initial capacitor voltage (dependent on initial conditions)

ζ = damping factor

ω_n = natural frequency $= \dfrac{1}{\sqrt{LC}}$

Comparing Equation (9.15) with Equation (9.10), we see that

$$\alpha_1 = y_0$$

$$\alpha_2 = \zeta\omega_n$$

with t replacing x. Therefore

$$\zeta = \frac{\alpha_2}{\omega_n} = \alpha_2 \sqrt{LC} \tag{9.17}$$

By measuring n data points on the envelope, i.e., (t_1, y_1), (t_2, y_2) ... (t_n, y_n) we can determine the best fit value for α_2, giving our best estimate for the damping factor, ζ.

9.4 MATLAB's polyfit Function

MATLAB refers to curve fitting with a polynomial as "polynomial regression." The `polyfit` function returns a vector of $m + 1$ coefficients that represent the best-fit polynomial of degree m for the (x_i, y_i) set of data points. The coefficient order corresponds to decreasing powers of x, that is,

$$y_c = a_1 x^m + a_2 x^{m-1} + a_3 x^{m-2} + \ldots a_m x + a_{m+1} \tag{9.18}$$

The vector $A = (a_1, a_2, \ldots, a_m, a_{m+1})$ containing the coefficients is obtained by running `A = polyfit(X,Y,m)`, where $X = (x_1, x_2, \ldots, x_n)$ and $Y = (y_1, y_2, \ldots, y_n)$.

MATLAB provides the `polyval(a,x)` function to calculate the approximated values $y_{c,i}$ at $(x_1, x_2, \ldots, x_n)$ for the fitted coefficients $(a_1, a_2, \ldots, a_{m+1})$:

$$y_{c,i} = a_1 x_i^m + a_2 x_i^{m-1} + a_3 x_i^{m-1} + \ldots a_m x_i + a_{m+1}$$

For calculating the MSE, `polyval` is useful as seen in Example 9.1.

Example 9.1

Given the following set of data points, find the best fit to polynomials of second, third, fourth, and fifth degree. Also, calculate the mean square error.

$$(x,y) = (-10,-980),\ (-8,-620),\ (-6,-70),\ (-4,80),$$
$$(-2,100),\ (0,90),\ (2,0),\ (4,-80),\ (6,-90),\ (8,10),\ (10,220)$$

```
% Example_9_1.m
% This program determines the best fit polynomial curve
% passing through a given set of data points for
% polynomial degrees 2 thru 5.
clear; clc;
```

```
% Provided data set
X = [ -10    -8   -6 -4   -2   0 2   4   6   8   10 ];
Y = [-980 -620 -70 80 100 90 0 -80 -90 10 220 ];
% Fit to polynomials of degree m:
m=2:5;
% Create a second set of x points over the same interval
% in order to plot our fitted curve
X2 = -10:0.5:10;
% Vector to keep track of MSE (to print at end)
MSE=zeros(length(m));
for i=1:length(m)
    fprintf('m = %i \n',m(i));
    % an mth-degree polynomial has m+1 coefficients:
    A = zeros(m(i)+1);
    % do the fit
    A = polyfit(X,Y,m(i));
    % compute the MSE
    Yc = polyval(A,X);
    MSE(i) = (1/length(X)) * sum((Y-Yc).^2);
    % print table
    fprintf('    x         y          yc \n');
    fprintf('----------------------------\n');
    for j=1:length(X)
        fprintf('%5.0f    %5.0f     %8.2f \n', ...
            X(j),Y(j),Yc(j));
    end
    fprintf('\n\n');
    % plot
    subplot(2,2,i);
    plot(X2,polyval(A,X2),X,Y,'o');
    xlabel('x'); ylabel('y'); grid;
    axis([ -10 10 -1500 500]);
    title(sprintf('Degree %d polynomial fit',m(i)));
end
% print computed MSE
fprintf('  m             MSE \n')
fprintf('----------------------\n');
for i=1:length(m)
    fprintf('  %g        %10.2f  \n',m(i),MSE(i))
end
```

PROGRAM OUTPUT

```
  m        MSE
-------------------
  2      32842.37
  3        2659.97
  4        2342.11
  5        1502.95
```

As would be expected, the MSE decreases as the order of the fitted polynomial increases. The polynomial fits are plotted in Figure 9.2.

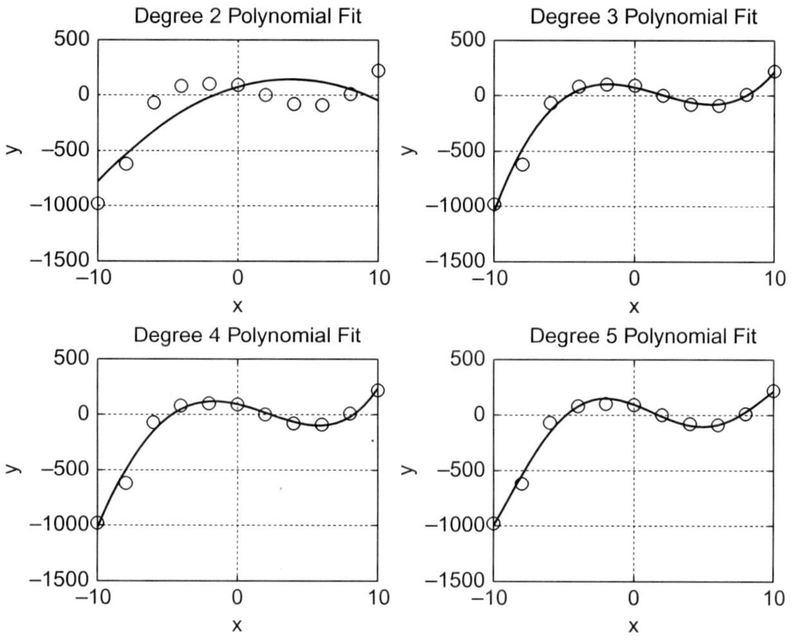

Figure 9.2 Polynomial fits using MATLAB's `polyfit` function for second-, third-, fourth-, and fifth-order polynomials.

Example 9.2

Figure 9.3 shows an RC circuit, and Table 9.1 shows a set of steady-state voltage amplitudes and phases that were measured in the lab for V_{IN} and V_{OUT} at the given frequencies.

We wish to fit the data to the best-possible first-order frequency response.

The RC circuit can be considered a first-order low-pass filter with a frequency response of the form

$$H(f) = \frac{n_0}{j2\pi f + d_0} \tag{9.19}$$

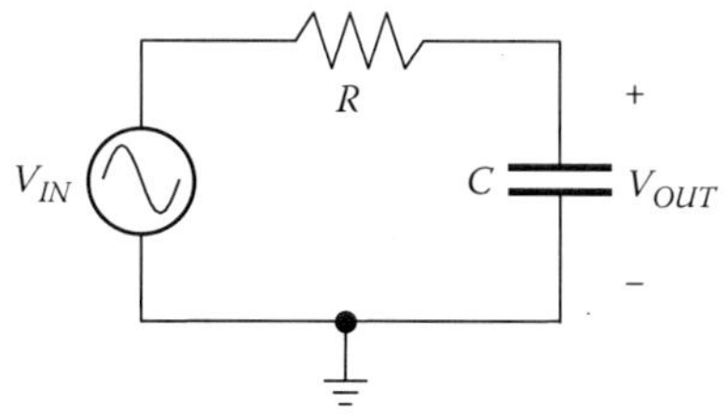

Figure 9.3 RC circuit with input sinusoidal voltage V_{IN} and output V_{OUT}.

Table 9.1 Laboratory-Measured Frequency Response of RC Circuit

Frequency (Hz)	V_{IN} *(volts peak-to-peak)*	V_{OUT} *(volts peak-to-peak)*	*Phase Difference between* V_{OUT} *and* V_{IN}
0	5	5	0
2,000	5	2.2	–60
4,000	5	1.2	–75
6,000	5	0.8	–80
8,000	5	0.6	–83
10,000	5	0.5	–85

where $H = V_{OUT}/V_{IN}$ is the frequency-dependent output-to-input ratio, and n_0 and d_0 are the numerator and denominator coefficients, respectively, to be determined. Because Equation (9.19) has the polynomial in the denominator, we start by rearranging it into a polynomial of the form of Equation (9.18) so that we can apply `polyfit`. This gives

$$\frac{1}{H} = \frac{1}{n_0} j2\pi f + \frac{d_0}{n_0} \tag{9.20}$$

Matching terms between Equations (9.20) and (9.18) shows that $a_1 = j2\pi/n_0$ and $a_2 = d_0/n_0$; thus, the inverse of the frequency response $1/H$ can be fitted by using `A = polyfit(f,1./H,1)`, where `f` is the vector of measured frequencies, and `H` is the vector containing measured values of V_{OUT}/V_{IN}. The MATLAB program follows:

```
% Example_9_2.m
% Fit lab-measured freq response to 1st order response
clear; clc;
% Lab-measured data from Table 9.1:
f =             [ 0  2e3 4e3 6e3 8e3 10e3 ];
V_in =          [ 5    5   5   5   5    5 ];
V_out =         [ 5  2.1 1.3  .8  .6   .5 ];
Phi_degrees =   [ 0  -60 -75 -80 -83  -85 ];
% Ratio of V_out to V_in is the magnitude of the
% frequency response:
H_mag = V_out ./ V_in;
% The phase is the measured phase difference (converted
% to radians)
H_phase = Phi_degrees * pi / 180;
% Express the complex freq response H as:
% mag * exp(j*phase)
H = H_mag .* exp(j*H_phase);
% Do polynomial fit to 1/H
A=polyfit(f,1./H,1);
% Compute coefficients of fitted freq response based
% polyfit results
```

```
n0 = 2*pi*j/A(1);
d0 = 2*pi*j*A(2)/A(1);
% Print fitted frequency response:
fprintf('Fitted frequency response:\n');
fprintf('     H(f) = %.0f / (j*2*pi*f + %.0f)\n',n0,d0);
fprintf('Pole location: %.0f rad/sec (%.0f Hz)\n',...
    d0, d0/(2*pi));
% For comparison purposes, calculate the fitted curve
% with fine precision. Use 100 log-spaced points from 1Hz
% to 1MHz
f_fine = logspace(0,6,100);
H_fit = n0 ./ (j*2*pi*f_fine + d0);
H_fit_mag = abs(H_fit);
H_fit_phase = angle(H_fit);
% Create Bode plot:
subplot(2,1,1);
loglog(f,H_mag,'o',f_fine,H_fit_mag);
axis([ 1e0 1e6 1e-3 2]);
legend('measured','fitted function');
ylabel('|H(f)|');
title('Fit of measured data to 1st-order freq response');
subplot(2,1,2);
semilogx(f,(180/pi)*H_phase,'o', ...
    f_fine, (180/pi)*H_fit_phase);
axis([ 1e0 1e6 -100 10]);
legend('measured','fitted function');
ylabel('\angleH(f) (degrees)'); xlabel('frequency (Hz)');

------------------------------------------------------------
```

PROGRAM RESULTS

```
Fitted frequency response:
      H(f) = 6204/(j*2*pi*f + 6842)
Pole location: 6842 rad/sec (1089 Hz)
```

The resulting plot is shown in Figure 9.4.

9.5 Cubic Splines

Suppose for a given set of data points, all attempted degree polynomial approximating curves produced points that were not allowed. For example, suppose it is known that a particular property represented by the data (such as voltage or absolute temperature) must be positive, and all the attempted polynomial approximating curves produced some negative values. For this case, the polynomial approximating function would not be satisfactory. The method of cubic splines eliminates this problem.

Given a set of $n + 1$ data points (x_i, y_i) for $i = 1, 2, \ldots, n + 1$, the method of cubic splines develops a set of n cubic functions such that $y(x)$ is represented by a different cubic function in each of the n intervals, and the set of cubics passes through the $n + 1$ data points.

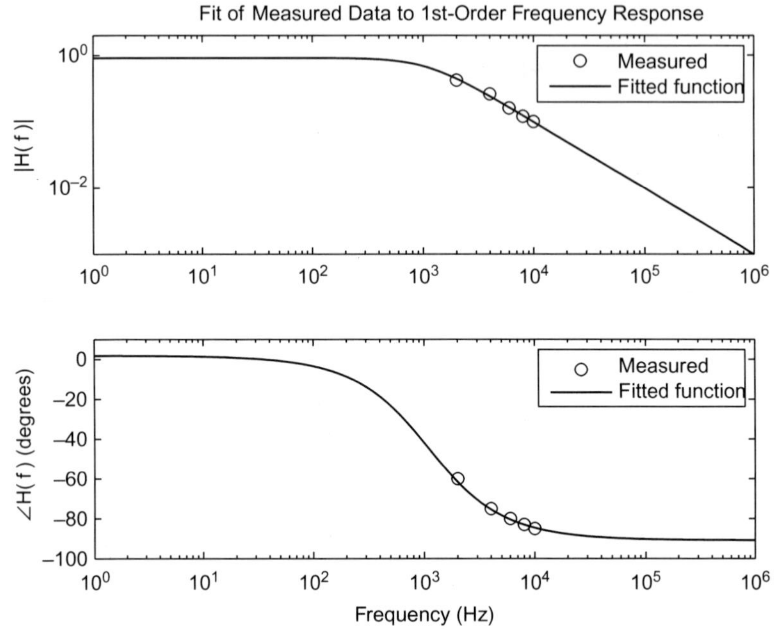

Figure 9.4 Fitted frequency response for a first-order RC circuit.

This is accomplished by forcing the slopes and curvatures to be identical for each pair of cubic functions that join at a given data point.

$$\text{Note: Curvature } K = \frac{\pm\dfrac{d^2y}{dx^2}}{\left[1+\left(\dfrac{dy}{dx}\right)^2\right]^{3/2}} \tag{9.21}$$

We see that if we satisfy the following set of equations, Equations (9.22), we will automatically satisfy both the slopes and the curvature at the connecting points. Thus, set

$$\begin{aligned} \left[y(x_i)\right]_{\text{int } i-1} &= \left[y(x_i)\right]_{\text{int } i} \\ \left[y'(x_i)\right]_{\text{int } i-1} &= \left[y'(x_i)\right]_{\text{int } i} \\ \left[y''(x_i)\right]_{\text{int } i-1} &= \left[y''(x_i)\right]_{\text{int } i} \end{aligned} \tag{9.22}$$

At the point x_i, the values y_i, y_i', and y_i'' must be the same for both the left interval (int i – 1), and the right interval (int i).

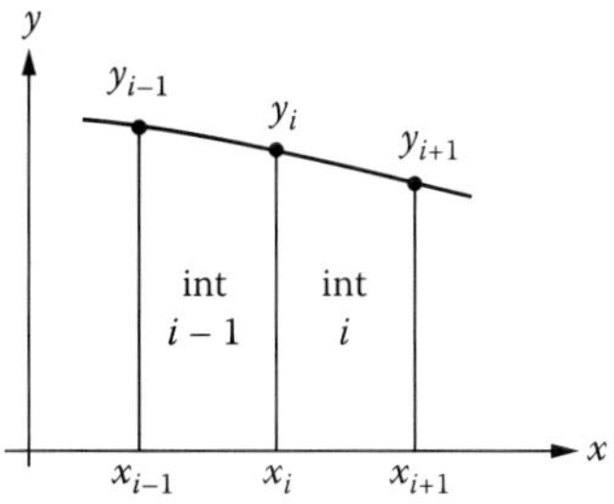

Figure 9.5 Two adjacent intervals in a cubic spline interpolation.

In the (i – 1) interval, $x_{i-1} \leq x \leq x_i$ (see Figure 9.5), and

$$y(x) = A_{i-1} + B_{i-1}(x - x_{i-1}) + C_{i-1}(x - x_{i-1})^2 + D_{i-1}(x - x_{i-1})^3 \tag{9.23}$$

where A_{i-1}, B_{i-1}, C_{i-1}, and D_{i-1} are the coefficients of the fitted cubic polynomial between x_{i-1} and x_i.

In the (i) interval, $x_i \leq x \leq x_{i+1}$, and

$$y(x) = A_i + B_i(x - x_i) + C_i(x - x_i)^2 + D_i(x - x_i)^3 \tag{9.24}$$

where A_i, B_i, C_i, and D_i are the coefficients of the fitted cubic polynomial between x_i and x_{i+1}.

This gives n – 1 equations and n + 1 unknowns.

Thus, values for $\frac{d^2y}{dx^2}$ at x_1 and x_{n+1} must be assumed to obtain the final two equations. Several alternatives exist for choosing these last two equations:

a. Assume $y''(x_1) = y''(x_{n+1}) = 0$. This is widely used and forces the splines to approach straight lines at the endpoints.
b. Assume $y''(x_1) = y''(x_2)$ and $y''(x_{n+1}) = y''(x_n)$. This forces the splines to approach parabolas at the endpoints.

9.6 The Function `interp1` for Cubic Spline Curve Fitting

MATLAB's built-in function `interp1` interpolates between data points by the cubic spline method.

Usage: `Yi = interp1(X,Y,Xi,'spline')`

where `X,Y` are the set of data points, and `Xi` is the set of `X` values at which the set of values `Yi` is to be returned.

Example 9.3

```
% Example_9_3.m
% This program uses interpolation by cubic splines to
% upsample an audio signal.
clear; clc;
% Define original data points for y(t) (time in microsec)
orig_t=[0  4  8 12 16 20 24  28  32  36 40  44 48 52 56];
orig_y=[.7 .9 .9 .7 .3 0 -.3 -.7 -.7 -.3 0  .3 .7 .7 .3];
% Define upsampled time points
upsampled_t = 0:60;
% Calculate interpolated data points using cubic splines
interp_y = interp1(orig_t,orig_y,upsampled_t,'spline');
% Print output to screen
fprintf('UPSAMPLING VIA CUBIC SPLINE FIT\n');
fprintf('time (microsec)  orig sample  upsample\n');
fprintf('-------------------------------------\n');
for i=1:length(upsampled_t)
    % Try to find the corresponding timepoint in the
    % original dataset for this upsampled timepoint with
    % MATLAB's "find" function.
    j = find(orig_t == upsampled_t(i));
    if j>0
        % if we found original value, print both orig and
        % interpolated.
        fprintf('%8.2f      %10.1f    %10.3f\n', ...
            upsampled_t(i),orig_y(j),interp_y(i));
    else
        % otherwise, just print interpolated value
        fprintf('%8.2f                     %10.3f \n', ...
            upsampled_t(i),interp_y(i));
    end
end
plot(orig_t,orig_y,'o',upsampled_t,interp_y);
xlabel('t (microsec)'); ylabel('y(t)'); grid;
title('Upsampling with Cubic Spline Interpolation');
legend('original','upsampled','Location','SouthWest');
```

PROGRAM OUTPUT (EXCERPT)

```
UPSAMPLING VIA CUBIC SPLINE FIT

time (microsec)   original sample    upsample
     0.00               0.7            0.700
     1.00                              0.770
     2.00                              0.827
     3.00                              0.870
     4.00               0.9            0.900
     5.00                              0.918
     6.00                              0.923
     7.00                              0.917
     8.00               0.9            0.900
     9.00                              0.872
```

```
10.00                               0.830
11.00                               0.774
12.00               0.7             0.700
13.00                               0.608
14.00                               0.506
15.00                               0.400
16.00               0.3             0.300
  .                                   .
  .                                   .
```

9.7 Curve Fitting with Fourier Series

Suppose an experimental data set $u(t)$ produces a plot as shown in Figure 9.6, and it is desired to obtain an analytical expression that comes close to fitting the data. Let us assume that the data ranges over the symmetric interval $[-L, L]$. If not, we can make it so by shifting the origin. In this case, the original abscissa data were for $0 \leq t \leq 10.5$ sec, and the data were shifted by letting $x = t - 5.25$. Then, the x domain is subdivided into 70 equal intervals with $\Delta x = 10.5/70 = 0.15$ sec.

Thus, $x_{i+1} - x_i$ is uniform over the entire domain. An attempt to fit a polynomial-approximating curve to these data did not produce an approximating curve that resembled the data and was thus not successful. However, the use of a Fourier series gives a reasonable analytical expression approximating the data. If u_c is the approximating curve, then by a Fourier series,

$$u_c(x) = a_0 + \sum_{m=1}^{\infty}\left(a_m \cos\left(\frac{m\pi x}{L}\right) + b_m \sin\left(\frac{m\pi x}{L}\right)\right) \tag{9.25}$$

where

$$a_0 = \frac{1}{2L}\int_{-L}^{L} u(x)\,dx \tag{9.26}$$

$$a_m = \frac{1}{L}\int_{-L}^{L} u(x)\cos\left(\frac{m\pi x}{L}\right)dx \tag{9.27}$$

$$b_m = \frac{1}{L}\int_{-L}^{L} u(x)\sin\left(\frac{m\pi x}{L}\right)dx \tag{9.28}$$

Using 30 terms in the series and Simpson's rule of integration, an approximating curve as shown in Figure 9.7 is obtained.

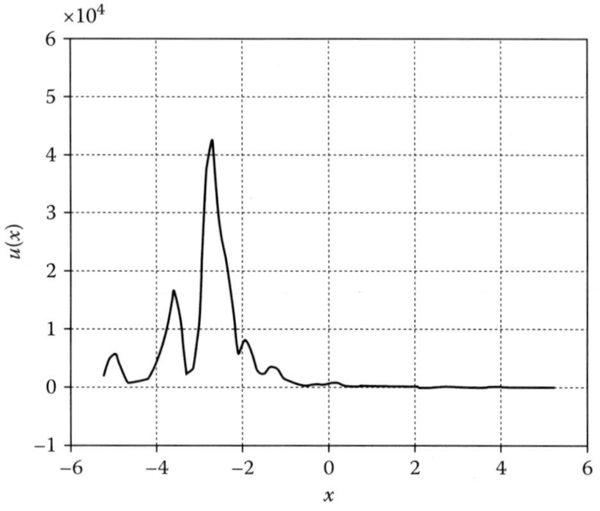

Figure 9.6 Experimental data of u versus x.

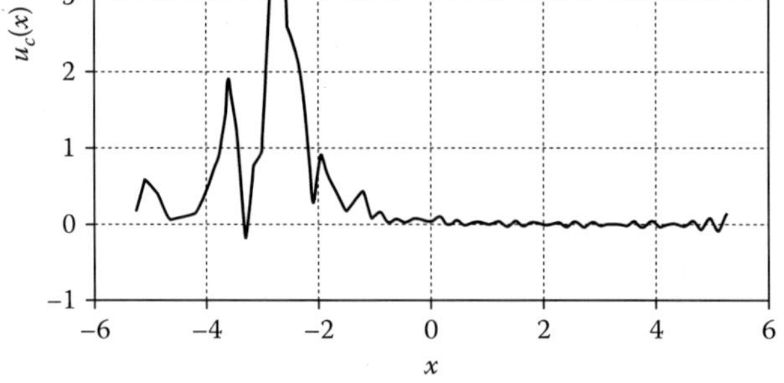

Figure 9.7 Fourier series fit u_c versus x for the data in Figure 9.6.

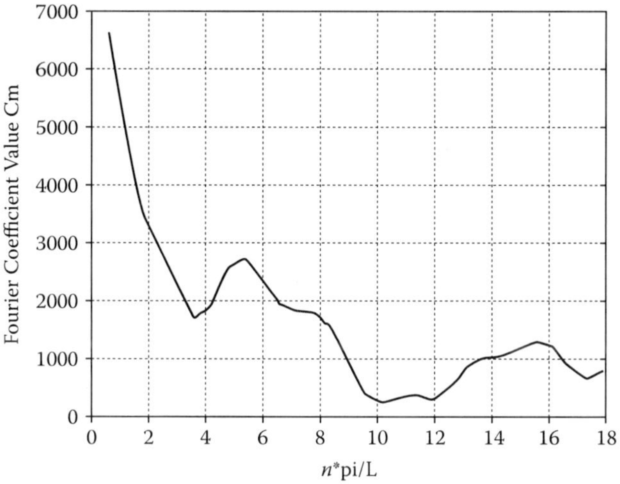

Figure 9.8 Fourier series coefficient amplitudes versus $\frac{n\pi}{L}$.

The $a_m \cos\left(\frac{m\pi x}{L}\right) + b_m \sin\left(\frac{m\pi x}{L}\right)$ terms can be simplified by applying the trigonometric identity $a\cos\beta + b\sin\beta = \sqrt{a^2+b^2}\,\sin(\beta+\varphi)$, giving

$$c_m = \sqrt{\left(a_m^2 + b_m^2\right)}$$

A plot of c_m versus $\frac{m\pi}{L}$ (neglecting the phase factor φ) is shown in Figure 9.8.

Projects

Project 9.1

Figure P9.1 shows a resistor-diode circuit using a type 1N914 silicon diode (D1) and a 10 kΩ resistor (R1). Table P9.1 shows a list of laboratory measurements of V_2 for various applied voltage levels of V_1 at room temperature (300 K).

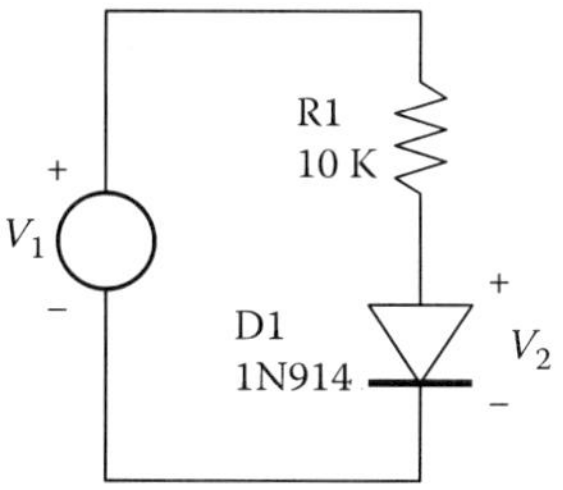

Figure P9.1 Diode-resistor circuit for laboratory measurement of diode I-V curve.

Table P9.1 Laboratory Measurements of Resistor-Diode Circuit

V_1 (volts)	V_2 (volts)
0.189	0.189
0.333	0.317
0.393	0.356
0.819	0.464
1.067	0.487
1.289	0.501
1.656	0.518
1.808	0.522
2.442	0.541
3.949	0.566
4.971	0.579
6.005	0.588
6.933	0.595
7.934	0.602
9.014	0.607
10.040	0.613
11.009	0.619
15.045	0.634
19.865	0.647
24.64	0.657
29.79	0.666

1. Use Kirchhoff's voltage law to calculate the diode current i_D in terms of V_1 and V_2.
2. Use the technique described in Section 9.3 to find the least-square fit of i_D and v_D (= V_2) to the formula

$$i_D = I_S \exp\left(\frac{v_D}{V_T}\right) \tag{P9.1}$$

In this case, you are using the raw data to find best-fit values for I_S and V_T. Plot both the lab data and your fitted curve on the same axes.

3. $V_T = kT/q$ is known as the *thermal voltage* (where k is the Boltzmann constant and q is the unit electric charge). For your best-fit value for V_T, what is the corresponding temperature value T (in kelvin)? Does this value seem reasonable?
4. A more accurate equation to model the diode is

$$i_D = I_S \exp\left(\frac{v_D}{nV_T}\right)$$

where n is the *ideality factor*. Find the best-fit value for n when $T = 300$ K.

5. The complete I-V model for the diode is

$$i_D = I_S\left(\exp\left(\frac{v_D}{nV_T}\right) - 1\right)$$

Is it reasonable that we neglected the –1 term in our curve fit? Why?

Project 9.2

The measured open-loop frequency response of the 741 op amp is shown in Figure P9.2.

1. Find the magnitude (in decibels) and phase (in degrees) of the frequency response by measuring directly from the plot. Note that the phase readings (on the right side of the plot) are denoted as "Phase Lag," which means that the readings should be interpreted as negative degrees. Enter the readings as two vectors in MATLAB.
2. Amplifier gain A is usually expressed in decibels (dB), where

$$A_{\text{dB}} = 20 \log A$$

Convert your decibel readings to absolute gains by dividing by 20 and then raising to the power of 10. Also, convert your degree readings to radians. Then, express the frequency response in complex polar form. Remember that $z = |z| e^{j\phi}$, where $|z|$ is the magnitude and ϕ is the phase angle.

3. Use MATLAB's `polyfit` function to find a fit to a frequency response of the form

$$H(f) = \frac{d_0}{(j2\pi f)^2 + n_1 j2\pi f + n_0}$$

Hint: get your fit working for $f \leq 1000$ h and then add the points for the higher frequencies one at a time. Because the polynomial is in the denominator, try to fit $1/H(f)$ instead of $H(f)$.

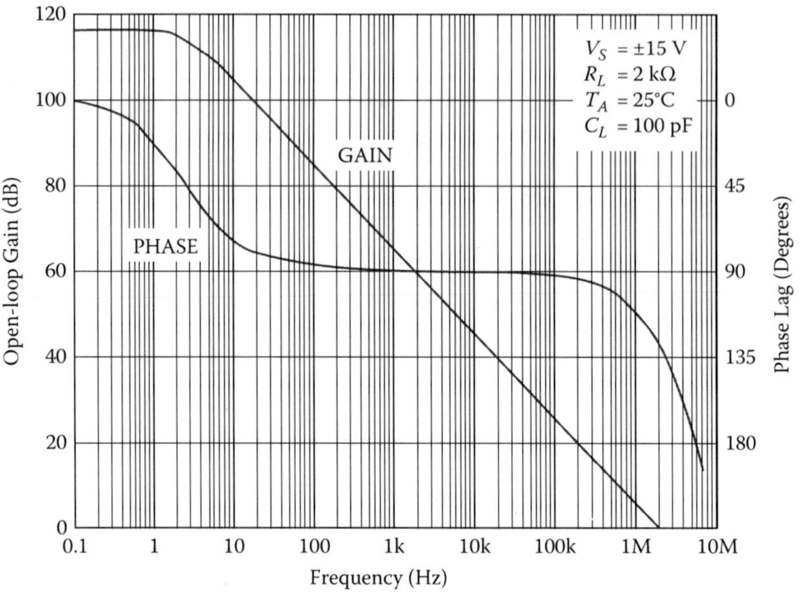

Figure P9.2 Frequency response of the 741 op amp. (With permission from Analog Devices, Inc.)

4. Find the locations of the poles for your fitted $H(f)$ by solving for the roots of the denominator.
5. Plot the measured results and the fitted results on the same set of axes. Does the fit seem reasonable? At what frequencies does, the fit fail, and why?

Project 9.3

Reuse the data for `orig_t` and `orig_y` from Example 9.3 to perform a curve fit using Fourier series. Begin by shifting t so that the data are symmetric around the origin such that $-L \le t \le L$ (where $L = 28\ \mu\text{sec}$). Then, proceed as follows:

1. Write a MATLAB program to calculate the first m Fourier coefficients. Use Simpson's rule (as described Chapter 5) to calculate the coefficients a_0, $a_1, a_2, \ldots, a_m$, and $b_1, b_2, \ldots, b_m$ as in Equations (9.26)–(9.28).
2. Generate three sets of Fourier coefficients for $m = 2$, $m = 4$, and $m = 6$.
3. Generate three fitted curves (for $m = 2, 4, 6$) by substituting your coefficients back into Equation (9.25). Plot on the same set of axes. When plotting the fitted curves, use 150 points on the horizontal axis over the range $-L \le t \le L$ (instead of the 15 points in `orig_t`). Also plot `orig_y` on the same axes, using the × symbol to indicate the points.
4. Explain qualitatively what happens for the case when $m = 6$.

Chapter 10

Optimization

10.1 Introduction

The objective of optimization is to maximize or minimize some function f (called the *object function*). You are probably familiar with determining the maxima and minima of functions using techniques from differential calculus. However, the problem becomes more complicated when we place *constraints* on the allowable solutions to f. As an example, suppose there is an electronics company that manufactures several different types of circuit boards. Each circuit board must pass through several different departments (such as drilling, pick-and-place, testing, etc.) before shipping. The time required for each circuit board to pass through the various departments is also known. There is a minimum production quantity per month that the company must produce. However, the company is capable of producing more than the minimum production requirement for each type of circuit board each month. The profit the company will make on each circuit board it produces is known. The problem is to determine the production amount of each type of circuit board per month that will result in the maximum profit. A similar type of problem may be one in which the object is to minimize the cost of producing a particular product. These types of optimization problems are discussed in greater detail in this chapter.

In most optimization problems, the object function f will usually depend on several variables, $x_1, x_2, x_3, \ldots, x_n$. These are called the *control variables* because their values can be selected. Optimization theory develops methods for selecting optimal values for the control variables $x_1, x_2, x_3, \ldots, x_n$ that either maximize or minimize the objective function f. In many cases, the choice of values for $x_1, x_2, x_3, \ldots, x_n$ is not entirely free but is subject to some constraints.

10.2 Unconstrained Optimization Problems

In calculus, it is shown that a necessary (but not sufficient) condition for f to have a maximum or minimum at point P is that each of the first partial derivatives at P be zero, that is,

$$\frac{\partial f}{\partial x_1}(P)=\frac{\partial f}{\partial x_2}(P)=\cdots=\frac{\partial f}{\partial x_n}(P)=0 \tag{10.1}$$

where the notation $\frac{\partial f}{\partial x_i}(P)$ indicates the partial derivative with respect to x_i evaluated at point P, that is, $\left.\frac{\partial f}{\partial x_i}\right|_{x=P}$. If n = 1 and the object function is $y = f(x)$, then a necessary condition for an extremum (maximum or minimum) at x_0 is for $y'(x_0)=0$.

For y to have a local minimum at x_0, $y'(x_0)=0$ and $y''(x_0)>0$.

For y to have a local maximum at x_0, $y'(x_0)=0$ and $y''(x_0)<0$.

For f involving several variables, the condition for f to have a relative minimum is more complicated. First, Equation (10.1) must be satisfied. Second, the quadratic form

$$Q=\sum_{i=1}^{n}\sum_{j=1}^{n}\frac{\partial^2 f}{\partial x_i\,\partial x_j}(P)\left[(x_i-x_i(P))((x_j-x_j(P))\right] \tag{10.2}$$

must be positive for all choices of x_i and x_j in the in the vicinity of point P, and Q = 0 only when $x_i = x_i(P)$ for i = 1, 2, … , n. This condition comes from a Taylor series expansion of $f(x_1,x_2,\ldots,x_n)$ about point P using only terms up to $\frac{\partial^2 f}{\partial x_i\,\partial x_j}(P)$. This gives

$$f(x_1,x_2,\ldots,x_n)=f(P)+\sum_{i=1}^{n}\frac{\partial f}{\partial x_i}(P)[x_i-x_i(P)]+\sum_{i=1}^{n}\sum_{j=1}^{n}\frac{\partial^2 f}{\partial x_i\,\partial x_j}(P)\left[(x_i-x_i(P))(x_j-x_j(P))\right] \tag{10.3}$$

If $f(x_1,x_2,\ldots,x_n)$ has a relative minimum at point P, then $\frac{\partial f}{\partial x_i}(P)=0$ for i = 1, 2, …, n and $f(x_1,x_2,\ldots,x_n)-f(P)>0$ for all $(x_1,x_2,\ldots,x_n)$ in the vicinity of point P. But, $f(x_1,x_2,\ldots,x_n)-f(P)=Q$. Thus, for $f(x_1,x_2,\ldots,x_n)$ to have a relative minimum at point P, Q must be positive for all choices of x_i and x_j in the vicinity of point P.

Since this analysis is quite complicated when f is a function of several variables, an iterative scheme is frequently used as a method of solution. One such method is the method of steepest descent. In this method, we first need to guess for a point where an extremum exists. Using a grid to evaluate the function at different values of the control variables can be helpful in establishing a good starting point for the iteration process.

10.3 Method of Steepest Descent

Consider a function f of three variables x, y, and z. From calculus, we know that the gradient of f, written as ∇f, is given by

$$\nabla f = \frac{\partial f}{\partial x}\hat{\mathbf{e}}_x + \frac{\partial f}{\partial y}\hat{\mathbf{e}}_y + \frac{\partial f}{\partial z}\hat{\mathbf{e}}_z$$

where $\hat{\mathbf{e}}_x, \hat{\mathbf{e}}_y,$ and $\hat{\mathbf{e}}_z$ are unit vectors in the x, y, and z directions, respectively.

At (x_0, y_0, z_0), we also know that $\nabla f(x_0, y_0, z_0)$ points in the direction of the maximum rate of change of f with respect to distance. A unit vector $\hat{\mathbf{e}}_g$ that points in this direction is

$$\hat{\mathbf{e}}_g = \frac{\nabla f}{|\nabla f|}$$

where $|\nabla f| = \sqrt{\left(\frac{\partial f}{\partial x}\right)^2 + \left(\frac{\partial f}{\partial y}\right)^2 + \left(\frac{\partial f}{\partial z}\right)^2}$.

To find a relative minimum via the method of steepest descent, we start at some initial point and move in small steps in the direction of steepest descent, which is $-\hat{\mathbf{e}}_g$. Let $(x_{n-1}, y_{n-1}, z_{n-1})$ be the new position on the nth iteration and (x_n, y_n, z_n) the old position. Then,

$$x_{n+1} = x_n - \frac{\frac{\partial f}{\partial x}(x_n, y_n, z_n)}{|\nabla f(x_n, y_n, z_n)|}\Delta s$$

$$y_{n+1} = y_n - \frac{\frac{\partial f}{\partial y}(x_n, y_n, z_n)}{|\nabla f(x_n, y_n, z_n)|}\Delta s \qquad (10.4)$$

$$z_{n+1} = z_n - \frac{\frac{\partial f}{\partial z}(x_n, y_n, z_n)}{|\nabla f(x_n, y_n, z_n)|}\Delta s$$

where Δs is some small length.

Example 10.1

Given

$$f(x_1,x_2) = 4 + 4.5x_1 - 4x_2 + x_1^2 + 2x_2^2 - 2x_1x_2 + x_1^4 - 2x_1^2x_2$$

Determine the minimum of f by the method of steepest descent, starting at point $(x_1,x_2) = (6,10)$. Use a $\Delta s = 0.1$ and a maximum of 100 iterations.

```
% Example_10_1.m:
% This program determines a relative minimum by the
% method of steepest decent. The function is:
% f(x1,x2) = 4+4.5*x1-4*x2+x1^2+2*x2^2
%                  -2*x1*x2+x1^4-2*x1^2*x2
% Note: this function has known minima at
% (x1,x2)=(1.941,3.854) and (-1.053,1.028). The
% functional values at the minima points are 0.9855 and
% -0.5134 respectively.
clear; clc;
% Define function and its partial derivatives
fx_func = @(x1,x2) 4+4.5*x1-4*x2+x1^2+2*x2^2 ...
    -2*x1*x2+x1^4-2*x1^2*x2;
dfx1_func = @(x1,x2) 4.5+2*x1-2*x2+4*x1^3-4*x1*x2;
dfx2_func = @(x1,x2) -4+4*x2-2*x1-2*x1^2;
% Define stepping parameters
ds=0.1;
max_iterations = 100;
% First guess
x1=6;
x2=10;
fx=fx_func(x1,x2);
% Print headings and initial guess to screen
fprintf('        x1          x2            fx \n');
fprintf(' 0:  %7.4f     %7.4f    %10.4f \n',x1,x2,fx);
for n=1:max_iterations
    % compute partial derivatives
    dfx1=dfx1_func(x1,x2);
    dfx2=dfx2_func(x1,x2);
    % compute magnitude of gradient
    gradf_mag=sqrt(dfx1^2+dfx2^2);
    % compute next values of x1 and x2 as per Eqn 10.4
    x1n=x1-dfx1/gradf_mag*ds;
    x2n=x2-dfx2/gradf_mag*ds;
    fxn=fx_func(x1n,x2n);
    fprintf('%2d:  %7.4f     %7.4f    %10.4f \n',...
        n,x1n,x2n,fxn);
    % if new value is larger than previous, then minimum
    % has been found
    if(fxn > fx)
        fprintf('A minimum has been found after ');
        fprintf('%d iterations\n\n',n);
        break;
        % otherwise, store new values over current ones
        % and continue
    else
```

```
        x1=x1n;
        x2=x2n;
        fx=fxn;
    end
end
if i >= max_iterations
    fprintf('Error: no solution found after ');
    fprintf('%d iterations\n',i);
else
    fmin=fx_func(x1,x2);
    fprintf('The relative minimum occurs at ');
    fprintf('x1=%.4f  x2=%.4f\n', x1,x2);
    fprintf('The minimum value for f=%.4f \n',fmin);
end

------------------------------------------------------------
```

PROGRAM OUTPUT (EXCERPT)

```
        x1          x2            fx
0:    6.0000     10.0000      683.0000
1:    5.9003     10.0077      622.7192
2:    5.8006     10.0155      566.2528
3:    5.7009     10.0233      513.4609
         .
         .
         .
89:   1.9936      4.0234        1.0001
90:   1.9638      3.9279        0.9883
91:   1.9495      3.8289        0.9901

A minimum has been found after 91 iterations
The relative minimum occurs at x1=1.9638 x2=3.9279
The minimum value for f=0.9883.
```

To obtain a more accurate result, we could rerun the program with revised starting values (from iteration 91) and use a smaller Δs. Alternatively, instead of starting at some arbitrary point as specified in the example, we can first use a grid program to establish a good starting point. In addition, a grid program may indicate that there is more than one relative minimum point.

Example 10.2

```
% Example_10_2.m: This program calculates the values of
% a specified function f(x1,x2) of 2 variables for
% determining a good starting point for the method of
% steepest decent. The range of interest is from
% -10.0 <= x1 <= 10.0 and -10.0 <= x2 <= 10.0.
clear; clc;
% Define function of interest:
fx_func = @(x1,x2) 4+4.5*x1-4*x2+x1^2+2*x2^2 ...
    -2*x1*x2+x1^4-2*x1^2*x2;
% Define grid endpoints and step size
x1min=-10.0;  x1max=10.0;  dx1=2.0;
```

```
x2min=-10.0;  x2max=10.0;  dx2=2.0;
% Define grid and calculate f(x1,x2) at each point
x1=x1min:dx1:x1max;
x2=x2min:dx2:x2max;
for i=1:length(x1)
    for j=1:length(x2)
        f(i,j) = fx_func(x1(i),x2(j));
    end
end
% Print heading
fprintf('------------------------------------');
fprintf('------------------------------------');
fprintf('------------------------------------\n');
fprintf('   x2  |                           ');
fprintf('                              x1\n');
fprintf('------------------------------------');
fprintf('------------------------------------');
fprintf('------------------------------------\n');
fprintf('       |');
for i=1:length(x1)
    fprintf('%7.1f  ',x1(i));
end
fprintf('\n');
fprintf('------------------------------------');
fprintf('------------------------------------');
fprintf('------------------------------------\n');
% Print values of f(x1,x2)
for j=1:length(x2)
    fprintf('%6.1f |',x2(j));
    for i=1:length(x1)
        fprintf('%8.1f ',f(i,j));
    end
    fprintf('\n');
end
```

PROGRAM RESULTS

```
----------------------------------------------------------------------------------
   x2  |                                 x1
----------------------------------------------------------------------------------
       |   -10.0     -8.0     -6.0    -4.0    -2.0     0.0     2.0     4.0      6.0      8.0     10.0
----------------------------------------------------------------------------------
 -10.0 | 12099.0 5488.0 2149.0 738.0 295.0 244.0 393.0 934.0 2443.0 5880.0 12589.0
  -8.0 | 11659.0 5184.0 1949.0 610.0 207.0 164.0 289.0 774.0 2195.0 5512.0 12069.0
  -6.0 | 11235.0 4896.0 1765.0 498.0 135.0 100.0 201.0 630.0 1963.0 5160.0 11565.0
  -4.0 | 10827.0 4624.0 1597.0 402.0  79.0  52.0 129.0 502.0 1747.0 4824.0 11077.0
  -2.0 | 10435.0 4368.0 1445.0 322.0  39.0  20.0  73.0 390.0 1547.0 4504.0 10605.0
   0.0 | 10059.0 4128.0 1309.0 258.0  15.0   4.0  33.0 294.0 1363.0 4200.0 10149.0
   2.0 |  9699.0 3904.0 1189.0 210.0   7.0   4.0   9.0 214.0 1195.0 3912.0  9709.0
   4.0 |  9355.0 3696.0 1085.0 178.0  15.0  20.0   1.0 150.0 1043.0 3640.0  9285.0
   6.0 |  9027.0 3504.0  997.0 162.0  39.0  52.0   9.0 102.0  907.0 3384.0  8877.0
   8.0 |  8715.0 3328.0  925.0 162.0  79.0 100.0  33.0  70.0  787.0 3144.0  8485.0
  10.0 |  8419.0 3168.0  869.0 178.0 135.0 164.0  73.0  54.0  683.0 2920.0  8109.0
```

Since the functional value at `(x1,x2) = (0,2)` is lower than the functional values at surrounding points, we suspect that there is a relative minimum in the vicinity of `(x1,x2) = (0,2)`. A second relative minimum appears to be in the vicinity of `(x1,x2) = (2,4)`.

10.4 MATLAB's `fminunc` Function

MATLAB provides the function `fminunc(FUN,X0)` to solve unconstrained optimization problems. The two arguments to `fminunc` are the function to optimize (`FUN`) and an initial guess (`X0`). `FUN` can be a function defined in a separate *.m* file or may be defined anonymously within the script. The output of `fminunc` is the minimum that is closest to the initial guess. Note that MATLAB does not have a separate function to find maxima. To find a maximum, redefine your function to return the negative value and then use `fminunc` to find the minimum.

Example 10.3

Given

$$y(x) = x^3 + 40x^2 - 200x + 12$$

Determine the minima and maxima.

```
% Example_10_3.m: Find the minima and maxima of
% y = x^3 + 40x^2 - 200x + 12
clc; clear;
% First, plot the function so that we can make some
% useful initial guesses:
x = -40:40;
for i=1:length(x)
    y(i) = x(i)^3 + 40*x(i)^2 - 200*x(i) + 12;
end
plot(x,y);
xlabel('x'),ylabel('y'), grid, title('y vs x');
% Next, find the minimum and maximum using MATLAB's
% anonymous function method (find first guesses by
% eyeballing plot).
[xmin,minvalue] = fminunc(@(x) x^3+40*x^2-200*x+12, 2 );
% Note: To find a maximum, instead find the minimum of
% the negative of the function.
[xmax,maxvalue] = fminunc(@(x) -(x^3+40*x^2-200*x+12),...
    -30 );
% Print results
fprintf('xmin=%.1f minvalue=%.1f, ',xmin,minvalue);
fprintf('xmax=%.1f maxvalue=%.1f\n',xmax,-maxvalue);
```

PROGRAM OUTPUT

```
xmin = 2.3 minvalue = -224.2, xmax = -29.0 maxvalue = 15063.0
```

Determine maximum and minimum values of y and compare with the results from the fminunc function.

10.5 Optimization with Constraints

In many optimization problems, the variables in the function to be maximized or minimized are not all independent but are related by one or more conditions or constraints. A simple example that illustrates the constraint concept follows.

Example 10.4

Suppose we wish to determine the maximum and minimum values of the objective function

$$f(x,y) = 2x + 3y \tag{10.5}$$

with the following constraints:

Lower bounds (LB): $x \geq 0, \ y \geq 0$
Upper bounds (UB): $x \leq 3, \ y \leq 3$
Constraint 1 (L1): $x + y \leq 4$
Constraint 2 (L2): $6x + 2y \geq 8$
Constraint 3 (L3): $x + 5y \geq 8$

The bounds are graphed in Figure 10.1. The MATLAB code that produces Figure 10.1 follows. Letters at the points of intersection were obtained by using the insert option on the MATLAB figure.

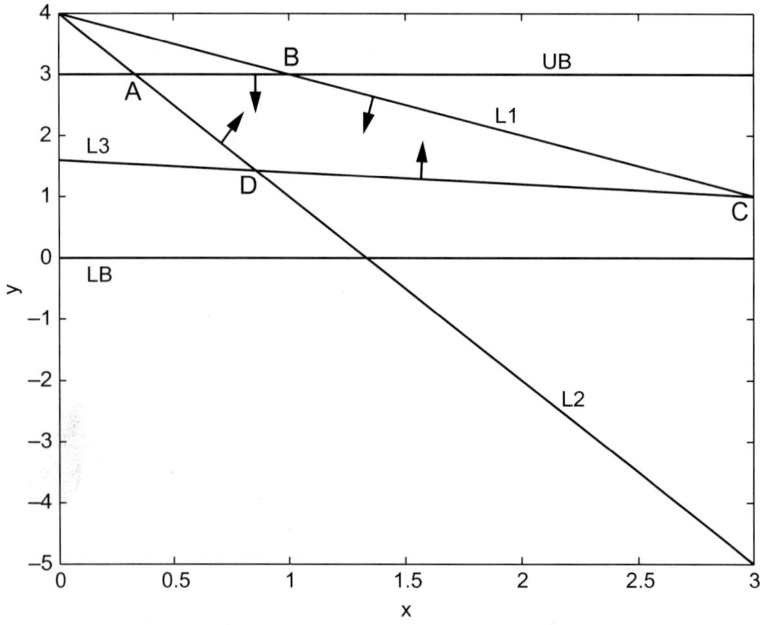

Figure 10.1 Allowable region for control variables in determining maximum and minimum points of the object function.

```
% Example_10_4.m
% To draw lines, specify two points on the line
% upper bound on y
x(1)=0; y(1)=3; x(2)=3; y(2)=3;
% upper bound on x
x1(1)=3; y1(1)=0; x1(2)=3; y1(2)=3;
% lower bound on y
x2(1)=0; y2(1)=0; x2(2)=3; y2(2)=0;
% lower bound on x
x3(1)=0; y3(1)=0; x3(2)=0; y3(2)=3;
% line L1
x4(1)=0; y4(1)=4; x4(2)=3; y4(2)=1;
% line L2
x5(1)=0; y5(1)=4; x5(2)=3; y5(2)=-5;
% line L3
x6(1)=0; y6(1)=8/5; x6(2)=3; y6(2)=1;
% plot the allowable region
plot(x,y,x1,y1,x2,y2,x3,y3,x4,y4,x5,y5,x6,y6)
xlabel('x'), ylabel('y'), title('y vs x');
```

For each constraint, we replace the inequality with an equal sign to draw lines for LB, UB, L1, L2, and L3 and then add an arrow to indicate the region corresponding to the inequality. This specifies the allowable region in which to consider the maximum and minimum values for function *f*.

We see in the graph that the allowable region for (x,y) in determining the maximum and minimum values for the object function *f* is the region enclosed by the polygon ABCD. For the specified object function, the minimum value of *f* is either on line L3 (between points D and C) or on line L2 (between points A and D). We can see this if we place a point P on line L3 and a point Q directly above it; then, the *x* values at points P and Q will be the same, but the *y* value at point Q will be larger than the *y* value of point P. Thus, *f* will be greater at point Q than *f* at point P. Thus, the minimum value of *f* is either on line L3 or on line L2.

The equation describing line L3 is

$$y = \frac{8}{5} - \frac{x}{5} \quad \text{(line L3)}$$

Substituting this expression for *y* into Equation (10.5) gives the value of *f* on line L3, which is

$$f = \frac{24}{5} + \frac{7x}{5} \quad \text{(on L3)}$$

The minimum value for *f* occurs at the lowest allowable *x* value on L3, which is at point D. Point D results from the intersection of line L3 and line L2. The equation describing line L2 is

$$y = 4 - 3x \quad \text{(line L2)}$$

The x coordinate at point D can be obtained by equating the y expressions for line L1 and line L2 giving the x value at point D, or $x_D = \frac{12}{14} = 0.8571$. At point D, the value of f is 6.00.

Substituting the expression for y on line L2 into Equation (10.5) gives the equation for f on line L2, which is

$$f = 12 - 7x \quad \text{(on line L2)}$$

The minimum value for f on line AD occurs at the maximum allowable value for x on AD, which is point D. Thus, in the allowable region, $f_{min} = 6.000$.

From Figure 10.1, we see that the maximum value of f will be either at point B or somewhere else on line L1. The equation describing line L1 is

$$y = 4 - x \quad \text{(on line L1)}$$

Substituting this expression for y into Equation (10.5) gives

$$f = 12 - x \quad \text{(on line L1)}$$

The maximum f occurs where x is a minimum on line L1, which is at point B. At point B, $x = 1$. Thus, $f_{max} = 11.0$.

10.6 Lagrange Multipliers

A more general and mathematical discussion of the optimization problem with constraints follows. Suppose we are given the object function $f(x_1, x_2, x_3, \ldots, x_n)$ in which the variables $x_1, x_2, x_3, \ldots, x_n$ are subject to N constraints, say

$$\begin{aligned} \Phi_1(x_1, x_2, x_3, \ldots, x_n) &= 0 \\ \Phi_2(x_1, x_2, x_3, \ldots, x_n) &= 0 \\ &\vdots \\ \Phi_N(x_1, x_2, x_3, \ldots, x_n) &= 0 \end{aligned} \tag{10.6}$$

Theoretically, the N x's can be solved in terms of the remaining x's. Then, these N variables can be eliminated from the objective function f by substitution, and the extreme problem can be solved as if there were no constraints. This method is referred to as the *implicit method* and in most cases is impractical.

The method of *Lagrange multipliers* provides the means for solving an extrema problem with constraints analytically. Suppose $f(x_1, x_2, x_3, \ldots, x_n)$ is to be maximized subject to constraints $\Phi_1(x_1, x_2, \ldots x_n)$, $\Phi_2(x_1, x_2, \ldots x_n), \ldots$, $\Phi_n(x_1, x_2, \ldots x_n)$ as in Equation (10.6). We define the *Lagrange* function F as

$$F(x_1, x_2, x_3, \ldots, x_n) = f(x_1, x_2, x_3, \ldots, x_n) + \lambda_1 \Phi_1(x_1, x_2, x_3, \ldots, x_n)$$
$$+ \lambda_2 \Phi_2(x_1, x_2, x_3, \ldots, x_n) + \cdots + \lambda_N \Phi_N(x_1, x_2, x_3, \ldots, x_n)$$

where λ_i are the unknown Lagrange multipliers to be determined. We now set

$$\frac{\partial F}{\partial x_1} = 0, \quad \frac{\partial F}{\partial x_2} = 0, \quad \frac{\partial F}{dx_3} = 0, \ldots, \frac{\partial F}{\partial x_n} = 0$$
$$\Phi_I = 0, \quad \Phi_2 = 0, \quad \Phi_3 = 0, \ \ldots, \Phi_N = 0 \tag{10.7}$$

(Note: $\dfrac{\partial F}{\partial \lambda_j} = 0$ implies $\Phi_j = 0$.)

This set of $n + N$ equations gives all possible extrema of f [1].

Example 10.5

A silo is to consist of a right circular cylinder of radius R and length L, with a hemispherical roof (see Figure 10.2). Assume that the silo is to have a specified volume V = 8400 m³. Find the dimensions R and L that make its surface area S a minimum. Assume that the silo has a floor of the same material. Note: $V_{\text{sphere}} = \frac{4}{3}\pi R^3$ and $S_{\text{sphere}} = 4\pi R^2$.

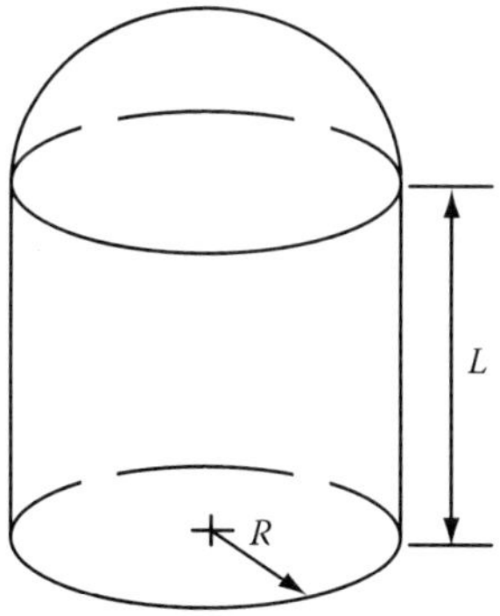

Figure 10.2 Silo consisting of a right circular cylinder topped by a hemisphere.

Solution:

$$V = \frac{2}{3}\pi R^3 + \pi R^2 L \tag{10.8}$$

$$\Phi = \frac{2}{3}\pi R^3 + \pi R^2 L - V = 0 \tag{10.9}$$

$$\begin{aligned} S &= 2\pi RL + \pi R^2 + 2\pi R^2 \\ &= 2\pi RL + 3\pi R^2 \end{aligned} \tag{10.10}$$

In this case, the surface area S is the function to be minimized, and the volume V is the constraint. The Lagrange function is

$$\begin{aligned} F &= S + \lambda\Phi \\ &= 2\pi RL + 3\pi R^2 + \lambda\left(\frac{2}{3}\pi R^3 + \pi R^2 L - V\right) \end{aligned} \tag{10.11}$$

The variables are R, L, and λ. Taking partial derivatives with respect to R and L gives

$$\frac{\partial F}{\partial R} = 2\pi L + 6\pi R + \lambda(2\pi R^2 + 2\pi RL) = 0 \tag{10.12}$$

$$\frac{\partial F}{\partial L} = 2\pi R + \lambda\pi R^2 = 0 \quad \rightarrow \quad \lambda R = -2 \text{ or } \lambda = -\frac{2}{R} \tag{10.13}$$

Substituting the value of λ from Equation (10.13) into (10.12) gives

$$2\pi L + 6\pi R - \frac{2}{R}(2\pi R^2 + 2\pi RL) = 0 \tag{10.14}$$

Equation (10.14) reduces to $R - L = 0$ or $R = L$.

Substituting this result into Equation (10.8) gives

$$\begin{aligned} V &= \frac{2}{3}\pi R^3 + \pi R^3 \\ &= \frac{5}{3}\pi R^3 \end{aligned}$$

For $V = 8400\text{ m}^3$,

$$R = \left(\frac{8400 \times 3}{5\pi}\right)^{1/3} = 11.7065\text{ m}$$

Substituting the values for R and L into Equation (10.10) gives $S = 2152.6\text{ m}^2$.

10.7 MATLAB's fmincon Function

MATLAB's function for solving optimization problems with constraints is `fmincon`. The `fmincon` function takes as arguments a user-defined function `FUN`, a starting point `X0`, plus additional arguments that depend on the type of constraints defined in the problem.

The function `FUN` defines the object function to be minimized. The vector `X0` is an initial guess of the control variables that minimizes the object function. MATLAB's `fmincon` handles four types of constraints:

1. Inequality constraints: The constraints involve one or more inequalities of the form $\mathbf{A} * \mathbf{X} \le \mathbf{B}$. Suppose the problem specifies three linear inequality constraints of the form

$$a_{11}x_1 + a_{12}x_2 + \cdots + a_{1n}x_n \le b_1$$

$$a_{21}x_1 + a_{22}x_2 + \cdots + a_{2n}x_n \le b_2$$

$$a_{31}x_1 + a_{32}x_2 + \cdots + a_{3n}x_n \le b_3$$

These constraints would be specified in MATLAB for use with `fmincon` as

```
A = [a11 a12 ... a1n; a21 a22 ... a2n; a31 a32 ... a3n]
B = [b1; b2; b3]
```

2. Equality constraints: The constraints involve one or more equalities of the form $\mathbf{A}_{eq} * \mathbf{X} = \mathbf{B}_{eq}$. Suppose the problem specifies two linear equality constraints of the form

$$\tilde{a}_{11}x_1 + \tilde{a}_{12}x_2 + \cdots + \tilde{a}_{1n}x_n = \tilde{b}_1$$

$$\tilde{a}_{21}x_1 + \tilde{a}_{22}x_2 + \cdots + \tilde{a}_{2n}x_n = \tilde{b}_2$$

where $\tilde{a}_{ij}$ and $\tilde{b}_i$ are the elements of $\mathbf{A}_{eq}$ and $\mathbf{B}_{eq}$, respectively. These constraints would be specified in MATLAB for use with `fmincon` as

$$\text{Aeq} = [\tilde{a}_{11}\ \tilde{a}_{12} \cdots \tilde{a}_{1n};\ \ \tilde{a}_{21}\ \tilde{a}_{22} \cdots \tilde{a}_{2n}]$$
$$\text{Beq} = [\tilde{b}_1;\ \ \tilde{b}_2]$$

3. Bounds: The constraints involve lower or upper limits of the form $\mathbf{X} \geq \mathbf{LB}$ and $\mathbf{X} \leq \mathbf{UB}$. Then, you would specify the bounds in MATLAB for use with `fmincon` as

$$\text{LB} = [l_1\ l_2 \cdots l_n]$$
$$\text{UB} = [u_1\ u_2 \cdots u_n]$$

where $x_1 \geq l_1, x_2 \geq l_2, \ldots, x_n \geq l_n$ and $x_1 \leq u_1, x_2 \leq u_2, \ldots, x_n \leq u_n$.

4. Nonlinear constraints: The constraints are defined by the function `[C,Ceq] = NONLCON(X)`, where `NONLCON` is a (user-defined) MATLAB function that specifies the nonlinear inequality constraints `C` and the nonlinear equality constraints `Ceq`. Suppose the problem specifies two nonlinear inequality constraints and one nonlinear equality constraint. The nonlinear inequality and equality constraint functions f_1, f_2, and f_3 need to be set up such that

$$f_1(x_1, x_2, \ldots, x_n) \leq 0, \quad f_2(x_1, x_2, \ldots, x_n) \leq 0 \quad \text{and} \quad f_3(x_1, x_2, \ldots, x_n) = 0$$

Then, in the function `NONLCON`, set `C(1)` $= f_1(x_1, x_2, \ldots, x_n)$, `C(2)` $= f_2(x_1, x_2, \ldots, x_n)$, and `Ceq(1)` $= f_3(x_1, x_2, \ldots, x_n)$.

A description of the many invocations of `fmincon` can be obtained by typing **`help fmincon`** in the Command window, some of which are described next.

Usage 1

```
X = FMINCON(FUN,X0,A,B) starts at X0 and finds a minimum X
to the function FUN, subject to the linear inequalities A*X <
= B. FUN accepts input X and returns a scalar function value F
evaluated at X. X0 may be a scalar, vector, or matrix.
```

This first version is used only if all the constraints are linear inequalities; that is, `A*X <= B`. In this case, the script starts at `X0` and finds control variables `X` that minimize the object function contained in `FUN` and returns the `X` values to the calling program. The initial guess `X0` is a column vector, and `A,B` describe a system of equations defining the inequality constraints.

Usage 2

```
X = FMINCON(FUN,X0,A,B,Aeq,Beq) minimizes FUN subject to
the linear equalities Aeq*X = Beq as well as A*X < = B. (Set
A = [] and B = [] if no inequalities exist.)
```

The second version is used if there are also linear equality constraints; that is, `Aeq*X = Beq`, where `Aeq` and `Beq` describe a system of equations describing the equality constraints. If there are no inequality constraints, then use `[]` for `A` and `B`.

Usage 3

```
X = FMINCON(FUN,X0,A,B,Aeq,Beq,LB,UB) defines a set of lower
and upper bounds on the design variables, X, so that a solution
is found in the range LB < = X < = UB. Use empty matrices for
LB and UB if no bounds exist. Set LB(i) = -Inf if X(i) is
unbounded below; set UB(i) = Inf if X(i) is unbounded above.
```

The third version is used if you wish to set lower and upper limits `LB` and `UB` to the control variables, where `LB` and `UB` are vectors containing the bounds on `X`.

Usage 4

```
X = FMINCON(FUN,X0,A,B,Aeq,Beq,LB,UB,NONLCON) subjects the
minimization to the constraints defined in function NONLCON.
The function NONLCON accepts X and returns the vectors C and
Ceq, representing the nonlinear inequalities and equalities
respectively. FMINCON minimizes FUN such that C(X) < = 0 and
Ceq(X) = 0. (Set LB = [] and/or UB = [] if no bounds exist, do
the same for A,B,Aeq,Beq if there are no linear inequality or
linear equality constraints.)
```

The fourth version is used if there are nonlinear constraints as defined in the function `NONLCON` of `X` as demonstrated in Examples 10.7 and 10.8.

Note that in all usages provided, we have invoked `fmincon` as returning a single vector, that is, the form `X = fmincon(FUN,X0,...)`. However, for convenience, we can also use the form `[X,FVAL] = fmincon(FUN,X0,...)`, which also returns `FVAL`, which is the minimum value of the object function.

Example 10.6

In this example, we use `fmincon` to determine the maximum and minimum values of the object function of Example 10.4 subject to the constraints specified in that example.

```
% Example_10_6.m: Linear programming example using
% MATLAB's fmincon function for optimization
% Object function: 2*x(1)+3*x(2)
% Lower bounds
%       x(1)>=0    x(2)>=0
% Upper bounds
%       x(1)<=3    x(2)<=3
% Inequality constraints
%       x(1)+x(2)<=4
%       6*x(1)+2*x(2)>=8
%       x(1)+5*x(2)>=8
clear; clc;
lb=[0; 0];              % Lower bound
ub=[3; 3];              % Upper bound
x0=[0; 0];              % Initial guess
Aeq=[];                 % No linear equality constraints
Beq=[];                 % No linear equality constraints
A=[1 1; -6 -2; -1 -5];  % Linear inequality constraints
B=[4; -8; -8];          % Linear inequality constraints
[xmin,fvalmin] = fmincon(@object_fmin,...
    x0,A,B,Aeq,Beq,lb,ub);
[xmax,fvalmax] = fmincon(@object_fmax,...
    x0,A,B,Aeq,Beq,lb,ub);
% Print min and max values:
fprintf('MIN\n');
fprintf('------------------------------\n');
fprintf('xmin(1)=%.4f  xmin(2)=%.4f \n',xmin(1),xmin(2));
fprintf('fmin=%.4f \n\n',fvalmin);
fprintf('MAX\n');
fprintf('------------------------------\n');
fprintf('xmax(1)=%.4f  xmax(2)=%.4f \n',xmax(1),xmax(2));
fprintf('fmax=%.4f \n',-fvalmax);
% object_fmin.m
% This function works with Example_10_6.m
function f = object_fmin(x)
f = 2*x(1)+3*x(2);
% object_fmax.m
% This function works with Example_10_6.m
function f = object_fmax(x)
f = -(2*x(1)+3*x(2));
```

PROGRAM RESULTS

```
MIN
------------------------------
xmin(1) = 0.8571 xmin(2) = 1.4286
fmin = 6.0000
MAX
------------------------------
xmax(1) = 1.0000 xmax(2) = 3.0000
fmax = 11.0000
```

Example 10.7

Solve for the minimum surface area of the silo in Example 10.4 using MATLAB's `fmincon` function.

```
% Example_10_7.m: This program minimizes the material
% surface area of a silo. The silo consists of a right
% cylinder topped by a hemisphere. Solve where the silo
% volume is 8400 m^3.
% Define the vector X = [R,L] where R is radius and L is
% length (as drawn in Figure 10.1)
% The function objfun_silo calculates the silo surface
% area and is the objective function to be minimized.
% The function confun_silo defines the constraint that
% the silo volume be fixed at 8400.
clear; clc;
global V;
V=8400;
% Define bounds: radius and length must be positive.
LB = [0,0];
UB = [];
% Initial guesses for R and L:
Xo = [10.0 20.0];
fprintf('This program minimizes the surface area\n');
fprintf('of a silo consisting of a right cylinder\n');
fprintf('topped by a hemisphere. The silo volume\n');
fprintf('is fixed at %.0f m^3.\n\n',V);
% Run the optimization.  We have no linear constraints,
% so pass [] for those arguments:
[X,fval]=fmincon(@objfun_silo,Xo, ...
    [],[],[],[],LB,UB,@confun_silo);
% Print results:
fprintf('Silo volume:          %9.3f m^3\n',V);
fprintf('Minimum surface area: %9.3f m^2\n',fval);
fprintf('Optimum radius:       %9.3f m\n',X(1));
fprintf('Optimum length:       %9.3f m\n',X(2));
-------------------------------------------------------------
% objfun_silo.m (object function for Example 10.7)
function SA = objfun_silo(X)
% Calculate surface area of silo.  The variables are:
% radius R = X(1), length of cylinder L = X(2)
SA = 2.0*pi*X(1)*X(2) + 3.0*pi*X(1)^2;
-------------------------------------------------------------
% confun_silo.m (constraint function for Example 10.7)
function [c, ceq] = confun_silo(X)
% Variables are:
% radius R = X(1), length of cylinder L = X(2).
global V;
% Nonlinear equality constraints:
ceq = pi*X(1)^2*X(2) + 2.0/3.0*pi*X(1)^3 - V;
% No nonlinear inequality constraints:
c = [];

-------------------------------------------------------------
```

PROGRAM RESULTS

```
Optimization Problem:
This program minimizes the surface area of a silo
consisting of a right cylinder topped by a hemisphere.
The silo volume is set at 8400   m^3
Silo volume:               8400.000 m^3
Minimum surface area:      2152.651 m^2
Optimum radius:            11.707   m
Optimum length:            11.706   m
```

Example 10.8

Suppose we now reverse Example 10.7 and determine the maximum volume of the silo described in Example 10.7 subjected to the constraint that the surface area of the silo is to be less than a specified amount, say 2152.6 m^2. The solution to the problem using MATLAB's `fmincon` follows:

```
% Example_10_8.m: This program maximizes the volume of a
% silo. The silo consists of a right cylinder topped by a
% hemisphere. The variables to optimize are radius 'R'
% and cylinder height 'L'.
% Let X(1) = R and X(2) = L.
% Eqn for surface area: S=3*pi*X(1)^2+2*pi*X(1)*X(2);
% Constraint: 3*pi*X(1)^2+2*pi*X(1)*X(2) <= 2152.6 m^2.
% We need to set up the constraint in the form:
% 3*pi*X(1)^2+2*pi*X(1)*X(2)- 2152.6 <= 0
% We wish to maximize the volume under the constraint.
% The equation for the volume, V, of the silo is given by
% V=2.0/3.0*pi*X(1)^3 + pi*X(1)^2*X(2).
% Since we wish to maximize V, we will need to place a
% minus sign in front of the expression for V and then
% minimize.
clear; clc;
global SAmax;
SAmax = 2152.6;
% Define bounds: radius and length must be positive.
LB = [0,0];
UB = [];
% Take an initial guess at the solution
Xo = [10.0 20.0];
fprintf('This program maximizes the volume of a silo\n');
fprintf('consisting of a right cylinder topped by a\n');
fprintf('hemisphere.  The maximum surface area is\n');
fprintf('fixed at %.1f m^3.\n\n',SAmax);
% Run the optimization.  We have no linear constraints,
% so pass [] for those arguments:
[X,fval]=fmincon(@objfun_silo2,...
    Xo,[],[],[],[],LB,UB,@confun_silo2);
SA = 3*pi*X(1)^2 + 2*pi*X(1)*X(2);
% Print results:
fprintf('Maximum surface area: %9.3f m^2\n',SA);
fprintf('Maximum volume:       %9.3f m^3\n',-fval);
```

```
fprintf('Optimum radius:        %9.3f m\n',X(1));
fprintf('Optimum length:        %9.3f m\n',X(2));
------------------------------------------------------------

% objfun_silo2.m (object function for Example 10.8)
function V = objfun_silo2(X)
% Compute volume of silo.  The variables are:
% radius R = X(1), length of cylinder L = X(2)
V = -(2.0/3.0*pi*X(1)^3 + pi*X(1)^2*X(2));
------------------------------------------------------------

% confun_silo2.m (constraint function for Example 10.8)
function [c, ceq] = confun_silo2(X)
global SAmax;
% Variables are:
% radius R = X(1), length of cylinder L = X(2)
% Nonlinear inequality constraint:
c = 3*pi*X(1)^2 + 2*pi*X(1)*X(2) - SAmax;
% No nonlinear equality constraints:
ceq = [];
------------------------------------------------------------
```

PROGRAM RESULTS

```
Optimization Problem:
This program maximizes the volume of a silo
consisting of a right cylinder topped by a hemisphere.
The maximum surface area is set at 2152.6 m^3
Maximum surface area: 2152.600 m^2
Maximum volume:       8399.701 m^3
Optimum radius:         11.706 m
Optimum length:         11.706 m
```

Example 10.9

Two machine shops, Machine Shop A and Machine Shop B, are to manufacture two types of motor shafts, shaft S1 and shaft S2. Each machine shop has two turning machines: Turning Machine T1 and Turning Machine T2. The following table lists the production time for each shaft type on each machine and at each location:

Time to Manufacture (minutes)				
	Machine Shop A		*Machine Shop B*	
	Shaft S1	*Shaft S2*	*Shaft S1*	*Shaft S2*
Turning Machine T1	4	9	5	8
Turning Machine T2	2	6	3	5

Shaft S1 sells for \$35, and shaft S2 sells for \$85. Determine the number of S1 and S2 shafts that should be produced at each machine shop and on each machine that will maximize the revenue for 1 hour of shop time.

```
% Example_10_9.m: Shaft Production Problem
% This program maximizes the revenue/hr for the
% production of two types of shafts, type S1 and type S2.
% There are two machine shops producing these shafts,
% shop A and shop B. Each shop has two types of turning
% machines, T1 and T2, capable of producing these shafts.
% Shop A:
%   Machine T1 takes 4 minutes to produce type S1 shafts
%   and 9 minutes to produce type S2 shafts.
%   Machine T2 takes 2 minutes to produce type S1 shafts
%   and 6 minutes to produce type S2 shafts.
% Shop B:
%   Machine T1 takes 5  minutes to produce type S1 shafts
%   and 8 minutes to produce type S2 shafts.
%   Machine T2 takes 3 minutes to produce type S1 shaft
%   and 5 minutes to produce type S2 shafts.
% Shaft S1 sells for $35 and shaft S2 sells for $85.
% We wish to determine the number of S1 & S2 shafts that
% should be produced at each shop and by each machine
% that will maximize the revenue/hr for shaft production.
% Let:
% X(1)=# of S1 shafts produced/hr by machine T1 at shop A
% X(2)=# of S2 shafts produced/hr by machine T1 at shop A
% X(3)=# of S1 shafts produced/hr by machine T2 at shop A
% X(4)=# of S2 shafts produced/hr by machine T2 at shop A
% X(5)=# of S1 shafts produced/hr by machine T1 at shop B
% X(6)=# of S2 shafts produced/hr by machine T1 at shop B
% X(7)=# of S1 shafts produced/hr by machine T2 at shop B
% X(8)=# of S2 shafts produced/hr by machine T2 at shop B
% Let r=total revenue/hr for producing these shafts:
%   r=35*(X(1)+X(3)+X(5)+X(7))+85*(X(2)+X(4)+X(6)+X(8))
clear; clc;
% Objective function: total revenue per hour for
% manufactured shafts. Have the function return a
% negative number because we are maximizing instead of
% minimizing.
revenue=@(x) -(35*(x(1)+x(3)+x(5)+x(7))+85*(x(2)+x(4)...
+x(6)+x(8)));
% Take a guess at the solution
Xo = [0 0 0 0 0 0 0 0];
% Lower and upper bounds:
LB = [0 0 0 0 0 0 0 0];
UB = [];
% We have linear inequality constraints.  We require that
% each machine make an integral number of shafts per 60
% minutes, so:
%   4*X(1)+9*X(2) <= 60
```

```
%    2*X(3)+6*X(4)  <= 60
%    5*X(5)+8*X(6)  <= 60
%    3*X(7)+5*X(8)  <= 60
A=[4  9  0  0  0  0  0  0;
   0  0  2  6  0  0  0  0;
   0  0  0  0  5  8  0  0;
   0  0  0  0  0  0  3  5];
B=[60  60  60  60]';
% We have no linear equality constraints, so pass [] for
% those arguments.
[X, rmax] = fmincon(revenue,Xo,A,B,[],[],LB,UB);
fprintf('Optimization Results:\n\n');
fprintf('No. of S1 shafts produced at shop A ');
fprintf('by machine T1: %2.0f\n',X(1));
fprintf('No. of S2 shafts produced at shop A ');
fprintf('by machine T1: %2.0f\n',X(2));
fprintf('No. of S1 shafts produced at shop A ');
fprintf('by machine T2: %2.0f\n',X(3));
fprintf('No. of S2 shafts produced at shop A ');
fprintf('by machine T2: %2.0f\n',X(4));
fprintf('No. of S1 shafts produced at shop B ');
fprintf('by machine T1: %2.0f\n',X(5));
fprintf('No. of S2 shafts produced at shop B ');
fprintf('by machine T1: %2.0f\n',X(6));
fprintf('No. of S1 shafts produced at shop B ');
fprintf('by machine T2: %2.0f\n',X(7));
fprintf('No. of S2 shafts produced at shop B ');
fprintf('by machine T2; %2.0f\n\n',X(8));
fprintf('The max revenue per hour: $%.0f /hour\n',-rmax);
----------------------------------------------------------
```

PROGRAM OUTPUT

```
Optimization Results:
No. of S1 shafts produced at shop A, T1: 0
No. of S2 shafts produced at shop A, T1: 7
No. of S1 shafts produced at shop A, T2: 30
No. of S2 shafts produced at shop A, T2: 0
No. of S1 shafts produced at shop B, T1: 0
No. of S2 shafts produced at shop B, T1: 8
No. of S1 shafts produced at shop B, T2: 0
No. of S2 shafts produced at shop B, T2: 12
The max revenue per hour: $3274/hour
```

Note: When the program is run, MATLAB gives diagnostic warnings to the screen that can be ignored. If a satisfactory solution is obtained, MATLAB will inform you by saying

```
Local minimum found that satisfies the constraints.
```

Exercises

Exercise 10.1

Use MATLAB's `fminunc()` function to find the maxima and minima of the following functions:

1. $f(x) = x^4 + 10x^3 - 20x - 15$
2. $f(x) = \dfrac{\sin^2(x - 0.75)}{x^2 - 1.5x + 0.5625}$
3. $f(x) = e^{-0.5x} \sin 2x$ (for $x \geq 0$)

Exercise 10.2

Use the method of steepest-descent to obtain the approximate position that makes f a relative minimum where

$$f(x_1, x_2) = 8x_1^2 - 20x_1x_2 + 17x_2^2 - 32x_1 + 40x_2$$

Use $(x_1, x_2) = (6, 4)$ as the starting point, $ds = 0.05$, and 200 steps.

Exercise 10.3

Use Lagrange multipliers to find the volume of the largest box that can be placed inside the ellipsoid

$$\frac{x^2}{a^2} + \frac{y^2}{b^2} + \frac{z^2}{c^2} = 1$$

so that the edges will be parallel to the coordinate axis.

Projects

Project 10.1

A silo consists of a right circular cylinder topped by a right circular cone as shown in Figure P10.1. The radius of both the cylinder and the base of the cone is R. The length of the cylinder is L, and the height of the cone is H. The cylinder, the cone, and the silo floor are all made of the same material. Write a program using MATLAB's `fmincon` function to determine the values of R, H, and L that will result in the minimum surface silo area for an internal silo volume of 7000 m^3.

Note: For a right circular cone,

$$V = \frac{\pi R^2 H}{3}$$

$$S = \pi R \sqrt{R^2 + H^2}$$

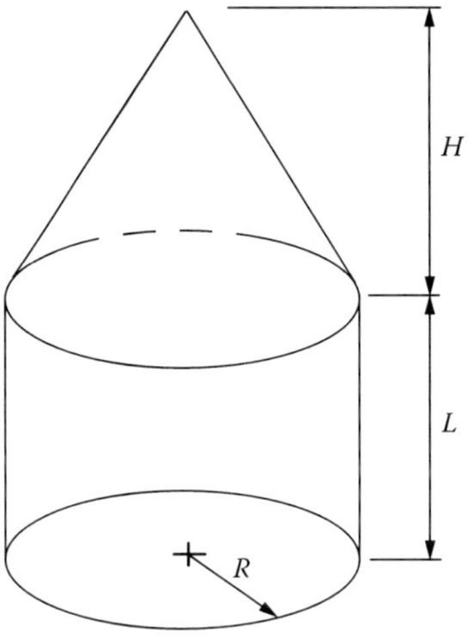

Figure P10.1 Silo consisting of a right circular cylinder topped by a right circular cone.

Project 10.2

A retail store sells computers to the public. There are eight different computer types that the store may carry. Table P10.2 lists the type of computer, the selling price, and the cost to the store. The store plans to spend $20,000 per month purchasing the computers.

The store plans to spend no more than 30% of its costs on computer types C1 and C2, no more than 30% on computer types C3 and C4, no more than 10% on computer types C5 and C6, and no more than 30% on computer types C7 and C8. The store estimates that it can sell 30% more of type C1 than C2, 20% more of type C3 than type C4, 20% more of type C5 than C6, and 60% more of type

Table P10.2 Retail Price and Manufacturing Cost for Computer Types C1 through C8

Computer Type	*Selling Price ($)*	*Cost ($)*
C1	675	637
C2	805	780
C3	900	874
C4	1025	990
C5	1300	1250
C6	1500	1435
C7	350	340
C8	1000	1030

C7 than C8. Use the `fmincon` function in MATLAB to determine the number of each type of computer that will provide the store with the most profit. Print out the number of each type of computer the store should purchase per month, the total profit per month and the total cost per month to the store.

Project 10.3

The Jones Electronics Corporation has a contract to manufacture four different computer circuit boards. The manufacturing process requires each of the boards to pass through the following four departments before shipping: etching and lamination (etches wiring into board); drilling (drills holes to secure components); assembly (installs transistors, microprocessors, etc.); and testing. The time requirement in minutes for each unit produced and its corresponding profit value are summarized in Table P10.3a.

Each department is limited to 3 days per week to work on this contract. The minimum weekly production requirement to fulfill a contract is shown in Table P10.3b.

Write a MATLAB program that will

1. Determine the number of each type of circuit board for the coming week that will provide the maximum profit. Assume that there are 8 hours per day, 5 days per week available for factory operations. Note: Not all departments work on the same day.
2. Determine the total profit for the week.

Table P10.3a Manufacturing Time for Various Circuit Board Types in Each Department

Circuit Board	*Etching and Lamination (minutes)*	*Drilling (minutes)*	*Assembly (minutes)*	*Testing (minutes)*	*Unit Profit ($)*
Board A	15	10	8	15	12
Board B	12	8	10	12	10
Board C	18	12	12	17	15
Board D	13	9	4	13	10

Table P10.3b Minimum Weekly Production Requirement for Various Circuit Board Types

Circuit Board	*Minimum Production Count*
Board A	10
Board B	10
Board C	10
Board D	10

3. Determine the total number of minutes it takes to produce all the boards.
4. Determine the total number of minutes spent in each of the four departments.
5. Print the requested information to a file.

Project 10.4

The XYZ oil company operates three oil wells (OW1, OW2, OW3) and supplies crude oil to four refineries (refinery A, refinery B, refinery C, refinery D). The cost of shipping the crude oil from each oil well to each of the refineries, the capacity of each of the three oil wells, and the demand (equality constraint) for gasoline at each refinery are tabulated in Table P10.4a. The crude oil at each refinery is distilled into six basic products: gasoline, lubricating oil, kerosene, jet fuel, heating oil, and

Table P10.4a Cost of Shipping per 100 Liters ($)

Oil Well	*Refinery A*	*Refinery B*	*Refinery C*	*Refinery D*	*Oil Well Capacity (liters)*
OW 1	9	7	10	11	7000
OW 2	7	10	8	10	6100
OW 3	10	11	6	7	6500
Demand (liters of gasoline)	2000	1800	2100	1900	

Table P10.4b Cost of Distillation per 100 Liters ($)

Oil Well	*Refinery A*	*Refinery B*	*Refinery C*	*Refinery D*
OW 1	15	16	12	14
OW 2	17	12	14	10
OW 3	12	15	16	17

Table P10.4c Distillation Products per Liter of Crude Oil

	Product Percentage per Liter from Distillation					
Oil Well	*Gasoline*	*Lubricating Oil*	*Kerosene*	*Jet Fuel*	*Heating Oil*	*Plastics*
OW 1	43	10	9	15	13	10
OW 2	38	12	5	14	16	15
OW 3	46	8	8	12	12	14

Table P10.4d Product Revenue per Liter ($)

Gasoline	*Lubricating Oil*	*Kerosene*	*Jet Fuel*	*Heating Oil*	*Plastics*
0.40	0.20	0.20	0.50	0.25	0.15

plastics. The cost of distillation per liter at each refinery from each of the oil wells is given in Table P10.4b. The percentage of each distilled product per liter is tabulated in Table P10.4c. The profit from each product is tabulated in Table P10.4d.

Using the `fmincon` function in MATLAB, determine the liters of oil to be produced at each oil well and shipped to each of the four refineries that will satisfy the gasoline demand and will produce the maximum profit. Print out the following items:

1. The liters produced at each oil well
2. The liters of gasoline received at each refinery
3. The total cost of shipping and distillation of all products
4. The total revenue from the sale of all of the products
5. The total profit from all of the products

Project 10.5

A second-order control system has a frequency response of the following general form:

$$H(s) = \frac{\omega_n^2}{s^2 + 2\zeta\omega_n s + \omega_n^2} \qquad \text{(P10.5a)}$$

where ω_n is the natural frequency (in radians/second), and ζ is the damping factor. The *step response* of a system is defined as its time-domain response to a unit step input. In the s domain, this corresponds to the product $H(s)\,U(s)$, where $U(s) = \frac{1}{s}$ is the Laplace transform of the unit step function $u(t)$. To find the time-domain step response $y(t)$, we find the inverse Laplace transform of $H(s)U(s)$:

$$\begin{aligned} y(t) &= \mathcal{L}^{-1}\left(H(s)U(s)\right) \\ &= \mathcal{L}^{-1}\left(\frac{\omega_n^2}{s^2 + 2\zeta\omega_n s + \omega_n^2} \times \frac{1}{s}\right) \end{aligned} \qquad \text{(P10.5b)}$$

By performing a partial-fraction expansion on Equation (P10.5b) and using inverse Laplace transform tables, we obtain

$$y(t) = \begin{cases} 1 - e^{-\omega_n t}\left(\cosh\sqrt{\zeta^2 - 1}\,\omega_n t + \dfrac{\zeta}{\sqrt{\zeta^2 - 1}}\sinh\left(\sqrt{\zeta^2 - 1}\,\omega_n t\right)\right) & \zeta > 1 \\ 1 - e^{-\omega_n t}\left(1 - \omega_n t\right) & \zeta = 1 \\ 1 - e^{-\omega_n t}\left(\cos\sqrt{1 - \zeta^2}\,\omega_n t + \dfrac{\zeta}{\sqrt{1 - \zeta^2}}\sin\sqrt{1 - \zeta^2}\,\omega_n t\right) & \zeta < 1 \end{cases} \qquad \text{(P10.5c)}$$

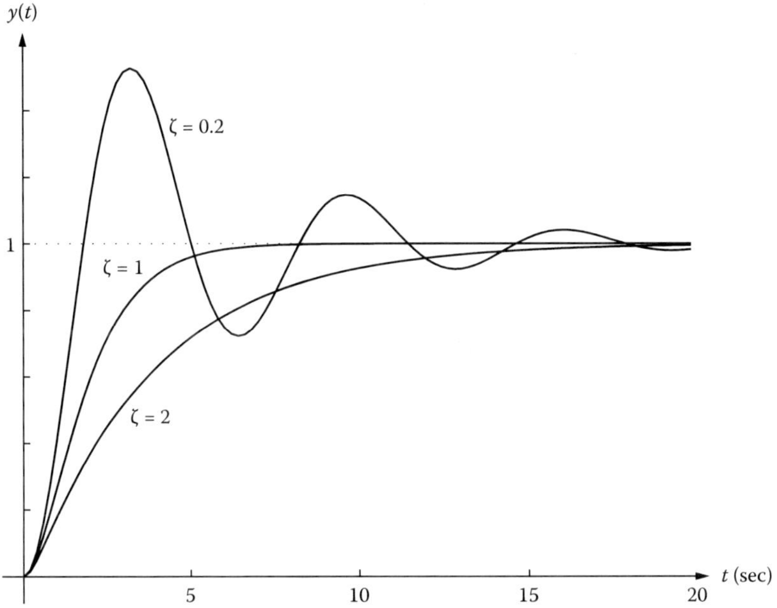

Figure P10.5 Settling time of an RLC circuit for $\zeta = 0.2$, $\zeta = 1$, and $\zeta = 2$.

The *settling time* t_S is defined as the time it takes for $y(t)$ to settle to its final value within some arbitrary range, typically 5% or 10%. Figure P10.5 shows the step response for three values of ζ for $\omega_n = 1$.

In this problem, we wish to find the optimum value of ζ to minimize the settling time.

1. Write a MATLAB function named `step_response(zeta, wn, t)` that calculates the unit step response of $H(s)$ as per Equation (P10.5c) as a function of ζ and ω_n over the given interval t. Confirm that your function is correct by plotting the step response for $\zeta = 0.2$, $\zeta = 1$, and $\zeta = 2$. Assume $\omega_n = 1$ and use the time interval $0 \le t \le 20$ sec in steps of 0.1 sec. Your results should match Figure P10.5.
2. Write another MATLAB function named `find_settling_time(zeta, wn, t, Etol)` that finds the settling time t_S of a waveform generated by `step_response()` to the tolerance specified by the `Etol` argument. The waveform $y(t)$ may be considered settled when the magnitude of its deviation from the final value is less than the desired tolerance, that is,

$$\left| \frac{y(t) - y(\infty)}{y(\infty)} \right| < E_{tol} \qquad \text{(P10.5d)}$$

where $y(\infty)$ is the final settled value of $s(t)$, and E_{tol} is the desired error tolerance (e.g., 5% or 10%). Thus, for example, to find the time t_S it takes for $y(t)$ to settle to 5% of its final value, the function should use the techniques described in Chapter 4 to find the root of the equation

$$\left|\frac{y(t)-1}{1}\right| - 0.05 = 0 \tag{P10.5e}$$

Note that in the underdamped case, $y(t)$ may oscillate in and out of tolerance before finally settling. Thus, you should search for the root of Equation (P10.5e) starting from the right side of the waveform (i.e., starting at $t = \infty$) rather than starting at $t = 0$. Then, you are sure to find the final settled value after the oscillations have died away.

3. Plot t_s for $0.2 \le \zeta \le 2$ in steps of 0.01 for a settling tolerance of 5%. Assume that $\omega_n = 1$. You might see some discontinuities in your plot for $\zeta \le 1$. What is the cause of the discontinuities?
4. Use MATLAB's `fminunc()` function to find the value of ζ that minimizes the settling time. Compare this value with your plot from part 3 above. Does your answer look correct?
5. Use the curve-fitting techniques of Chapter 8 to fit your data for t_s versus ζ to a fourth-order polynomial with MATLAB's `polyfit()` function. Rerun your minimization on the fitted polynomial. Does the answer seem more accurate?

Reference

1. Wylie, C.R., *Advanced Engineering Mathematics*, McGraw Hill, New York, p. 596.

Chapter 11

Simulink

11.1 Introduction

Simulink® is used with MATLAB® to model, simulate, and analyze dynamic systems. Common uses are for solving differential equations, modeling feedback systems, and signal processing.

With Simulink, models can be built from scratch or additions can be made to existing models. Simulations can be made interactive, so a change in parameters can be made while running the simulation. Simulink supports linear and nonlinear systems, modeled in continuous time, sample time, or combinations of the two.

Simulink provides a graphical user interface (GUI) for building models as block diagrams, using click-and-drag mouse operations. By using scopes and other display blocks, simulation results can be seen interactively while the simulation is running. The program includes a comprehensive library of components ("blocks") from which to construct models. Additional application-specific "toolboxes" are also available.

11.2 Creating a Model in Simulink

1. Click on the Simulink icon on the menu bar in the MATLAB window or type `simulink` in the MATLAB Command window. This brings up the Simulink Library Browser window (see Figure 11.1).

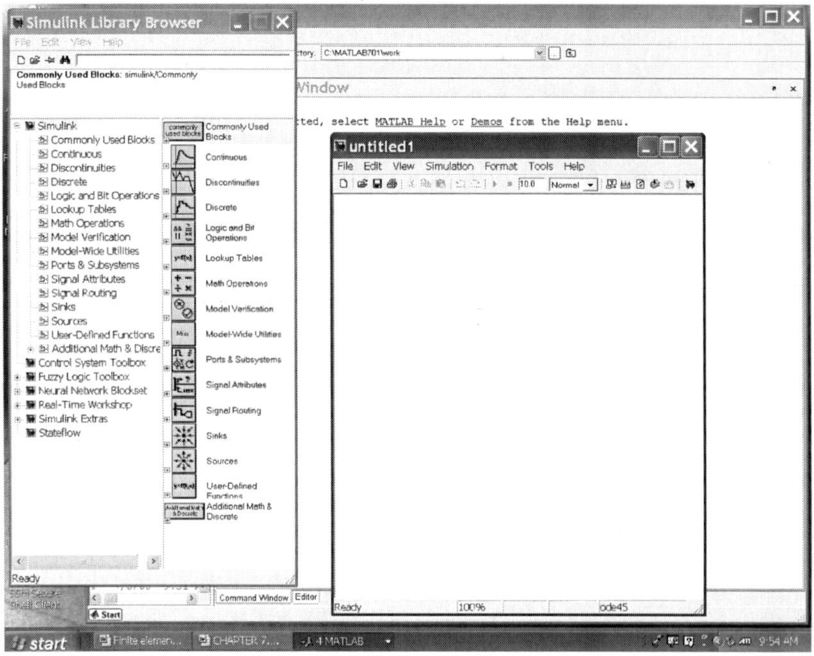

Figure 11.1 Simulink Library Browser and untitled model window. (From MATLAB, with permission.)

2. Click on *File* in the Simulink Library Browser window. Select *New–Model* (for a new model) or *Open* for an existing model. This will bring up an untitled model window (for the case of a new model) or an existing model window.
3. To create a new model, you need to copy blocks from the Library Browser window into the new model window. This can be done by highlighting a particular block and dragging it into the model window. To simplify the connections of blocks, you may need to rotate a block 90° or 180°. To do this, highlight the block, click on *Format* in the menu bar, and then select *Rotate Block* (for 90°) or *Flip Block* (for 180°).

Simulink has many categories for displaying the library blocks; those of interest for this chapter are Commonly Used Blocks, Continuous, Discontinuities, Math Operations, Ports & Subsystems, Signal Routing, Sinks, Sources, and User-Defined Functions.

Common blocks that will be used repeatedly in this chapter are Constant, Clock (from the Sources library); Product, Gain, Sum (from the Math Operations library); Integrator (from the Continuous library); Scope, Display,

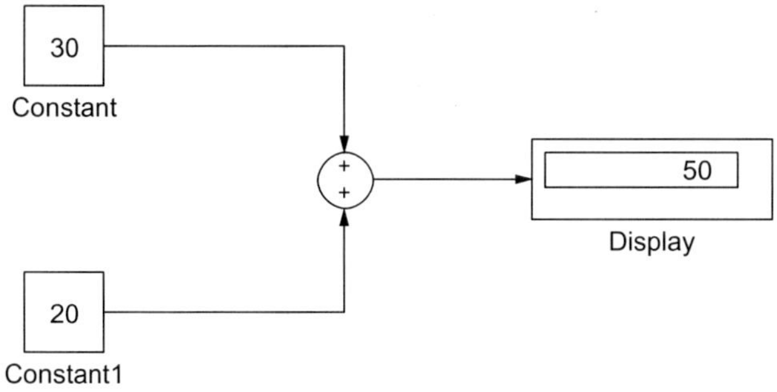

Figure 11.2 Constants, Sum, and Display blocks for addition.

To Workspace (from the Sink library); Relay (from the Discontinuities library); Switch, Mux (from the Signal Routing library), and Fcn (from the User-Defined Functions library).

11.3 Typical Building Blocks in Constructing a Model

1. Addition of two constants with displayed output (see Figure 11.2). To set the value for a constant, double click on the block and edit the constant value. To run the program, click on *Simulation* in the menu bar and select *Start*; alternatively, click the Play button (►) in the menu bar.
2. Subtraction (see Figure 11.3). To make the Sum block perform a difference, double click on the block and edit the list of signs.
3. Product of two blocks (see Figure 11.4).
4. Division of two blocks (See Figure 11.5).

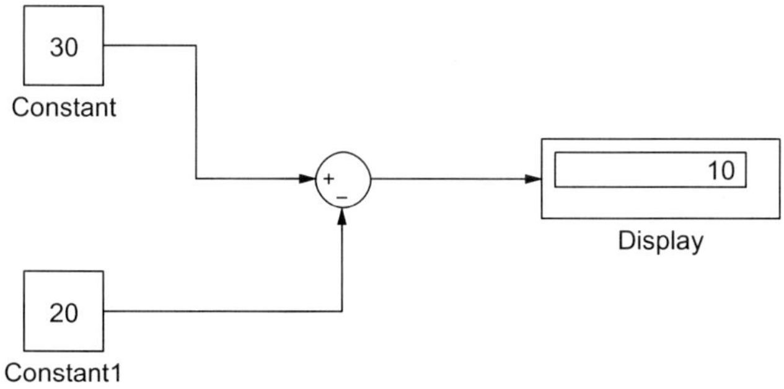

Figure 11.3 Constants, Sum, and Display blocks for subtraction.

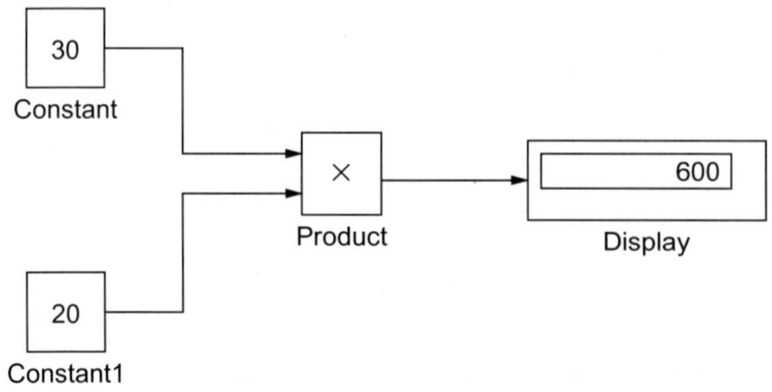

Figure 11.4 Constants, Product, and Display blocks for multiplication.

5. Integrate a sine wave (see Figure 11.6). In the sine wave block parameters, set the frequency to 2 rad/s. To view the output waveform, first click the Play button (►) and then double click on the scope block to open the plot. Then, right click on the plot and select *autoscale*. The resulting waveform is the integral of *sin* 2*x*:

$$\int_0^t \sin 2x\,dx = -\frac{1}{2}\cos 2x\Big|_0^t = -\frac{1}{2}(\cos 2t - 1) = \frac{1}{2}(1 - \cos 2t) \tag{11.1}$$

Note that because the integrator has a (default) initial condition of zero, the resulting waveform will vary from zero to one.

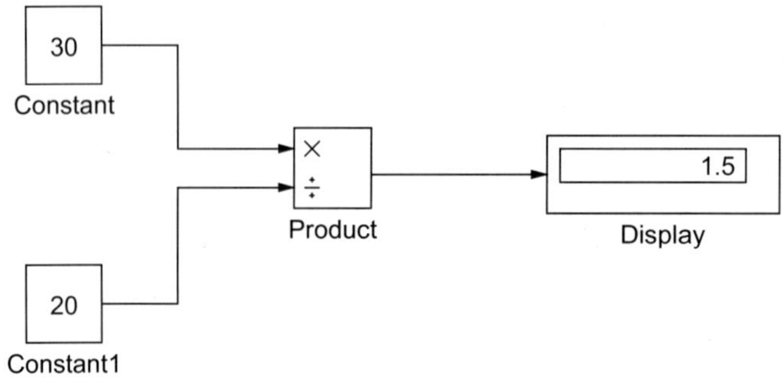

Figure 11.5 Constants, Product, and Display blocks for division.

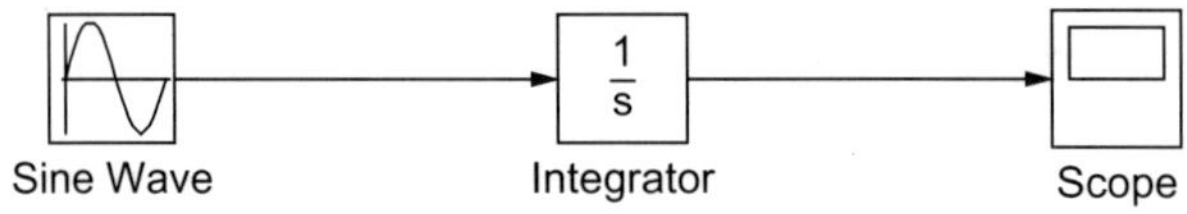

Figure 11.6 Sine wave, Integration, and Scope blocks.

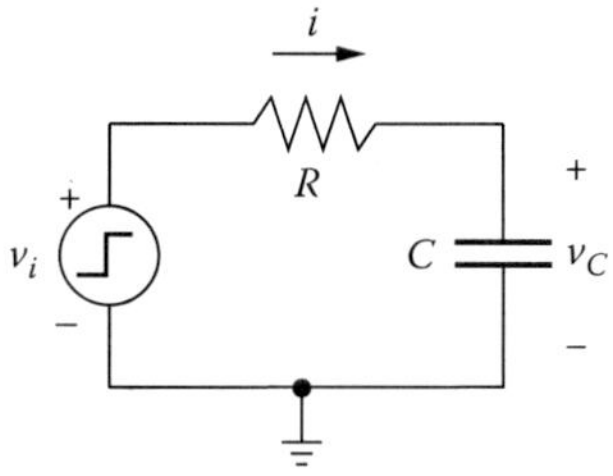

Figure 11.7 First-order RC circuit.

6. Solution of a simple ordinary first-order differential equation. The method of solution is illustrated in Example 11.1, which considers the step response of an RC circuit.

Example 11.1

For the series RC circuit of Figure 11.7, we examine the capacitor voltage v_C with respect to time in response to a unit step input voltage. The governing equation (as derived in Example 6.1) is

$$\frac{dv_C}{dt} = \frac{1}{RC}(v_i - v_C) \tag{11.2}$$

where

$$R = 10\ \text{k}\Omega$$
$$C = 4.7\ \mu\text{F}$$
$$v_i = \begin{cases} 0\ \text{V} & \text{for } t \le 0 \\ 1\ \text{V} & \text{for } t > 0 \end{cases}$$

The block diagram for Equation (11.2) is shown in Figure 11.8, and the resulting scope output is shown in Figure 11.9.

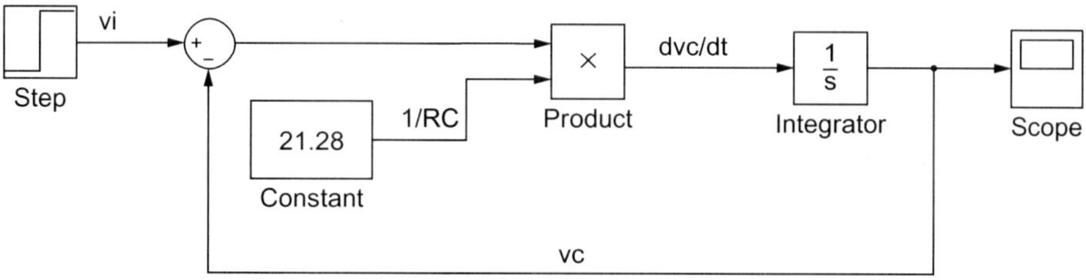

Figure 11.8 Block diagram for solving Equation (11.2).

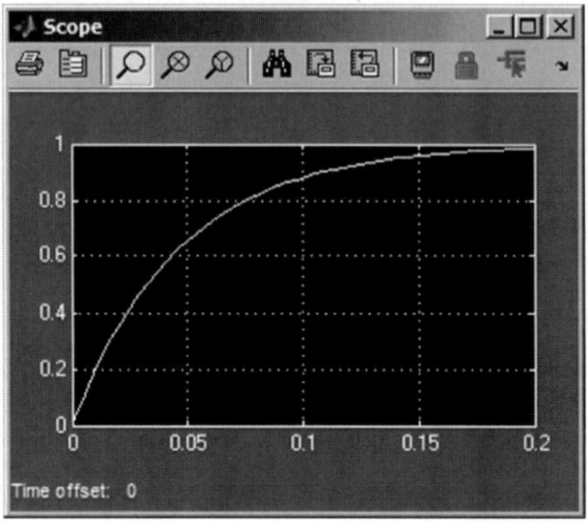

Figure 11.9 Scope output of RC circuit.

11.4 Tips for Constructing and Running Models

1. To connect lines from the output of a block to the input of a second block, place the cursor on the output of the first block, right click on the mouse, and drag the line to the input of the second block.
2. To connect a point on a line to the input of a block, place the cursor on the line, right click on the mouse, and drag the line to the input of the block.
3. To add alphanumeric information above a line, use the left button and double click above the line and a text box will appear. Type in the desired label and click elsewhere to complete.
4. To view the results on a scope, double click on the scope to make a graph appear. To select the graph axis, right click on the graph and select *axis properties* or *autoscale*. In most cases, selecting autoscale is sufficient. You may also click on the binoculars icon to autoscale the graph.
5. To set initial conditions for an integrator, double click on the block and edit the initial condition line.
6. By default, Simulink runs over a time interval of 0 to 10 sec. These times are inappropriate for many models (e.g., high-frequency circuits). To edit the start and stop times, click on *Simulation* in the menu bar, select *Configuration Parameters*, and edit the start and stop time boxes. Alternatively, you can adjust the stop time in the menu bar (the start time defaults to zero).

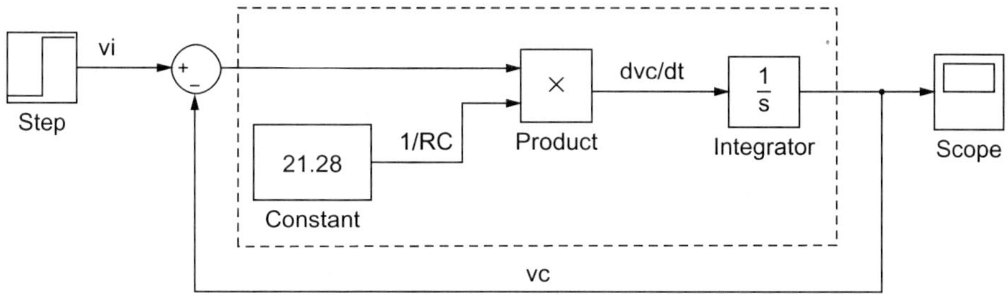

Figure 11.10 Constructing a subsystem.

7. To run the simulation, click on *Simulation* in the menu bar and choose *Start*. Alternatively, click the Play button (►) in the menu bar.

11.5 Constructing a Subsystem

Suppose we build a large system consisting of many blocks, and we wish to reduce the number of blocks appearing in the overall block diagram. This can be done by creating a subsystem. The subsystem will appear as a single block. To create a subsystem, place the cursor in the vicinity of the region that is to become a subsystem and right click the mouse. This produces a small dashed box that can be enlarged by dragging the mouse over the region enclosing the number of blocks to be included in the subsystem (Figure 11.10). When the mouse button is released, a drop-down menu appears. Select *Create Subsystem* to cause the multiple blocks to be replaced with a single subsystem block.

In Figure 11.11, the constant, product, and integrator blocks have been combined into the subsystem. This particular subsystem has one input and one output, but in general, a subsystem may have multiple inputs and outputs. By double clicking on the subsystem, you may view its components (see Figure 11.12).

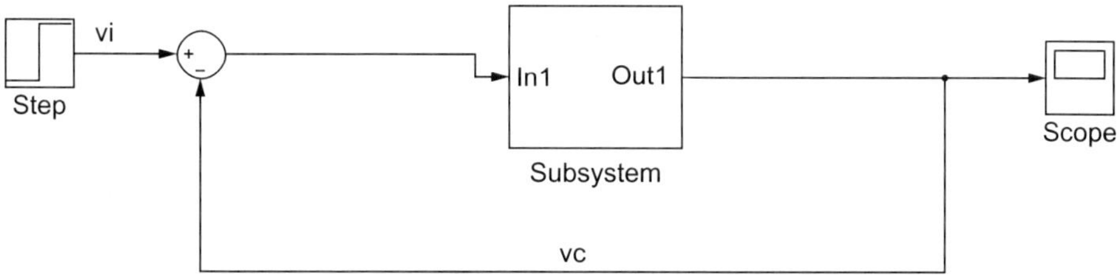

Figure 11.11 Block diagram with subsystem for solving Equation (11.2).

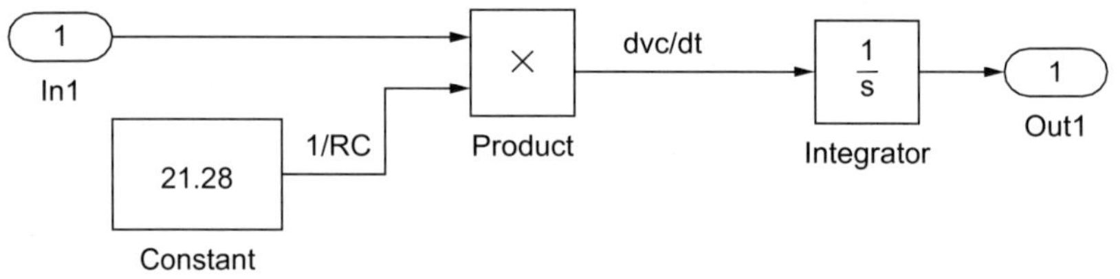

Figure 11.12 Subsystem model.

11.6 Using the Mux and Fcn Blocks

An alternative to the block diagram for Example 11.1 is shown in Figure 11.13. In this solution, Simulink's Mux and Fcn blocks are used to solve the problem. The Mux block allows you to select among multiple inputs (to adjust the number of inputs, double click on the block and edit the number of inputs). The uppermost input is designated $u[1]$, the one below is designated $u[2]$, and so on. In this example, the output from the Mux block should go to the input of the Fcn block.

The purpose of the Fcn block is to allow arbitrary mathematical and MATLAB functions to be defined within the model. In this case, the math expression in the Fcn block is used to implement Equation (11.2) in terms of the $u[]$'s.

11.7 Using the Transfer Fcn Block

A common method for solving circuit problems is to substitute complex impedances for the capacitors and inductors and then solve like a resistive circuit. For the RC circuit, the impedance of the resistor is simply $Z_R = R$, and the impedance of

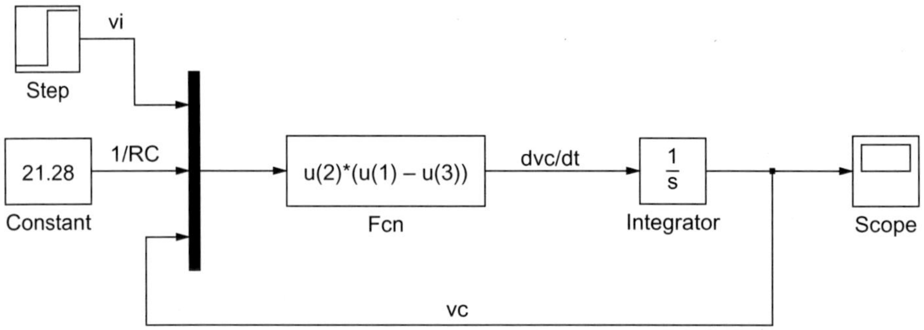

Figure 11.13 Block diagram for solving Equation (11.2) using the Mux and Fcn blocks.

the capacitor is $Z_C = \frac{1}{Cs}$ (where $s = j\omega$). Then, the capacitor voltage is simply the output of a resistive divider:

$$v_C = \frac{Z_C}{Z_R + Z_C} v_i$$

$$= \frac{\frac{1}{Cs}}{R + \frac{1}{Cs}} v_i$$

$$= \frac{\frac{1}{RC}}{s + \frac{1}{RC}} v_i$$

$$= H(s) v_i$$

where $H(s) = \dfrac{1/RC}{s + 1/RC}$ is commonly referred to as the *transfer function*. In Simulink, the Transfer Fcn block allows direct entry of a transfer function into your model as shown in Figure 11.14.

11.8 Using the Relay and Switch Blocks

Relays and switches are used in designs to enable a low-power device (e.g., an electronic controller) to control a high-power system (e.g., a boiler or furnace). Simulink has Relay and Switch blocks that can be used to simulate these types of systems.

Example 11.2

In a home heating system, a temperature sensor is used to switch the boiler on and off to heat the house to a comfortable temperature. However, because most boilers do not turn on and off instantaneously (i.e., they take a few minutes to heat up after turning on and take time to cool after turning off), the control of the room temperature requires some hysteresis to avoid cycling the boiler on and off too often (which causes excessive wear on the boiler). This concept can be represented by a simple differential equation in

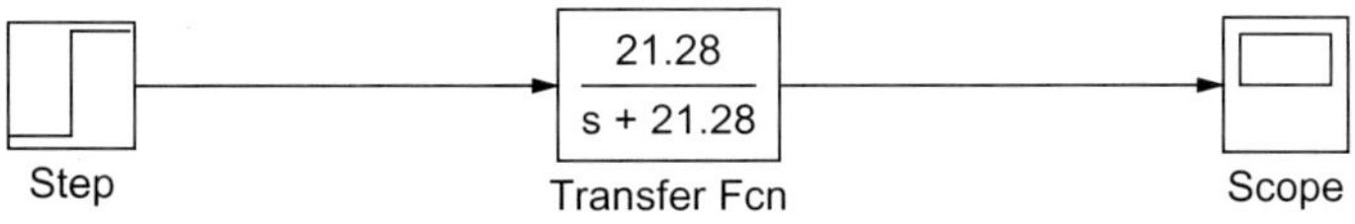

Figure 11.14 Block diagram using the Transfer Fcn block.

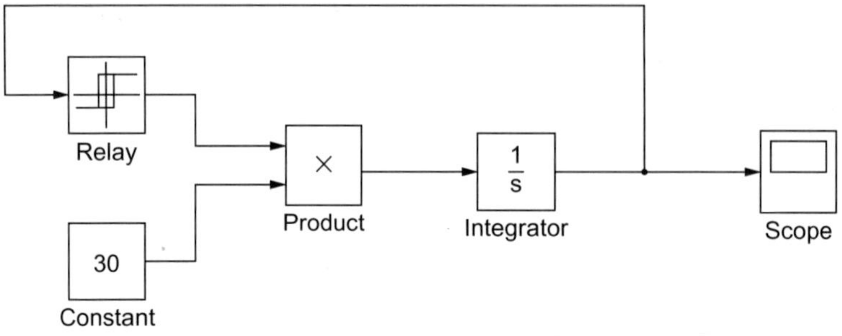

Figure 11.15 Block diagram using the Relay block from Example 11.2.

which the temperature T is set to fluctuate at a constant rate between 20°C and 22°C :

$$\frac{dT}{dt} = c \quad \text{where} \quad c = \begin{cases} 30 & \text{if } T \leq 20 \\ -30 & \text{if } T \geq 22 \end{cases}$$

The block diagram for this system consists of an Integrator, a Constant, a Relay, a Product, and a Scope (Figure 11.15). The Relay is used to invert the sign on c depending on whether the relay is on or off. The Relay parameters may be edited by double clicking on the Relay block and setting the parameters to the following values:

Switch point on = 22
Switch point off = 20
Output when on = –1
Output when off = +1

We assume that the initial room temperature is T = 18°C, and this value is entered into the parameters for the Integrator block. At the start of the simulation, $T \leq 20$; thus, the Relay switch is off, and the output of the Relay is +1, causing T to increase. The Relay output will remain +1 until T reaches 22, at which point the Relay will turn on and its output will be –1, causing T to decrease. The Relay output will remain –1 until T reaches 20, at which point the Relay will turn off and its output becomes +1 again. This process will continue until the simulation end time is reached. The output of the Scope is shown in Figure 11.16.

Example 11.3

Some problems may involve a function that varies in time for $0 \leq t \leq t_1$ and is constant for $t_1 < t \leq t_2$. This type of function can best be modeled with the Switch block that implements a DPST (double-pole, single-throw) switch with an additional terminal to control the opening and closing of the switch.

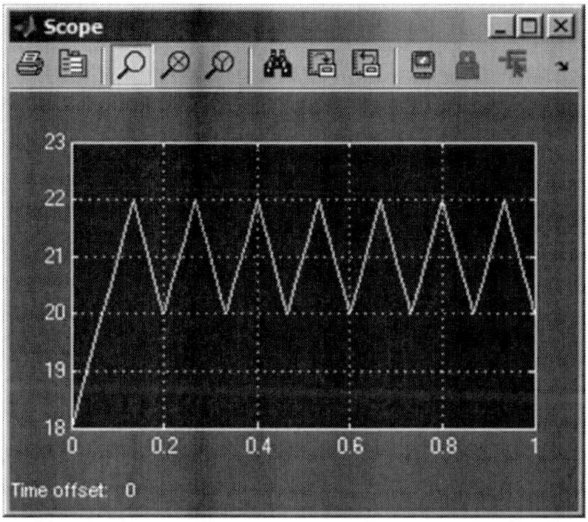

Figure 11.16 Scope output of Example 11.2.

Suppose

$$y = \begin{cases} 5t & \text{for} \quad 0 \le t \le 10 \\ 50 & \text{for} \quad 10 < t \le 20 \end{cases}$$

The Simulink model for this problem is shown in Figure 11.17. The parameters for the Switch are as follows (note that terminal u1 is the top switch input, u2 is the middle [control] input, and u3 is the bottom switch input):

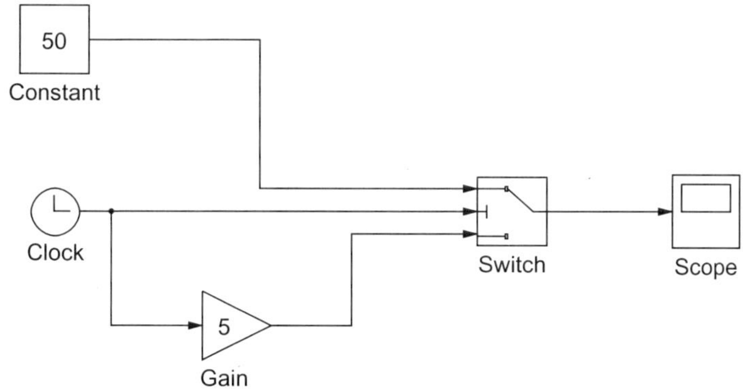

Figure 11.17 Block diagram using the Switch block from Example 11.3.

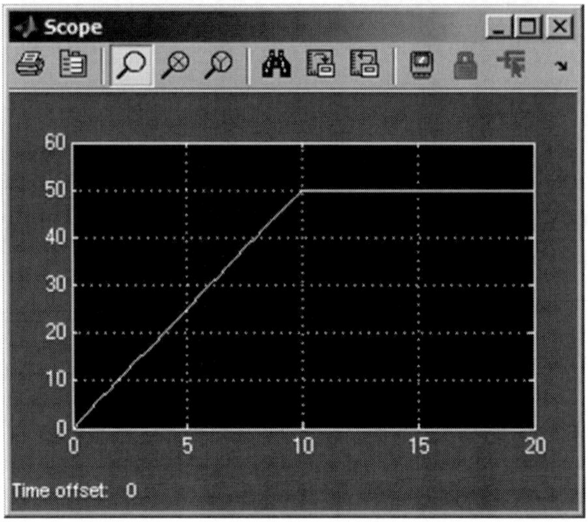

Figure 11.18 Scope output of Example 11.3.

Criteria for passing first input: u2 ≥ Threshold
Threshold: 10

The resulting output is shown in Figure 11.18. Note that we use the Clock block to obtain a value for *y* that is proportional to the elapsed time.

11.9 Trigonometric Function Blocks

Functions such as sine, cosine, and tangent can be obtained via the Trigonometric Function block located in Simulink's Math Operations library. The input to this block is the argument to the desired trig function. If the argument involves the independent variable *t* (as in *sin* ω*t*), then we can use the Clock block to obtain the value of *t*. This is shown in Figure 11.19, where we compute the value of cos 2*t*.

Example 11.4: Simulation of an RLC Circuit

In Section 2.17, we studied the parallel RLC circuit. If we use a sinusoidal input current to the circuit in Figure 2.14 and assume that the switch closes at $t = 0$, the governing equation is

$$\frac{d^2 i_L}{dt^2} + \frac{1}{RC}\frac{di_L}{dt} + \frac{1}{LC} i_L = \frac{1}{LC} I_o \sin \omega t \tag{11.3}$$

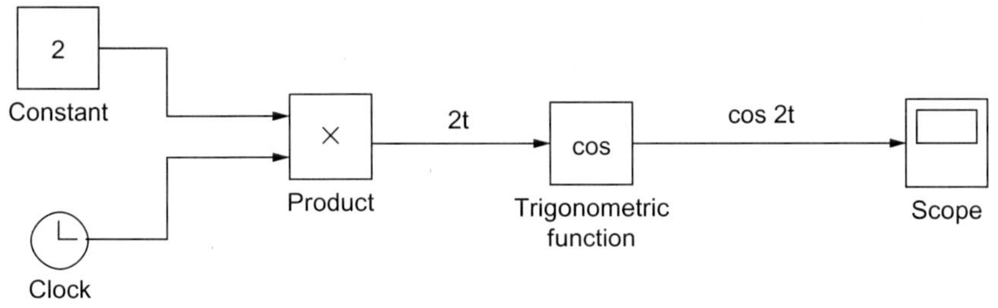

Figure 11.19 Block diagram using the Clock, Product, and Trigonometric Function blocks.

where the circuit is "driven" by a sinusoidal current of frequency ω and magnitude I_0. The Simulink model in Figure 11.20 solves this second-order differential equation with the following circuit values and initial conditions:

$C = 1\ \mu F$
$L = 10\ mH$
$R = 2000\ \Omega$
$I_o = 5\ mA$
$\omega = 2000$ radian/sec
$i_L(0) = 2\ mA$
$i_L'(0) = 0$

The output of the simulation is shown in Figure 11.21. Simulation and workspace parameters for this example are as follows:

Simulation time:
 Start time: 0.0
 Stop time: 0.015
Solver options:
 Type: Variable step
 Solver: ode45 (Dormand-Prince)
 Maximum step size: auto
 Minimum step size: auto
 Initial step size: auto
 Relative tolerance: 1e-3
 Absolute tolerance: auto
Workspace parameters:
 Variable name: i
 Limit data points to last: inf
 Decimation: 1
 Sample time (-1 for inherited): -1
Save format: array

Note that you can export Simulink output values into MATLAB variables for further manipulation or for printing. You can do this with the *To Workspace*

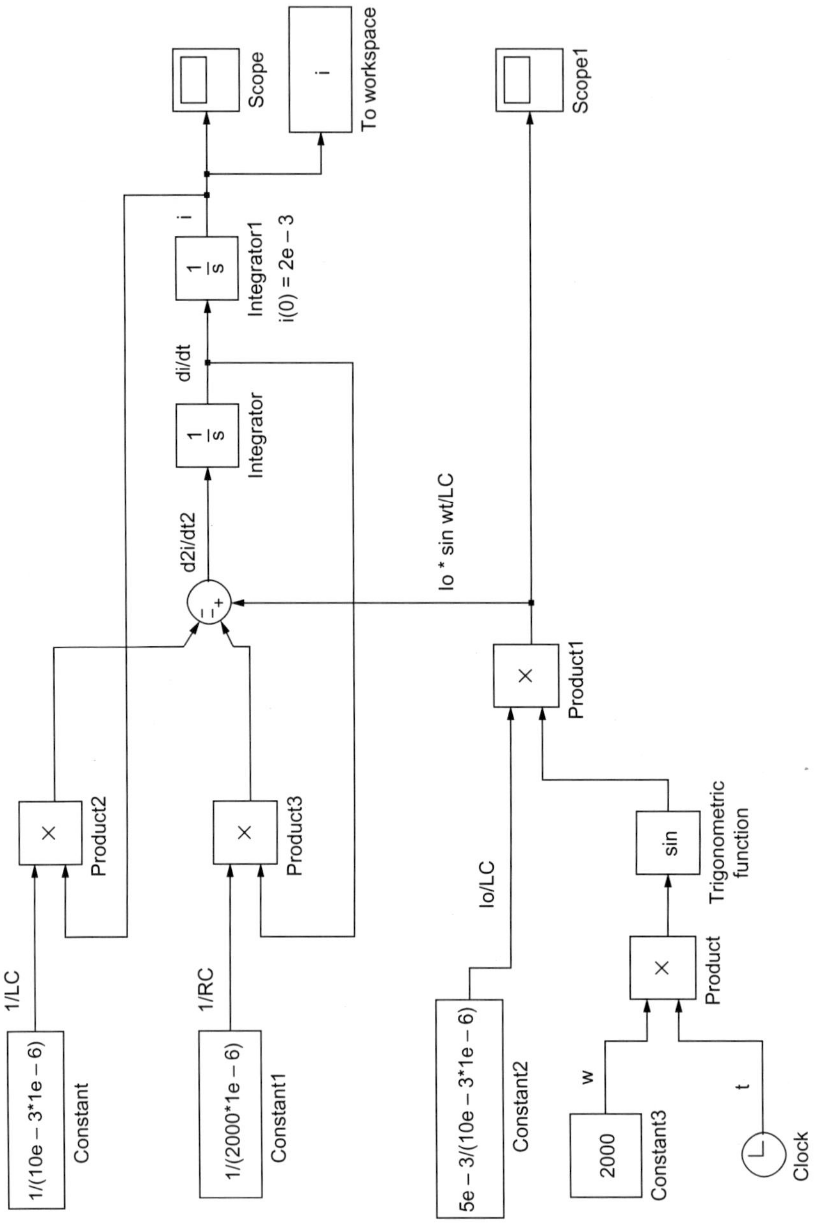

Figure 11.20 Block diagram for solving the second-order differential equation of Equation (11.3).

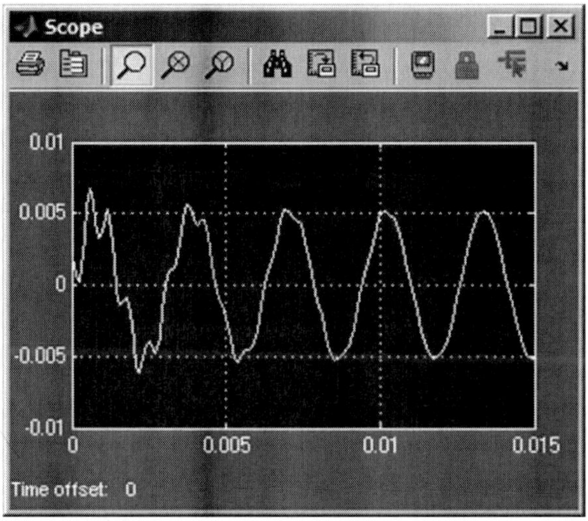

Figure 11.21 Scope output of Example 11.4.

block as shown in Figure 11.20. After the simulation is run, those variables become available for use in any MATLAB program. When using To Workspace, be sure that the *Save Format* property is set to *Array*.

Exercises

Exercise 11.1

Implement the following function in Simulink:

$$y = 5t^2 + 4t + 2$$

1. Using one Clock block, three Constants, two Multipliers, and a Sum.
2. Using one Clock block, three Constants, a Mux block, an Fcn block, a Scope block, and two To Workspace blocks. The scope block should give a plot of y versus t. Also, create a MATLAB program that constructs a table of y versus t in the Command window.
3. Using one Constant and two Integrators.

Projects

Project 11.1

A *decision circuit* is used in a communication system to decide whether a received digital signal is a logical one or zero. It then outputs its decision using onboard logic levels. For example, in the RS-232 serial communication protocol [1], the nominal logic levels to represent a logical one or zero are ±12 V. However, typical logic levels on a computer motherboard are +5 V and 0 V. We can use a relay block in Simulink to examine the behavior of a decision circuit that implements these requirements in the presence of noise that is induced in the RS-232 cable due to fluorescent lights, radio waves, and so on.

1. Use Simulink's Signal Generator block (from the Sources library) to generate a binary signal of alternating ones and zeros using RS-232 logic levels at a rate of 1200 bits/sec. (Note: 1200 bits/sec is *not* the same as 1200 Hz.)
2. Add white noise to your RS-232 signal with a Band-limited White Noise block (from the Sources library) and a Sum block. Set the parameters on the white noise to be 2×10^{-4} for the noise power and 1×10^{-5} for the sample time. View the resulting noisy binary signal with a Scope block and confirm that it still looks like a binary signal (albeit with noise).
3. Use a Relay block to convert your RS-232 binary signal from +12 V (for a one) and –12 V (for a zero) into +5 V (for a one) and 0 V (for a zero). Use 0 V for both the switch-on and switch-off points for the relay. Run the simulation for 0.01 sec and view the resulting output from the relay with a scope. You should see some errors on the relay output due to the noise on the input.
4. We now quantify the bit errors on the relay output as follows:
   a. First, we need to generate a "perfect" (i.e., noiseless) version of the relay output for comparison purposes. Thus, make a copy of your existing blocks (including Signal Generator, Relay, and Scope) within the current model but omit the Noise Generator in the copy. Then, run the simulation again for 0.01 sec and confirm that you have both perfect and noisy versions at the outputs of your two relays.
   b. Next, create an error signal by subtracting the two relay outputs with a Sum block.
   c. Next, generate the magnitude of the error signal with an Abs (absolute value) block (from the Math Operations library). The purpose of this is to make sure that the error signal is always positive so that it may be easily counted.
   d. Finally, send the output of your Abs block to an Integrator block (with an initial condition of zero) and use a Display block to monitor the output of your integrator. The purpose of the integrator is to provide a running total of all of the detected errors.
5. Run the simulation for 0.01 sec on your complete model containing dual relays with cumulative error detection. At the end of the simulation, you should wind up with a positive value at the output of the integrator. Also, try running the integration for 1 sec and see that you have even more errors.
6. One method of improving the error performance of this decision circuit is to insert hysteresis into the relay to increase the noise margins. To observe this, modify the relay switch-on and switch-off values to +0.5 and –0.5 and rerun the simulation for a 1-sec interval and confirm that you see fewer errors. Try the various sets of switch-on and switch-off values listed in Table 11.1 and complete the table. What happens if you use too much hysteresis?

Project 11.2

Repeat Project 6.3 for a Sallen-Key circuit with a step and impulse input, but this time use Simulink to construct a simulation of the system. Scope output should be for v_{out} and v_1 versus t. Set the end time to $t = 0.0001$ sec and print out the block diagram, impulse response, and step response.

Table 11.1 Cumulative Errors for the Decision Circuit of Problem 11.1 for Various Amounts of Hysteresis

Switch-on and Switch-off Values	*Cumulative Error Detected at Integrator Output (per second)*
0, 0	
+0.5, −0.5	
+2, −2	
+5, −5	
+8, −8	

Project 11.3

A swinging kitchen door in a restaurant weighs $m = 20$ kg and has a spring to cause it to close automatically (with spring constant $k = 300$ N/m) and a piston damper to prevent it from slamming (with damping coefficient $c = 150$ N-sec). We wish to simulate this door as an RLC circuit in Simulink. Assume that the door position x varies over the range $-1 \leq x \leq 1$ meter, where −1 and 1 correspond to the door being fully open in either direction, and zero corresponds to the closed position.

1. Set up a model in Simulink to describe the second-order differential equation for a series RLC circuit (refer to Appendix A for the proper equation). Assume that the door position x is analogous to the capacitor voltage v_C. For R, L, and C, use the analogous values c, m, and $1/k$, respectively. Use the initial condition $x = 1$ (i.e., the door is fully open at $t = 0$) and no forcing function (analogous to zero input voltage). Run the simulation for 5 sec. Is this door underdamped or overdamped?
2. Now, assume that the piston damper breaks off the door, causing a zero value for the damping coefficient c. What happens when you rerun the simulation? Is this what would happen in real life? Why or why not?
3. After replacing the damaged piston damper, the repairperson mistakenly sets the damping coefficient to 50 N-sec. What happens when you rerun the simulation? Does this match what would happen in real life?
4. Interpret these results back to the RLC circuit. What happens in an RLC circuit for $L = 20$, $C = 1/150$, and an initial capacitor voltage of 1 V when R changes value from 150 Ω to 0 Ω to 50 Ω?

Reference

1. McNamara, J., *Technical Aspects of Data Communication*, 3rd ed., Butterworth-Heinemann, Oxford, UK, 1988.

Appendix A: RLC Circuits

The resistor-inductor-capacitor (RLC) circuit is used repeatedly as an example in this text and its behavior is derived in detail in this appendix. In electrical engineering, this simple second-order system is used directly in circuit theory, signal processing, and control theory. In addition, many non-circuit problems lend themselves to being modeled with RLC, including phase-lock loops, transmission lines, and non-electrical problems such as the spring-dashpot problem in mechanical engineering, the resonance of sound waves in acoustics, and even the flow of automobiles on a highway during a traffic jam.

There are two basic topologies of RLC circuits: series and parallel (see Figure A.1). All other configurations can generally be reduced to either of these two by transforming with Thévenin or Norton equivalent circuits [1] (Figure A.2), so we only analyze the basic two here. In the series case, the input variable is a voltage and the output is the current; in the parallel case, the opposite is true (current in, voltage out).

A.1 Direct Analysis with Differential Equations

Starting with the series circuit, we model the resistor, inductor, and capacitor voltage-current relations using their respective constituent relations:

$$v_R = i_R R \tag{A.1}$$

$$v_L = L\frac{di_L}{dt} \tag{A.2}$$

$$i_C = C\frac{dv_C}{dt} \tag{A.3}$$

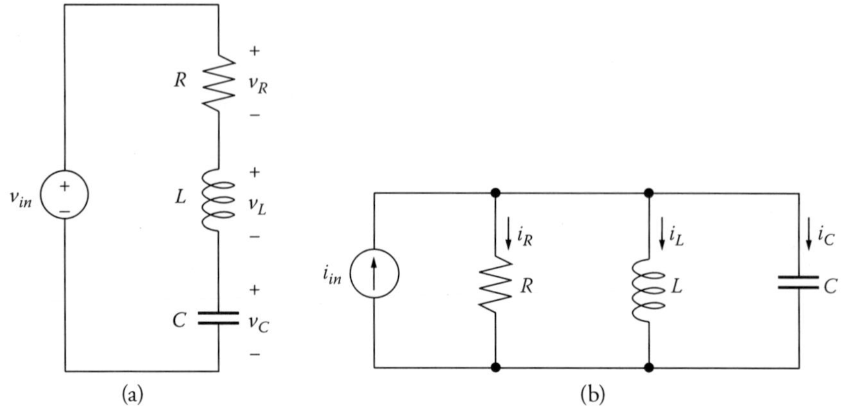

Figure A.1 **(a) Series RLC circuit, (b) Parallel RLC circuit.**

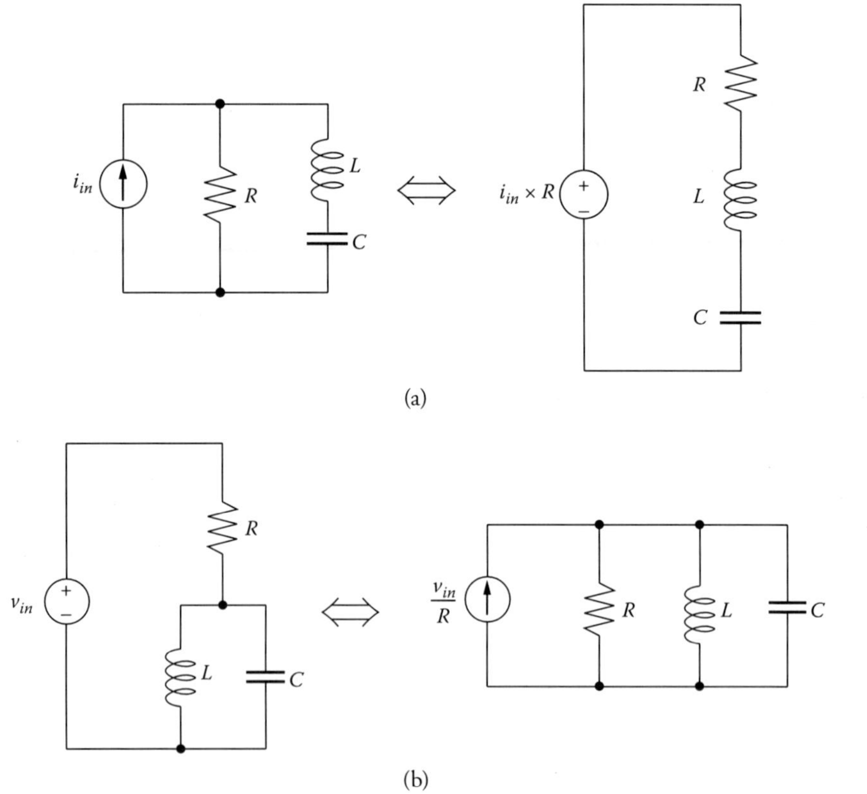

Figure A.2 **Any RLC network can usually be converted to either the series or the parallel configuration by applying (a) Thévenin's and (b) Norton's theorems to convert a series voltage source and resistor into a parallel current source and resistor.**

where v_R, v_L and v_c are the voltages across the resistor, inductor, and capacitor respectively, i_R, i_L and i_C are their respective currents, and R, L and C are their respective component values in ohms, farads, and henries.

Applying Kirchhoff's voltage law around the RLC loop gives

$$V_{in} - v_R - v_L - v_C = 0 \tag{A.4}$$

In the series case, all of the components have the identical current and thus we define $I_{out} = i_R = i_L = i_C$. Substituting Equations (A.1) and (A.2) into (A.4) and rearranging gives

$$I_{out}R + L\frac{dI_{out}}{dt} + v_C = V_{in} \tag{A.5}$$

Now substituting Equation (A.3) into (A.5) gives

$$RC\frac{dv_C}{dt} + LC\frac{d^2v_C}{dt^2} + v_C = V_{in}$$

$$\Rightarrow \frac{d^2v_C}{dt^2} + \frac{R}{L}\frac{dv_C}{dt} + \frac{1}{LC}v_C = \frac{V_{in}}{LC} \tag{A.6}$$

Equation (A.6) is a second-order differential equation for v_C which can be solved via standard techniques. The "driving function" $V_{in}(t)$ and the two initial conditions $v_C(0)$ and $i_L(0)$ are necessary to obtain a complete solution. To solve for $v_C(t)$, we choose a particular solution which satisfies the differential equation for nonzero $V_{in}(t)$, and then we choose a homogenous solution (by setting $V_{in}(t) = 0$) which allows us to satisfy the initial conditions. This approach is demonstrated in Example 6.1. Finally, once we have solved Equation (A.6) for v_C, we can obtain I_{out} by applying Equation (A.3).

By a similar analysis, we can solve the parallel RLC circuit by applying Kirchhoff's current law to obtain

$$\frac{d^2i_L}{dt^2} + \frac{1}{RC}\frac{di_L}{dt} + \frac{1}{LC}i_L = \frac{I_{in}}{LC} \tag{A.7}$$

Note that Equations (A.6) and (A.7) have similar form and thus by solving a single differential Equation, we can solve both the series and parallel RLC circuits.

A.2 Analysis via Circuit Theory

A common method for solving RLC circuits is to apply simple circuit theory where we model the resistor, inductor, and capacitor with their complex impedances Z_R, Z_L, and Z_C:

$$Z_R = R$$

$$Z_L = Ls$$

$$Z_C = \frac{1}{Cs}$$

where $s = j\omega$ is the complex frequency. Applying Ohm's law to the series RLC circuit of Figure A.1a gives

$$\begin{aligned} I_{out} &= \frac{V_{in}}{Z_R + Z_L + Z_C} \\ &= \frac{V_{in}}{R + Ls + \frac{1}{Cs}} \end{aligned}$$

$$\Rightarrow \frac{I_{out}}{V_{in}} = \frac{\frac{1}{L}s}{s^2 + \frac{R}{L}s + \frac{1}{LC}} \tag{A.8}$$

Similarly, applying Ohm's law in the parallel case gives

$$\begin{aligned} V_{out} &= I_{in}\left(Z_R \parallel Z_L \parallel Z_C\right) \\ &= \frac{I_{in}}{\frac{1}{R} + \frac{1}{Ls} + Cs} \end{aligned}$$

$$\Rightarrow \frac{V_{out}}{I_{in}} = \frac{\frac{1}{C}s}{s^2 + \frac{1}{RC}s + \frac{1}{LC}} \tag{A.9}$$

Note that the input-output relations in Equations (A.8) and (A.9) have similar form and are considered to be "second-order" systems because the highest term in their denominators is s^2. We can rewrite these equations into the general form for second-order systems:

$$H(s) = \frac{Ks}{s^2 + 2\zeta\omega_n s + \omega_n^2} \tag{A.10}$$

where $H(s)$ is the *transfer function*, ω_n is the *natural frequency*, ζ is the *damping factor*, and K is a constant scaling factor. Matching terms between Equations (A.3), (A.2), and (A.1), we see:

$$\text{Series RLC circuit: } \omega_n = \frac{1}{\sqrt{LC}},\ \zeta = \frac{R}{2}\sqrt{\frac{C}{L}},\ K = \frac{1}{L}$$

$$\text{Parallel RLC circuit: } \omega_n = \frac{1}{\sqrt{LC}},\ \zeta = \frac{1}{2R}\sqrt{\frac{L}{C}},\ K = \frac{1}{C}$$

The physical meanings for natural frequency and damping factor become apparent when we observe the frequency behavior for $H(s)$. The Bode plot for Equation (A.10) is shown in Figure A.3, where we assume that $\omega_n = 1000$ and ζ has the

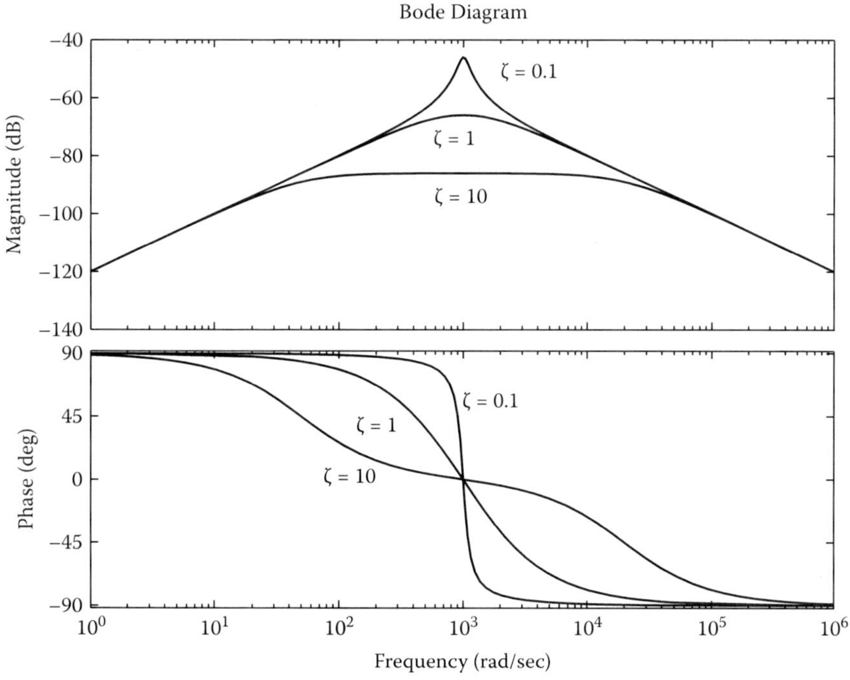

Figure A.3 Bode plot of an RLC circuit for ω_n = 1000 rad/s and ζ values of 0.1, 1, and 10.

values 0.1, 1, and 10. Note that the plots are centered around ω_n and fall off symmetrically as $\omega \to 0$ and $\omega \to \infty$. Thus, $H(s)$ is a *bandpass filter* with a passband centered around ω_n. This is confirmed when we examine Equation (A.10) at the low and high frequency limits and at $s = j\omega_n$:

$$\text{at low frequencies:} \quad \lim_{j\omega \to 0} |H(j\omega)| = \frac{K(0)}{0^2 + 2\zeta\omega_n(0) + \omega_n^2} = 0$$

$$\text{at high frequencies:} \quad \lim_{j\omega \to \infty} |H(j\omega)| = \frac{K(\infty)}{\infty^2 + 2\zeta\omega_n(\infty) + \omega_n^2} = 0$$

$$\text{at } \omega_n\text{:} \quad |H(j\omega_n)| = \frac{Kj\omega_n}{(j\omega_n)^2 + 2\zeta\omega_n(j\omega_n) + \omega_n^2} = \frac{K}{2\zeta\omega_n}$$

Thus, $H(s)$ approaches zero at low and high frequencies and has a peak value at the natural frequency which is dependent on the damping factor. Traditionally, the values for ζ are classified into three types: underdamped ($\zeta<1$), overdamped ($\zeta>1$), and critically damped ($\zeta = 1$). For the underdamped case in Figure A.3 ($\zeta = 0.1$), $H(s)$ has a tall narrow peak that indicates *resonance* at the natural frequency, i.e., only input signals at (or very near to) the natural frequency will be passed by the filter. For the overdamped case ($\zeta = 10$), there is no peak at all but rather there is simply a wide flat passband. The critically damped case ($\zeta = 1$) has the narrowest passband without resonance, the implications of which will become clear momentarily when we examine the transient response.

An alternative representation of the standard form of Equation (A.10) is

$$H(s) = \frac{Ks}{s^2 + \dfrac{\omega_n}{Q}s + \omega_n^2} \tag{A.11}$$

where Q is the *quality factor* and is an indication of the height and width of the resonant peak in the Bode plot. Note that by comparing Equations (A.11) and (A.10), we see that $Q = \dfrac{1}{2\zeta}$ and thus the quality factor and damping factor are simply two different ways of expressing the same idea. The choice between whether to use Q or ζ is dependent on the application, with Q usually being used in filter design and ζ in control theory. A *high-Q* filter ($Q > 1/2$) is one which has high resonance and is typically used in oscillator design or tunable circuits, and a *low-Q* filter ($Q < 1/2$) has no resonance at all. An *intermediate Q factor* ($Q = 1/2$) corresponds to a critically damped response.

The damping factor is further illustrated by examining the step response $s(t)$. From system theory, we know that

$$s(t) = h(t) * u(t)$$

where $h(t)$ is the system impulse response (i.e., the inverse Laplace transform of $H(s)$), $u(t)$ is the unit step function, and the "*" operator indicates convolution. In order to avoid doing the convolution, we solve in the Laplace domain where the convolution operator transforms to multiplication. Thus, the s-domain step response $S(s)$ is

$$S(s) = H(s) \times \frac{1}{s}$$

where we have used the transform relation $\mathcal{L}(u(t)) = \frac{1}{s}$. By factoring the denominator of $H(s)$, we obtain

$$S(s) = \frac{Ks}{\left(s + \omega_n\left(\zeta + \sqrt{\zeta^2 - 1}\right)\right)\left(s + \omega_n\left(\zeta - \sqrt{\zeta^2 - 1}\right)\right)} \times \frac{1}{s} \tag{A.12}$$

Performing a partial-fraction expansion for the case where $\zeta \neq 1$ gives

$$S(s) = \frac{K}{2\omega_n\sqrt{\zeta^2 - 1}}\left(\frac{-1}{s + \omega_n\left(\zeta + \sqrt{\zeta^2 - 1}\right)} + \frac{1}{s + \omega_n\left(\zeta - \sqrt{\zeta^2 - 1}\right)}\right) \tag{A.13}$$

Knowing the Laplace transform relation $\mathcal{L}(e^{at}) = \frac{1}{s - a}$, we can inverse transform Equation (A.13) to obtain

$$s(t) = \frac{K}{2\omega_n\sqrt{\zeta^2 - 1}}\left(-e^{-\left(\zeta + \sqrt{\zeta^2 - 1}\right)\omega_n t} + e^{-\left(\zeta - \sqrt{\zeta^2 - 1}\right)\omega_n t}\right) \tag{A.14}$$

In the case where $\zeta > 1$, Equation (A.14) can be algebraically rearranged to obtain a sinh function, and in the case where $\zeta < 1$, Equation (A.14) can be rearranged into a sine function.

In the special case where $\zeta = 1$, Equation (A.12) becomes:

$$S(s) = \frac{Ks}{(s + \omega_n)^2} \times \frac{1}{s} \tag{A.15}$$

This equation can be inverse transformed with the Laplace transform relation $\mathcal{L}(te^{at}) = \frac{1}{(s - a)^2}$.

Summarizing, the step response of the RLC circuit for all values of ζ and zero initial conditions is

$$s(t) = \begin{cases} \dfrac{Ke^{-\zeta\omega_n t}}{2\omega_n\sqrt{1-\zeta^2}} \sin\sqrt{1-\zeta^2}\,\omega_n t & \text{for } \zeta < 1 \\ Kte^{-\zeta\omega_n t} & \text{for } \zeta = 1 \\ \dfrac{Ke^{-\zeta\omega_n t}}{2\omega_n\sqrt{\zeta^2-1}} \sinh\sqrt{\zeta^2-1}\,\omega_n t & \text{for } \zeta > 1 \end{cases} \tag{A.16}$$

The step response is plotted in Figure A.4 where we assume that $\omega_n = 1000$ and ζ has the values 0.1, 1, and 10. Note that for the underdamped case (ζ = 0.1), the transient response has an oscillatory component (due to the sine term) which dies out over time (due to the exponential term). In the overdamped case (ζ = 10), the response has no oscillatory behavior and is a sum of decaying exponentials. The critically damped case (ζ = 1) can be seen to have the fastest decay without any oscillatory component.

Note that in Equation (A.16), the sine term in the underdamped case has an "effective" frequency that is dependent on the damping factor and the natural frequency. We may define this "damped frequency" ω_d as

$$\omega_d = \sqrt{1-\zeta^2}\,\omega_n \tag{A.17}$$

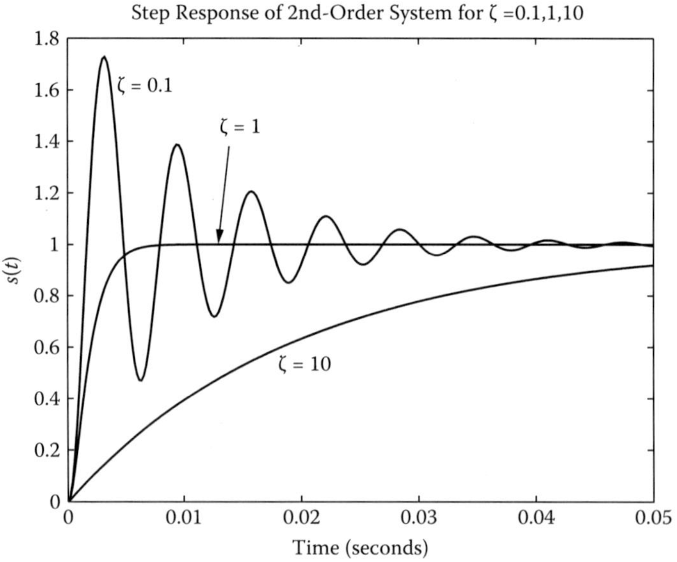

Figure A.4 Step response of an RLC circuit for ω = 1000 rad/s and ζ values of 0.1, 1, and 10.

and thus for the underdamped case, the step response may be rewritten as

$$s(t) = \frac{Ke^{-\zeta\omega_n t}}{2\omega_d} \sin \omega_d t \qquad \text{for } \zeta < 1 \tag{A.18}$$

Because the damping factor can be hard to measure directly, the damped frequency can be useful for measuring ζ because it may be easily read from the oscillatory step response on an oscilloscope screen. If both the damped and natural frequencies are known, then from Equation (A.17),

$$\zeta = \sqrt{1 - \frac{\omega_d}{\omega_n}}$$

A.3 Application: Signal Processing

In the previous section, we derived the bandpass response for the standard-form transfer function of Equation (A.10). However, it is also possible to obtain a lowpass and highpass response from an RLC circuit. Figure A.5 shows the series RLC circuit where the system outputs are taken as the voltages v_R, v_L, and v_C across the three circuit elements. Applying the relation for a voltage divider for impedance circuits, we can obtain

$$\frac{v_R}{V_{in}} = \frac{R}{R + Ls + \frac{1}{Cs}} = \frac{\frac{R}{L}s}{s^2 + \frac{R}{L}s + \frac{1}{LC}} \tag{A.19}$$

$$\frac{v_L}{V_{in}} = \frac{Ls}{R + Ls + \frac{1}{Cs}} = \frac{s^2}{s^2 + \frac{R}{L}s + \frac{1}{LC}} \tag{A.20}$$

$$\frac{v_C}{V_{in}} = \frac{\frac{1}{Cs}}{R + Ls + \frac{1}{Cs}} = \frac{\frac{1}{LC}}{s^2 + \frac{R}{L}s + \frac{1}{LC}} \tag{A.21}$$

Note that Equations (A.19), (A.20), and (A.21) all have the same denominator (and thus the same natural frequency and damping factor) but different numerators. The resulting Bode magnitude plots (Figure A.5) show that the resistor voltage has a bandpass response, the inductor voltage has a high-pass response, and the capacitor voltage has a low-pass response. For the underdamped case, all three responses will have a resonant peak at the natural frequency.

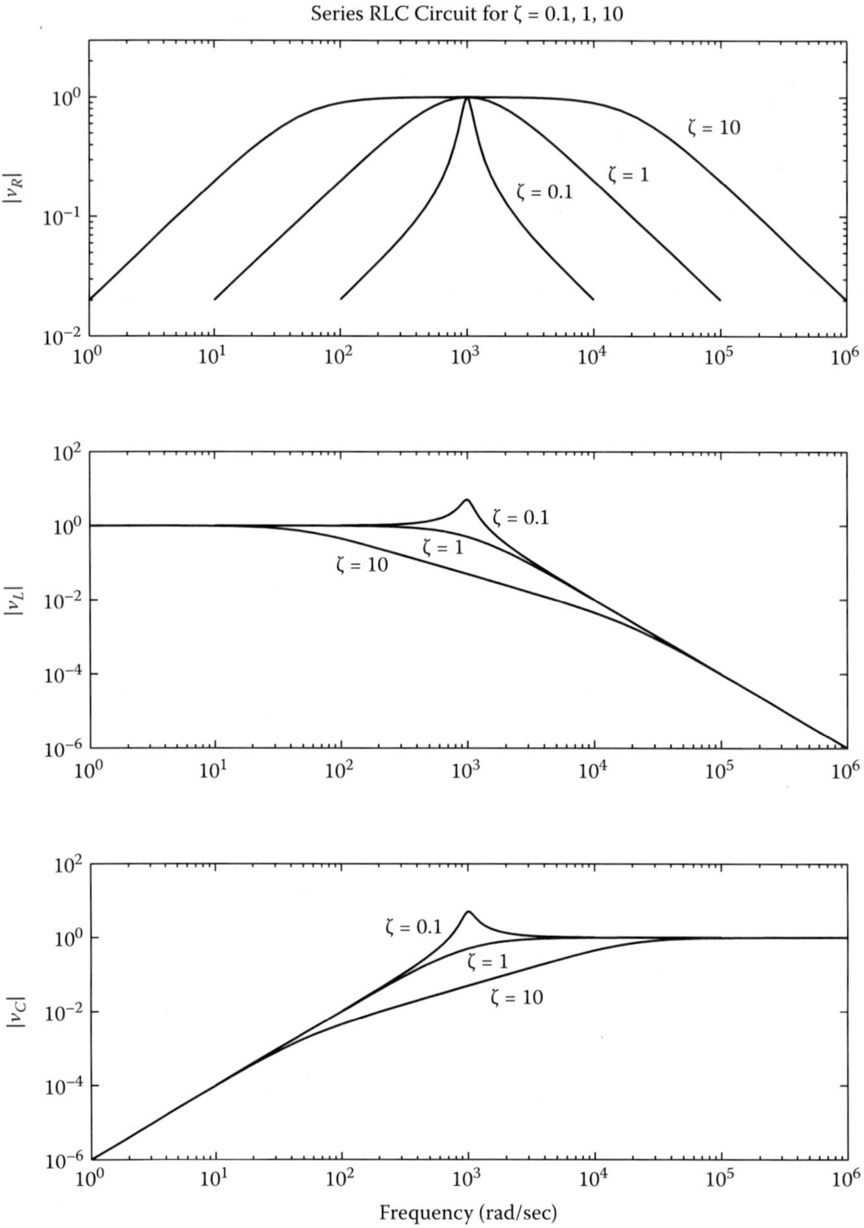

Figure A.5 Bode plot (magnitude portion only) showing the bandpass, high-pass, and low-pass responses for ω = 1000 rad/s and ζ values of 0.1, 1, and 10.

A.4 Application: Spring-Dashpot System

A problem from mechanical engineering which may be modeled with an RLC circuit is the "spring-dashpot" system consisting of a mass, a spring, and a damper. A common household example of a spring-dashpot system is a pneumatic door closing mechanism (Figure A.6) where the door is the mass, a spring closes the door, and a pneumatic piston is used to adjust the closing speed. If the piston is incorrectly adjusted, then the door either closes too slowly (overdamped) or too rapidly with a few bounces (underdamped). If adjusted just right (critically damped), then the door closes as quickly as possible without slamming and without any oscillation.

From physics, the force applied to a mass due to an attached spring is defined as

$$F_{\text{spring}} = -kx \tag{A.22}$$

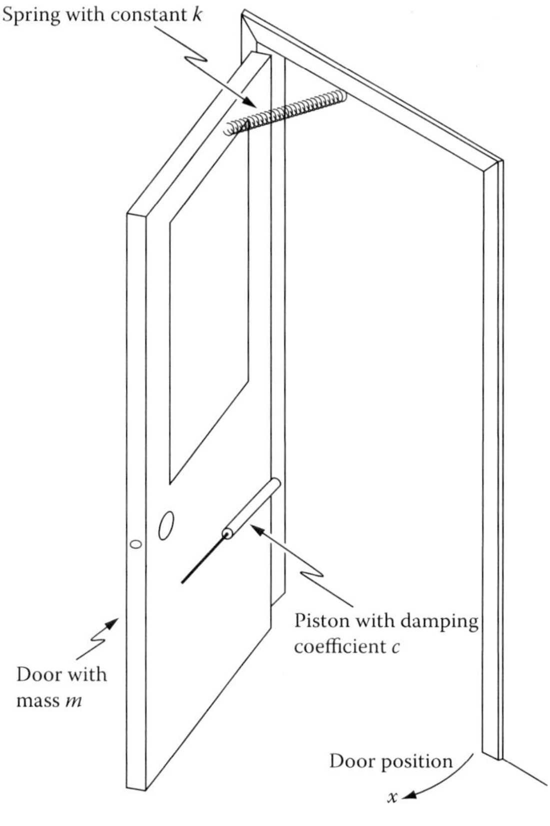

Figure A.6 Example of a spring-dashpot system: automatic door-closing mechanism.

where k is the spring constant (in units of newton/meter) and x is the position of the door attached to the spring (in meters).

The damping force in the pneumatic piston is proportional to the velocity $x' = \frac{dx}{dt}$ of the door:

$$F_{\text{damper}} = -cx' \tag{A.23}$$

where c is the damping coefficient of the piston (in units of newton-seconds).

The sum of the forces on the door $F_{\text{total}} = F_{\text{spring}} + F_{\text{damper}}$ must obey Newton's second law $F_{\text{total}} = m\frac{d^2x}{dt^2}$, and thus

$$mx'' = -kx - cx'$$

$$\Rightarrow x'' + \frac{c}{m}x' + \frac{k}{m}x = 0 \tag{A.24}$$

Equation (A.24) has the same form as Equation (A.6) where $R = c$, $L = m$, and $C = 1/k$. Thus, we can model the door/spring/damper system as a series RLC circuit (which we have already solved mathematically) where the piston corresponds to the resistor, the mass of the door corresponds to the inductor, and the spring corresponds to the capacitor.

Reference

1. Johnson, D.E., Hilburn, J.L., and Johnson, J.R., *Basic Electric Circuit Analysis, 4th ed.*, Prentice Hall, 1990.

Appendix B: Special Characters in MATLAB® Plots

MATLAB® allows the use of Greek and special characters in its plot headings and labels. The method for doing this based on the TeX formatting language [1] and is summarized in this appendix.

MATLAB provides the functions `title`, `xlabel`, `ylabel`, and `text` for adding labels to plots. These labels can include Greek and special characters by applying the character sequences as shown in Table B.1. These sequences all begin with the backslash character (\) and can be embedded in any text string argument to `title`, `xlabel`, `ylabel`, and `text`. Subscripts and superscripts may also be applied by using the _ and ^ operators. For example, the sequence V_o is written as `V _ o`, and 10^6 is written as `10^6`. If the subscript or superscript is multiple characters, then use curly braces to delimit the string to be subscripted, for example, V_{out} is generated with `V _ {out}`.

Example B.1

The following MATLAB script shows how to use special characters in a plot.

```
% Example_B_1.m
% This script shows example usage of special characters in
% MATLAB plots.
% Plot a 1MHz sine wave over the interval 0<t<2 microsec
t = 0:2e-8:2e-6;
fo = 1e6;
xout = sin(2*pi*fo*t);
plot(t*1e6,xout);
title('Plot of sin(2\pif_{o}t) for f_{o} = 10^6 Hz');
xlabel('time (\museconds)');
ylabel('x_{out}(t)');
text(1.5,0.3,'\omega = 2\pi \times f_{o}');
----------------------------------------------------------------------
```

The resulting plot is shown in Figure B.1.

Table B.1 Special Symbols for Use in MATLAB Plots

Character Sequence	*Symbol*	*Character Sequence*	*Symbol*	*Character Sequence*	*Symbol*
\alpha	α	\upsilon	υ	\sim	~
\beta	β	\phi	ϕ	\leq	≠
\gamma	γ	\chi	χ	\infty	∞
\delta	δ	\psi	ψ	\clubsuit	♣
\epsilon	ε	\omega	ω	\diamondsuit	♦
\zeta	ζ	\Gamma	Γ	\heartsuit	♥
\eta	η	\Delta	Δ	\spadesuit	♠
\theta	θ	\Theta	Θ	\leftrightarrow	↔
\vartheta	ϑ	\Lambda	Λ	\leftarrow	←
\iota	ι	\Xi	Ξ	\uparrow	↑
\kappa	κ	\Pi	Π	\rightarrow	→
\lambda	λ	\Sigma	Σ	\downarrow	↓
\mu	μ	\Upsilon	ϒ	\circ	°
\nu	ν	\Phi	Φ	\pm	±
\xi	ξ	\Psi	Ψ	\geq	≥
\pi	π	\Omega	Ω	\propto	∝
\rho	ρ	\forall	∀	\partial	∂
\sigma	σ	\exists	∃	\bullet	•
\varsigma	ς	\ni	∍	\div	÷
\tau	τ	\cong	≅	\neq	≠
\equiv	≡	\approx	≈	\aleph	ℵ
\Im	ℑ	\Re	ℜ	\wp	℘
\otimes	⊗	\oplus	⊕	\oslash	∅
\cap	∩	\cup	∪	\supseteq	⊇
\supset	⊃	\subseteq	⊆	\subset	⊂
\int	∫	\in	∈	\o	ο

Table B.1 Special Symbols for Use in MATLAB Plots (Continued)

Character Sequence	*Symbol*	*Character Sequence*	*Symbol*	*Character Sequence*	*Symbol*
`\rfloor`	⌋	`\lceil`	⌈	`\nabla`	∇
`\lfloor`	⌊	`\cdot`	·	`\ldots`	...
`\perp`	⊥	`\neg`	¬	`\prime`	′
`\wedge`	∧	`\times`	×	`\0`	∅
`\rceil`	⌉	`\surd`	√	`\mid`	|
`\vee`	∨	`\varpi`	ϖ	`\copyright`	©
`\langle`	⟨	`\rangle`	⟩		

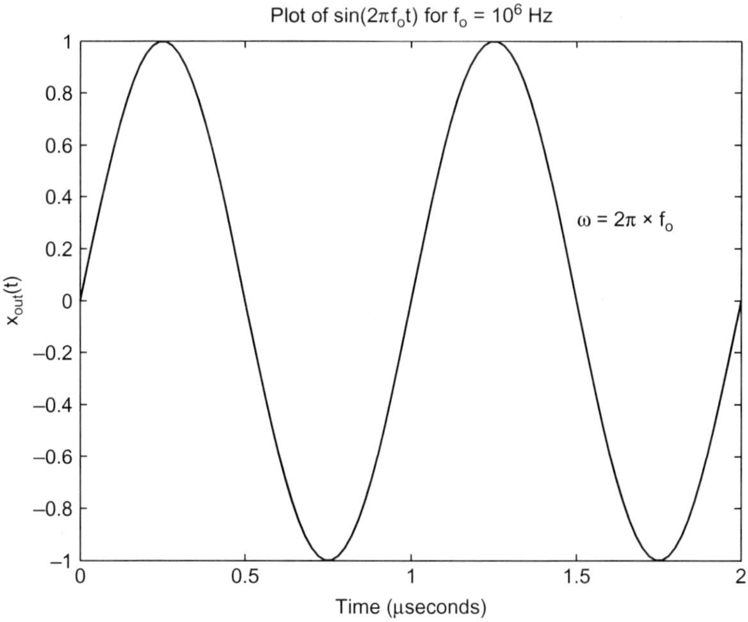

Figure B.1 Example usage of Greek letters, special characters, subscripts, and superscripts in a MATLAB plot.

Reference

1. Knuth, D.E., *The TeXbook*, Addison Wesley, Boston, 1984.

MATLAB® Function Index

This index contains a list of the MATLAB commands used in this book and the pages on which they are introduced.

Simulink Blocks

Index

D

G

H

I

K

L

M

N

O

Q

R

S